Prentice Hall PTR MCSE Series at a Glance

Prentice Hall PTR, the leader in professional computer publishing, is pleased to offer the very best in MCP training. The following chart positions our books within the framework of the various options offered by Microsoft®.

The Microsoft Certified Program (MCP) offers certification exams in the following advanced fields:

- MCSE
- MCSE + Internet
- MCSD
- MCP + Site Building
- MCP + Internet

Microsoft Certified Systems Engineers (MCSE) are required to pass four MCP operating system exams (or core exams) and two MCP elective exams. Microsoft Certified Systems Engineers with a specialty in the Internet (MCSE + Internet) are required to pass seven MCP operating system exams and two MCP elective exams. Microsoft Certified Professionals with a specialty in the Internet (MCP + Internet) are required to pass three MCP exams that provide a valid and reliable measure of technical proficiency and expertise.

Exam	Prentice Hall Title	MCSE Certification Credit	MCSE + Internet Certification Credit	MCP + Internet Certification Credit
70-058	*Core MCSE: Networking Essentials*, Keogh, 0-13-010733-6	1 of 4 Core Requirements	1 of 7 Core Requirements	NA
70-067	*Core MCSE*, Dell, 0-13-082861-0	1 of 4 Core Requirements	1 of 7 Core Requirements	1 of 3 Requirements
70-068	*Core MCSE*, Dell	1 of 4 Core Requirements	1 of 7 Core Requirements	NA
70-073	*Core MCSE*, Dell	1 of 4 Core Requirements	1 of 7 Core Requirements	NA
70-098	*Core MCSE*, Dell	1 of 4 Core Requirements	1 of 7 Core Requirements	NA
70-028	*MCSE: Administering Microsoft ® SQL Server™ 7*, Byrne, 0-13-010795-6	1 of 2 Elective Requirements	1 of 2 Elective Requirements	NA
70-059	*MCSE: Internetworking with Microsoft® TCP/IP on Microsoft Windows NT 4*, Hoffman, 1999	1 of 2 Elective Requirements	1 of 2 Elective Requirements	1 of 3 Requirements
70-079	*MCSE/MCSE + Internet: Implementing and Supporting Microsoft® Internet Explorer™ by Using the Microsoft Internet Explorer Administration Kit*, 1999	NA	1 of 7 Core Requirements	NA
70-081	*MCSE: Implementing and Supporting Microsoft® Exchange Server 5.5*, Goncalves, 0-13-923525-6	1 of 2 Elective Requirements	1 of 2 Elective Requirements	NA
70-085	*MCSE: Implementing and Supporting Microsoft® SNA Server 4*, Mariscal, 1999	1 of 2 Elective Requirements	1 of 2 Elective Requirements	NA
70-086	*MCSE: Implementing and Supporting Microsoft® Systems Management Server 2*, Vacca, 0-13-020226-6	1 of 2 Elective Requirements	NA	NA
70-087	*MCSE: Implementing and Supporting Microsoft® Internet Information Server 4*, Dell, 1999	1 of 2 Elective Requirements	1 of 7 Core Requirements	1 of 3 Requirements
70-088	*MCSE: Implementing and Supporting Microsoft® Proxy Server 2*, Clark, 1999	1 of 2 Elective Requirements	1 of 2 Elective Requirements	NA

MICROSOFT CERTIFIED SYSTEMS ENGINEER SERIES

JIM KEOGH

CORE MCSE: NETWORKING ESSENTIALS

Prentice Hall PTR
Upper Saddle River, NJ 07458
http://www.phptr.com

Library of Congress Cataloging-in-Publication Data

Keogh, James Edward
Core MCSE : networking essentials / Jim Keogh.
p. cm.
Includes bibliographical references and index.
ISBN 0–13–010733–6
1. Electronic data processing personnel—Certification.
2. Microsoft software—Examinations—Study guides. 3. Computer networks. I. Title.
QA76.3.K46 1998
004.6—dc21 98-31329
CIP

Editorial/Production Supervision: Nicholas Radhuber
Acquisitions Editor: Jeffrey Pepper
Editorial Assistant: Linda Ramagnano
Marketing Manager: Miles Williams
Development Editor: Jim Markham
Manufacturing Manager: Alexis R. Heydt
Cover Design Director: Jerry Votta
Cover Design: Scott Weiss
Interior Design: Gail Cocker-Bogusz

Prentice-Hall, Inc.
A Simon & Schuster Company
Upper Saddle River, NJ 07458

Prentice Hall books are widely used by corporations and government agencies for training, marketing, and resale.

The publisher offers discounts on this book when ordered in bulk quantities. For more information, contact Corporate Sales Department, Phone: 800-382-3419; fax: 201-236-7141; email: corpsales@prenhall.com; or write Corporate Sales Department, Prentice Hall PTR, One Lake Street, Upper Saddle River, NJ 07458.

Printed in the United States of America

10 9 8 7 6 5 4 3 2 1

ISBN 0-13-010733-6

Prentice-Hall International (UK) Limited, *London*
Prentice-Hall of Australia Pty. Limited, *Sydney*
Prentice-Hall Canada Inc., *Toronto*
Prentice-Hall Hispanoamericana, S. A., *Mexico*
Prentice-Hall of India Private Limited, *New Delhi*
Prentice-Hall of Japan, Inc., *Tokyo*
Simon & Schuster Asia Pte. Ltd., *Singapore*
Editora Prentice-Hall do Brasil, Ltda., *Rio de Janeiro*

This book is dedicated to Anne, Sandra, and Joanne without whose help it could not have been written.

CONTENTS

PREFACE

Corporations throughout the world are converting to Windows NT networks, which is creating high demand for qualified technicians to design and run those networks. Until recently, IS recruiters were in a dilemma. They had no sure-fire way of knowing if the technician they hired had the skills to do the job.

This changed in recent years with the onset of the Microsoft® Certified Systems Engineer program. Microsoft's certificate program requires network engineers and those seeking to take on such roles to pass six tests prepared by Microsoft. If they pass, Microsoft certifies them as a network engineer giving them professional recognition—and a ticket to a rewarding career.

IS recruiters now have an objective tool to use when assessing the skills of a candidate for a network technicians position. The MCSE certificate tells the IS recruiter that the candidate met Microsoft's standards for a network technician.

This book is designed to help you take your first step towards receiving your MCSE certificate. You'll need to pass six tests to qualify for the certificate and the test every MCSE candidate must pass is Networking Essentials. The Networking Essentials test challenges your basic understanding of network technology and how to implement Windows NT in a real-life situation.

Whom Is This Book For?

I assume that you have a basic understanding of computers enough to know how to maneuver around Microsoft Windows 95, which has a similar interface to Windows NT 4.0. This means you'll know how to click the mouse, locate the Start button, display and highlight selections on a menu.

I don't assume you know anything about computer networks nor Windows NT 4.0 although a general knowledge of such will let you skip the basics and get to more challenging topics. Everything you need to know about networks and Windows NT 4.0 to take the Networking Essentials test is presented in this book.

Much of the Network Essentials test addresses generic networking issues that cross all product lines. The test does not exclusively cover Windows NT networking. This means I don't expect you to have access to Windows NT 4.0. However, you'll find having access to Windows NT 4.0 very useful when learning about Windows NT 4.0 networking tools.

I also assume that you are likely to be rusty on test-taking skills, so I've included an appendix that reviews some of the basic techniques for studying and taking a test. Following the steps contained in that appendix will relieve test anxiety and give you an edge when sitting for the test.

And I threw in a few sample tests to let you practice your skills before you enter the test room. You'll find questions on the sample tests very similar to the ones on the Network Essentials test. I expect to you to take the sample test as if you were taking the real test. Don't cheat and look up the answers until you have completed the test. And be sure you don't exceed the time limit.

I also expect you to review the material in the book that covers questions you missed on the sample test. This is a proven method used to strengthen your weak points.

About the Microsoft Certified Systems Engineer (MCSE) Tests

Microsoft decided that there are four areas of knowledge a certified systems engineer should possess. These are networking, clients, Windows NT 4.0 server, and the Windows NT 4.0 Enterprise server.

The network component is addressed in the Networking Essentials course and test-referred to as 70-058. The client component is satisfied with either the Implementing and Supporting Windows NT Workstation 4.0 course/test (70-073) or Implementing and Supporting Microsoft Windows 95 course/test (70-063).

Both server components are satisfied by the Implementing and Supporting Windows NT Server 4.0 course/test (70-067) and the Implementing and Supporting Windows NT Server 4.0 course/test (70-068).

In addition to these required tests, you must pass two of ten possible electives. Requirements for the MCSE certification can change, so I suggest you stop by *www.microsoft.com* for the latest information.

An advantage of the MCSE program is that you don't have to attend classes to become certified. All that is necessary is to pass the tests. This means if you already have the skills to implement and support Windows 95, then you can sit for the test. If you pass, then you've completed a requirement to become certified.

If you don't have these skills, you can use books and courseware material to learn at your own pace. You'll find all the necessary material you'll require to become certified in the Microsoft Certified Program.

What You'll Need

Unlike other computer books you've purchased, you don't require any hardware or software to use this book. Chapters 1 through 8 provide the information you need to learn to pass the Network Essentials test.

You will find it useful to have available Windows NT 4.0 with administrator rights when you read Appendix A. Appendix A provides a step-by-step guide to set up, use, and troubleshoot a Windows NT 4.0 network. You'll be able to practice using these steps only by having access to Windows NT 4.0.

You'll also need a PC with a CD drive to use the CBT course that is provided on the CD. This course provides you with an online, hands-on-learning supplement to this book. You won't need this to pass the course, but it's well worth a look for it provides an interactive way to prep for the test.

How This Book Is Organized

A network is composed of a complex hodgepodge of computer components that can baffle even the most skilled computer programmer. You are probably wondering how you are going to learn this imposing technology after skimming through the pages of this book. There are abstract modeling concepts you need to master, new terminology to memorize, and techniques that you must be able to apply when designing a network.

I have taken particular care to present these topics in a simple, logical way that is very similar to how you and I learn. You'll begin your education using the same technique as is used in building a skyscraper. You start with an empty hole, which represents a void in your knowledge about networks, and then slowly fill the hole with the terms and concepts used in data communications. You will end up with a solid foundation on how a basic network functions.

With the foundation in place, you begin to learn more challenging network concepts, which aren't difficult to understand because I relate the new material to topics you have already learned. At the end of each chapter you'll find a synopsis of the chapter followed by a little quiz you can use to test your knowledge about lessons presented in the chapter. These questions are similar to those found on the Network Essentials certification test.

In the first chapter, you'll receive an overview of networking beginning with the fundamentals of information, data, and computer networks. When you're finished with Chapter One, you'll have a good idea of what is in store in the remaining pages of the book.

Chapter Two explores the network model that specifies the rules called protocols that network software and hardware manufacturers must follow. These rules enable error-free data communications between unlike computers. You won't need to learn the details of these protocols, but you will develop an understanding of what they are and how you can implement specific protocols on a network.

In Chapter Three I introduce you to how computers, cables, and other network components are assembled. The technical term for this is called the network topology. A number of different topologies can be used to provide the most efficient data communication network for an organization. You'll know the advantages and disadvantages of each topology by the time you finished this chapter.

Chapter Four begins your look into the depths of networks with a penetrating look at network architecture. You'll learn about Ethernet, Token Ring, and other blends of hardware and software that enable network resources to be shared amongst computers. These terms may sound a bit imposing now, but they'll be second nature to you before long.

In Chapter Five you take a step back for a broad look at computer networks. Here you'll learn about servers and clients and how the network operating system manages the flow of data across the network. You'll explore how clients communicate with the network through the use of a redirector and about the various kinds of services that are typically available on the network. Once you have the big picture of network operations, you're ready to move ahead to the details.

Chapter Six shows you the information you need to manage a network. Yes, networks are smart, but you're smarter. You'll learn about user accounts and group accounts and how network-monitoring tools are used to identify bottlenecks on the network. A bottleneck slows down the flow of data causing network performance to falter. This is a nuts-and-bolts kind of chapter that shows you buttons to push to get the network rolling.

In Chapter Seven you are introduced to Wide Area Networks (WAN). A WAN is used to extend your Local Area Network beyond the walls of the building. It is in this chapter where you learn about Asynchronous Transfer Mode (ATM); Public Switched Telephone Network (PSTN); and other network technologies that lets computers on your LAN communicate with the outside world.

Chapter Eight brings you into the real-life, imperfect world of networks. All of us assume networks run smoothly without any problems once the connections are made and the network is activated. Unfortunately, this is not always the case in the real world. In this chapter you'll learn to handle day-to-day problems such as network security, how to prepare for a network disaster, and how to troubleshoot network problems when they occur. You might say this is the chapter that gives you the tools to become a professional network engineer.

I round off the book with four important appendixes. The first contains hands-on exercises that show you step by step how to perform various network-engineering tasks using Windows NT 4.0 network features. You'll find this to be a valuable resource even after you pass your Network Essentials test. You'll learn everything you need from setting up user accounts to using network-monitoring tools to troubleshoot the network.

The next appendix gives your mind a wake-up call to prepare for the test. It has probably been more than a few months since you've sat in a classroom taking a test. You're likely to have forgotten those test-taking tricks you used back in school. All of them and more will come back to you after reviewing this appendix.

The third appendix is a glossary of buzzwords you should know. I found reviewing the glossary a good way to test your knowledge of networking terms and concepts.

The fourth appendix is the answers to the chapter review questions.

About the CD

I found a great companion CD to this book. It is a CBT CD that contains online, interactive courses covering Network Essentials topics. CBT offers a variety of CD-based courseware that is designed to fine-tune your knowledge about Network Essentials and other topics in the Microsoft Certification program.

CBT has a course for each area of the Network Essentials test. I reviewed all of them and decided to include the Network Essentials: Network Troubleshooting course with this book. You'll find it is a good representative sample of the quality of the other courses.

The course is easy to install. Follow the directions that accompany the CD. You'll have the choice to either install the course on your hard disk or use it interactively from the CD. I preferred to install the courses on the hard disk because this frees my CD player for playing a little music while studying.

You'll notice a listing of the available course displayed on your screen when you select CBT from the Program listing. The list contains the name of the course(s) you installed. You can install additional courseware from the CD contained in this book or from others purchased from CBT by using an installation program provided on the CD.

Once you begin a course, you'll find yourself reading text on the screen then clicking a few buttons to go forward or backward in the course. Watch out for sneak pop quizzes. They'll appear suddenly and you'll be graded too. Fortunately, if you're stumped by any question, you can click a button and get the answer.

The grades measure your performance in the course. You can always skip quizzes and ignore the grade, but you'll be missing out on an excellent feature of the course. You need this feedback to tell you how close you're coming to your goal—to pass the Networking Essentials test.

CTB courseware also contains Windows NT 4.0 screens that can be used to simulate using the features of Windows NT 4.0. For example, you can interact with Windows NT 4.0 screens to set up user accounts and group accounts and run the network monitor along with other features. This gives you the opportunity to develop your hands-on skills if you don't have access to Windows NT 4.0 or lack administrator's rights to Windows NT 4.0 on your computer.

Special thanks to CBT Systems for permission to use some of the artwork in their excellent computer-based training modules. Please see the advertisement in the back of this book for more information about how you can receive their full line of products.

ONE

Inside Computer Networks

▲Chapter Syllabus

Just a year ago, I overheard a fellow worker give directions to a popular restaurant. She did this over the telephone and I didn't give it a second thought until I heard her mention German street names. It then struck me and made me pause for a few moments; I began reflecting on the technology we have come to take for granted.

She was speaking with her husband as he was driving on the Autobahn. We were working in New Jersey. As he asked questions, she typed away on her keyboard—letting her computer search the Internet for maps, restaurants, and gas stations all within his vicinity. She was even able to find the menu to the popular restaurant, which she relayed to her husband.

I'm sure neither of them gave it a second thought that they were communicating as if they were home. Yet their words were transmitted around the globe in a fraction of a second, as was her search for information on the Internet.

Next, she sent an email to our corporate travel department requesting that they make travel arrangements so that she could join her husband when he arrived in Paris. Within a few hours, her reservations were set and airline tickets were delivered to her desk.

She dispatched another email to her boss, stating that she'd be leaving early Thursday, but would dial into the company's network when she arrived in Paris and work from her hotel room on Friday. All this took place in minutes without her leaving her desk.

The telephones, mobile phones, Internet, intranet, extranet and corporate networks . . . all these electronic highways make it possible for anyone to work and communicate from anywhere in the world. It seems like magic. How does all this happen? In this chapter, we'll explore the concepts of networking, which will provide a foundation on which you can learn to design and manage a network.

MCSE 1.1 Information

Information zips from one computer to another computer in less than a second, even if the other computer is miles away. However, what you and I recognize as information is different from how it appears to computers and computer networks.

We use lines and ovals to construct a set of symbols that we know as the alphabet and numbers. Each symbol (letter) is associated with other symbols in a particular order to form a word such as Paris. A word is related to other words to convey information, as in the case: I'll be in Paris Thursday night.

We are not cognoscenti of graphic constructs that form the words we read and write. Instead, subconsciously our brains assemble these images into letters, group letters into words then conjure images associated with the word or group of words; we consciously recognize these associations as information.

However, because a computer is a box of switches etched into chips, it lacks this ability. These switches are similar to a light switch in that the switch can be on or off, which is called a **state.** The challenge facing computer scientists many decades ago was to figure a way to encode our ability to catalog information into a switch.

The binary number system, which contains only two numbers (zero and one), became the obvious way to denote the state of a switch. Zero represents the off state and one the on state. Although two numbers could hardly be used to represent more than two letters of our alphabet, a combination of switches could be used to encode the complete alphabet.

Each switch, referred to as a **bit** can represent one of two values, or in this case one of 2 letters. Two bits can represent one of four values, or four letters and so on. In trying to decide on a common format, computer scientists settled on using eight bits or 1 **byte** to represent 1 piece of information or one letter. One byte can represent 256 unique values, which is more than sufficient to encode our alphabet and numbers. We know the switch as a bit and eight switches a byte.

Each letter of our alphabet is assigned to one of the 256 unique values as specified in the **ASCII code** or the **EBCIDIC code,** depending on which coding system is used by the computer. Mainframe computers typically use the EBCIDIC code, whereas most other computers use the ASCII code.

When a key is pressed on the keyboard, the **Operating system,** which consists of programs that enable the computer to process information, translates the keystroke into the appropriate setting of eight switches (byte) corresponding to the keyboard character. An application program, such as a word processor, can access the byte and interpret the byte as an ASCII or EBCIDIC character.

The Signal

One of the magical features of a computer network is how our words are able to flow through a wire connected to our computer. How are these words sent over long distances? The answer is each bit of the word travels on a signal.

Let's return to high school physics to see how this works. When you were a youngster, you probably dropped a stone in a pond of still water. The stone pushed a few water molecules, which in turn pushed a few more water molecules. You noticed the water moving up, then down to form a wave that traveled in all directions from the impact area.

Waves (Figure 1–1) have at least two characteristics that can be easily recognized. These are the height of the wave, which is the distance above the still water line (called the **baseline**), and the **frequency** of the wave, which is the number of waves that occur within a specified time over a specified distance.

The height of the wave is called the **amplitude** and the number of waves is called the **frequency**. You have probably heard these terms used in connection with radio, with AM referring to amplitude modulation, and FM referring to frequency modulation.

Vibrations of water molecules cause the wave you create in a pond. The more something vibrates, such as with water molecules, the higher the frequency of the wave. This becomes familiar when we think about the vibration of air molecules.

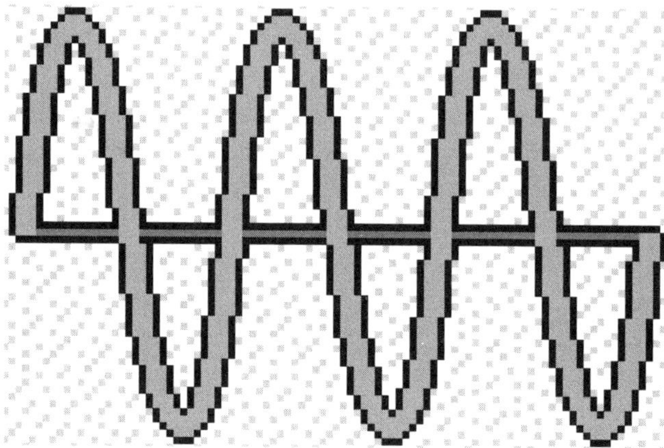

Figure 1–1. *A wave has two characteristics: height and frequency.*

Air molecules are in constant vibration from things moving through the air. We don't notice all these vibrations because we are not in tune with their frequencies. However, we are in tune with a specific range of frequencies called sound waves because those are the frequencies that are detected by our ears.

Waves are categorized according to the **electromagnetic spectrum**, which groups frequencies into subcategories that consist of a range of frequencies. One of these ranges is called **sound waves**. There are also radio waves, microwaves, infrared waves, ultraviolet waves, and light waves.

All these categories of waves have the same fundamental elements, which are frequency and amplitude. However, you probably realize that each category has its own characteristics. This is why microwaves can be used to heat food (among other uses) and light waves are used to illuminate a darkened space.

Just as with waves in a pond, waves described in the electromagnetic spectrum travel from the source of the wave (called the **transmitter**) in a continuous **pulse** until the energy pushing the wave dissipates. The distance the wave can travel is dependent on the category of wave and the amount of energy used to transmit it.

Radio waves, for example, travel in all directions and can be detected by a receiver that is enclosed within walls. In comparison, microwaves travel in one direction as long as an obstacle, such as a wall, does not disrupt them.

A transmitted wave is commonly referred to as an **analog signal**, which is the transport mechanism used to carry information over a distance. Energy that powers the wave is supplied by a fluctuating electrical current.

Imagine a small circuit that contains a battery, a light, and a switch. With the switch off, no electricity flows and the light remains off. With the switch on, electricity is flowing and the light is on. By tapping the switch on and off, you are creating a wavelike signal on the circuit.

Encoding Information

The electromagnetic spectrum is the keystone to every computer network, for this is the fundamental mechanism by which information is transmitted. The question that comes to mind is the following: How is information attached to the transmitted wave?

In the simple light-switch circuit, you noticed that there was voltage or there wasn't voltage. This concept parallels the method used to encode information inside your computer. No voltage could represent a bit value of zero and voltage can represent a bit value of one. You can visualize this as the height of the wave. In a no-voltage state (zero), you'd see the wave at the baseline. In a voltage state (one), you'd see the wave at its full height above the baseline.

The fluctuation of the wave is called **modulation**, which is a term you associate with a **modem**, which stands for modulation and demodulation. **Modulation** is the process of encoding information into a wave and **demodulation** is the process of decoding the information from the wave back to the binary values used by the computer.

A typical network uses a more sophisticated method of encoding and transmitting data than described in the simple light circuit. A transmitter sends a **signal** (wave) of a steady frequency and amplitude even when no data is transmitted. This signal is called a **carrier signal**.

Information is encoded on the carrier signal by alternating the amplitude of the signal based on the binary value of the data being transmitted. The receiver of the signal subtracts the standard amplitude of the carrier signal from the signal received, then decodes the difference in the binary value.

The Connection

Various paths can be used to carry the transmitted signal to a **receiver**. In the case of radio waves, the air is the highway enabling waves of data to move in all directions. Any receiver within the area of the transmitted signal can pick up the signal, then translate the signal into information. Typically, this is in the form of sound waves generated by the speaker of the radio receiver.

The conduit for moving computer data is typically a **cable**, although infrared and radio transmitters are used in hybrid networks. A cable (Figure 1–2) is a cylinder of one or more wires that physically connects one com-

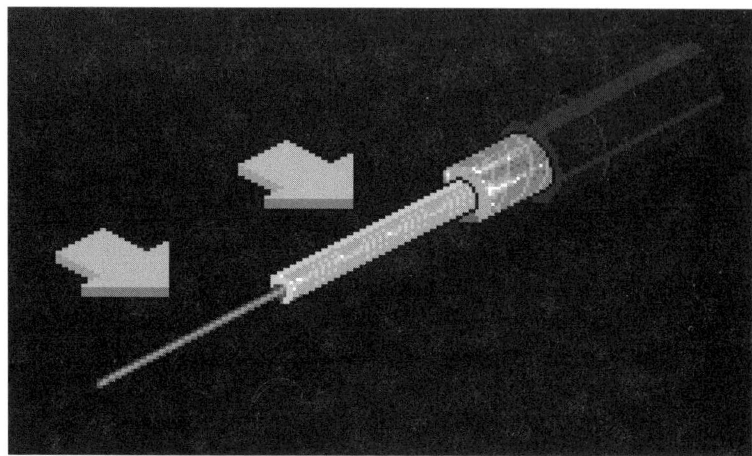

Figure 1–2. *A cable transmits a signal protected from interference by sheathing.*

puter to another computer. An electrical signal flows through the cables and creates a carrier signal.

A cable sits inside a sheathing that isolates the signal from external interference. **Interference** occurs when another transmitted signal using the same frequency enters the cable and conflicts with the transmission. Interference is sometimes referred to as noise. You've probably seen this occur in radio transmissions when a signal from a stronger radio station interrupts a station with a weaker signal operating on the same frequency. The sheathing absorbs conflicting signals and isolates the cable and the carrier signal from external influence.

A network card, also known as a network adapter or nic card, inside the computer serves as a transceiver and connects the motherboard to the network cable. A **transceiver** is a device that sends and receives a signal. It also encodes and decodes data transmitted over the network.

MCSE 1.2 A Computer Network

Not too long ago, data transfer was cumbersome. The only practical method of exchanging data was to print information, then if necessary rekey the information into another computer. Soon this process improved with the advent of the sneaker net, which saw data copied on to a floppy disk then "transmitted" or physically carried to other computers using foot power. Data transfer was slow, but reliable as long as the disk wasn't lost in transit.

Sneaker net lost its esteem as the transfer method of choice with the onset of modems. A **modem** is a telephone for a computer; it enables a computer to call and connect to another computer using public telephone lines. This is similar to how you and I make a telephone call. Once a connection is made, information can be transmitted from one computer to another over the telephone lines.

Modems are much faster than sneaker net, but still fall far short of the computer networks we see today. There are serious drawbacks to using a modem. For example, only two computers can be linked together at the same time. Furthermore, each computer requires its own telephone line and the public telephone system lacks the infrastructure to efficiently transmit computer data, although this is dramatically changing. Also phone lines can be very noisy.

An effiecient way to circumvent the public telephone network is by directly connecting modems of two nearby computers using a special cable called a **NULL Modem Cable**. This cable tricks the modem into thinking it is connected to a telephone line.

However, even a NULL Modem Cable can't meet the ever-increasing demand for highly reliable, cost-efficient sharing of information between lots of computers at the same time. Business sees electronic information sharing as a major way to reduce operating cost and dramatically increase the speed at which business is conducted. Yet not too many years ago, the computer industry couldn't deliver the technology. This sparked a revolution in data communications.

Today, more than two computers can "talk" to each other without having to use a modem. Businesses create private computer networks by linking all their computers together.

All computer networks consist of the same basic elements: two or more computers that use network cards to connect to each other via a cable. It is from this basic model that more elaborate networks are built, which you'll learn about throughout this book.

The sole purpose of a computer network is to transfer information between computers or from a computer to another network device such as a printer, modem, and/or fax which are referred to as a **peripheral**.

Every device (computer or peripheral) on the network is assigned a unique address; such addresses are similar to the address of a house, where the streets are the network cables. An address uniquely identifies the computer or peripheral to all other computers on the network.

Information is sent to a computer or peripheral by encapsulating the information into one or more electronic envelopes called a **data packet**. A data packet (Figure 1–3) has characteristics that are similar to the envelopes we use

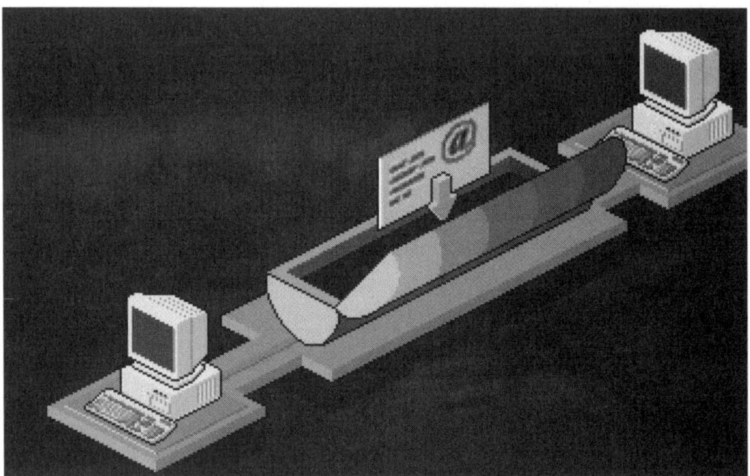

Figure 1–3. *A data packet is like an envelope that contains data transmitted across the network.*

to send letters. For example, a data packet contains a destination address, a return address, and can hold a limited amount of information.

The **destination address** is the network address of the computer or peripheral that will receive the information. The **return address** is the network address of the computer or peripheral sending the information. The amount of information that can be contained in the data packet is determined by the network operating system, i.e., the group of programs that facilitate data transfer.

Often, a user needs to transfer amounts of information larger than the size of the data packet. When this occurs, more than one data packet is used to transmit the information. This is similar to using two envelopes when mailing an especially thick document.

The network card creates and delivers the data packet to the network operating system, which ships the packet along the cable to the destination address. A network card in the destination computer or peripheral receives the packet from the network operating system, then disassembles the data packet. Disassembling strips the transmitted information from the packet information and stores the transmitted data on the destination computer or peripheral.

At times, data packets can be delivered in disarray, making it impossible for the information to be extracted from the data packet. This is commonly caused by interference with the signal carrying the packet. When this occurs, the return address contained in the data packet is used by the destination computer to send a request to resend the damaged data packet.

The Birth of Computer Networks

You'll learn throughout this book that there are a variety of types of computer networks, but all of them have their origins with the small printer networks used decades ago to reduce the cost of printing. One of the first networks involved joining a few computers to a common printer, thus eliminating the need to purchase a printer for every computer.

Technology improved and by 1980 the data communications industry saw the first full-blown computer network that enabled information to be shared amongst computers. This was the birth of the **local area network (LAN)**.

A LAN is indeed local in that computers must be within 600 feet of each other. In the 1980s, LANs reduced the dependency on modems by providing a reliable and efficient way to exchange information.

However, the limitations of private business LANs dampened the full potential cost savings and efficiency demanded by the business community. Independent, isolated, private LANs could not meet the increasing demands of businesses to connect all their computers together to provide a seamless data communications infrastructure that allowed computers to communicate with other computers and peripherals from anywhere in the world.

Furthermore, businesses needed a facility to handle electronic mail, voice mail, and the centralization of office applications such as spreadsheets, word processors, and database applications. Their goal was to reduce cost and increase the efficiency of supporting thousands of users throughout their organization. The solution was to create a network design that used LANs as building blocks for much wider and industrial-strength computer networks.

LANs have become an efficient building block for industrial strength networks. They enable organizations to reduce cost by sharing resources such as printers among computers and provide a shared link to outside services such as to the Internet.

Organizations are also able to centralize data to a centralized location on the LAN such as a database server. Access to the data can be controlled and shared with computers on the network.

Peer-to-Peer Computer Networks

Today's computer networks are enhanced versions of the simple model, where two computers using network cards are connected together using cables. Embellishments to the simple model include a server, clients, a mechanism to connect servers and clients, and information and devices to be shared by clients.

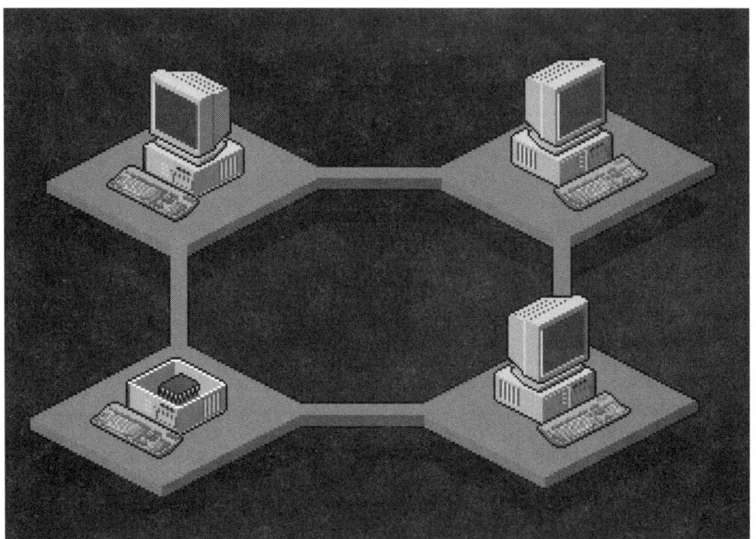

Figure 1–4. *A peer-to-peer computer network.*

A **server** is a computer on the network that contains data files, program files, and other resources that can be accessed by computers connected to the network. A **client** is a computer connected to the network. Cables or a variety of wireless technologies, called the media, are used to link together clients and servers.

All computer networks fall into two general groups. These are peer-to-peer and server-based networks. A **peer-to-peer network** (Figure 1–4), also known as a **work group**, is where each computer on the network is both a client and a server.

Each client can access the resources (i.e., hard disk) of all the other clients. A client on the network can access any other client's files, although those files are on another client's hard disk.

The peer-to-peer network does not have a centralized system administrator. A **system administrator** is the person responsible for maintaining and managing the network and server. Typically, the system administrator, also has the job of backing up the server and setting access permissions for individual users.

In a peer to peer network each user is responsible for administrating his computer and must back up information stored on his hard disk, grant or deny access to directories, files, and other resources on his computer.

A peer-to-peer network is very cost-effective, because a dedicated server is not required, and the business does not need to retain the services of a network administrator. The network operating system to run a peer-to-peer network is built into Microsoft NT Workstation, Windows for Workgroups, or Windows 95/Windows 98. A network operating system manages the exchange of data between computers.

Small workgroups that occasionally share the same files will find a peer-to-peer network a good network solution. However, not all businesses would be properly served by a peer-to-peer network. For example, a peer-to-peer network is not a server-based network. There is no central depository for data files, programs, and other resources on the network. In addition, a peer-to-peer network can serve no more than ten clients, all of which must be located within the vicinity of each other.

Also, all users assume the role of network administrator and must maintain and upgrade software. They must also enforce data security procedures. Therefore, any business that expects to see network growth should avoid creating a peer-to-peer network. Instead, from the onset they should consider and create a server-based design.

Here are things to remember about a peer-to-peer network:

- Less than 10 computers, relatively close to each other, can be connected together to a peer-to-peer network
- Each user is responsible for security for their own computer, therefore peer-to-peer networks should not be used in situations that require sophisticated security.
- Each user administrates his computer. The user must backup disk drives and handle software and hardware upgrades.
- A peer-to-peer network does not contain a central repository for data and programs.

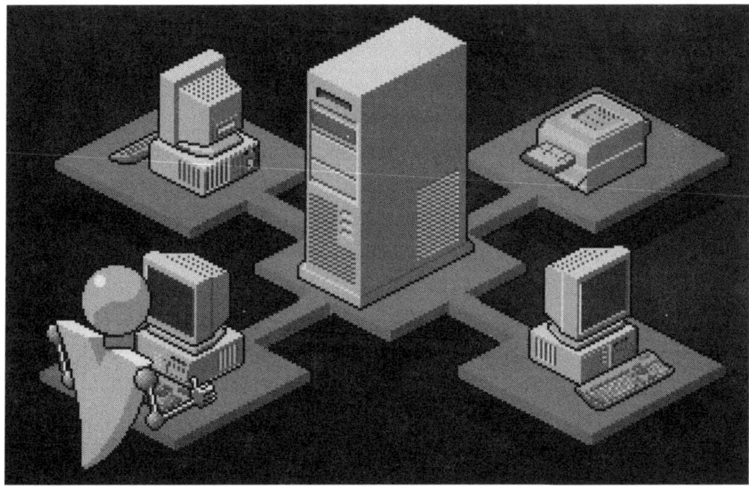

Figure 1–5. *A server-based computer network.*

Server-Based Computer Networks

A server-based network (Figure 1–5) is the best model for most computer networks. It centralizes shared data files, programs, and resources to one or more specially configured computers and is called a server. A **server** has many of the hardware elements found on a desktop computer, including a network card and a unique address on the network. However, it is not used as a client. Instead, the server runs a network operating system that is optimized to manage network operations and to efficiently respond to requests from clients.

A server-based computer network offers a more secure environment than the alternative peer-to-peer network. The key to a server-based network is centralization. All network administration, network security, and network maintenance are managed by the network administrator.

Users are only concerned with using proper login procedures to access the network and correct steps to access network resources. Installing and upgrading hardware and software backups as well as ensuring network security is the responsibility of the network administrator. In contrast, each user in a peer-to-peer network undertakes these duties.

Centralization also provides reliability and consistency in network administration. A trained technician follows standard procedures when performing administrative chores. Therefore, there is uniformity in access control policy, software installations, and other network operational issues.

One of the key roles a server plays in a computer network is to provide network security. The network administrator, based upon a network security policy established by the organization, grants each user access to the network. Permission to use resources is called an **access right**, which is associated with a **network ID** and sometimes called the user or login ID.

Each ID is unique and must be entered when the user logs into the network. An ID is also associated with a password, which consists of a series of characters known only to the user. The network operating system grants access to the network only if both the ID and the password match those stored on the server.

Unlike a peer-to-peer network, a server-based network is scalable, which means the network can grow as additional clients are added to the network. As new clients connect, network traffic increases. At some point, the number of users connected can cause a degradation of network performance. **Network traffic** is a term that refers to the amount of data that travels across the network.

Degradation of network performance is commonly caused by the inability of the server to adequately respond to requests by clients. Network designers overcome this problem by placing specialized servers on the network to spread the task of responding to requests among several servers. Each specialized server handles a specific type of request. Here are the more common kinds of servers:

- **File server** is a central repository for data. Requests for data from a network computer are passed along to the appropriate file server by the network operating system. The file server sends the data to the user if the user has access rights to the data. The data is not sent if the user hasn't been granted access rights.
- **Printer server** manages the flow of information to network printers. Files that are to be printed are transmitted from the user's computer to the printer server where it is placed on the print queue. Files on the print queue are sent to the printer on a first come first serve basis.
- **Mail server** is the central repository for electronic mail. E-mail sent to another user on the network is transmitted to the destination user's mailbox on the mail server. Users retrieve their mail by using e-mail software on their computer to request files from their mailbox on the mail server.
- **Fax server** is connected to one or more fax modems. Users who need to send a fax and have access rights to the fax modem, transmit the fax file to the fax server where the file is queued, then sent when a fax modem is free. Likewise, the fax server receives and stores faxes designated for users on the network.
- **Communications server** acts as a gateway between computers on the network and computers outside the network. This includes communicating with other networks, mainframe computers, and remote computers that need to enter the network via modem and telephone lines.
- **Application server** contains the server side of database applications. Data and database applications reside on the application server and respond to queries for data from clients. Application servers are sometimes referred to as a computer server because the server uses its own CPU to process part of the application.

An application server processes the request, and then sends back to the client the data matching the request. This differs from a database stored on a file server, in which the client requests a copy of the database file. In this case, all the data is downloaded to the client, which places unnecessary traffic on the network.

MCSE 1.3 Network Operating System

A **network operating system** such as Windows NT is the software responsible for transmitting data throughout the network. Think of the network operating system as the software needed to operate the network similar to a PC operating system such as Windows 98 that is needed to operate a PC. The network operating system organizes computers into groups called **domains** and enables clients within the domain to access network resources (i.e., servers, files, programs, printers, and modems). The network operating system is also responsible for storing and accessing information on the server, much like the operating system of the client.

Servers have become increasingly sophisticated in recent years, as manufacturers continue to rush in order to make industrial-strength servers both flexible and scalable. For example, the installation of multiple CPUs on one server is called **symmetric multiprocessing**; to divvy the workload from network traffic among the processors requires flexibility in the network operating system.

Network operating systems must also be able to support multiple platforms, which is the mixture of computers from a variety of manufacturers (i.e., workstations and PCs). Such systems must be able to handle files and directory names of up to 255 characters and file sizes larger than a billion gigabytes (an **exbyte**).

Businesses have come to rely heavily on computers. For many businesses, if the computer network isn't operating properly, then neither is the business. Therefore, a network operating system must be of industrial strength and be able to manage network traffic around the clock. It must also automatically react to disasters, such as when a critical server on the network stops working.

Typically, network designers build redundancy into the network. **Redundancy** is the duplication of servers and critical data on the network. For example, networks used for security transactions on Wall Street have servers and databases that store every trade received by the firm. If the primary server malfunctions, trading operations are automatically switched to the backup server; this is done in a fraction of a second, without risk of losing any transactions.

While network designers can incorporate redundancy in a network design, they must rely on the network operating system to switch to the secondary server/database when a problem arises. This is referred to as a **fault-tolerant network operating system**.

Here's how a fault-tolerant network operating system works. During normal operations, the network operating system transports new and updated data to both the primary and backup servers. Requests for data, such as by a processing program or a client, are funneled to the primary server.

However, such requests are immediately directed toward the backup server when the network operating system detects no response from the primary server. Requests continue to be processed without a disruption to network service.

Recently, in order to capitalize on the advantages of each type of network, designers have merged peer-to-peer based networks with server-based networks. What has resulted is a hybrid network, where the server-base component runs the Windows NT Server (or another network operating system), but clients use theWindows NT Workstation or Windows 95.

Resources (i.e., files, programs, modems) are centrally managed on the server and made available to clients. However, using the peer-to-peer component of the hybrid network, clients can also use the resources available on any other computer.

Network Considerations

Much thought is required to design a computer network using the few network components that are briefly discussed in this chapter. Network designers must answer several critical questions before embarking on a design. The most important question is to determine why the business needs a computer network.

The answer to this question establishes a clear objective for the network designers. For example, management of a Wall Street firm may respond to the question by stating that the firm needs to process 10,000 security transactions a day for 15,000 clients located around the globe.

Network designers must translate this need into **network specifications** that can meet this objective. However, coming up with a viable solution requires careful analysis and understanding as to how the network will be used by the business.

A computer network must meet the needs of the organization. In the Wall Street example, management wanted the network to handle 10,000 security transactions a day, however the firm processed only 1,000 transactions a day with an annual growth rate of 500 transactions a day.

The gap between today's reality and projected growth is addressed by designing computer networks that are scalable. Networks created to meet today's business needs must allow room for expansion without the need to overhaul the network.

There are four factors that must be considered when analyzing the network needs of an organization. These are:

- Size: You must know the type and number of computers that need connectivity.
- Location: You must know where these computers are located.
- Current Needs: In the Wall Street example, network designers need to know the category of users, such as traders, trading assistants, back office staff, and client contact staff as well as how often each group will use the network (i.e. lookup information, enter trades).
- Projected Needs: What are the future needs of the organization such as increases or decreases in employment? Typically an increase in network connections and network traffic is seen when employment increases. Likewise, an increase in business transactions also will increase network traffic.

This is similar to the analysis used by highway designers who need to estimate the maximum number of vehicles that will use the highway. However, instead of projecting the number of vehicles, network designers estimate the number of data packets transmitted at the same time across the network.

In addition to assessing network traffic, network designers must also consider other needs of the business, such as levels of security, response time to the users, and the expense of building the computer network.

Response time is the delay from the time the client computer requests a resource to the time the client receives access to the resource. We have come to expect all computers to respond instantaneously to our requests and measure response time in fractions of a second.

Our tolerances for delays typically fall within a range of expectation. For example, we demand an immediate response whenever we enter data into a computerized data entry form. Yet, we expect to wait for a response to an inquiry we make to a database.

Network designers must anticipate the **user's tolerance range** when planning a computer network. This is similar to the highway designer who knows drivers can tolerate a fifteen second delay; start to become frustrated at a thirty second delay; and become irate at a delay over forty-five seconds.

Therefore, a balance is struck between the user's occasional frustration in peak traffic periods and the economical considerations of building a more robust electronic highway.

■ Summary

The words we create and transmit over a computer network are translated many times into words the computer and the computer network understand. We create our words by typing letters on the keyboard. The computer recognizes those keystrokes as numeric values associated with each letter; these values are based on one of two types of translation charts called the ASCII or EBCIDIC code. The EBCIDIC code is typically used on mainframe computers and the ASCII code on other computers.

Each ASCII or EBCIDIC code value is stored inside the computer, using eight binary digits (bits) commonly called a byte. Each bit can have one of two values: a zero or a one, which is represented by the state of a "switch" inside the computer.

The computer's operating system, the network card, and the network operating system work together to transfer each bit of information across the network and deliver the bits to another computer. The destination computer then reassembles these bits into bytes and into the transmitted information.

Transmission occurs across the network in many ways. Typically, electricity is fluctuated into a wavelike form called a carrier signal. The fluctuations occur at a fixed rate, for instance a frequency. The value of the bit (zero or one) is encoded in the height of the wave, called the amplitude, by the sending computer. The receiving computer decodes the wave heights into values of the bits.

Bits of data can flow among computers using various paths—the most common is a cable. A cable comes in various types, but typically contains one or more solid pieces of copper that conduct electricity with little interference from other signals.

Computers are connected to cables through a network adapter card, which, among other duties, transmits and receives data across the network. This is a LAN (local area network).

LANs fall into two general categories. These are peer-to-peer and server based. A peer-to-peer network is where computers on the LAN have access to each other's resources, that is, printers, modems, and files on the hard disk. There is no central device such as a server on a peer-to-peer network.

The advantage of a peer-to-peer network is that there is no costly server and no need to hire a network administrator, because each user acts as the administrator for his or her computer.

The major drawback of a peer-to-peer network is that each user must have the technical skills necessary to manage resources on his or her computer. This includes data security, data integrity, and software maintenance.

A server-based LAN is one where there is a central device called a server that typically contains the network operating system and shared resources such as files, programs, and devices.

The advantage of a server-based LAN is that a network administrator is assigned the job of managing network resources: network and data access, maintaining software, and troubleshooting network problems. The disadvantage is the expense of the server and of the employee.

LANs for under ten users are typically peer-to-peer networks, while large LANs are server-based. The software that runs a LAN is called the network operating system. An industrial-strength network operating system must be able to handle a network that consists of multiple servers and multiple CPUs within the same server. This is called symmetric multiprocessing.

Multiple servers are used for redundancy processing and storage, for example duplication of data on more than one server. This provides a fault-tolerant network. If one server becomes inoperable, another server can take over without losing data or stopping network traffic.

▲ Chapter Review Questions

▲ Fill in the Blanks

1. *A _____________ network is one that does not use a server.*

Data is represented as a series of __________.

2. *______ and _________ are codes used to represent characters on the keyboard as a numeric value.*

3. *A _______________ is used to connect computers to a network.*

3. *Computers and other devices are identified on the network by their ____________.*

▲ True/False

1. *(T/F) All computer networks have a server.*
2. *(T/F) A network/system administrator must be assigned to every computer network.*
3. *(T/F) A computer on a network is called a client.*
4. *(T/F) Access rights allow a user to turn on a computer.*
5. *(T/F) Too much network traffic can cause a degradation of network response to users.*
6. *(T/F) Less than 30 computers, relatively close to each other, can be connected together to a peer-to-peer network*

▲ Multiple Choice

1. *What is a scalable network?*
   A. More than one network adapter card can be installed in a computer.
   B. The size of the packet changes over time.
   C. Lightweight cable can be used to speed up network traffic.
   D. The network can grow as additional clients are added to the network.
   E. Planners use a model to design the network.

2. *Computers are grouped together into:*
   A. Cable links
   B. Domains
   C. Shared application groups
   D. Units of clients
   E. Buildings

3. *Symmetric multiprocessing means:*
   A. A network operating system can access multiple CPUs.
   B. Packets pass through every computer on the network.
   C. A specially designed network adapter card.
   D. Networks are connected together using a router.
   E. Two wires are used in the network cable.

4. *Network redundancy is used to:*
   A. Reduce network traffic
   B. Build a bridge to another network
   C. Link computers to a printer
   E. Provide uninterrupted access to data when a network server becomes inoperable
   F. Link computers to a modem

5. *A file server:*
   A. Processes request for data
   B. Enables computers on the network to share files stored in a central location
   C. Sends email to the Internet
   D. Joins two networks together
   E. Sends faxes over the telephone line

▲ Open Ended

How does fault-tolerant protect data on a network?

When would you use a peer-to-peer network?

What is the purpose of the network operating system?

How does information you want transmitted over the network translated into a group of bits?

Is network response time important. If so, why?

TWO

The Network Model

▲Chapter Syllabus

Communication among computers appears to be a simple task, especially when you and I press a few keys on the keyboard and information is transmitted in a fraction of a second to a computer miles away.

Even those who assemble a computer network from parts can have a similar perception, since they simply insert network cards inside computers, connect cables, then install network software to have computers "talk" with each other.

In reality, network **communications** is complicated.

Over the last few decades, network engineers have created a plan that outlines the steps necessary for computers to communicate with each another over a computer network. The plan is called the Open Systems Interconnection reference model (**OSI**), which was created in the late 1970s, then revised in the mid 1980s by the International Standards Organization (**ISO**).

The ISO in an organization made up of representatives from countries around the world. Its purpose is to develop standards that are accepted globally. Products that are manufactured to adhere to these standards are compatible with each other. The United States representative to IOS is the American National Standards Institute (ANSI). Late in the 1970s, the ISO developed a theoretical network model the first version of which is the Open Systems Interconnection (OSI) reference model.

The **OSI model** establishes networking standards for manufacturers. Hardware and software manufacturers that adhere to these standards are assured that data will flow seamlessly among computers using their products regardless of the make of the computer or the operating system running on the computer.

You'll learn about the OSI model in this chapter and how it is used to simplify the complex task of transmitting data across the network. You'll also explore a more detailed view of how computer networks function.

MCSE 2.1 Data Transfer

Data communication between computers follows the same basic steps regardless of the type of computer network in use. Inside the sending computer, software identifies the information that is to be transmitted, then breaks up the information into small pieces of data called packets that can be efficiently sent across the network. The address of the destination computer is added to the data as well as other information used for timing and error checking before the data is transmitted.

The network operating system delivers the data to the destination computer, which then strips away the address, timing, and error checking information before reassembling the data back into the information.

You can imagine the complex set of procedures that must be followed by the network hardware and software to accomplish these tasks. These procedures are called **protocols**. A protocol is a set of rules describing how each step in the data communication process is performed. Protocols used to communicate across multiple LANs are known as **routable protocols** and those designed for a single LAN are called **nonroutable protocols**.

Protocols for data communications are defined in two popular standards. These are the **OSI model** and the **IEEE's Project 802**, which beefed up the OSI standards for how network cards send and receive information on a network.

Both standards are important to understand, since they provide a framework for learning the details of how a computer network functions. With this understanding, you'll be able to quickly focus on trouble spots on a computer network.

In addition to the ISO and IEEE, the International Telecommunications Union (ITU), which was known as the Comite Consultantif Internationale de Telegraphie et Telephonie (CCITT), also created protocols that complement some of the OSI layers.

MCSE 2.2 Inside the OSI Model

The birth of local area networks (LAN) in the late 70s saw a rapid demand by the business community for an efficient way to exchange information among computers. However, a major obstacle in meeting this demand was the lack of uniformity among hardware and software manufacturers. Each computer manufacturer could use any number of operating systems that could make data communications impractical.

A solution to this potential roadblock to development of computer networks was the OSI model. A model is a description of how something will look and function. The **OSI model** divided data communications into seven distinct tasks. Each task called a **layer**, describes an aspect of data communication (Figure 2–1) and outlines the protocols required to complete the task. Table 2–1 contains the OSI layers.

Figure 2–1. *Each data packet is passed through each layer of the OSI model, where appropriate information is stripped from the data packet.*

Table 2–1 *The OSI Layers*

Data Communications Steps	Description
1. Physical Layer	Sends/receives packets.
2. Data Link Layer	Prepares the packet for transport.
3. Network Layer	Inserts addressing and sequencing information to the packet.
4. Transport Layer	Handles errors
5. Session Layer	Inserts traffic control information into the packet and begins the session with the other computer.
6. Presentation Layer	Encrypts and formats the information that is being transmitted.
7. Application Layer	Accepts a request for network services from an application.

Each layer receives the information from the previous layer, provides a service or takes an action according to the OSI model, then passes the information to the next layer in the model through an interface. An **interface** is a programmatic way in which a layer can interact with another layer. This is similar to how you use the File Manager in Windows to tell the operating system which file you want to use. The File Manager is your interface to the computer.

Data flows down the layers beginning with the Application Layer when data is being sent across the network. Each layer communicates with the layer above or below it. When data is being transmitted, data is generated by the Application Layer and each preceding layer adds header information to the data. The process is reversed when data is received. Data arrives at the Physical Layer, then passes up to the other layers. Each layer strips away its associated header information until the Application Layer receives just the data.

The transmission process begins with the **Application Layer**. The Application Layer works on the client or server level and makes the network services available to any computer program or application running on the client. A client is another name for a computer connected to the network.

For example, a programmer who develops an e-mail program only needs to make a request to the Application Layer to send a message to another client on the network. The e-mail program provides the Application Layer with required information, then the Application Layer begins the transmission process. It is the Application Layer's job to offer network services such as database access and file transfer to applications like the Windows File Manager and the Windows Explorer.

The Application Layer passes the information that is to be transmitted to the **Presentation Layer**, sometimes referred to as the **translator**. The Presentation Layer translates the information into a format for transmission across the network. This is referred to as an **intermediate data format**, which is the format that can be used by the rest of the OSI model.

It is at this layer where the data is encrypted, compressed and required server resources are identified by a utility called the redirector. Compression is a routine whereby the size of the information is reduced before entering the network.

On Microsoft networks, the redirector works at this level. The **redirector** is a service that represents network information to the applications. This occurs when the Windows Explorer wants the directory of a network drive. The Windows Explorer sends the request just as it does for a local drive, however the redirector intercepts the request and redirects the request to the network server.

Reformatted information is passed from the Presentation Layer to the **Session Layer**. The Session Layer establishes a connection between two applications running on two different computers. This connection is called a **session** and manages the connection between the two computers. The Session Layer controls the communication process by synchronizing tasks with checkpoints in the data flow. **Checkpoints** are signals inserted in the data flow to determine if a communications error occurred. If the receiving computer doesn't receive a checkpoint, then the Session Layer retransmits the data.

Let's say you want to save a file to a network server. The Session Layer on your computer opens the connection with the network server's Session Layer. Once both Session Layers acknowledge the open connection, then data transfer begins. The Session Layers close down the connection once the last packet containing the file is acknowledged by the network file server.

Once the session is established and checkpoints are in place, the information is handed-off to the **Transport Layer** that packetizes the information and is responsible for error checking. Packetizing is the process of dividing large amounts of information into manageable packets, also known as frames, and combines small pieces of information going to the same address into a single packet. A packet is composed of the address of the originator client; the destination client's address; routing information; the data; and a verification and error correction scheme called **cyclical redundancy check** (CRC). Packet size varies according to the different protocols being used.

The next step in the transmission process is the **Network Layer**, typically working on a router, where logical addresses are translated into physical addresses on the network. A logical address is typically a name that represents the actual (physical) address of the destination client on the network. For example, an e-mail might use "Bob Smith" as the logical address for the person. However, the physical address for the computer with an IP address might be something like 147.107.55.151.

The Network Layer also determines the path along the network to use to deliver the packet and avoid any traffic problems along the way such as network traffic congestion and size restrictions. A network component such as a router may reject the packet as being too large to handle. The Network Layer has the job of repackaging the information into smaller packets and re-transmitting the packets.

Packets created by the Network Layer are transferred into frames and sent to the **Data Link Layer**. In large networks, bridges typically work at this level. It is the responsibility of the Data Link Layer to assure packets are transmitted without errors. Once a packet is sent, the destination client returns an acknowledgement message to the sending client. However, if an acknowledgement isn't received, the Data Link Layer resends the packet.

The **Data Line Layer** is comprised of two sub-layers. These are the Logical Link Control (LLC) and the Media Access Control (MAC). The Logical Link Control maintains the link between the two computers while data is sent over the physical network connection. The link is maintained through **Service Access Points** (SAPs) which is a series of interface points that other computers use to communicate with higher network protocol stack levels.

The Media Access Control sub-layer is responsible for permitting computers to alternate sending data on the physical network medium. It is this sub-layer that determines when a data packet can be sent and that the data packet is received without errors.

The last step in data communication process is for the bit stream representing a frame to be sent over the cable. A bit stream is an electronic signal encoded with a series of zeros and ones which represent the frame. This is handled by the **Physical Layer** that manages the physical layer communication such as being responsible for the defining of the pin connection of the cable to the network card. A cable is comprised of several wires each transmitting a unique signal and terminated by a pin. Each pin connects to a connector on the network card. Typically, hubs, repeaters, and transceivers operate at the Physical Layer.

The reverse process occurs at the destination computer where the Physical Layer receives the bit stream that is passed along to the Data Link Layer to acknowledge receipt of packet. The Network Layer provides the Data Link Layer with the source computer's address for sending the receipt. The Transport Layer removes the information from the packet, then passes the data to the Sessions Layer where checkpoints are reviewed. Next, the Presentation Layer translates the intermediate format back to the original format which is made available to the Application Layer, then to programs running on the destination computer.

The seven layers of the OSI reference model are grouped into services. These are the Networking Services, Transport Services, and the Application

Network Services. The Networking Services are comprised of the Physical Layer and the Data Link Layer. The Transport Services Layer contains the Network Layer and the Transport Layer. the Application Layer, Presentation Layer, and the Session layer are within the Application Network Services.

A Look at IEEE's Project 802

The IEEE Project 802 focused on protocols for transmitting bit streams between computers on a network. It complements and enhances the physical layer and data-link layer of the OSI model. Protocols for Project 802 are divided into 12 groups, each handling a group of different network devices such as network cards and cables. Table 2–2 contains the Project 802 groups.

One of the major contributions Project 802 has made to data communications is to enhance physical and the data-link layer (Figure 2–2) protocols to allow more than one computer to access the network without disrupting each other's communication.

This enhancement created an additional protocol for the data-link layer. The additional protocol divided the layer into sublayers called the logical link control (LLC), which handles flow control and the media access control (MAC), which handles network access and responds to errors. LLC requires the use of logical interface points known as service access points (SAPs) to manage data communications. MAC handles all the communication to the network adapter card.

Table 2–2 *IEEE Project 802 Groups*

Project Group Number	Group Name
802.1.	Internetworking
802.2.	Logical Link Control (LLC)
802.3.	Carrier Sense Multiple Access with Collision Detection (CSMA/CD) LAN
802.4.	Token Bus LAN
802.5.	Token Ring LAN
802.6.	Metropolitan Area Network (MAN)
802.7.	Broadband Technical Advisory Group
802.8.	Fiber-Optic Technical Advisory Group
802.9.	Integrated Voice/Data Networks
802.10.	Network Security
802.11.	Wireless Networks
802.12.	Demand Priority Access Land

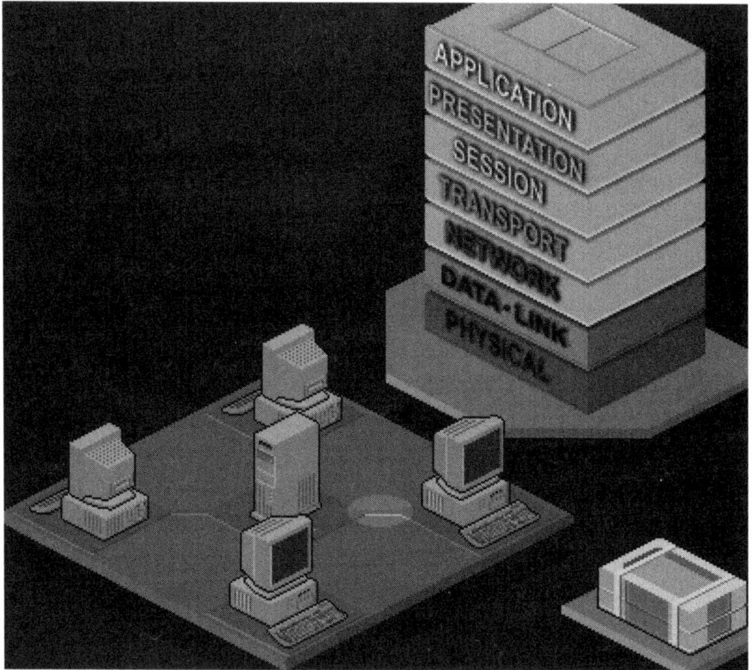

Figure 2–2. *Project 802 defines the physical components of the network.*

IEEE 802.3

The IEEE 802.3 defines the **Carrier Sense Multiple Access with Collision Detection** (CSMA/CD) standard for the **Media Access Control** (MAC) sublayer of the Data Link Layer of the OSI Model. CSMA/CD, also called the contention method, is a way to assure that all clients and servers on a network have the opportunity to transmit data.

CSMA/CD, which is used in **Ethernet networks**, requires network computers to sense if there is traffic on the network before it transmits data. Sometimes this is referred to as listening for the network to be free before sending data. No other computer may transmit data until data currently being transmitted on the network has reached its destination.

CSMA/CD has a distance limitation. The drop-off in signal called attenuation occurs beyond 1.5 miles of network cable. It is at that point when it is difficult to detect network traffic. Clients and servers can find themselves transmitting data at the same time as another computer.

Data collision occurs when multiple transmissions occur simultaneously. 802.3 requires computers to listen for data collisions. Once detected, computers that transmitted the data wait a random time period then retransmit their data.

IEEE 802.5

The IEEE 802.5 defines the **token ring** standard for the Media Access Control (MAC) sub-layer of the Data Link Layer of the OSI Model. 802.5 is a way of avoiding data collisions and the need to re-send data across the network.

A **token** is a small data packet that is passed among clients and servers on the network. A computer that holds the token is the only computer on the network that can transmit data.

The first computer to log onto the network generates the token, which is called a free token because the token does not contain any data. This computer then has the opportunity to transmit data or pass the free token to another computer.

Free tokens are passed to the nearest active upstream computer called the Nearest Active Upstream Neighbor (NAUN). Tokens that contain data are passed to the nearest active downstream computer called Nearest Active Downstream Neighbor (NADN).

The computer that receives the token determines if the token is a free token or if the token contains data. If the token is free, then the computer has the same options as the first computer. That is to send data or pass on the token.

If the token contains data, the computer reads the destination address. If the destination address is that of the computer, data is copied from the token and processed by the upper layer protocols. The computer then toggles two bits in the token and passes the token to its NADN.

The token continues its trip around the network. When the token returns to the computer that originated the transmission (the source address), the computer verifies that the two bits were toggled. This indicates the data was received. Next, the computer removes the data from the token and creates a free token again, then passes the token to NAUN.

If the destination address is not that of the computer, then the data is left intact and the token is passed to the NADN.

This process continually repeats as the token is passed around to all the active computers on the network.

Protocols 802.3, also known as the **Ethernet protocol**, and 802.4 for Token Passing are of particular importance, since they specify how packets are transmitted and received over the network.

Robert Metcalfe and David Boggs developed Ethernet back in the 1972. They were researchers in Xerox's Palo Alto research Center (PARC) and were working on a way to enable several computer systems to connect to each other and share resources. The first commercial version was released in 1975 and enabled the transmission of data amongst 100 computers. This network reached 1 km and transmitted data at 3 Mbps.

The Ethernet protocol requires that the originator of the transmission hold off from sending a message until it is sure no communication is occurring on the network. Simply stated, the network must be silent, otherwise transmission cannot be initiated.

Every client receives all the packets sent along the network, which are transmitted at 10 MBPS. Clients ignore those packets that do not contain their address. Those addressed to the client are acknowledged by the client, letting the originator client know delivery has taken place.

Token Passing uses a similar approach to manage network traffic. However, no client can transmit a packet without first having a token. A token is a special packet sent across the network. A client who has the token is the only client who can transmit information. Once the transmission is completed, the client releases the token, making it available to another client. You'll learn more about how clients access the network later in this chapter.

MCSE 2.3 Protocols

The OSI reference model and the IEEE Project 802 are not programs. Instead they are rules, called standards, that govern each step in the data communications process. Anyone who writes a program to complete a data communications task must be sure their program protocol adheres to the appropriate standard, otherwise their program will not be able to communicate with other network data communications programs.

Figure 2–3. *A protocol suite is a group of complementary protocols that address all data communications needs of a client.*

A protocol is grouped together with complementary protocols to address all the data communications needs of a client. The group of protocols is called a protocol stack or protocol suite (Figure 2–3). Each member of the stack handles a specific aspect of the communications process. There are a number of protocol stacks besides the OSI reference model, as listed in Table 2–3. All of these have protocols that correspond to the OSI reference model.

The OSI layered architecture approach provides several benefits. First, it avoids conflict among data communications programs by isolating data communications tasks to one layer. Furthermore, only one protocol needs to be changed in the protocol stack if a data communications rule is modified.

Each protocol influences how manufacturers of network software and hardware design their products. For example, the application protocol determines how programs such as Word and Excel gain access to network services, whereas the physical protocol establishes the design rules for cable and network card manufacturers.

A protocol stack must be associated with a network card, which is the circuit board inside the computer where network cables are attached, by using software available in the operating system. This association is called the **binding** process, which gives the network designer flexibility when creating a network.

A client can use multiple protocol stacks, which enables a client to communicate with various networks without the need to change communication software. A client could have several protocol stacks, each of which could be bound to the same network adapter card. Likewise, each network adapter card in a client could have its own protocol stack.

You can imagine that multiple protocol stacks on the same computer could cause conflict for the client's operating system. However, protocol stacks are used sequentially, based on the order in which they were bound, which is called the **bounding order**. The first protocol stack bound to the client is used first. If it fails, the client's operating system automatically uses the next bound protocol stack to initiate network communications. Tables 2–4, 2–5, and 2–6 contain the most common protocol stacks used in the industry.

Table 2–3 *Common Network Protocol Stacks*

Network	Protocol Stack
Apple Computer	AppleTalk
Digital	DECnet
IBM	Systems Network Architecture (SNA)
Novell	NetWare
International Standards Organization (ISO)	Open Systems Interconnection reference model (OSI)
The Internet	TCP/IP

Table 2–4 *Common Application Protocols*

Network Protocol	Description
Advanced Program to Program Communication (APPC)	Peer-to-peer SNA protocol (IBM)
AppleTalk	Networking (Apple)
AppleTalk Files (AFP)	Remote file access (Apple)
File Transfer Access and Management (FTAM)	File access protocol (OSI)
File Transfer Protocol (FTP)	File transfer (Internet)
Novell NetWare Core (NCP)	Redirectors and client shells (Novell)
Server Message Blocks (MS SMB)	Redirectors and client shells (Microsoft)
Simple Mail Transfer (SMTP)	Transferring email (Internet)
Simple Network Management (SNMP)	Monitor networks (Internet)
Telnet	Processing data locally on a remote host (Internet)
X.400	International email transmissions (CCITT)
X.500	File and directory services across several systems (CCITT)

PPP and SLIP Internet Protocols

There are two popular protocols used to transmit Internet Protocol packets over telephone and serial connections. **Internet Protocol packets** are used to transmit data over the Internet, intranet, and extranet. These are **Point-to-Point Protocol** (PPP) and the **Serial Line Internet Protocol** (SLIP), both of which are commonly in use in a dial-up connection to the Internet.

SLIP and PPP are similar in that each allows for **point-to-point TCP/IP** serial connection that can be used in Ethernet and Token Ring networks, and satellite links. Satellite links are used to transmit data across vast areas where it isn't economical to use a cable or other wireless connections.

Table 2–5 *Common Transport Protocols*

Transport Protocol	Description
AppleTalk transaction protocol (ATP)	Sessions and data transport (Apple)
Datagram Delivery Protocol (DDP)	Data transport (Apple)
Name Binding Protocol (NBP)	Sessions and data transport (Apple)
Network Basic IO System Extended User Interface (NetBIOS NetBEUI)	Sessions and data transport (IBM)
NWLink	Similar to the IPX/SPX protocol (Microsoft)
Sequential Packet Exchange (SPX)	Sequenced data exchange (Novell)
Transmission Control Protocol (TCP)	Guaranteed delivery of sequenced data. (Internet)

Table 2–6 *Common Network Protocols*

Network Protocols	Description
Internet Protocol (IP)	Packet forwarding routing (Internet)
Internet Work Packet Exchange (IPX)	Packet forwarding routing (Novell)

In a satellite link, data is transmitted from a ground station to a satellite. The signal is then relayed to another ground station directly or to another satellite, then to a ground station.

SLIP is an old, reliable protocol because it has been around for years. SLIP is simple and is widely used. However, SLIP has outlived its usefulness since it lacks features required by today's technology.

The SLIP protocol provides the functionality of the Physical Layer of the OSI Reference Model by controlling the data flow from the modem to the remote computer.

PPP is a newer protocol that contains many of the features missing in SLIP, and it is gradually replacing SLIP as the protocol of choice.

Although both SLIP and PPP transmit IP packets, there are differences between them that you must taken into consideration when deciding which of the two protocols to use with your network.

SLIP

- SLIP is a single protocol transport technology where only one protocol, such as TCP/IP, can be handled at the same time. This is not a severe limitation, however, because it is common to have only one TCP/IP Internet connection.
- The **IP address** of the local computer and that of the remote computer must be known to SLIP to create the connection. An IP address uniquely identifies a computer on the Internet, intranet, and extranet. Typically when you connect to the Internet, your Internet Service Provider assigns an IP address to your local computer dynamically. This poses a problem for SLIP because software that uses SLIP does not recognize dynamic IP addresses. You must manually assign the IP address to your computer to complete the connection.
- SLIP has a less efficient packet throughput than PPP because SLIP does not offer header compression. SLIP transmits the complete IP and TCP headers. However, there is a version of SLIP called Compressed SLIP (SCLIP) that incorporates compression.

- There is no built-in error checking in SLIP. All error checking and error corrections are made by the hardware.
- There are no encryption abilities.

PPP

- PPP can handle multiple protocols at the same time. For example, PPP transports IP, NetBEUI, and IPX simultaneously over one connection. However, this robust feature is rarely used due to the common use of a single TCP/IP Internet connection.
- IP addresses of the local computer and the remote computer are automatically recognized by PPP. PPP negotiates these and other configuration parameters with the server as it makes the connection.
- PPP transmits compressed IP and TCP headers rather than the whole header. Only parts of the headers that changed are transmitted. This gives PPP a more efficient packet throughput than SLIP.
- Enhanced security login is another key feature of PPP. There are two ways in which PPP handles automatic logins. These are through use the Password Authentication Protocol (PAP) and by using the Challenge Handshake Authentication Protocol (CHAP).
- PPP provides the Physical Layer and the Data Link Layer of the OSI Reference Model that gives the modem the same capabilities as a network interface card.
- Error checking is provided by PPP as part of the Data Link Layer mechanism.

Avoid Confusion

There are two factors about SLIP and PPP that can be confusion.

- A new protocol called **PPTP** can be found in Windows NT 4.0. This is not PPP. PPTP is **Point-to-Point Tunneling** used to create a **secure network link.**
- SLIP is sometimes thought as being faster than PPP. This belief is fostered by the size of packets used by SLIP and PPP. The SLIP packet is three bytes smaller than the PPP packet. This reduced packet size has little impact on data transmission.

A Closer Look at Popular Protocols

In addition to the OSI and IEEE standards, there are nine widely adopted protocols issued to manage network communications. These are APPC, AppleTalk, DECnet, IPX/SPX, NetBEUI, NWLink, TCP/IP, X.25, ATM, and XNS.

IBM's **Advanced Program to Program Communication** (APPC) protocol is a critical piece to their Systems Network Architecture (SNA). The most important advantage of APPC is that it establishes rules allowing any computer to directly exchange data with any other computer regardless of manufacture or operating system.

A less robust protocol is **AppleTalk** created by Apple Computer. AppleTalk's major emphasis is to provide a network that links Apple's Mac computers together, enabling them to share resources such as printers and data files.

Digital Equipment developed a network protocol called **Digital Network Architecture** (DNA), which uses the DECnet protocol for Ethernet LANs and for wide area networks (WANs). A **WAN** extends a buildingwide network to locations within a several mile radius, typically using fiber optic instead of cables for transmissions. Two advantages of **DECnet** are that it is compatible with the TCP/IP and meets OSI standards and packets can be routed across networks. Digital Equipment frequently revises the DECnet protocol. Each revision is called a **phase**, which is identified by a Roman numeral.

Novell developed the Internetwork Pack Exchange/Sequenced Packet Exchange (IPX/SPX) group of protocols to transmit packets quickly on a LAN. The major ingredient in IPX/SPX is the relatively small size of a packet. IPX/SPX packets contain less control information than other protocols, primarily because IPX/SPX is not a routing protocol. That is, it cannot be used to exchange data between networks.

The **NetBEUI** protocol is akin to IPX/SPX in that it has been around since the beginning of LANs (in the 1980s) and in that it also does not provide routing capabilities. When NetBEUI was first released, it was joined with the **NetBIOS** protocol. However, ties were broken when NetBIOS, the session layer, was combined with a more robust transport layer than NetBEUI.

However, its major advantage is that the NetBEUI protocol is compatible with DOS-based networks. Microsoft distributed the NetBEUI protocol as **MS NET**, which was Microsoft's first networking system. Microsoft's current protocol is called **NWLink**; it is an enhancement to the NetBEUI and IPX/SPX protocols that is routable.

The most popular protocol is the **Transmission Control Protocol/Internet Protocol** (TCP/IP). TCP/IP is the protocol used to access the Internet and intranets. TCP/IP is a routable protocol that is widely used to exchange information between any computer on any network and handles communication between networks. TCP/IP has overtaken the **Xerox Network System** (XNS), which was an important player in LANs based on Ethernet since the 1980s. At that time, the **XNS** protocol provided a greater transmission of packets along the network than other protocols.

Another long-standing protocol (X.25) is also being challenged by **TCP/IP. X.25** is the protocol used by packet switching networks to link terminals to mainframe computers. An increasing number of firms are using a TCP/IP network to achieve the same results.

TCP/IP is not without drawbacks. It is a very large protocol stack and is slower than other protocols. Furthermore, clients using DOS can experience a degradation of network performance. However, installing Windows NT or Windows 95 on the DOS client can easily rectify this.

NetWare

NetWare based on Xerox network System contains the IPX/SPX protocol suite and is a server-centric architecture. **Server-centric** means that computers make a request for files and other services from a network server.

Table 2–7 *Major protocol suites and their relationship to the OSI reference model.*

OSI Model	NetWare Protocols	Internet Protocols	AppleTalk Protocols	Digital Network Architecture Protocols (DNA)	Systems Network Architecture Protocols (SNA)
Application	SAP NCP	FTP Telnet SMTP NFS	AppleTalk	FTAM MAILbus NVTS Naming Service	DIA SNADS DPM User applications
Presentation	SAP NCP	FTP Telnet SMTP NFS	AFP	ASN.1	APPC CICS IMS
Session	SAP NCP	FTP Telnet SMTP NFS	ADSP ZIO PAP ASP	ISO 8327 Session Control	APPC CICS IMS
Transport	IPX SPX NLSP NCP RIP	TCP UDP DNS	ADSP ATP NBP RTMP	ISO 8073 NSP Naming service	APPN VTAM
Network	IPX SPX NLSP RIP	RIP OSPF ICMP IP ARP	DDP	CLNS CONS	NCP
Data Link	LSL		LocalTalk AARP	Ethernet v.2 HDLC DDCMP	Token ring SDLC X.25
Physical	MLID		LocalTalk EtherTalk TokenTalk	Ethernet v.2	Token ring v.35 RS-232-C X.25

NetWare protocols can be used with TCP/IP and other protocols because NetWare protocols are modular in design and is not limited to the Internetwork Packet Exchange (IPX) protocol and The Sequenced packet Exchange protocol (SPX). Table 2–7 shows the relationship between NetWare protocols and the OSI reference model.

At the highest level of the OSI reference model, NetWare uses the Service Advertising Protocol (SAP) and the NetWare Core Protocols (NCP); You'll notice that a number of protocols work at more than one layer of the OSI reference model.

SAP is responsible for the session administration for the transfer of files. This works on the Application Layer to provide active service advertisement and at the Session Layer to administrate the session. Each network service such as a files server or a printer server broadcasts a SAP packet every 60 seconds to let each network node the service is available. The SAP packet also contains the address of the service that broadcasts the SAP packet. Traffic caused by SAP can cause a bottleneck on the network. In such a case, the network administrator can disable SAP.

NCP contains several function calls that handle the interchange of information between the computer and the server. NCP is responsible to provide reliable delivery of packets. In some situations, NCP makes PSX unnecessary. NCP works on the Application Layer taking on the role of the redirector. On the Presentation Layer, NCP handles translations of data. On the Session Layer, it administrates data transfer. And on the Transport Layer NCP manages connection services, errors control and is responsible for the complete control of the end-to-end flow.

The Transport Layer and Network Layer responsibilities are handled by the Internetwork Packet Exchange (IPX) protocol; the Sequenced Packet Exchange protocol (SPX); the Network Link Services Protocols (NLSP); the Routing Information Protocol (RIP) and NCP.

IPX handles logical network and service addressing, routing selections and services responsible for connection. At the center of IPX is the datagram service that transmits data over the entire network rather than using a direction connection. However, IPX is not suitable for all network communications such as to a print server because it does not send an acknowledgement when a data packet is received. An alternative protocol is SPX.

SPX has similar responsibilities to IPX. SPX uses virtual circuits identified as connection Ids. In addition, SPX acknowledges receipt of a data packet and retransmits the data packet if the acknowledgement is not received.

RIP is responsible for routing through the use of distance-vector route discovery method. This determines the number of hop count, which is the number of intermediate routers between the sender's address and the destination address. Periodically RIP broadcasts routing table information over the network that can create a bottleneck. NSLP provides an alternate solution that reduces the opportunity for a bottleneck to occur.

NLSP uses the link-state route discovery method. Routing information is only broadcast across the network when routing information changes, therefore reducing the chance of a bottleneck.

At the Data Link Layer of the OSI reference model is the **Link Support Layer** (LLS) and the **Multiple Link Interface Driver** (MLID). The LLS is the interface between the MLD and the Network Layer and uses the **Open Data-Link Interface** (ODI) specification. ODI enables easy configuration of client software using the same programs without concerns about the type of network card that is installed in the computer. MLID is the network driver and communicates with the network card.

Internet Protocols

In the 1970s the Department of Defense funded the **Internet** project which set out to connect educational institutions and government installations. The official name for the project was **Advanced Research Projects Agency Network**. The protocols used for data exchange over the Internet are called the Internet Protocols suite.

The **Internet Protocols suite** was developed prior to the OSI Reference Model and used the **Internet Model** sometimes called the **DOD Model**. The Internet model consisted of four layers that handled the same tasks as is outlined in the OSI Reference Model (Table 2–8). The four layers are **Process/Application; Host-to-Host; Internet**; and **Network**.

There are four Internet protocols that operate at the Application Layer, Presentation Layer, and the Session Layer of the OSI Reference Model. These are File Transfer Protocol (FTP), Telnet, Simple Mail Transfer Protocol (SMTP), and Network File System Protocol (NFS).

Table 2–8 *A comparison between the OSI Reference Model and the Internet Model.*

OSI Reference Model	Internet Model
Application Layer	Process/Application
Presentation Layer	Process/Application
Session Layer	Process/Application
Transport Layer	Host-to-Host
Network Layer	Internet
Data Link Layer	Network
Physical Layer	Network

FTP is responsible for transferring files between network nodes such as from a client to a server. FTP establishes a connection with the remote node and administrates the session. It transfers the file and releases the connection once the transfer is completed. This occurs at the Session Layer.

FTP also translates data into a machine-independent file format at the Presentation Layer. And at the Application Layer, FTP provides file services.

Telnet is the protocol used for remote terminal emulation and can emulate a remote host's terminal. At the Session Layer, telnet uses the half-duplex method for dialog control. Telnet also handles connection with the remote node, transfers files and breaks the connection once file transfer is completed. Telnet also handles data translation into an intermediate format (the Presentation Layer) and provides the application (the Application Layer) with access to the remote host.

SMTP is used for routing e-mail. Internet e-mail applications communicate with SMTP and uses TPC and IP to send e-mail over the network.

NFS provides files services and remote operation services. NFS, which was developed by Sun Microsystems, makes a remote file system appear as if it was part of the local file system.

The Transport Layer has three Internet Protocols. These are Transmission Control Protocol (TCP), User Datagram Protocol (UDP), and the Domain name System (DNS). TCP provides the Network Layer with addressing for network services. **TCP** is responsible for assigning port ID sometimes called connection ID to virtual circuits. It is also responsible for providing a full-duplex, transport service to other protocols. TCP uses sequential number to fragment and reassemble messages as well as enhanced error checking through the use of acknowledgements.

UDP transports datagrams. UDP is more efficient than TCP because it lacks the overhead process of acknowledging receipt of datagrams. UDP uses the port address that is a pointer to a process to deliver datagrams. The port address is not a connection identifier as used in TCP.

DNS provides name-to-addressing mapping through the use of a distributed database system. DNS uses the service-provider initiate method of name-to-address resolution.

There are five Internet protocols that work on the Network Layer. These are Internet Protocol (IP); Routing Information Protocol (RIP); Open Shortest Path First protocol (OSPF); Internet Control Message Protocol (ICMP); and Address Resolution Protocol (ARP).

IP handles addressing, switching, route selection, and connection services. IP uses logical network addresses and the **packet-switching method.** It dynamically handles route selection and provides error control connections.

IP data packets has an IP header that contains the source and destination address and a sequence number if more than one data packet is used to transfer a message. A checksum digit is also appended to the data packet as a method of error checking. A calculation is performed on the header information by the source computer that results in the **checksum** digit. The same calculation is performed when the data packet is received. If the checksum digits match, then the destination compute knows that the data packet was received error free. If the digits don't match, then the data packet is retransmitted.

An IP address is 4 bytes and must be unique for each network node. There are four classes of IP addresses. These are denoted as Class A, Class B, and Class C. A **Class A** address use the first bye to identify the network and the last three bytes to identify the host. The first byte must be in the range from 0 to 127. Organizations that have a small number of networks and large number of nodes use this class.

Class B address uses the first two bytes to identify the host and the last two bytes to identify the host. The value of the first bye is from 128 to 191. Universities and commercial organizations use this class.

Class C address uses the first three bytes of the address to identify the network and the last byte to identify the host. The first byte can range from 192 to 223 and is used by organizations that have as mall number of nodes.

Data packets sometimes called **IP datagrams** are routed differently through the network depending on the condition at each hop between the originator and the destination points. If a hop becomes unavailable, an alternative hop is used.

RIP periodically broadcasts routing table over the network and can cause bottlenecks to occur. **OSPF** is used in place of RIP. OSPF is a link state routing protocol and determines the state of a route. If the route is not in operation then another route is taken to the destination node.

ICMP enhances the error handing and control process of IP. ICMP notifies the IP when a link is down or there is congestion on the network. This enables other layers to reroute the data packet.

ARP maps node names to IP addresses and maintains name-to-address tables. If a node name is unknown, ARP sends a discovery packet across the network. The destination node then sends to the ARP the necessary address information.

AppleTalk Protocols

AppleTalk protocol suite is designed to connect Macintoshes together and connect it to other network. The AppleTalk protocol works at the Presentation Layer of the OSI Reference Model and provides networking services to applications that run on the Macintosh.

At the Presentation Layer is AppleTalk filing Protocol (AFP). AFP facilitates file sharing and translates local file system commands into a format that can be understood by the network file system. AFP also verifies login information (Ids and passwords) and encrypts the login information before it is transmitted over the network.

Working at the Session Layer are four protocols. These are Zone Information Protocol (ZIP), Printer Access Protocol (PAP), and AppleTalk Session Protocol (ASP).

ZIP is used to organize network devices into zones, which is a subset of a network. Routers and other network nodes to map between network names and zones use ZIP.

PAP permits sessions to be started by both the service provider and the service requestor. As such PAP is used to connect between workstations and file services and between printer servers and workstations.

ASP is the protocol that establishes, maintains, and disconnects sessions with the remote node. ASP can provide multiple sessions with the same service provider when requests are made individually by a node that request the service.

There are four protocols that work on the Transport Layer. These are ADSP discussed earlier and AppleTalk Transaction Protocol (ATP), Name Binding Protocol (NBP), and Routing Table Maintenance Protocol (RTMP).

ATP is responsible for acknowledging the delivery of data packets and initiate retransmission is the data packet is not acknowledge.

NBP has the job of matching addresses to logical device names. NBP is also responsible for acquiring the address for name of a node.

RTMP creates and maintains routing tables that are used to dynamically route data packets over the network.

Datagram Deliver Protocol (DDP) works on the Network Layer and with the RTMP, NBP, and ZIP to deliver data packets. DDP uses the complete address of the destination node to route data packets over the network. The address contains the logical network address, node address and socket number.

At the Data Link Layer and the Physical Layer are four protocols. These are LocalTalk Link Access Protocol (LLAP), EtherTalk LocalTalk Link Access Protoco (ELAP), TokenTalk LocalTalk Link Access Protoco (TLAP) and AppleTalk Address Resolution Protocol (AARP).

LLAP sometimes called LocalTalk handles multipoint connections, data synchronization, flow control, and error control.

ELAP uses Ethernet protocol's contention access, collision detection standard. Likewise, **TLAP** is AppleTalk's implementation of the Token Ring Protocol.

AARP has the responsibility to map AppleTalk addresses to the physical to Ethernet and Token Ring addresses.

Digital Network Architecture Protocols

In 1974, Digital Equipment Corporation developed **DECnet**, which is the implementation of Digital Network Architecture protocols (DNA). Table 2–2 compares the **DNA model** to the OSI Reference Model.

At the Applications Layer, DNA has four protocols. These are File Transfer, Access, and Management (FTAM), MAILbus, Network Virtual Terminal Service (NVTS), and Naming Service.

FTAM is recognizes certain document types that can be transferred. These include text and binary files. However, vendors can create customized implementation of the FTAM protocol.

MAILbus is the protocol that handles messaging for remote clients and is used for e-mail services. **NVTS** provides virtual terminal access to network nodes. It translates data from the local terminal format to the network format. **Naming Service** is responsible for addressing and OSI directory services.

Workings on the Presentation Layer are two protocols. These are Abstract Syntax Notation One with Basic Encoding Rules (ASN.1with BER) and Session Control. **ASN.1 with BER** has the task of establishing generic file syntax. This enables unlike computer systems to exchange files. **Session Control** is a proprietary protocol that manages sessions between nodes. It resolves logical names with physical addresses, manages the connection, and selects the protocol stack.

On the Session layer are two protocols. These are the Session Control that is mentioned earlier and ISO 8327. **ISO 8327** protocol opens, maintains, and closes sessions between network nodes similar to the Session Control protocol. It negotiates connections, translates data in half-duplex, can handle multiple connections for each session and synchronize packet transfer.

At the Transport layer are three protocols. These are ISO 8073, Network Services Protocol (NSP), and also the Naming Service, which is discussed earlier.

ISO 8073 is also known as the Connection-Oriented Transport Protocol Specification enables different classes of network services to be tailored to specific implementation requirements. Flow control, error control and data packet sequencing can determine which class to select.

NSP is one of the original protocols and is used for flow control and can handle full-duplex channels.

Working on the Network Level is two protocols. These are Connectionless-Mode Network Service (CLNS) and Connection Oriented Network Service (CONS).

CLNS is a connectionless service responsible to manage communication between two devices and performs simple routing functions other than network routing. It also determines routes through the network.

CONS is a connection oriented service that provides link-state route discovery and dynamic rout selection. It also handles Network Layer data packet sequence control, flow control and error control.

The Data Link Layer has three protocols. These are Ethernet v.2, HDLC, and DCMP.

Ethernet v.2 is the basis for IEEE 802.3. It uses Carrier Sense Multiple Access with Collision Detection (CSMA/CD) to access the media. It can transmit at 10 Mbps data using coaxial cable and uses a different frame format than the IEEE 802.3 standards.

HDLC provides asychronous or synchronous service, half-duplex or full duplex, point-to-point or multipoint topologies. Error control, flow control and frame sequencing.

DDCMP provides flow control and point-to-point connections. It also defines the data frame format and command frame format.

Systems Network Architecture Protocols (SNA)

Systems Network Architecture Protocols evolved from IBM's proprietary networking SNA architecture started in 1974. The IBM created the seven-layer SNA Model that is the basis for the OSI Reference Model. Table 2–9 shows the relationship between these models.

The Applications Layer contains four protocols. These are Document Interchange Architecture (DIA), SNA Distributed Services (SNADS), Distributed Data Management (DMM), and User Applications.

DIA is responsible for translating documents into a standard format that can be translated into a format the destination computer can understand. It also coordinates file transfer, document retrieval and document storage. **SNADS** is the protocol that distributes files using the store-and-forward technique. It also provides the facility for e-mail distribution. **DPM** is responsible for providing remote access to files over the network. It makes remote files appear local to clients. **User Applications** are applications that require network services.

There are five protocols working at the Presentation Layer. These are Ad-

Table 2–9 *A comparison between the OSI Reference Model and the SNA Model. The SNA Model was the basis for the OSI Reference Model.*

OSI Reference Model	SNA Model
Application Layer	Transaction Services
Presentation Layer	Presentation Services
Session Layer	Data Flow Control
Transport Layer	Transmission Control
Network Layer	Path Control
Data Link Layer	Data Link Control
Physical Layer	Physical Control

vanced Program-to-Program Communication (APPC), Customer Information Control System (CICS), and Information Management System (IMS).

APPC provides addressing and segment sequencing in addition to end-to-end flow control. It also is responsible for administration of the session and half-duplex control. **CICS** provides input and output commands for the SNA and is used for building transaction-processing applications. It manages half-duplex control and session management. **IMS** is similar to CICS in that it is used for building transaction-processing applications and handles half-duplex control and session management. IMS enables more than one application to schedule transactions and to share databases.

At the Transport Layer are two protocols. These are Advanced Peer-to-peer networking (APPN) and Virtual Telecommunications Access Method (VTAM).

APPN enable s peer-tp-peer network communications between multiple physical unit type 2.1 devices. It also offers flow control, directory services and route discovery. **VTAM** control data flow and data communication on an SNA network. It can control both single and multiple domains, handles addressing, end-to-end flow session administration, and data transfer.

There is only one protocol working at the Network Layer. This is Network Control Program (NCP). **NCP** is responsible for routing, gateway services, physical and logical addressing and static route selections.

The Data Link Layer has three protocols. These are Token Ring, SDLC, and X.25.

Token Ring uses the token passing access method to transmit data over the network. The network must be either a physical star topology or a logical ring topology. This is the basis for the IEEE 802.5 standard. **SDLC** provides half-duplex and full-duplex connections using either a dedicated leased line or a dial-up line. It adds link level headers to the data packets received from the Network Layer and generates specific control messages. **X.25** is the Wide Area Network standard for packet switching and provides a permanent or switched vital circuits. X.25 uses channel addressing which is similar to logical network addressing. The difference is that X.25 maintains an address for each connection.

Working at the Physical Layer is four protocols. These are the Token Ring and X.25, both previously discussed, and v.35 and RS-232-C.

MCSE 2.4 Packets

Throughout this book, we've been talking about **data packets**, which are at the center of how information is transported between computers in a computer network. In this section, we'll take a closer look at the structure of a data packet that is assembled by the data-link layer protocol.

One of the more imposing problems that computer network engineers faced was developing an efficient mechanism to get information from one computer to another. The term efficient is subjective. However, all of us know when something such as a computer network is inefficient.

End users, which you and I are whenever we communicate over a computer network, tend to measure the efficiency of a computer network by response time. An instantaneous reaction by the network to our request is deemed very efficient. The longer the response time of the network, the less efficient we believe it to be.

Two critical factors influence the response time of a computer network: the number of clients wanting to/or transmitting messages and the amount of information contained in each transmission. Other factors discussed throughout this book also influence response time.

The best way to visualize how the number of messages and the size of a message impacts the performance of the network is to think of the computer network as a highway of trucks carrying boxes. Boxes are information; the highway is the computer network; and each truck is a packet sent by a client on the network.

There is a limited number of trucks that can be on the highway at the same time. Longer trucks such as tractor trailers carry more boxes (information) than shorter trucks such as a pickup truck, but tractor trailers take up more space on the highway, which reduces the number of trucks that can be on the highway at any one time. Clients sending the other trucks will experience a delay during a heavy rush-hour period.

The data-link layer protocol reduces response times by defining a standard packet size, which is similar to designing a standard sized truck in the highway analogy (Figure 2–4). Information to be transmitted across the net-

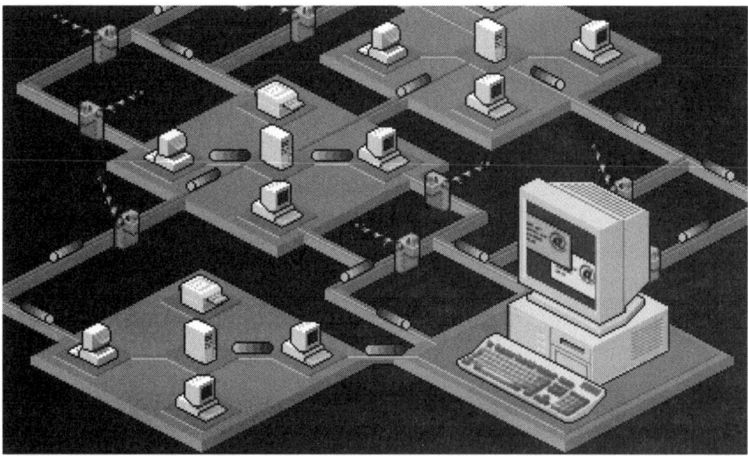

Figure 2–4. *Data packets carry data across the network to other clients.*

work to another computer must fit within the standard sized packet. The actual size is determined by the data-link layer protocol used on the network and range from 512 bytes to four Kilobytes.

Information larger than the size of a packet must be broken down into more than one packet by the data-link layer. The data-link layer on the destination client's system reassembles the packets back into the original information. Standard packet sizes give each client the same opportunity to transmit information regardless of the amount of the information that is being transmitted.

Computer networks are exposed to another type of delay called **retransmission**. Retransmission occurs when a corrupted packets is received by the destination client. In such cases, the destination client asks the originating client to retransmit the packet, which doubles the time it takes to transmit the single message.

Packet Details

A data packet is similar to the envelope we use to send correspondence through the mail. It contains a specific structure consisting of the packet header, the packet information, and the packet trailer.

The **packet header** is like the outside of the envelope and contains four kinds of encoded data. The first is data that signals the network operating system that a packet is ready to be transmitted across the network. Once this signal is received, the packet is queued for its turn on the network, depending on the protocols used for transmission. You may think of this as the stamp on the envelope. The postal service ignores envelopes without stamps because the envelope isn't ready to be sent.

The next two components are the address of the client sending the packet and the address of the destination client. The last component in the packet header is information used to synchronize the transmission with network traffic.

The packet trailer typically contains encoded information used by the destination client to determine if there were errors in the packet information. This is called the cyclical redundancy check (CRC), which requires the originator client to use packet information in a calculation, then encode the results of the calculation in the packet trailer.

The destination client performs the same calculation on the packet when it arrives, then compares the results to the packet trailer. If the result matches the trailer, then the designation client assumes that the packet was received error free, otherwise the destination client uses the originator client's address in the packet header to request a retransmission of the packet.

Packet Transmission

Once the data-link layer creates the packet, the physical layer, through the network adapter card sends each byte of the packet across the network. The packet is received by every client network card that is connected to the network (Figure 2–5). Each network card "reads" the destination address of the packet, then compares it with its own encoded address from its network card.

If the addresses match, then the network adapter card sends an interrupt message to the destination client's operating system, indicating a network transmission was received. However, if the address of the network adapter card and the destination address of the packet differ, then the packet is ignored. This process is called **packet directing**.

Many computer networks provide a **broadcast service** feature to clients. A broadcast service is used by any client on the network to send information to all network clients without having to include all their address in the packet header. This is similar to addressing letters to all postal customers in a community.

All packets require a destination object including those packets that are transmitted using a network broadcast service. However, a special broadcast address is used in the packet header in place of a unique destination address used in a typical transmission. A **broadcast address** is one in which every network card on the network is recognized as its own address.

You could say each client has two addresses. One address is their unique address on the network and the other is a shared address with all

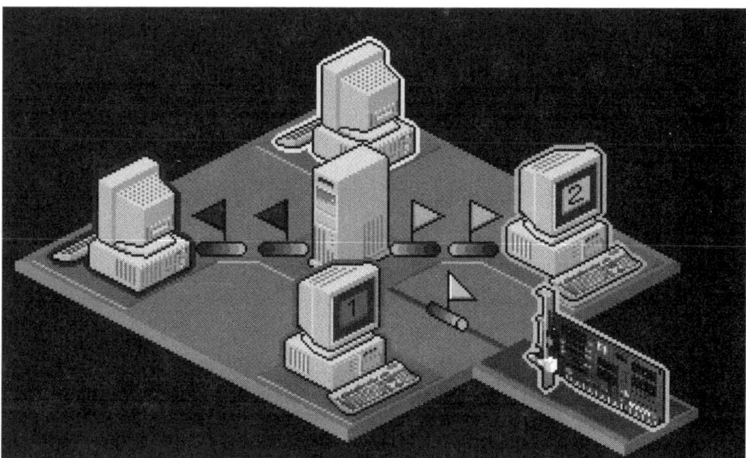

Figure 2–5. *The network adapter card in every client receives each data packet and determines if the data packet is addressed to its client.*

other clients. This is like a person able to receive postal mail using either the unique combination of zip code, street, and house number and being able to receive junk mail addressed to all houses in a particular zip code.

Multiple computer networks are used within a business. Typically, a LAN handles communications among a group of clients located within the same vicinity. However, businesses have a need to transmit packets to any of their LANs. This is made possible by connecting the LANs using a device called a router.

A **router** is a network device whose job it is to redirect packets that are addressed to clients outside of the originator's client's LAN. Part of the packet's destination and origination address identifies the LAN also called segment.

Think of a router as a regional postal distribution center where letters addressed to people located in another state are redirected to another local post office. In this example, the local post office is a LAN and the regional postal distribution center is a router.

MCSE 2.5 Device Drivers

Thanks in large part to IBM, computer manufacturers have used an open architecture philosophy when designing their computers. Open architecture means that anyone can enhance the capability of a computer by creating devices that connect to the motherboard (main circuit board) of the computer.

The term device describes a broad category of hardware such as modems, printers, scanners, and network adapter cards. Each of these devices speaks its own language. That is to say, each device uses a set of encoded vocabulary words to perform its job. However, the computer and other devices it interacts with probably use a different set of encoded vocabulary. This can cause a communication gap.

This is very similar to an American visiting England and being told someone is going to "ring you up." The American knows this to mean that someone is going to "call them on the telephone." Both expressions mean the same thing. However, the words need a bit of translation before successful communication can take place.

Devices also need an interpreter to translate to and from the computer and other devices. This interpreter is called a **device driver**. Actually, a device driver is a program that receives information in one language, then outputs the information using another language.

Device drivers are the keystone to the success of the open architecture philosophy. Independent manufacturers can create specialty hardware products which can be used with a variety of computers if these device drivers exist to communicate with the computer.

Device drivers are typically supplied with the device on a CD, disk, or can be downloaded from the Internet. They must be installed on the computer before the computer's operating system will recognize and communicate with the device (Figure 2–6). Device drivers are unique to each device and device drivers are written for a particular make and model of a network card to be used with a particular computer/operating system. In the case of the network card, it is contained within the data-link layer.

However, the more common popular device drivers are distributed with most operating systems such as Microsoft NT and Windows 95. This is commonly referred to as the **hardware compatibility list** (HCL), which the operating system manufacturer has tested to assure compatibility with the operating system.

Furthermore, operating systems that support **Plug and Play** (PnP) will automatically use the proper device driver the first time the computer is turned on after the device is installed.

Plug and Play compatible means the operating system identifies new devices installed in the computer, then configures the device automatically without any user interaction. If the device driver cannot be found, the operating system displays a message prompting the user to install the device driver.

Computer networks use a device driver called a network driver that handles communication translations between the networking operating system's redirector and the network card.

Figure 2–6. *Device drivers are supplied on a CD, disk, or can be downloaded from the Internet.*

The **redirector** is a program that handles the duties of a mail carrier to take the packet from the network card at the originator client and deliver the packet to the network cards of all the other clients on the network.

In the early days of computer networks, one protocol stack could be bound to each network driver and **network interface card** (NIC). However, this posed a dilemma when networks expanded and multiple protocols such as TCP/IP and IPX/SPX were being used.

The brunt of the concern was for servers that needed to communicate with various kinds of client computers. Rather than installing in a server multiple network interface cards each having a different protocol bound to it, developers created **driver interfaces** that allow multiple protocols to be bound to the same network interface card.

There are two driver interfaces commonly in use. These are the **Open Driver Interface** (ODI) and the **Network Driver Interface Specifications** (NDIS). ODI was developed by Novell and Apple and is used in Novell's NetWare networks. NDIS was developed by Microsoft and used in Microsoft networks.

Both ODI and NDIS enabled the creation of device drivers for network interface cards without regards to the protocols that will be used for the network interface card.

Device Driver and Protocol Maintenance

Typically, device drivers and protocols must be manually installed on a computer using an interface provided by the operating system. For example, device drivers and protocols are installed in Windows NT by using the Control Panel. Others can be installed using a setup program that is distributed with the device.

Installation procedures are defined by the operating system. However, the same procedure is typically used for all device drivers and protocols. As part of the installation procedures, device drivers and protocols may need to be fine-tuned to the operating system and hardware. This is called configuring the device driver or the protocol.

Configuration procedures vary with the device, but typically require **DIP** switches to be set or jumpers to be repositioned on the network adapter card. **DIP** switches are tiny toggle switches grouped together into one or more sets physically attached to the network card. A jumper is a tiny plastic component that is used to connect two of three prongs protruding from the network card to set parameter.

Newer network adapter cards are configured by using software run from the computer or by being **PnP** compatible. There are no DIP switches to set or jumpers to reposition on the device.

A **network administrator**, who is the person responsible for maintaining a computer network, must remove and upgrade device drivers and protocols when appropriate if the network or client operating system is upgraded.

Not all upgrades to the operating system require that the device driver or protocol be upgraded. Typically, the device or protocol provider will announce if the existing device driver or protocol must be upgraded.

Upgrades are available from the device manufacturer and are commonly delivered by downloading the device driver from the device manufacturer's web site. The upgrade is also available as part of the operating system HCL list. Upgrading procedures are identical to the installation procedures.

MCSE 2.6 Network Traffic Control

Imagine the traffic flow along a busy computer network of a typical business. It reminds me of rush-hour traffic, where packets of data are like cars and trucks rushing to be the next on the highway. The problems facing highway traffic are also present on a computer network.

Data traffic on the cables of a computer network could easily come to a swift halt if it weren't for network traffic control procedures called access methods. The access method is akin to the rules of the road, which if followed practically guarantee successful transmission of data to any client on the network.

Early attempts to develop a robust network of computers were thwarted when several computers tried to send packets across the network at the same time. As you can imagine, the second packet transmission interfered with the first, causing the loss of both packets. None reached their destination.

In an effort to address this problem, network engineers created various access methods to control the flow of packets on the network. Table 2.7 contains a listing of four popular access methods.

One of the original access methods is Carrier Sense Multiple Access Method with Collision Detection (CSMA/CD). Clients on networks that use CSMA/CD, also known as the Contention Method, must test the network for an existing packet before transmitting its own packet. However, nothing prevents the client from transmitting even if another transmission is under way.

Collisions between packets do occur. However, CSMA/CD requires clients to test the network to determine if their packet collided with another packet. If a collision is detected, then clients who transmitted a packet must resend their packet.

Table 2–7 *Popular Access Methods for Computer Networks*

Access Method	Network Type	Communication Type
Demand Priority	100VG-AnyLAN	Hub Based
Carrier Sense Multiple Access Method with Collision Avoidance (CSMA/AD)	LocalTalk	Broadcast Based
Carrier Sense Multiple Access Method with Collision Detection (CSMA/CD)	Ethernet	Broadcast Based
Token Passing	Token Ring/ ArcNet	Token Based

This scenario sets up the possibility for a total stoppage of network traffic when clients detect a collision, then attempts to retransmit packets immediately. Obviously, this will likely cause another collision of packets, requiring each client to repeat the process over again.

Network engineers anticipated networks being virtually locked by collision and retransmissions. They built into CSMA/CD a routine that forced each client whose packet was involved in the transmission to pause, then retransmit the packet at random intervals. This statistically lowered the chances that a network lock caused by responses to packet collisions would occur.

CSMA/CD performs well under many circumstances. However, there are serious drawbacks that must be considered when deciding on this access method. The first concern is the need to retransmit packets that are involved in a collision. This increases network traffic. Four transmissions happen instead of two transmissions for every collision.

Fortunately, data transmission speeds on most networks are more then adequate to counteract the effects of this unnecessary traffic. However, network traffic in a typical business is dramatically growing. As more clients join the network, there is the increasing likelihood of packet collisions. There could be a point when this additional traffic would degrade the performance of the network unless a network administrator assigned new clients to less traveled network segments.

Another serious limitation of CSMA/CD is that clients who transmit packets must test the network to determine if a collision has occurred. The problem is this electronic test is only good for networks of under 1.5 miles. Beyond this point, the signal of the collision is too weak to be detected by the client.

In an effort to overcome the deficiency of the CSMA/CD access method, network engineers came up with an access method that avoids collisions rather than detecting them. This access method is called the **Carrier Sense Multiple Access Method with Collision Avoidance** (CSMA/AD).

The CSMA/AD access method requires clients to send a signal to the network operating system that it intends to transmit a packet. A return signal informs the client whether there is currently a packet in transit. If so, the client holds off transmission, then repeats this step until an all-clear signal is received, at which time the new packet is sent.

On the surface, CSMA/AD appears to be a better solution to network traffic control than CSMA/CD since it checks the network traffic before sending a packet. However, network engineers found this to be a less desirable access method because of the increased traffic on the network caused by clients signaling their intent to send a packet. CSMA/CD actually slows network traffic when compared to the CSMA/CD access method.

Contention among clients to transmit packets and collisions of packets on the network are avoided when **Token Passing** is used as the access method to the network. A **token** is a special packet that is sent along the network to every client by the network operating system. A client has the choice of accepting the token packet or ignoring it.

When a client accepts the token packet, the client can transmit its own data packet across the network. Only when that data packet successfully reaches its destination will the client release the token packet back to the network. If a client ignores the token packet, then the token is delivered to the next client and continues its path until a client accepts the token.

The advantage of Token Passing is efficiency in transporting a packet with a low risk of retransmission. Token Passing does not eliminate retransmissions. A packet can still be corrupted during the trip, which will require the destination client to request a retransmission. However, there will not be a retransmission due to a collision with another packet.

The disadvantage of Token Passing is that a client must wait to receive the token packet before it can send its data packet. The client must wait for all the other clients on the network to ignore the token before the waiting client has the right to transmit across the network. This delay is built into the network regardless of whether the waiting client is the only client desiring to send a packet.

The most recently developed access method is called IEEE 802.12 **Demand Priority**. The Demand Priority approach, created for use with the 100 MBPS Ethernet standard (100VG-AnyLAN), defines the cabling required for the network as well as the method used by clients to transmit packets.

There are four pairs of wires used with the Demand Priority access method, allowing clients to transmit and receive packets at the same time. This feature reduces contention among clients for the use of the network, but does not eliminate the chance that two clients would attempt to transmit a packet at the same time.

In a network using Demand Priority, the network administrator can establish a priority for data transmission. The network hub polices transmission priority. The **network hub**, also known as a repeater, is a device connected to all clients and devices (i.e., printers) called end nodes on the network.

The purpose of the hub is to receive transmitted packets, then redirect the packets to the destination address. It is the hub that will detect contention among two clients attempting to transmit a packet. The hub will allow only one of them to complete the transmission based on the priority established by the network administrator. Whenever two packets have the same priority, the hub alternates between the two clients.

You can think of a hub as a bus station that is the destination for all buses. Passengers leave their bus, then enter the station to find their next connection to continue their trip to their ultimate destination.

The major advantage of the Demand Priority access method is that clients send and receive packets using two electronic pathways, one for sending and the other for receiving packets. This design increases the efficiency of the network.

This is similar to the enhancement a telephone has over a two-way radio used for CB and on boats. Telephones enable two people to talk and listen at the same time because a separate wire is used for transmitting and receiving. Whereas, a twoway radio has only one communication path, either allowing a person to transmit a signal or listen for a receiving signal, but not both.

The use of the hub to control traffic flow is another improvement the Demand Priority access method brings to the way clients access the network. Packets are no longer broadcast to every client. Instead, all packets are sent to one destination—(the hub) where they are reviewed, then sent directly to their ultimate destination.

■ Summary

Computer networks consists of a physical network (i.e., computer network cards and cables) and a logical network that defines how information will be transmitted among computers on the network (standards, protocols and software).

The OSI reference model and IEEE's Project 802 define the logical computer network. Both of these set guidelines for the development of network software and hardware, so that products created by different manufacturers can communicate with each other.

The OSI reference model divides network communications into seven tasks call layers. These are as follows:

1. Physical Layer
2. Data-link layer
3. Network Layer
4. Transport Layer
5. Session Layer
6. Presentation Layer
7. Application Layer

The data transmission process begins with the application layer, which gathers information from an application then moves through subsequent layers until the physical layer sends the data across the network. Data received from the network goes through the reverse process, beginning with the physical layer and ending with the application layer, which makes the data available to an application.

Data communication follows strict rules, called protocols, that specify how a particular task is to be performed. A protocol isn't a program or a piece of hardware. Instead, it is the algorithm for handling data communications. There are a number of data communications protocols, the most common being TCP/IP. TCP/IP is the protocol for communicating on the Internet.

Information is divided into small pieces of data that are then encapsulated with other information into a data packet. A data packet is like an envelope in that it contains the address of the computer sending the data, the address of the destination computer, synchronization information, the data, and an error-checking value called the cyclical redundancy check (CRC).

CRC requires the originator of the message to perform a calculation based on the data in the packet. The result of this calculation is stored at the end of the packet. When the packet is received, the destination computer performs the same calculation, then compares the results with the value stored in the packet. If the values match, the destination computer assumes the data was received error-free, otherwise a retransmission request is made.

Computers on the network, also known as clients, see all packets, but read data contained in packets addressed to them and ignore all other packets. There are commonly two kinds of addresses: the unique address of the client and a broadcast address. A broadcast address is one in which all clients on the network read as if it is their own unique address.

Packets travel the network similar to how cars travel a highway. Like highway traffic, there can be traffic congestion on a computer network when multiple computers try to send packets at the same time.

Network operating systems control network traffic by using the Carrier Sense Multiple Access Method with Collision Detection (CSMA/CD); Carrier Sense Multiple Access Method with Collision Avoidance (CSMA/AD); Token Passing; or Demand Priority.

CSMA/CD requires each computer that sends a packet to test that the network is free, then send the packet and listen for a collision between its packet and one on the network. If a collision is detected, then the originators of both packets must retransmit the packet.

CSMA/AD requires each computer that sends a packet to first signal its intention on the network, then send the packet. This method is slower than CSMA/CD because the signal creates additional network traffic.

Token Passing passes a special packet called a token to each computer on the network. A computer that receives the token can transmit its own data packet. Once the data packet is received, the computer generates and transmits a new token packet. This method avoids data packet collisions on the network, because only one computer can transmit at any point in time.

Demand Priority requires network traffic to use four pairs of wires: two for sending data packet and two for receiving data packets. All data is transmitted to a central network connection called a hub. The hub reroutes data packets to the appropriate computer. The hub also enforces the transmission priority that is used to decide which of two data packets received simultaneously by the hub is processed first. Computers on the network only receive data packets addressed to them. There are no broadcast messages.

▲ Chapter Review Questions

▲ Fill in the Blanks

1. *A ____________ is a set of rules used to define how to communicate among computers on the network.*

2. *The ____________ and the ____________ are the addresses stored in a data packet.*

3. *Error checking is performed by using the ____________ that performs a ____________ on the data, the stores the results in the ____________ of the packet.*

4. *The three parts of a packet are ____________, ____________, and __________.*

5. *A token is a ____________ that is received in turn by every computer on the network.*

▲ True/False

1. *(T\F) The Application Layer transmits the packet on the network.*
2. *(T\F) Demand Priority broadcasts all the transmitted packets to every computer on the network.*
3. *(T\F) A computer using CSMA/AD signals the network its intent to send a packet.*
4. *(T\F) TCP/IP is the network adapter card used to transmit information across the Internet.*
5. *(T\F) A router is used to redirect packets to computers located on other networks.*
6. *(T\F) The Application Layer of the OSI Reference Model is found on a client.*

▲ Multiple Choice

1. *What is the Binding Order?*
   A. The order that links cable to the network adapter card.
   B. The order in which the protocols are bound to the network card.
   C. The method the Application Layer communicates with the Physical Layer.
   D. The way the parts of a packet are joined together.
   E. The technique used to link routers to segments.

2. *Packets received by a computer are:*
   A. Stripped of everything but the data, then the data from one or more packets is reassembled into the transmitted information.
   B. Retransmitted to the router.
   C. Sent directly to the application.
   D. Re-addressed and returned to the network.
   E. Stacked segmented.

3. *A protocol stack is:*
   A. Packets queued to be transmitted.
   B. A special packet used to signal the network operating system.
   C. A group of protocols that work together to handle network communications.

D. Control flow software stored in a router.

E. The upper layer in the binding process.

4. *________ is a single protocol transport technology where only one protocol, such as TCP/IP, can be handled at the same time.*

   A. SLIP

   B. PPP

   C. IP

   D. IPX

   E. NDIS

5. *The _______ defines the token ring standard for the Media Access Control (MAC) sub-layer of the Data Link Layer of the OSI Model.*

   A. IEEE 802.11

   B. IEEE 802.5

   C. IEEE 803.8

   D. IEEE 802.10

   E. IEEE 802.9

6. *Two driver interfaces that allow multiple protocols to be bound to the same network card are the ________________ and the ____________________.*

   A. Open Driver Interface and Network Driver Interface Specifications

   B. PPP and SLIP

   C. IP and IPX

   D. IEEE 802.1 and IEEE 802.4

   E. None of the above.

▲ Open Ended

Communicating devices are using incompatible line protocols. Verify that the devices are configured for the same or compatible protocols. If one computer initiates a connection using PPP, the other computer must be capable of using PPP.

THREE

Topologies and the Connection

▲Chapter Syllabus

Any time I install a new network connection, I receive the same response from the end user, "where is the network?" Most are disappointed with the installation because they expect to see a new electronic contraption attached to their computer or at least fancy software to dazzle coworkers who lack such a connection.

I simply point to the cable coming from behind the computer and show them the network file server on their system. That's all there is until their application software taps into network services and opens a vast new world giving them capabilities they rarely appreciate.

We tend to overlook the network technology because its complex design of cables, computers, network adapter cards, software, and other components do their work invisibly. Even logging into the network has become transparent, since this typically occurs when we start our computer. Many believe they are simply logging into their personal computer and not the network.

So far in this book, you've explored the logic of network design and the concept of how information is exchanged on the network. In this chapter, you'll learn about the physical components of the network. I like to call this the nuts and bolts of a computer network.

MCSE 3.1 Topology

Every computer network has basically the same components. These are cables (or wireless connections), network cards that transmit and receive information, clients, and software that makes all these components work together. Remember, a client can be any network device (computer, hub, printer, modem, etc.)

These are the building blocks of a computer network and can be assembled in various ways to exchange information efficiently among computers. The way in which components are assembled is called the design, or the topology, of the network. There are six topologies used in the design of a computer network; these are bus, star, ring, token passing, hubs, mesh and hybrid. The choice of design is dependent upon factors relating to the installation, which will be presented later in this book.

Bus Topology

A bus topology (Figure 3–1) requires that all the clients on the network be connected to common cable. This cable is known as the **trunk**, segment, or **backbone**. Every data packet that is transmitted on the bus network are received by every network client. When a packet is received by a client, the

Figure 3–1. *A bus topology is where clients are connected to the same cable.*

client checks the destination address against its own address. Data packets not addressed to the client are ignored, otherwise the data packet is accepted and processed by the client.

The signal encoded with a data packet travels the complete length of the cable, then bounces back when the end of the cable is reached. This is called **signal bounce**; the bouncing continues until the signal loses energy and dissipates. Only one client can transmit at a time.

Signal bounce has a serious effect on network traffic, since the reflected signal can interfere with newly transmitted signals on the cable. This is especially critical on a bus topology because only one client at a time can transmit a signal. It can be difficult to troubleshoot.

Network engineers solved this problem by developing a network terminator. A terminator connects to the ends of the cable and absorbs the network signal, preventing the signal from bouncing back along the cable.

Therefore, a signal carrying a data packet is picked up by all clients, one of which accepts the data packet. When the signal reaches the end of the cable, the terminator removes the signal from the cable.

Network clients do nothing to the signal being transmitted on the network. Clients simply receive the signal, then accept the data packet or ignore it. The network operating system has the responsibility of keeping transmissions moving along the cable.

The network is not dependent on any client. That is, a client can malfunction and the network will continue to operate. This is why a bus topology network is called a **passive topology**. Clients do not play a key role in network operations.

A bus network is easy to construct, expandable and highly reliable, although it is susceptible to slow performance when there is heavy network traffic and can experience a network outage because of a break in the trunk. A break in the trunk causes the signal to avoid the terminator. Therefore, the network experiences signal bounce.

A break in the cable is rarely caused by a cut cable. Instead, it is commonly caused by an improper network connection to a client or a network device (i.e., a printer). A loose connection has the same effect as an unterminated cable. Breaks are hard to track down on a bus network, because every client and device on the network could be suspect. Fortunately, a network outage does not shut down a client's operation. Instead, clients work as a stand-alone computer until the network is back in operation.

Star Topology

The star topology (Figure 3–2) gets its name from the arrangements of cables leading from clients to a central device, which is called a **concentrator** or a **hub**. Clients on a star network transmit and receive data packets to and

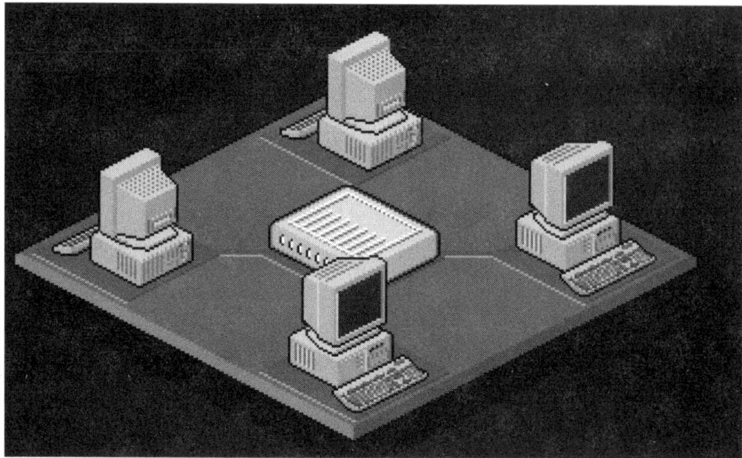

Figure 3–2. *A star topology wherein cables lead from clients to a hub.*

from the concentrator. They are not connected directly to other network clients. It is the job of the concentrator to redirect data packets to the appropriate client.

Each client on the network only receives data packets addressed to it. Other data packets never enter the client's network card, which reduces the amount of network traffic clients must handle.

The concentrator is able to detect if a client is not connected to the network and, therefore, returns to the sender data packets addressed to the unavailable client. All other network operations continue uninterrupted. That is, the failure of one client does not disable the entire network.

However, network services to clients become unavailable if the concentrator malfunctions. Clients on a star network use 10BaseT network cards, and can also be 100 MB cards, which automatically detect trouble with the concentrator. The client then stops any transmission of data packets and operates as a stand-alone computer until the concentrator becomes operational.

Star networks are:

- Easy to set up and maintain
- Expandable
- Has centralized management
- Since each client is connected to the other concentrator and not to other clients, clients don't have to wait for the network to be free before transmitting.

Ring Topology

Conceptually, a ring network (Figure 3–3) requires each client to be connected consecutively to the single circular cable. This differs from a bus network in that there are no ends to the ring network that must be sealed with a terminator.

Data packets pass clockwise from one client to the next. If the data packet isn't addressed to the client, the client resends the data packet to the next client. In doing so, the client adds new energy to the signal, which is similar to a repeater that strengthens the signal allowing the data packet to travel a further distance on the network.

The ring network actually resembles the physical design of a star network in that all clients are directly connected to a hub, which facilitates the transmission to each client in the order of the ring network.

However, each client on the network has an active role in network communications. So if one client is not working properly, then there is a good chance the entire network will fail. Finding the problem is time-consuming. This depends on the network operating system and associated components (i.e., network cards). Some ring networks, such as those created by IBM, automatically ignore inactive clients.

Ring Networks:

- Has to have a closed circuit to function.
- Performance is normally consistent
- The entire network is disrupted to add new clients

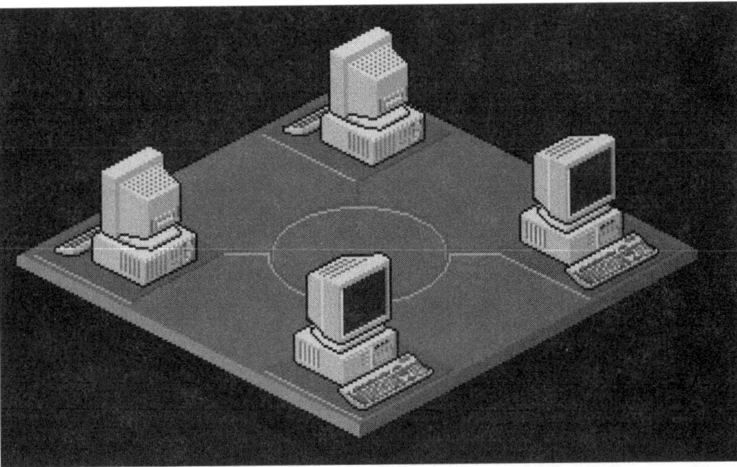

Figure 3–3. *A ring topology, wherein each client is connected consecutively to a single cable.*

Token-Ring Topology

A token ring is a ringlike topology in that clients are connected together to form a ring and each data packet is transmitted to each client on the network. However, a special packet called a token is used to control transmissions on the network.

The token packet is delivered to clients clockwise along the network. The client has the choice to accept the token and transmit a data packet or pass the token along to the next client on the ring. This is called token passing. Actually, the token packet is sent to the hub, which sends it to the next client. Token packets can travel more than 10,000 times around the network per second.

If the token is accepted, only that client has permission to transmit a data packet. The token packet is modified to include addresses, data, and other information necessary to create a data packet. The modified token packet becomes the new data packet and is sent to the hub for delivery to the destination client. Once the destination client acknowledges receipt of the data packet, the client that sent the data packet creates a new token packet and passes it to the next client via the hub.

Hub Topology

A **hub** (Figure 3–4) is a central processing device and is used with the star and ring topologies as a concentrator for network traffic. Networks use one of two kinds of hubs, either passive or active hubs.

A **passive hub** acts as a connector box, and is also referred to as a wiring panel. It is here where cables from all clients come together to form a joint connection. A passive hub only provides connectivity among network clients. It does not interrupt transmissions on the network.

An **active hub**, also known as multiport repeaters, joins together clients. However, it also has intelligence to boost the signal along the network (like a repeater) and in some cases to redirect data packets to the appropriate client.

LANs which connect multiple Hubs are sometimes called a hierarchial topology because it can look like an organizational chart.

Hub topology has become very popular as a means of dividing networking requirements into smaller, serviceable LANs called segments. A hub enables network administrators to monitor and manage network traffic; link together other segments; mix and match cabling used by various clients (i.e., fiber optics, coaxial); and to isolate network disruption to a single segment.

Hub Topology:

- Easy to expand
- The rest of the network is not affected when one client goes down.

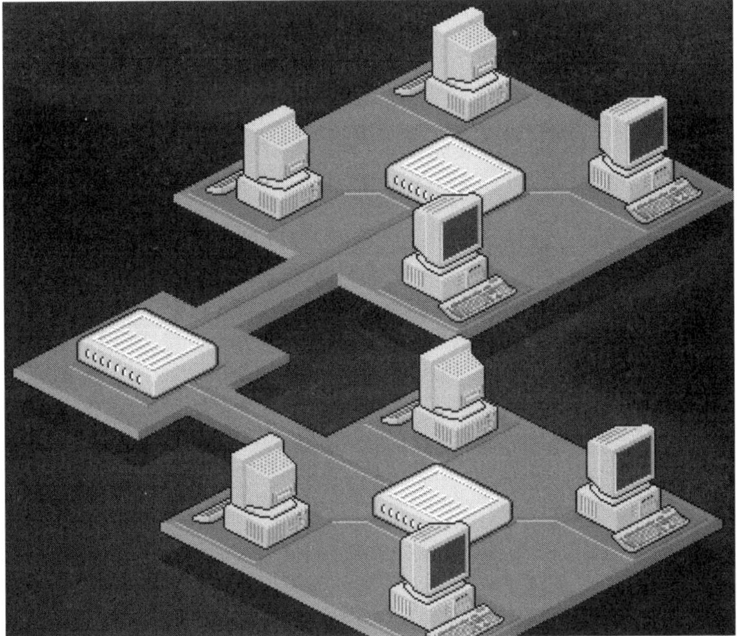

Figure 3–4. *Hub topology connects clients to a central device called a hub.*

Hybrid Topology

Network designers are able to reduce the disadvantages of each topology by creating networks that combine topologies. What results is a mixture of networks, which is commonly called a hybrid network. There are two common hybrid networks. These are a star bus and star ring hybrid topology.

As the name implies, the star bus topology combines the star topology and the bus topology into one large network. The network is divided into several smaller networks, each one uses a star topology where clients are directly linked by cable to a concentrator or hub.

A star bus network typically would have several concentrators, each being the central device for the smaller network. Concentrators are connected together using the bus topology, where a single cable is used to connect each concentrator to the next concentrator on the network. Therefore, network concentrators are linked together in a bus topology, while clients of the smaller networks use the star topology to connect to its network concentrator.

The star bus topology provides a unique way to control traffic flow on the network. Traffic between concentrators is typically less demanding than traffic among clients. Therefore, the bus topology is a more direct and efficient design for connecting concentrators. However, the start topology enables an efficient means of using the concentrator to avoid transmission conflicts among clients.

Another advantage of the star bus topology is that it enables the network to be expanded to meet the growing needs of the organization. For example, if network response time is slow because of an increase in traffic, clients can be transferred to a different segment with its own concentrator or an entirely new segment can be created and linked to the network.

The star ring topology combines the best of the star and the ring networks. This is commonly referred to as the star wired ring network. Similar to the star bus network, the star ring network divides the network into smaller networks, each having a concentrator or hub used to connect network clients. The concentrators are joined together using a master concentrator sometimes called the main hub in the form of a ring.

The advantage of a star ring network is similar to that of the star bus network, in that network traffic is handled by a topology that best suits the volume of traffic and that the network is scalable.

A hybrid network reduces the chance that a complete network failure will occur. For example, only clients directly linked to a concentrator will lose access to network services if the concentrator malfunctions, other clients would continue to work unaffected by the outage on the segment except when a client attempts to access another client on the affected segment.

Mesh Topology

A Mesh topology contains redundant links between devices to provide fault tolerances. When one link goes down, the other link maintains connectivity. The mesh topology also guarantees communication channel capacity. However, they are difficult to install and to reconfigure and are costly to maintain.

Only a small number of devices can be linked to a Mesh topology, otherwise the network becomes unmanageable. For example, five devices would require 10 connections. Organizations that require a Mesh topology usually install a hybrid Mesh where some, but not all devices have redundant links.

MCSE 3.2 Network Cables

Once a network topology is selected, attention must be given to how clients, servers, and other devices are connected together. There are two common methods used to connect network devices. These are by cables or by using a wireless connection. The cables are often referred to as **media.**

Many LANs are connected using cables. A cable consists of one or more wires wrapped in a protected sheathing. The wires are a conduit for a signal transmitted by a network card. There are over 2,000 kinds of cables on the market. However, these can be grouped into three familiar categories. These are coaxial, twisted pair, and fiber optics.

A coaxial cable contains a single core of copper wire similar to the wire used for your cable television connection. Twisted pair consists of at least two strands of wire twisted together. You'll recognize this as the wire connected to your telephone. Fiber optics consists of a thick tube of polished glass that transmits a light beam. You won't find fiber-optic cables around your home, yet. Plans are underway to replace cable television cables and telephone lines with fiber-optic cable in the future.

Cables are susceptible to two critical influences. These are stray signals (interference) that can interfere with data packets and the ability to transmit a signal over a distance without losing the signal strength. The loss of signal strength is called attenuation.

All cables are affected by these influences. However, each category of cable addresses these problems differently, which is one of the reasons network designers choose a particular cable for a network. Other factors entering into the choice of cable include the amount of information that will be transmitted; the length of the network; the installation restrictions; and the cost allocated to building the network.

Coaxial Cables

Coaxial cable (Figure 3–5) is the choice of many network designers because it is reliable, cost-effective, and easy for technicians to pull through walls and crawl spaces. It also has a high resistance to interference, a low rate of atten-

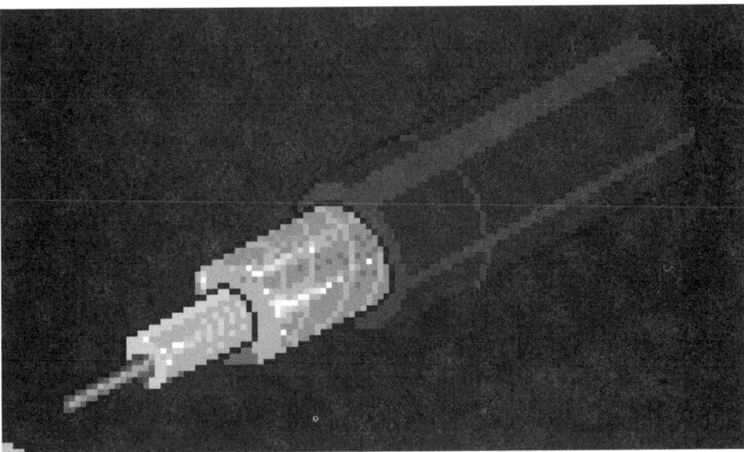

Figure 3–5. *Coaxial cable is reliable and cost-effective.*

uation, and can handle fast voice, data, and video transmission speeds over long distances.

The copper core of the coaxial cable is surrounded by a three-layer protected sheathing that consists of an outer rubberlike cover (sometimes made of Teflon or plastic), followed by a **braided metal shield** and **foil insulation** that separates the shield from the copper core. This is called a dual shielded coaxial cable, which refers to the metal shield and the foil insulation.

The shield and the foil insulation protect the signal traveling on the cable from ambient signals of similar frequencies that are in the environment around the cable. Ambient signals are unwanted signals that can corrupt data packets transmitted on the network. You've probably experienced similar interference when you hear a radio station's signal while listening to your telephone. Wires inside your telephone or the telephone line itself inadvertently picks up the radio signal, which is then transmitted to the telephone receiver.

Shielding around the cable absorbs stray frequencies, also known as noise, before they reach the copper core of the cable. Networks within environments that are susceptible to higher occurrences of noise than the average office building will require additional shielding on the cable. In such cases, network designers use quad-shielded coaxial cables that consist of two layers of braided metal shielding and two layers of foil insulation.

The core of a coaxial cable is either a single solid strand of copper or several strands of copper. It carries the data packets among computers on the network. In addition to being susceptible to noise, a coaxial cable can receive signals from adjacent wires. This is called **crosstalk**, wherein two signals cross over to each other's wire. The foil insulation around the core, called the **dielectric insulation**, reduces the occurrence of crosstalk by acting as a ground for the shield. The foil insulation also prevents the shield from touching the copper, which would disrupt the transmission of data packets.

Coaxial cable is available in two types. A thin cable called **thinnet** and a thick cable called **thicknet**.

Thinnet Coaxial Cable

A thinnet coaxial cable has all the characteristics of a coaxial cable, but the thickness of the cable is 0.25 inches, which makes this a perfect candidate whenever network cables must be snaked through a restricted area of a building.

Thinnet is used in many network installations because it is flexible and can directly connect to a network adapter card, yet the cable still can carry a signal 600 feet before attenuation is realized. For signals that must travel beyond 600 feet, a different kind of cabling is used or a repeater is connected to the thinnet. A **repeater** is a device that receives, amplifies, and retransmits the signal on a network.

A thinnet cable is a member of the RG-58 family of cables. RG-58 is one of several standards created by cable manufacturers to group cables that have similar characteristics. The RG-58 family has a 50-ohm impedance. **Impedance** is the resistance the cable has on an alternating current passing through the cable. **Ohms** are a measurement of resistance. Table 3–1 contains a listing of cables that fall within the RG-58 family.

Thicknet Coaxial Cable

A thicknet coaxial cable (Figure 3–6), which is more difficult to install than thinnet and is more costly, is better known as the standard Ethernet because of its use in the early Ethernet networks. As the name implies, a thicknet cable with a diameter of 0.5 inches is thicker than the thinnet cable. The larger diameter enhances the transmission distance. Attenuation isn't realized for 1,600 feet.

Both thicknet and thinnet are used in networks found in most buildings. The thicknet is used as the main trunk line to carry data packets across long distances, such as between floors in a building. In this implementation, the thicknet is referred to as the **backbone**.

Thinnet is used to connect clients and hubs to a transceiver that joins together the thicknet and the thinnet. The **transceiver** exchanges signals from the thicknet and the thinnet, enabling clients to communicate with other clients located outside their area.

A **vampire tap** also known as **piercing tap** is used to break into the sheathing of the thicknet cable to make the physical connection between the transceiver and the thicknet cable. The connect between the transceiver and the clients' network adapter card is made using a DB-15 connector, also known as the **Attachment Unit Interface** (AUI) port connection, which is connected to the thinnet cable commonly called a **drop cable**.

Besides the vampire tap and the DB-15 connector, there are other kinds of connectors used to connect thinnet and thicknet coaxial cables. These connectors are called the **British Naval Connector** (BNC) and are typically soldered or crimped to the end of the coaxial cable. **Three** types of BNC are described in Table 3–2. BNC terminator absorbs signal bounce back.

Table 3–1 *Cables in the RG-58 Family*

Family Name	Description
RG-58 /U	Core: solid copper
RG-58 A/U	Core: stranded wire
RG-58 C/U	C/U Military specifications. Core: stranded wire

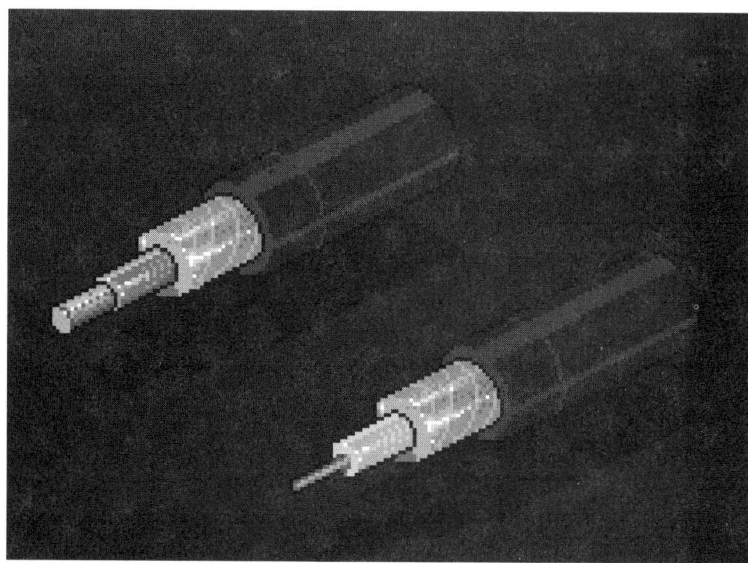

Figure 3–6. *The top cable is thicknet coaxial cable and the bottom is thinnet.*

Fire Regulations and Coaxial Cables

Whenever a cable of any kind is placed in the space between the false ceiling and the floor above in a building, called a **plenum**, the cable must meet specific fire code regulations because a burning cable could be lethal to the occupants of the building.

The cable industry grades a cable by the sheathing around the cable. There are two common grades: **Polyvinyl Chloride** (PVC) and Plenum. Fire officials have serious concerns over cables that have a PVC covering. Poisonous gases are given off when the PVC coating burns. The noxious gas emanating from PVC cables located in the plenum will circulate freely throughout the building.

Fire regulations in many states prohibit the use of PVC grade cables in the plenum and other areas of the building. Instead, fire officials require

Table 3–2 *Types of BNC Connectors*

Connector Type	Description
BNC T Connector	Connects the network adapter card to the coaxial cable.
BNC Barrel Connect	Connects two lengths of thinnet cable together.
BNC Terminator	Terminates ends of a bus network cable.

plenum grade cables. Sheathing on a plenum grade cable is fire resistant, meaning it will take longer to burn than other grade cables.

Furthermore, only a small amount of smoke is produced when a plenum grade cable reaches its flash point. As you would expect, the additional protection provided by a plenum grade cable isn't achieved without drawbacks. Plenum grade cables are more difficult to install because the added protection makes them less flexible than other grade cables and it is more costly than PVC grade cables.

Twisted-Pair Cable

Twisted-pair cable is more recognizable as the standard telephone wire that contains two or more copper stranded wires twisted around each other. The twisting action is used to reduce interference from electrical devices. Twisted-pair cable is ideal for economical LAN connections that can handle up to 100 MBPS. There are two types of twisted-pair cable (Figure 3–7). These are unshielded (UTP) and shielded (STP).

The most common twisted-pair cable is Category 3 UTP, which meets the 10Base T specification. It contains two copper wires that are insulated and can be successfully used in a LAN up to 325 feet. UTP cables are certified for a particular use by the Electronic Industries Association and The Telecommunications Industries Association (EIA/TIA) 568 Commercial Building Wiring Standard. The standards are specified by category number, as listed in Table 3–3.

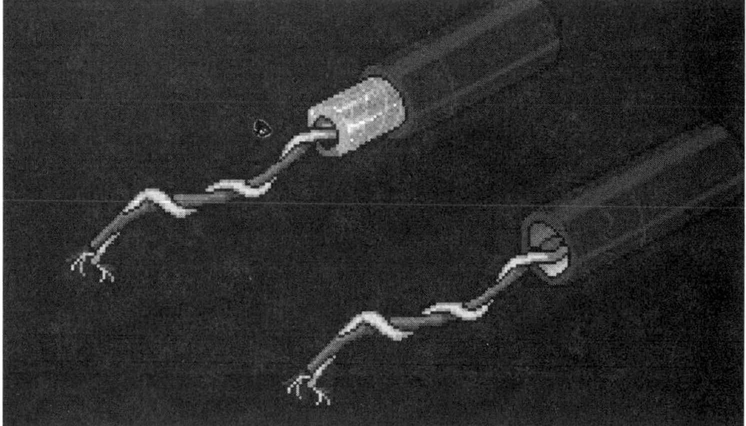

Figure 3–7. *Twisted-pair cable is available in shielded (top) and unshielded (bottom) form.*

Table 3–3 *Category of Twisted-Pair Wires*

Category	Description
1	Two-twisted pair. Telephone cables before 1983 are certified to carry voice but not data.
2	Four-twisted pairs. Certified to carry data up to 4 MBPS.
3	Four-twisted pairs with three twists per foot. Certified for data up to 10 MBPS.
4	Four-twisted pairs. Certified to carry data up to 16 MBPS.
5	Four-twisted pairs. Certified to carry data up to 100 MBPS.

UTP is widely used for LANs because UTP is installed through many existing buildings as part of the building's telephone system. Typically, not all the UTP telephone pairs are used for telecommunication. Extra cables are installed in anticipation of future needs.

If the existing UTP cabling is certified for data, then these cables can be included in the network design, which reduces the cost of running cables. However, an uncertified UTP is likely to expose the LAN to interference caused by other communication signs. This is called crosstalk.

Crosstalk (Figure 3–8) and other kinds of interference can be greatly reduced by using a shielded twisted-pair cable (STP). STP cable contains a braided sheathing of woven copper around the twisted-pair cable; in addition, each pair within the cable is surrounded by a foil wrap. These protection measures enable STP cables to transmit data faster and over greater distances than a UTP cable.

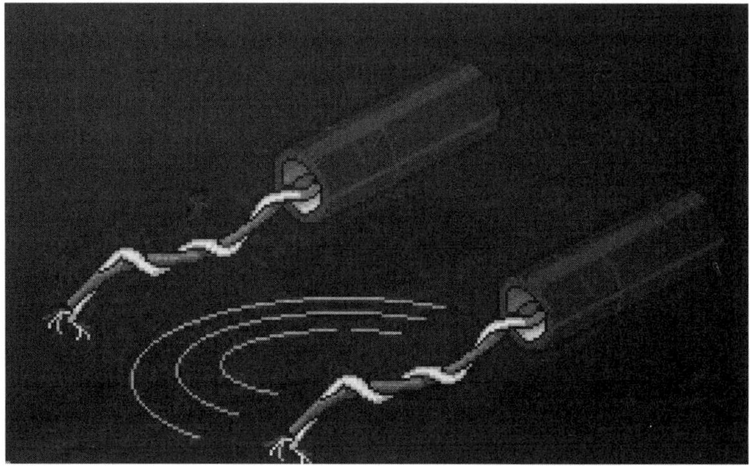

Figure 3–8. *Crosstalk occurs when a signal from one cable is inadvertently received by another cable.*

Twisted-pair cables are connected to components of a LAN, for instance a network card using the RJ-45 which is similar to the RJ-11 connector used to connect your telephone cable.

Both the RJ-45 and RJ-11 (Figure 3–9) are similar in appearance, except the RJ-45 connector is almost double the size of the RJ-11. This is because the RJ-45 contains eight cable connections and the RJ-11 has four cable connections.

Twisted-pair cables typically run from clients and network devices located throughout a floor of a building to wall plates. The plates are similar in appearance to an electrical outlet, except the wall plate accepts only an RJ-45 connector.

From the wall plate, the twisted-pair cable connects to a centrally located room called a communication closet. In there, twisted-pair cables flow onto distribution racks and shelves and eventually into expandable patch panels, where they are connected to the backbone of the building's data network system.

Fiber-Optic Cable

Fiber optic cable (Figure 3–10) is not a cable in the traditional sense, as it does not contain any wires. Instead, a fiber-optic cable consists of one or more long glass tubes that transmits pulses of light. These light pulses are encoded with a binary value that represents a bit in a data packet.

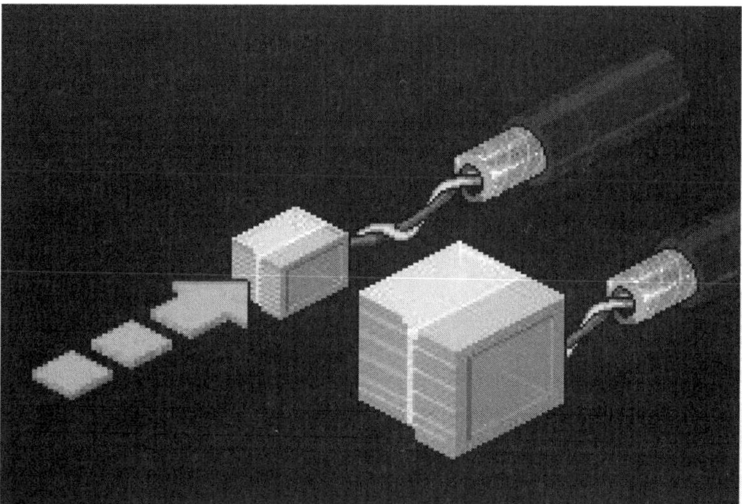

Figure 3–9. *Twisted-pair cable uses an RJ-45 connector (top) or the slightly large RJ-11 connector (bottom).*

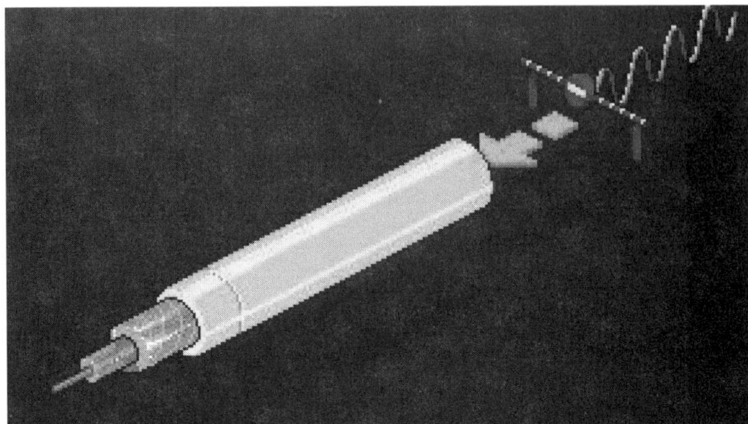

Figure 3–10. *Fiber-optic cable is a long glass tube that transmits data as light pulses.*

Signals carried by fiber-optic cable travel at 100 MBPS, much faster and over longer distances than electronic signals on copper cables. In the near future, speeds of 1 giga byte per second (GPS) will be reached.

At the center of the fiber-optic cable are two very thin tubes known as the **core**; they are made of glass although some fiber-optic cables use plastic instead. Plastic has less capacity than glass to transmit light pulses over long distances.

Each tube of the core is covered with a cladding made of a concentric layer of glass and an outer coating of Kevlar fibers and plastic. Each tube carries a separate light signal one direction. One carries data being sent and the other data being received.

Fiber-optic cables offer many advantages over traditional wire cable. In addition to increased speed, light waves do not experience attenuation and interference the way wire cables do. Furthermore, fiber-optic cable cannot be physically tapped, which results a secured network. A physical tap means that someone intercepts and possibly copies the signal transmitted on the cable.

There are two drawbacks using fiber-optic cable. First, fiber-optic cable is expensive to install. Prices vary, but are typically the same price level as thicknet. The other concern is with the installation itself. Special skills are required to properly connect fiber-optic cable to network devices.

The IBM Way

In 1984, IBM established its own standards and specifications that complement cable industry standards. However, there are several components of the IBM system that are different from cable industry standards.

One of those components is the cable connector. A cable connector is a device used to join two cables together or it joins the cable to a client's network adapter card. Cable industry standards require cable connectors to be either a male or female connector.

A male connector has prongs while the female connector contains holds, one for each prong. In contrast, the IBM connector has no prongs or holds (Figure 3–11). This is known as hermaphroditic and uses a face plate and distribution panel to join the connectors.

Another IBM convention is the classification used to identify a cable. Table 3–4 shows these classifications and the association each has with the American Wire Gauge (AWG) standards.

Baseband–Broadband Transmission

There are two common ways in which a data packet is sent across the network, regardless of which cable is in use. These are called **baseband transmission** and **broadband transmission.**

At the heart of these two methods is the concept of frequency. As discussed in Chapter 1, frequency is a wave of electricity or light, in the case of a fiber-optic network, that is encoded with the data packet. The number of waves in the signal per second is known as the signal's frequency. You are probably more familiar with a radio station broadcasting on a particular frequency in the radio-wave band of frequencies.

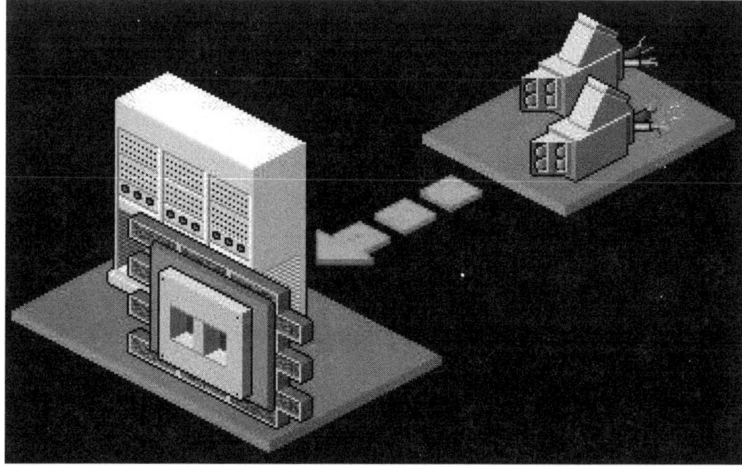

Figure 3–11. *The IBM cable connector has no prongs or holds.*

Table 3–4 *IBM and Standard Cabling Types*

Type	Industry Standard Equivalent	Description
1	Shielded Twisted Pair (STP)	Shielded two-pair of 22 AWG wires (telephone).
2	Shielded Voice and Data Cable	Shielded six-pair of twisted pair. Two pairs of 22 AWG for data. Four pairs of 26 AWG for voice.
3	Voice Grade Cable	Unshielded, four solid twisted-pair 22 or 24 AWG cables
4	Not yet defined	
5	Fiber-Optic Cable	Two 62.5/1/25 micron multimode optical fibers.
6	Data Patch Cable	Dual shielded two 26 AWG twisted-pair stranded cables.
7	Not yet defined	
8	Carpet Cable	Dual shielded, flat jacket, twisted-pair 26 AWG cables. One-half the distance of Type 1 cable.
9	Plenum	Dual shielded, fire resistant, twisted-pair cables.

A cable can carry one or more frequencies at the same time. Each frequency transmitted along the cable is called a **communication channel** and is measured in terms of the **cable's bandwidth**. A **bandwidth** is the difference between the lowest and highest frequencies transmitted along the cable. A cable with a large bandwidth can transmit more data per second than a cable having a small bandwidth.

Network cards used by network devices (i.e., printers) must be adjusted to account for the frequency of the network signal(s). This process is called **tuning the card** or device; it is similar in concept to how you tune a radio to the frequency of a radio station.

Baseband transmission uses a single frequency for all transmissions. Therefore, a baseband network has only one bidirectional communication channel. Clients and other devices use the channel to both send and receive data packets. Signals carried long distances on a baseband network must be given a boost to prevent data loss owing to a weak signal. This extra energy is given by a device called a **repeater**. Baseband uses a digital signal.

Broadband transmission consists of multiple communication channels that enable simultaneous communication along the network. A broadband network has the bandwidth capacity to handle data, voice, and video transmissions. Broadband signals too can become weakened over long distances and require a boost from a device called an **amplifier**.

Broadband transmission is unidirectional, which requires two communication channels to complete a transmission (send and receive). Network engineers have developed two methods to address the unidirectional limitation of baseband transmission. They are using a midsplit broadband configuration or a dual cable broadband configuration.

The **midsplit broadband** configuration divides the entire bandwidth into transmission and receiving channels. This enables half the frequencies in the bandwidth to be used for sending data (one bit per frequency) and the other half of the frequencies for receiving (one bit per frequency).

The **dual cable broadband** configuration requires the use of two different cables attached to each client and network device. One cable is used to transmit data and the other to receive data.

MCSE 3.4 Choosing the Right Topology and Cable

With all the options of topology and cables discussed in this chapter, the question that you are probably asking yourself is how should you choose the right combination of components for a network.

There is no easy answer to this question, since the criteria for each network is unique. However, you can use an approach that will help to narrow your options to an acceptable and affordable set of components. There are four major factors you must consider. These are budget constraints; the distance between the furthest client or network device; the anticipated data traffic along the network; and the degree of data security.

The first step in planning the network is to determine the data communications needs of the organization. This must include the current demands (0–3 years) and a forecast of future demands (4+ years). Current demands must be addressed immediately within the plan for the network and the plan must also consider the foundations necessary for future demands.

For example, a simple computer network can use bus topology to connect together a few clients. This might address the current needs of the organization. However, a star bus topology might be a wiser choice since all the clients connect directly to a hub. New hubs can be added to the network as demand grows for network services, such as adding more clients to the network or increasing data traffic flow. Multiple hubs can be connected together using a bus, thus allowing all clients to interact with each other. If one hub becomes inoperable, only a small group of clients lose network services. This design allows for a scalable network that also addresses budgetary concerns. The cost of adding hubs and client connectivity to the network can be allotted in future budgets.

Cabling considerations center around the need for bandwidth and security. Bandwidth determines the number of communication channels available for data transmission. A workgroup network typically does not require a large bandwidth, since data traffic is relatively low. However, high bandwidth is required for a backbone firmwide network, where 100 or more clients are constantly demanding network services. Multiple communication channels are necessary to maintain an acceptable network response time.

Once you've forecasted the bandwidth needs, then you can choose the cable(s) for the network. More than one type of cable can be used in a typical firmwide network. For example, an ideal candidate for the corporate backbone and hub-to-hub bus connection is fiber-optic cable, since this provides the largest available bandwidth. Thicknet cabling is a viable alternative to fiber optics in this situation. However, thinnet or twisted-pair cables are ideal to connect clients and network devices to a hub.

The distance of the network must be considered when choosing cabling. Every type of cable has a maximum length. Afterwards you must use a repeater to extend the signal to other cable segments.

Another factor that must be considered when selecting a cable is whether or not the cable will be exposed to an area where electrical or electronic devices are in use, such as electric motors. These devices can emit signals that could be picked up by the network cable and corrupt data transmission. You can avoid this problem by using cables that are sufficiently insulated, as described previously in this chapter.

The last factor you must consider is that of data security. It is technically feasible for a cable to be tapped, which allows an intruder to copy the data traffic. Rarely does this occur in most computer networks. However, fiber optics should be used in networks that require foremost data security. Keep in mind that a secured cable is not a guarantee of data security. Other measures such as encryption must be implemented to provide additional security measures.

MCSE 3.5 Wireless Connection

One of the most exciting developments in data communication is with the growing acceptance of a cableless data transfer among clients and devices on a network, for instance, utilizing wireless connections. A wireless connection uses radio, microwave, or light waves to transmit data packets from a client or device across the air to another client or device. In practice, it is very similar to a radio broadcast signal.

Although the name implies that no cables are used to connect clients and other devices, a typical wireless network is a hybrid network that is a mixture of wireless and cable connectivity. Network designers combined network components such as various cabling alternatives and wireless connections to create the most cost-efficient network.

For example, a wireless component of a network is ideal for making the network available to clients that are away from the network cable, such as a traveling sales representative. Likewise, wireless links are used in areas that prohibit the installation of cables, such as in a temporary location or in buildings where laws prevent modification of the structure to install cables.

Wireless networks are divided into two broad categories based on the ownership of the wireless transmitter. These are **privately owned transmitters** and **public carriers** used for mobile computing, such as those owned by SPRINT, AT&T, and MCI.

The privately owned category is subdivided into two types called LAN and Extended LAN. A wireless LAN links clients within the vicinity of each other, whereas an Extended LAN connects clients a couple of miles apart.

Clients and other devices on wireless LAN contain a network adapter card that is connected to a transmitter, called an **access point**, via a cable. The transmitter is typically located on a wall, which gives the signal an uninterrupted path to a wall-mounted receiver located on the far side of the room. Data packets are transmitted over the airwaves to the receiver, which is also connected to network clients by a cable.

The second type of privately owned is the Extended LAN. The expanded LAN is similar to the wireless LAN except the transmitter and the receiver are typically located outside the buildings and form an electronic data communication bridge called a wireless bridge. Using spread-spectrum radio technology, this can transport data packets up to 25 miles away from the transmitter (as is discussed later in this chapter).

Microwave communication is commonly used for a wireless bridge (Figure 3–12). The signal uses a frequency in the microwave spectrum to transmit information point to point over short and long distances. The **wireless bridge** links buildings located across the parking lot or miles away, as long as there are no physical obstructions between the two points.

This physical limitation of microwave transmission can be overcome by creating a network of microwave relay stations. Assume that a firm has two office buildings, one on either side of a mountain. A microwave communications link would seem impossible because the mountain obstructs the line-of-sight transmission.

However, a microwave relay station could be installed at the top of the mountain. The microwave signal from an office building could be beamed to the relay station, which then retransmits the signal to the microwave receiver on the other building.

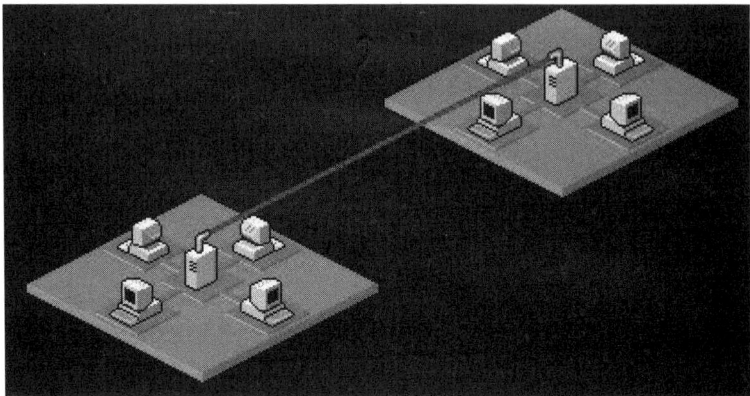

Figure 3–12. *A microwave transmitter/receiver can create a wireless bridge between two buildings.*

Another solution to the **line-of-sight** limitation imposed by microwave technology is to send the microwave signal to a satellite. The **satellite** is a microwave relay station that redirects the signal to an earth microwave receiving station.

Satellites are owned and operated by a service provider. The provider leases time to other companies for use of the satellite relay. Firms who use this service either transmit their data signals to a satellite up-link station owned by the service provider or use their own satellite up-link facility. The choice is dependent on the amount of time the firm will use the satellite relay. Most firms don't own their own satellite up-link stations.

Types of Wireless Network Transmissions

There are four ways in which data packets are transmitted over a wireless portion of a network. These are infrared transmission, laser transmission; narrow-band radio transmission (also known as single frequency), and spread-spectrum radio transmission.

The **infrared spectrum** is a group of frequencies in the light frequency range of the electromagnetic spectrum. The infrared transmitter encodes bits of the data packet into pulses of infrared waves. The waves carry the signal to the receiver, which decodes the pulse back into bits that are then passed along to the destination client.

Infrared communication have transmission rates of about 10 MBPS due to the broad bandwidth available in the infrared spectrum. However, infrared signals are also generated by natural sunlight, which can be a source of interference unless the network infrared signal is stronger than ambient infrared waves.

There are four common ways to incorporate an infrared device into a network. These are broadband optical telepoint links, scatter infrared links, line-of-sight links, and reflective links.

A **broadband optical telepoint link** is used to transmit a broadband signal no more than 100 feet to the receiver. Data communication is likely to be disrupted beyond this distance due to light sources around the office.

The **scatter infrared** link has a lower transmission rate when compared with a broadband optical telepoint link because the infrared signal uses broadcast transmission to send the signal in all directions around the transmitter. This is similar to radio transmission.

Any receiver tuned to the broadcast frequency is able to receive the data packet. However, one of the major drawbacks to the scatter infrared link is speed. Rather than focusing energy into one direction, the energy powering the signal is distributed in all directions. This weakens the signal, as the infrared signal bounces around the office giving multiple clients the opportunity to receive the same signal.

The **line-of-sight link** (also known as point-to-point transmission) requires that an uninterrupted line of sight exists between the sender's transmitter and the destination client's receiver—such as in microwave transmissions discussed earlier in this chapter. This is called **line of sight**. A wall or other obstacle between the transmitter and receiver will cause a break in the communication connection.

The **reflective link** is similar to the line-of-sight method, except a reflector such as a mirror is typically located in the corner of the floor. Each client and device must have their transceiver (antenna) pointed at the reflector. The line of sight between each client and the reflector must be unobstructed. An infrared signal is transmitted to the reflector, which redirects the signal to any client or device within the reflective borders of the mirror.

A **laser transmission** has many of the properties found in infrared transmission. That is, a laser is a range of frequencies in the light spectrum. A digital signal can be encoded into the laser wave as pulses of light. A laser signal must be directly aimed at the receiver (line of sight). An obstacle between the transmission and the receiver blocks the transmission.

Narrow Band and Spread Spectrum

Narrow band and spread-spectrum transmissions are similar to (yet different from) than infrared and laser transmissions. They're similar in that bits representing data packets are encoded into a wave of energy. They're different in that the frequency of the wave is in the radio spectrum not the infrared spectrum.

These radio waves are of a high frequency and can be transmitted in approximately a two to three square mile (5000 sq meters) area and about 800 feet indoors. Although these waves do not have the same line-of-sight restrictions as found in infrared and laser transmissions, they cannot be transmitted through certain material such as steel.

Furthermore, a special license is required from the Federal Communications Commission (FCC) before any signal is transmitted. Firms that use radio-based data transmissions typically do not hold their own FCC license. Instead, they subscribe to a service provided by a public communications carrier.

Narrow band uses a signal radio frequency to transmit data packets at a rate of approximately 4.8 Mbps. Network transceivers are tuned to the same frequency as the transmitter. However, a serious concern among firms that use narrow band transmission is data security.

Data is transmitted across the airwaves like any radio signal. The firm broadcasting the signal can only vary the strength of the signal to control the distance the signal will travel. Any receiver tuned to the frequency within the broadcast area will receive the signal.

Unlike a typical radio broadcast that transmits sound waves, the narrow band signal carries encoded data that must be decoded. The receiver must be able to decode the data. Authorized receivers will have the key to decode the data. Those unauthorized receivers could learn the key to the code by analyzing patterns within the signal. This is not an easy task. However, with enough time and using computer analyses, it is theoretically possible for an unauthorized person to decode the data encoded on the radio signal.

Many firms that use this technology encrypt their data. Encryption adds another level of patterns that must be examined to derive the key to the encryption algorithm. Again, with sufficient time and computer power, many—(not all) encryption algorithms can be theoretically broken.

The major drawbacks of the narrow band are that a single frequency is used for transmission and it is slower. An unauthorized person is given a steady stream of encoded and possibly encrypted data to analyze simply by tuning into the correct frequency.

An alternative to the narrow band approach is the spread-spectrum radio technology, which is commonly used in wireless bridges that connect remote locations to an Extended LAN.

Spread-spectrum technology also encodes bits of data packets into a radio signal. However, more than one radio frequency is used for the transmission. This adds a degree of complexity that when combined with other data security measures (i.e., data encryption) makes the signal practically secure. (Of course, most data security violations don't occur by taping the transmission. Instead, violations are committed by employees of the firm, who have direct access to the data.)

Hop, sometimes called **channel** instead of hop, timing is used in a spread-spectrum radio transmission to distribute transmission over a range of radio frequencies. Hop timing refers to the technique of changing (frequency hopping) the transmission frequencies at a regular interval during the transmission. Only authorized transceivers "know" which frequency to use and when to tune to the frequency.

However, this extra degree of security isn't without a drawback. The interruption in data transmission when changing frequencies and retransmissions to address communications errors can slow down the data transmission rate to 250 kilobits per second (KBPS).

Mobile Computing

Computer networks have grown from a cable linking two clients together to networks using wireless communication to bridge distances between two or more networks. In both cases, the network client is at a stationary location such as on the desktop. However, advancements in communication technology have progressed to a point where clients no longer need to be stationary. They can be anywhere and still transmit and receive data packets across the network by a branch of wireless communication technology. This is called mobile computing.

Mobile computing technology links clients such as laptop computers, personal digital assistants (PDA), and even desktop computers located on a boat, plane, car, or truck with traditional LANs and WANs using a broadcast signal with a maximum data exchange rate of 19.2 KBPS.

Mobile computing technology is organized into three general categories. These are cellular networks (Figure 3–13), packet-radio communication, and microwave satellite communication.

Cellular networks (CDPDs) use public cellular telephone technology to transmit data packets from the mobile client to the LAN. CDPD requires a cellular network adapter (sometimes this is a modem) to encode bits of the data packet into the wireless signal used by the cellular network. Some adapters simply provide a connection to a cellular telephone and the cellular telephone handles the transmission just as if voice communication was being transmitted. Other adapters have cellular telephone capabilities built into the adapter.

In either case, the signal is transmitted continuously (like a radio signal) to a local cellular telephone antenna. From there, the signal is amplified and retransmitted over the cellular telephone network's cable to the public telephone system and reaches the firm's LAN through a network modem connection.

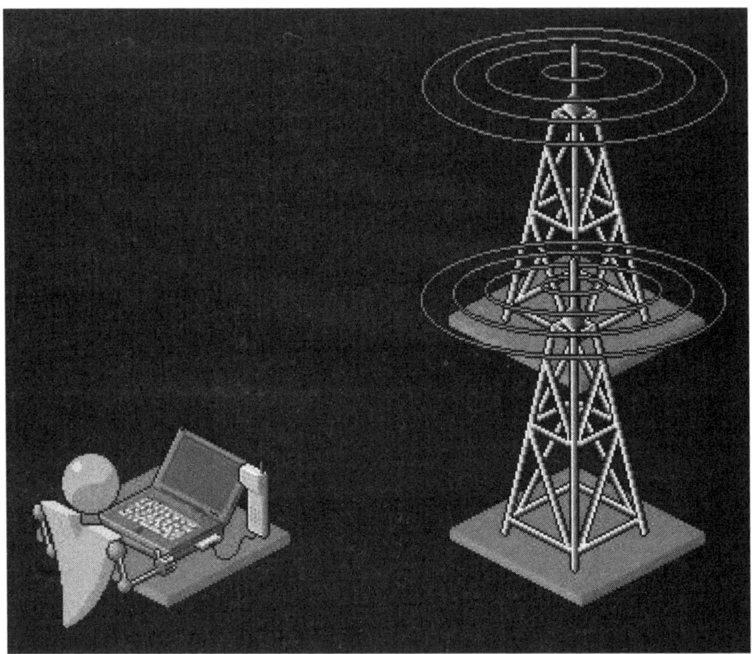

Figure 3–13. *A cell phone can be used to connect a laptop computer to the office LAN.*

In contrast, **packet-radio communication** is not a continuous transmission of information. Instead, the information is packetized similar to the method used to transmit information on a LAN. That is, the data packet contains the source and destination addresses, piece of the information being transmitted; and error-checking data.

Packets are then transmitted using microwave technology to a satellite that is called an up link. The satellite retransmits the signal back to earth to a receiving station specified by the destination address in the packet.

MCSE 3.6 Network Cards

The link between a client or a network device and the network cable is the **network card**, which is inserted into an expansion slot in a client printer, or network server. An expansion slot (Figure 3–14) is an outlet within the device that physically connects the network card to the bus of the device.

You can consider the **bus** as the cabling etched into the motherboard of the device that handles transmission among the CPU, keyboard, memory, and other components inside the device. Once the network card is inserted

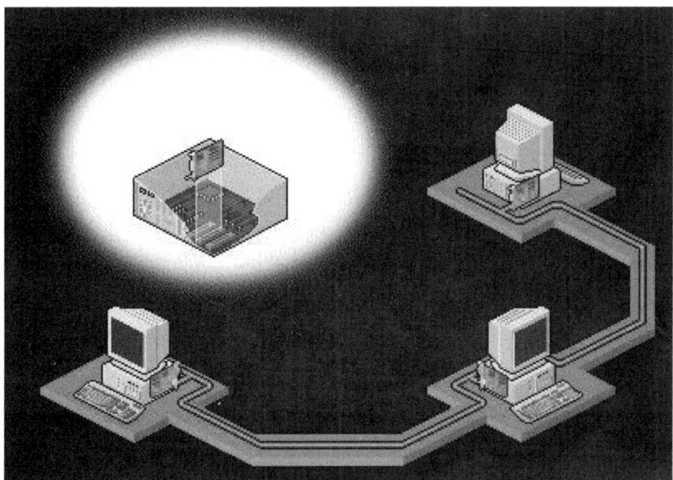

Figure 3–14. *A network adapter card is inserted into a PC and is used to connect the PC to the LAN.*

into an expansion slot and software provided by the network card is loaded on to the device, the card is treated by the device as if the card is an original component of the motherboard design.

The bus contains several etched wires called **a path**, each of which transmits a bit of information. A bus is classified by the number of paths used for transmission. Most computers use a 32-bit bus. Older models use a 16-bit or 8-bit bus.

A practical way to understand the importance of the number of paths in a bus is to relate the paths to the transmission of a character. As discussed in Chapter 1, a character (i.e., letter or number) is encoded as eight binary values. Each binary value is called a bit and eight are called a byte.

An 8-bit bus has eight paths and each can transport a bit at the same time. This is called **parallel transmission**. Therefore, one character at a time can be transmitted along the bus at the same time. Two characters can be transmitted at the same time if a 16-bit bus is used and four characters if a 32-bit bus is used.

The network card has an address called the I/O port address on the device's bus. This address is determined by the configuration of the network card, which is discussed later in this chapter. Whenever communications software wants to send data across the network, the software tells the CPU to move the data from an address in the device's memory to the address of the expansion slot that contains the network card.

The network card then converts the information into a data packet, then transmits the data packet across the network cable. Data transmission across the network is performed a bit at a time. This is called **serial transmission.** Therefore, the network adapter card must take the parallel data received from the bus and convert it to serial data.

Prior to transmitting a data packet across the network, the network card conducts a handshaking routine with the destination network card. **Handshaking** is the method by which network cards agree on the details as to how they will transmit and receive data packets.

Factors agreed upon between the two network cards that are trying to communicate are the size of the data, transmission timing, data confirmation, and data transmission. These factors can be different for each network card even if they are produced by the same manufacturer.

For example, an older model network card may lack features found in a newer model. The newer model typically has the features found in older models, for instance, they are backward-compatible. The handshaking routine determines the common factors between two network cards, which are then used for transmitting data packets.

The data size factor determines the amount of data that is transmitted at one time and the maximum amount of data that can be held in the receiving network card's memory. Data beyond this amount will overflow the memory.

The timing factor determines the amount of time that will elapse between each transmission. This typically reflects the amount of time it takes the receiving network card to process a data packet and get ready to receive another data packet.

The confirmation factor sets the time delay before the receiving network card will transmit a confirmation signal and the amount of data that is to be received before a confirmation is transmitted.

For example, network cards may agree that a confirmation will be transmitted not more than a second after each data packet is received. The network card that transmitted the packet will not suspect that data has not been received.

The remaining factor is transmission speed. The rate at which data packets can be transmitted across the network is dependent upon the sender's and receiver's network card's **transmission rates.** The fastest common rate of both cards determines the rate at which data packets will be transmitted.

Once the handshaking routines are completed, the destination network card awaits incoming messages and processes the data packet by stripping all but the data from the packet, then stores the information in memory. The network card then notifies the communication software that data has arrived.

The network card's intelligence comes from a combination of etched logic in the card's circuit board and from a special kind of read-only program called firmware, which is stored on a chip in the network card. It is here where the data-link layer's LLC and MAC features reside (see Chapter 2 for details).

Each network adapter card must have a unique address on the network. A network address is created by each network adapter card, rather than a central source on the network. Each network adapter card manufacturer is assigned a block of network addresses by the IEEE. These addresses are burned into a chip on the card.

Setting Up the Network Card

Network cards that are not **Plug and Play** (PnP) compliant require that certain settings on the card be configured before it can be used to connect a client to the network. **Configuration** means some of the rules that determine how the card and the client communicate must be established by moving jumpers (Figure 3–15) or DIP switches on the network card.

There are four common features that must be configured on every network card. These are the base memory address, the base I/O port address, the IRQ number, and the transceiver.

The **base memory address**, also known as the RAM start address, determines the location within the client's memory that can be used as the network card's memory buffer for temporary storage of data packets. Only net-

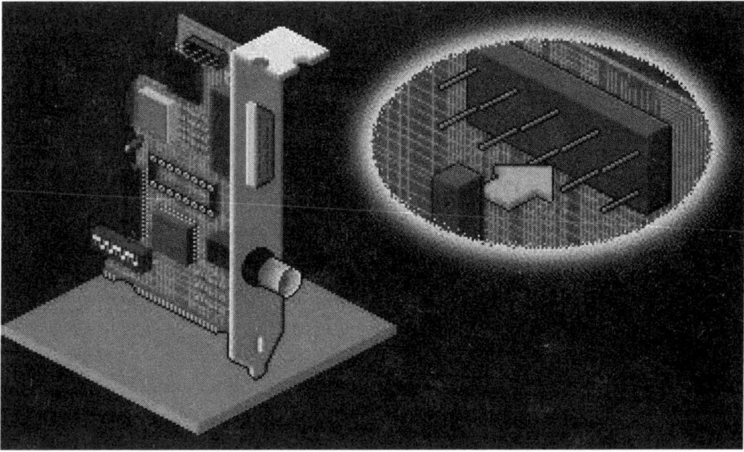

Figure 3–15. *Jumper connections enable you to choose which circuits to use on the network adapter card.*

work cards that use client memory require the base memory address to be configured. Other network cards contain their own memory on the card.

The base memory address must be reserved for exclusive use by the network card. Otherwise, the data stored in that area will be overwritten by another driver and corrupted. The base address memory of D8000 (or D800 on some computers where the last digit is dropped) is a common address for network cards.

Some network cards enable you to determine the size of the buffer, which is typically 16K or 32K. A word of caution. Reserving a large buffer for the network card provides more room to store data packets, but it also reduces the memory available for other applications running on the client. It is common for the buffer to be set to the maximum size during installation of the network card. The buffer size is reduced if degradation of performance is realized in other applications.

The **base I/O port address** is the address used by the client's CPU to communicate with the network card. Every device connected to the client has a unique base I/O port address. Table 3–5 contains a listing of common

Table 3–5 *Base I/O Port Addresses Commonly Not Used As Defaults for Other Devices*

Base I/O Port Address	Comment
210 to 21F	Unassigned
20 to 2F	Unassigned
240 to 24F	Unassigned
250 to 25F	Unassigned
260 to 26F	Unassigned
280 to 28F	Unassigned
290 to 29F	Unassigned
2A0 to 2AF	Unassigned
2B0 to 2BF	Unassigned
2C0 to 2CF	Unassigned
2D0 to 2DF	Unassigned
2E0 to 2EF	Unassigned
300 to 30F	Network Adapter Card (default)
310 to 31F	Network Adapter Card (default)
330 to 33F	Unassigned
340 to 34F	Unassigned
350 to 35F	Unassigned
360 to 36F	Unassigned
380 to 38F	Unassigned
390 to 39F	Unassigned
3A0 to 3AF	Unassigned
3E0 to 3EF	Unassigned

base I/O port addresses that are typically not used as defaults for common devices. Check the availability of base I/O port addresses by reviewing the documentation that came with the client before configuring the network card. Addresses are represented as hexadecimal numbers.

The **interrupt line (IRQ)** is the communications path used by the network card to get the attention of the CPU. For example, once a data packet is received and processed by the network card, the card sends a signal called an interrupt along the interrupt line to the CPU. This tells the CPU to stop what it is doing and provide service to the network adapter card. The service could be to inform the application program waiting for the data packet that the information is available in memory.

Every device installed in the computer has a dedicated interrupt request line. The logic etched into the CPU determines the priority of each interrupt message it receives. The CPU reacts to the highest priority first.

Interrupt request lines are numbered and referenced with IRQ preceding the line number such as IRQ2. The network adapter card must use an unassigned IRQ line. You can use MS Diagnostic (MSD) or in windows 95 use the system info to list IRQ lines that already are assigned. Table 3–6 contains default assignments for IRQ lines.

The transceiver setting determines whether an internal or external transceiver is used with the network adapter card. Some cards have an inter-

Table 3–6 *Set the Network Adapter Card's Interrupt to an Unassigned IRQ Line*

Interrupt Request Line (IRQ)	Typical Usage
2	EGA.VGA graphics adapter
3	COM2, COM 4 or bus mouse (Recommended as second choice for a network adapter card)
4	COM 1 COM 3
5	LPT2 (Default for many network adapter cards)
6	Floppy Disk Drive Controller
7	LPT2
8	Real-Time Clock
9	EGA.VGA graphics adapter
10	Unassigned
11	Unassigned
12	PS/2 Mouse
13	Math Coprocessor
14	Hard Disk Drive Controller
15	Unassigned

nal transceiver, but also have a connection for an external transceiver. The default is usually the internal transceiver.

The Choice of Network Cards

There are two major factors that influence the types of network cards you select for a network. These are the kind of computer (client/server) and the cabling used to connect to the network.

PC client and servers fall into four categories called data bus architectures. These are: industry standard architecture (ISA), extended industry standard architecture (EISA), Micro Channel, and peripheral component interconnect (PCI). A network card you select needs to support the data bus architecture of your computer.

ISA is the data bus architecture introduced by IBM in the 1980s. It uses 16-bit expansion slot to connect device interface cards directly to the motherboard. Each 16-bit expansion slot can accept either an 8-bit or a 16-bit device interface card, such as the network card.

By the late 1980s, firms that made IBM clones realized that IBM was getting ready to introduce the **Micro Channel** data bus architecture, which was designed to replace the ISA architecture. Micro Channel, use in IBM's PS/2 computers, could be used in either a 16-bit or 32-bit bus.

In an effort to counter IBM's move, a consortium of clone manufacturers introduced **EISA**, a 32-bit data bus architecture offering many of the advantages of Micro Channel while still maintaining backwards compatibility with ISA device interface cards.

PCI is the data bus architecture found on Pentium computers and the Power Macintosh. This is a 32-bit bus that is designed to automatically configure Plug ard Play compatible components.

A recent development in network computing is the introduction of a diskless client. A diskless client has no local disk drive (i.e., neither a hard nor floppy drive), which prevents employees from copying data. Application programs and data files that were typically stored on a local drive are now stored on one or more servers over the network.

Designers of a diskless client had to overcome a major obstacle. That is, how to install the client's operating system so the client could connect to the network. The operating system for most clients is stored on a local disk. Whenever a computer is powered up (booted), the operating system is loaded into memory and various processes are run before the computer is ready to be used. Without the operating system installed in the computer, the computer cannot connect to the network.

The solution to this dilemma is to install the operating system in a **PROM** (programmable read-only memory) chip located on the network card. This is called a **Remote Boot PROMS** network card. This program contains and loads the operating system, then makes the network connection and displays the network login prompt on the screen.

Choosing a Network for Performance

Network cards have features that help enhance the processing of data packets, which results in better all-around performance of the network. Data packets travel at nearly the speed of light over the network cables. However, network cards are unable to process data packets as quickly.

Network engineers incorporated features in network cards to ease this bottleneck. Efficient use of memory is one of the first places they looked to improve throughput performance. Network could take in data packets quickly, but couldn't process them at the same pace. Network engineers decided to store incoming data packets in memory, which is called **a buffer** or **cache**. Then the data packets are processed from memory rather than from the stream of data flowing from the network.

Memory must be allocated by the network card before data packets can be stored. There are several memory techniques used to allocate memory. These are: allocating part of a client's memory, called **direct memory access** (DMA); **shared memory access** for storage; providing memory on the network card. Memory on the network card is either used during the transfer process or not used at all. This feature enables network technicians to fine-tune the network card for performance by allocating more or less of the client's memory for data communications.

A network card can also make available its own memory buffer to the client's CPU. This is called **shared adapter memory** and is used to reduce data transfer while processing the data packets. This technique requires data packets to be stored and processed directly on the network card. The network card's memory, which contains the processed information, is then made available to the CPU without having to relocate the information from the network card's memory to the client's memory.

Another feature similar to shared adapter memory is RAM buffering. **RAM buffering** is where the network card has its own memory used to store incoming data packets until they are processed. However, this memory is not available to the client's CPU.

The processing power of the client's CPU is also a factor that can slow down the processing of data packets. The network adapter card at times could have to wait for the CPU to move data from the card's allocated memory to another memory site in the computer.

Network engineers overcame this potential problem and increased processing perform by 70 percent by designing network adapter cards that have their own CPUs, which can temporarily use the client's bus to move incoming information to the client's memory. This technique is called bus mastering.

Summary

There are several common topologies used in computer networks. These are a bus, star, ring, token ring, hub, and a mixture of two or more topologies, which is called a hybrid.

Bus topology uses a backbone or trunk to connect to each client and server on the network. Data packets travel to each client and server, which ignores those data packets not addressed to it. However, a break or intermittent cable in the cable can cause signal bounce, which effectively brings down network operations.

In a star topology, clients and servers are connected together using a central device called a concentrator or hub. Data packets are sent to the hub, which redirects it to the destination computer. If a client is inoperable or the cable linking the client to the concentrator is broken, the network remains operational. However, network operations come to a standstill if the concentrator malfunctions.

The ring topology requires clients to be connected consecutively to each other creating a single circular cable. Data packets pass clockwise from one client to the next. If the data packet isn't addressed to the client, the client resends the data packet to the next client. In doing so, the client adds new energy to the signal (similar to a repeater) that strengthens the signal. This allows the data packet to travel a further distance on the network.

If one client is not working properly, then there is a good chance the entire network will fail. Finding the problem is time-consuming. This depends on the network operating system and associated components (i.e., network adapter cards). Some ring networks, such as those created by IBM, automatically ignore inactive clients.

Token-ring topology is similar to the ring topology, except a special packet called a token is passed to each client on the network. Only one token is allowed. A client that receives the token can insert address, information, and error-checking data to the packet. This transforms the token packet to a data packet. The data packet is then transmitted across the network. Once the data packet is received, the client creates a new token packet and sends it to the next client on the network. However, if a client does not need to transmit a data packet, the token packet is passed to the next client unchanged.

Hub topology connects clients, servers, and network devices to a central point called a hub. The hub either provides simple connectivity (a passive hub) or retransmits the signal as a repeater (an active hub).

A hybrid topology uses a combination of other topologies. For example, a start-bus hybrid topology uses a star topology to link clients to a hub and a bus topology to link multiple hubs together.

Components of a network are connected to each other by a cable. There are three categories of cables. These are coaxial, twisted pair, and fiber optics. Coaxial cables are similar to the cables found on your cable television connection and are divided into two subcategories. These are thinnet and thicknet. Thinnet uses a coaxial cable of a smaller diameter than thicknet. Typically, thinnet is used to connect clients and servers to a concentrator or hub and thicknet (also called the backbone) is used to connect concentrators or hubs.

Twisted pair is the cable you find attached to your telephone. This is used to connect clients and servers to a concentrator or hub. Fiber optics is a cable to transmit light waves and is typically used similarly to thicknet.

Transmission across cable is conducted using one of two common methods. These are baseband and broadband. Baseband transmission uses a single frequency called a communication channel to transmit and receive data packets. In contrast, broadband uses more than one frequency for communication. The number of frequencies used in broadband transmission is called bandwidth.

Broadband transmission provides two way (send and receive) paths by using midsplit broadband configuration, which divides the bandwidth into a transmitting and a receiving set of frequencies. An alternative method is dual cable broadband configuration, which uses two cables.

Networks also use wireless connections to locations where it is not feasible to use cable. Radio, microwave, or light waves are used to transmit data packets from a client or device across the airwave to another client or device. This is very similar to a radio broadcast signal.

Common wireless transmission methods are infrared transmission; laser transmission; narrow-band radio transmission, also known as single frequency; and spread-spectrum radio transmission.

Infrared and laser transmission methods encode data packets in light waves. There cannot be any obstruction between the transmitter and the receiver, otherwise there will be a break in transmission. This is called the line-of-sight requirement.

Narrow-band radio transmission is similar to a radio broadcast, where a single signal is transmitted in all directions from the antenna. The same is true about spread spectrum radio transmission, except more than one frequency is used for the broadcast. At a predetermined time the transmitter and the receiver jumps to another frequency, which provides a degree of data security. Each jump is called a hopping. Typically, narrow band and spread spectrum are provided by a commercial communications carrier because an FCC license is required to broadcast the signal.

Mobile computing is the latest type of wireless connection found in computer networks. These are used to link computers in the field to a firm's network. There are three kinds of technology used in mobile computing.

These are cellular networks and packet-radio communication using microwave communication.

Cellular networks use the public cellular telephone networks to transmit signals from a remote client to the public telephone systems. Eventually, the signal is linked to the firm's LAN through the telephone lines.

Packet-radio communication breaks information into transmission packets similar in design to a data packet, then transmits the packet to a satellite using microwave transmissions. The satellite serves as a microwave relay station and redirects the packets to the earth station identified by the address in the transmission packet.

Clients and servers are connected to cables using a network card. A network card must be compatible with the client/server and with the cabling used to connect to the network.

Network cards must be selected by the features they offer, such as bus mastering, where the card temporarily controls the flow of data in the client. These special features increase the performance of network communication.

▲ Chapter Review Questions

▲ Fill in the Blanks

1. *A ______________ topology connects all clients and servers together using a single cable called a trunk.*

2. *The ______________ is a special packet used in a token ring topology that allows a client to control data transmission across the network.*

3. *Sending data to a satellite is called ___________ ____________.*

4. *_____________ is the name given to a signal lost over long distances on a cable.*

5. *____________ is used on a bus network to stop signal bounce.*

▲ True/False

1. *(T/F) Thinnet is flexible enough to be used to connect clients to the network.*

2. *(T/F) An infrared signal does not experience interference.*

3. *(T/F) A laser signal is used to transmit data to a satellite.*

4. *(T/F) A microwave relay station can be used to transmit a signal over an obstruction.*

5. *(T/F) Frequency hopping occurs when a technician configures a network adapter card.*

6. *(T/F) Ethernet 10BaseT topology uses fiber optic cables.*

7. *(T/F) Microwave communication is based on lin of sight technology.*

8. *(T/F) Coaxial cables are used in thinnet and thicknet networks.*

9. *(T/F) Wireless communications offer cost savings over the connection-oriented communications because cabling is required to link remote sites.*

▲ Multiple Choice

1. *What is crosstalk?*

A. Technology use in diskless clients.
B. A combination of topologies.
C. Two signals cross over to each other's wire.
D. The T-connector used to join together two cables.
E. Interference caused by ambient light.

2. *Why are twisted-pair cables twisted?*

A. Improves the connectivity to a client.
B. Increases the resistance to noise from electrical devices.
C. Strengthens the cable.
D. Required by fire code.
E. Improves the transmission of light signals.

3. *An Extended LAN is:*

A. Connections to clients a couple of miles away.
B. Joins together thicknet and thinnet.
C. Allows the devices such as a printer to connect to the LAN.
D. A design that uses multiple hubs on the network.
E. A variation of a coaxial cable network.

4. *A reflective link is:*

A. A signal that bounces from a terminator back along the cable.
B. The shield around a cable.
C. Increases the power of a transmitted signal.
D. A reflector such as a mirror is located typically in the corner of the floor to reflect infrared signals.
E. Used by network adapter cards to ignore data packets not addressed to it.

5. *What is the I/O Port Address?*
   A. The address of the network adapter card on the client's bus.
   B. The address of the client on the network.
   C. The address of the printer on the network.
   D. The frequency used in narrow-band radio communication.
   E. The frequency used in baseband transmission.

6. *Which of the following characterizes fiber optic transmission.*
   A. radio interference
   B. very loud bandwidth
   C. high data transmission speed
   D. frequently used for drop connections between clients and hubs
   E. very low cost.

7. *A token ring uses a ___________ topology.*
   A. bus
   B. star
   C. mesh
   D. hybrid
   E. relay

▲ Open Ended

Explain the handshaking procedure of network adapter cards.

Why must plenum cables be used in certain installations?

When would you use wireless communication in a network?

How do you decide the proper network adapter card to use?

What are the ways a network adapter card can improve network communication performance?

F O U R

Inside Network Architecture

▲Chapter Syllabus

MCSE 4.1 Ethernet

MCSE 4.2 Token Ring

MCSE 4.3 AppleTalk

MCSE 4.4 ArcNet

Network architecture conjures images of a highly sophisticated body of technical knowledge that requires a Ph.D. from MIT to comprehend. At least these were my thoughts when I first encountered the term. This is not the case. In fact, you have already learned much about network architecture by reading the previous chapters.

The term network architecture refers to the overall implementation of protocols, networking standards, and topologies in a computer network to deliver a consistent result. It is the coming together of network components to bring data communications to fruition.

The focal point of network architecture is the specification that describes how components are assembled to form a network. The specification is the well-designed plan that assures results, if they are adhered to during the installation of the network.

Specifications identify the type of cable to use; the arrangement of hubs and repeaters; the distance between network components; and the number of nodes allowed on a network. You'll explore these and more in this chapter.

MCSE 4.1 Ethernet

Ethernet is one of the first network architectures to be implemented and is still the most widely used in the public and private sector. Ethernet dates back to the 1970s when Robert Metcalfe and David Boggs at Xerox Palo Alto Research Center (PARC) developed a design to transfer data amongst 100 computer over a 1-kilometer cable at a transmission rate of 2.94 MPBS.

The original design dwarfs today's technological capabilities. However, at the time it surpassed previous networking efforts. Soon thereafter an industry consortium lead by Xerox devised a more robust Ethernet architecture that moved data at 10 MBPS and has become the foundation of Ethernet networks used today which can handle data transfers of 10 MBPS or 100 MBPS.

Ethernet, which follows IEEE 802.3 standards, uses baseband and bus topology although the star topology is also found in some Ethernet networks as well as support for broadband (Figure 4–1). Each client and network device is connected to the same cable, which carries data packets called frames over a single communication channel. The cable can be thicknet cables, thinnet cables, or UTP. Clients on the network are responsible for providing

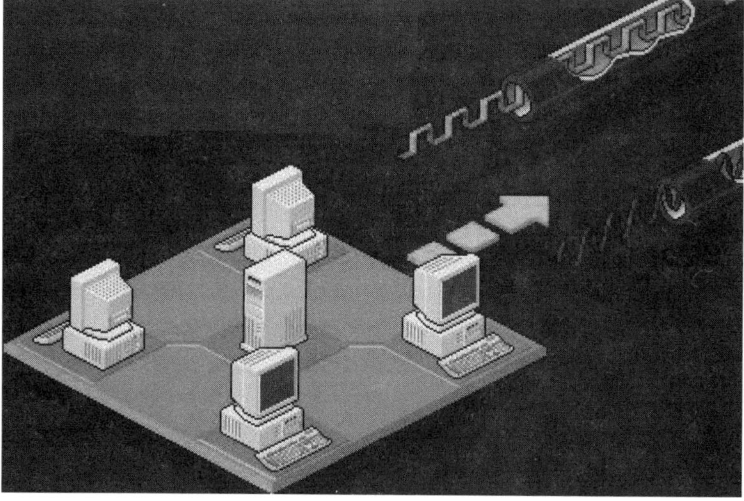

Figure 4–1. *Ethernet supports bus and start topologies and baseband and broadband.*

the energy to transmit frames around the network making Ethernet as passive network.

Ethernet clients use the **CSMA\CD** network access method to send frames. That is, frames are transmitted then the originator monitors the network to determine if the frame collided with another transmission. If so, then both frames must be retransmitted Figure 4–2.

A **frame** in concept is like an envelope that can hold between 46 bytes and 1,500 bytes of information. This is data that is exchange between clients. In addition to the data size, additional 18 bytes are required to successfully transport the information across the network.

The first byte in the frame indicates the beginning of the frame called a **preamble**. Next are the **destination address** and the **source address** followed by an indicator of the network layer protocol called the **type**. One of two protocols is used: IP or IPX depending on the network. **IP** is the Internet protocol and **IPX** is the protocol used on Novell's NetWare networks. Information that is being transmitted appears next in the frame. The frame ends with the **cyclical redundancy check** (CRC) value that is used to determine if the frame was transmitted successfully.

Ethernet is still evolving. The current standard provides a data transmission rate of 10 MBPS using one of four topologies: 10BastT, 10Base2, 10Base5, and 10BaseFL. However, a new Ethernet standard is emerging with a data rate of 100 MBPS.

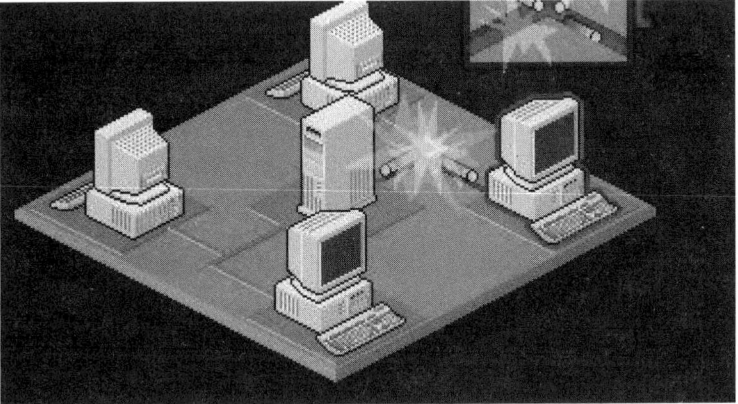

Figure 4–2. *Ethernet uses the CSMA/CD network access method. Clients re-send data packets whenever a collision is detected on the network.*

Ethernet Topologies

Ethernet technology is well suited for an array of common network operating systems including those sold by Microsoft (Windows 95, NT Workstation, NT Server, MS LAN Manager, and Windows For Workgroups), AppleShare, Novell NetWare, and IBM LAN Server.

An important advantage of Ethernet is that can be reconfigured to meet the changing network demands. Computer networks tend to grow rapidly as more clients are connected to the network. This results in increasing network traffic that can soon exceed the capabilities of the network.

However, Ethernet is based on segmentation technology which divides the network into groups of clients connected to the same central point called **hub**. If performance on a segment decreases, a technician can easily transfer some clients to a less populated segment which restores a smooth traffic flow of if necessary a new segment can be added to the network.

Ethernet 10BaseT Topology

The name **10BaseT** and the three other topologies in the current Ethernet standard seem to be a strange way of referencing a topology. However, the name describes the topology. The 10 represent the data transfer rate in MBPS. **Base** refers to the single communication channel used for communication and the **T** indicates **unshielded twisted pair** (UTP) is used as the cabling for the network although **shielded twisted pair** (STP) can also be used.

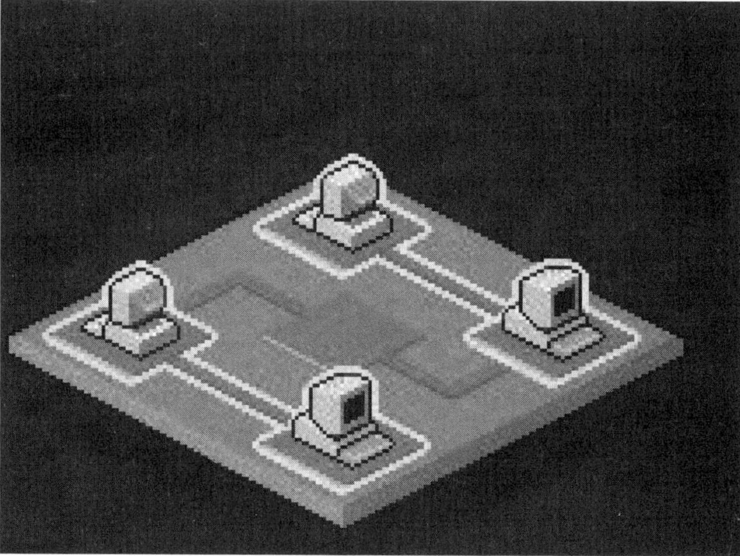

Figure 4–3. *Ethernet can be used to divide a crowded network into segments.*

At the center of the 10BaseT topology is a hub (Figure 4–4) that is used to connect clients to the network and as a **multi-port repeater**. A repeater receives a signal then retransmits the signal along the network. The hub has multi-ports to allow the signal to be retransmitted to more than one network client.

You probably recognize this as a star topology rather than the bus topology required in the Ethernet specifications. The star topology enables the efficient connectivity of clients to the network. However, data transmission follows the bus topology within the hub, which is also referred to as a star bus topology.

The network-end of **drop cables** leading from clients is found in one location typically in a communications closet. Cables are joined to the network using a patch panel (Figure 4–3) that contains many female connectors each enabling a client to connect to the network. The hub is also connected to the patch panel. Some network configurations may not use a **patch panel** and directly connect drop cables from the client to the hub.

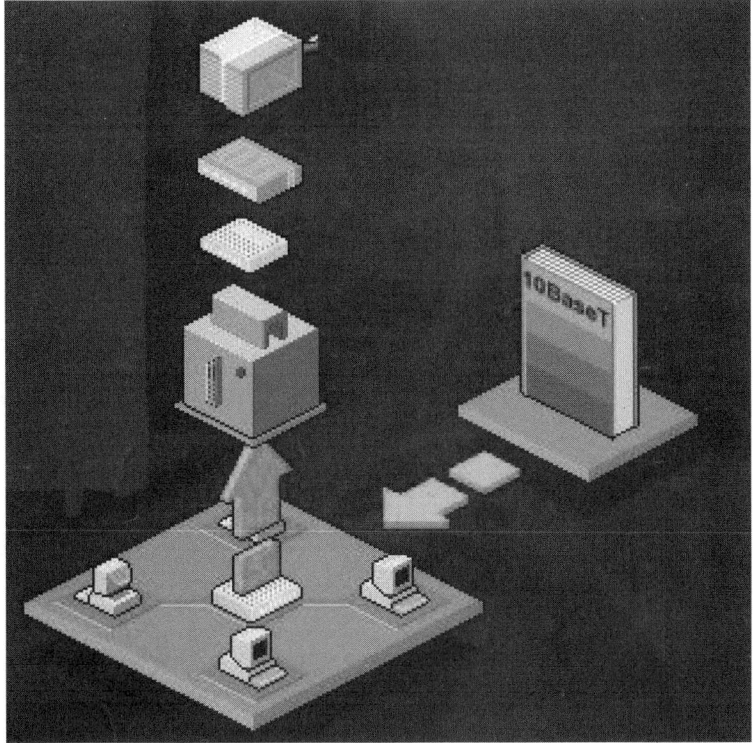

Figure 4-4 *10BaseT uses twisted pair or IBM cable, a hub, and repeaters to connect clients.*

A twisted pair cable (IBM category type 3,4, and 5) connects a client to the patch panel. The cable must be at least 8 foot and not more than 328 feet, otherwise the signal might be unstable. The distance can be extended between the maximum length by placing a repeater between the client and the patch panel. The repeater gives the signal the extra energy to reach the patch panel.

No more than 1,024 clients can be connected to the 10BaseT network. Networks that require more clients to be connected should use more than one 10BaseT network and link them together using a network backbone.

Ethernet 10Base2 Topology

You interpret the 10Base2 name as a topology that transmits data at a rate of 10 MBPS using baseband, single communication channel. However the 2 indicate the length of the cable between the client and patch panel or hub is twice than of a 10BaseT topology which is about 200 meters or 656 feet. The minimum cable distance is 20 inches, far less than the 8-foot minimum in the 10BaseT. The length of the distance is determined in part by the cabling requirement for the 10Base2 topology. The 10Base2 requires the use of thinnet coaxial cable.

A 10Base2 network is designed around the **5-4-3 thinnet rule** (Figure 4–5) which specifies the number of cable segments, clients, and repeaters that can be connected together to form the network.

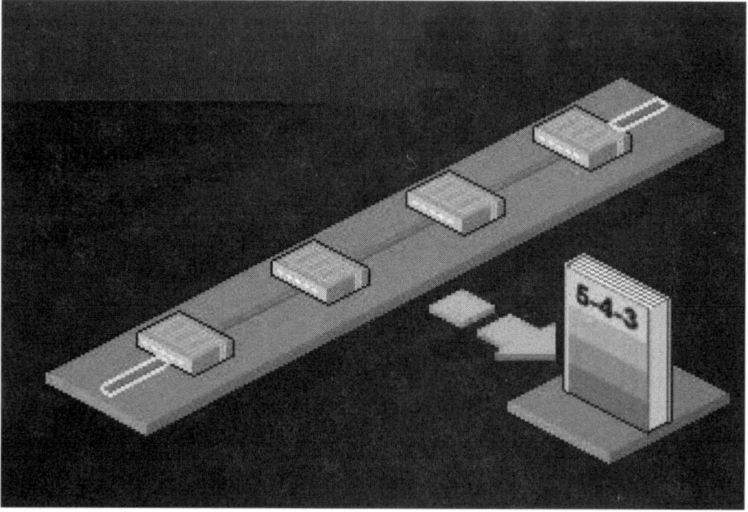

Figure 4–5 *The thinnet rule defines the number of cables segments, clients, and repeaters to be used to form a thinnet.*

Five cables segment are used to connect four repeaters. However, only three of the five segments can connect to clients. Two of the five cable segments must not attach to any clients.

Each of the three cable segments that connect to clients use a bus topology to connect multiple clients to the network. A cable from the repeater connects to a client's network adapter card using a BNC T connector. The **BNC T connector** (Figure 4–6) has three openings. Two are used to connect the ends of a thinnet cable and the other connects directly to the client's network adapter card. The 10Base2 specification does not permit a thinnet cable to be used between the network adapter card and the BNC T connector.

A thinnet cable is then connected to the next client on the cable segment. This process continues until all the clients on the segment are connected. A **BNC terminator** is used to terminate the end of the thinnet cable leading from the last client.

Each segment of the network (i.e. the cable segment from the repeater) can have no more than 30 computers along a cable not exceeding 607 feet in length. However, the overall network length can be no more than 3,035 feet and contain a maximum of 1,024 computers.

Ethernet 10Base5 Topology

The 10Base5 topology, also known as the **standard Ethernet**, specifies at 10 MBPS transmission rate using single channel baseband technology

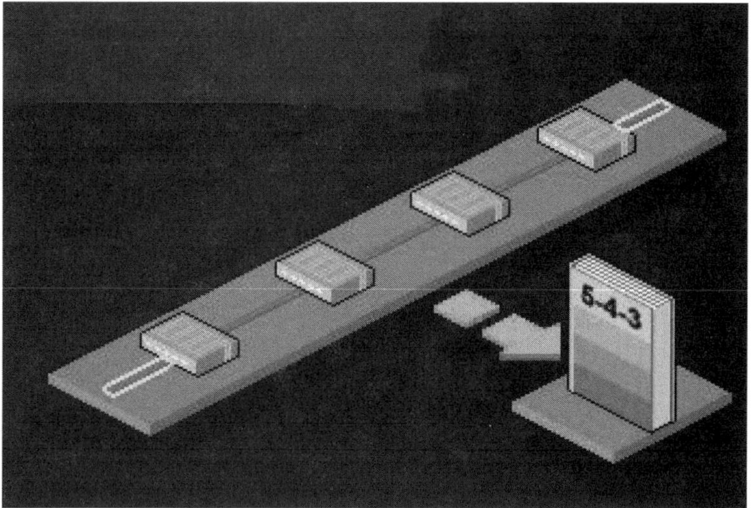

Figure 4–6 *A thinnet network requires transceivers, thinnet cable, T connector, BNC Barrel connector, BNC terminator, and repeaters.*

over a thicknet cable and extends the distance of the 10BaseT specifications by five times to 16,400 feet.

There can be a maximum of five backbone segments that connect four repeaters and as in the 10Base2 topology, three of those segments directly connect to clients. This is called the 5-4-3 thicknet rule. Each of the three segments used to connect clients can have no more than 100 clients connected to it.

Clients are connected to the thicknet cable via a **transceiver** A transceiver is a device that is clamped on to the thicknet cable using a **vampire tap** (Figure 4–7) and handles low level network transmissions between the computer and the network.

A transceiver cable is used to connect the transceiver to the computer's network adapter card. The length of the transceiver cable is not relative to the calculation of the maximum length of the network. Only, the length of the thicknet cable itself is used in this measurement. However, the length of the transceiver cable cannot exceed 164 feet.

Ethernet 10Base FL Topology

A more recent Ethernet topology to be defined by the IEEE is 10Base FL. This specification has a data transfer rate of 10 MBPS using baseband communication technology. However, fiber optic cables are used instead of copper cables.

10Base FL topology provides for the same kind of service offered by 10Base 5, except the maximum length of the 10Base FL topology is about 32,800 feet.

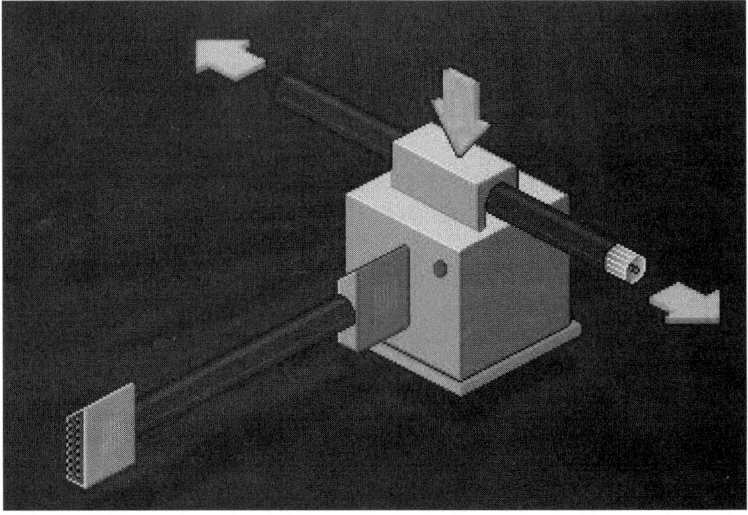

Figure 4–7 *A vampire tap is used to connected clients to the backbone.*

100 MBPS Standard

With the increasing demand for higher data transfer speeds, the IEEE has developed an enhanced Ethernet standard called 100 MBPS which provides the bandwidth required by graphic and imaging applications for image storing, video conferencing and computer aided design and manufacturing.

The 100 MBPS standard is divided into two topologies. These are 100BaseVB-AnyLAN and 100BaseX, which are sometimes called, fast Ethernet. Both topologies are backward compatible with the cabling used in other Ethernet topologies such as 10BaseT. However, these new standards can vastly increase the speeds at which information is exchanged over the network.

100VG-AnyLAN Topology

The name 100VG-AnyLAN implies the nature of the standards. The 100 infers the data transfer rate is 100 MBPS while the **VG** signifies the network is designed to handle voice communications called voice grade. The **AnyLAN** represents that the specifications work with either Ethernet or Token Ring network technology.

The 100VG-AnyLAN uses a star configuration. Clients are connected to a segment hub and segment hubs are connected to a central hub, which bridges data communications across segment hubs.

A multitude of cabling options is available with 100VG-AnyLAN including twisted pair, fiber optics, and IBM's Category type 3,4 and 5. However, additional cabling is typically required for a 100VG-AnyLAN network when compared with a 10BaseT network. This is because the maximum distance between a client and the hub is 420 feet.

A key feature in the 100VG-AnyLAN specification is the improve control over data flow by having the hub remove individually addressed frames for privacy reasons and the use of demand priority. Demand priority is a set of rules where by frames are assigned a priority level. The hub processes frames having a high priority before those with a low priority thereby assuring the most important information continues to flow in case a bottleneck arises at the hub.

100BaseX Topology

100BaseX is an enhanced version of 10BaseT that uses UTP and IBM's category type 5 cable to form a star bus configuration. 100BaseX uses CSMA/CD for network access along a baseband data channel.

The 100BaseX specification is divided into three subgroups each of which refers to the type of cabling used in the for the network. These are

100BaseT4 which uses 4 pair of UTP or IBM's category type 3,4,5 cable; 100BaseTX which uses 2 pair of UTP or STP or IBM's category type 5 cable; and 100BaseFX which uses 2 strand fiber optic cable.

MCSE 4.2 Token Ring

IBM developed the Token Ring as a robust network generally adheres to the IEEE 802.5 standard although there are some differences such as the number of stations allowed on a STP ring.

Token Ring architecture takes its name from the token ring method of accessing a network, which is also used as the networking accessing method for this architecture. At the center of a token ring network is a hub, which uses drop cables to connect to client in a star topology.

The hub is wired in such a way to create a physical ring, which is required for token ring access to the network. This is called a star wired ring topology. The first client to become active on the network generates the token and has the choice of transmitting data or sending the token to the next physical client on the ring.

Cabling for the token ring architecture consists of shielded or unshielded twisted pair or IBM type 1, 2 or 3 cables, which can communicate data over a single communications channel at rates of either 4 MBPS or 16 MBPS. The actual transfer rate is determined by the speed of each network adapter card of the clients involved in the transmission.

The originator client encapsulates data into a frame. The **frame** is composed of bytes that represent control information or the data itself. At the beginning of the frame is an indicator called the **start delimiter**, which identifies the frame to the destination client.

Next, is the **access control information** that is used to identify if the frame is a token to used for data transmission. Access control information is also used to set the frame's priority when the frame reaches the hub. High priority frames are transmitted before low priority frames.

The third piece of information in the frame contains media access control information that is used by either every client on the network or the end client. This is called **frame control data**, which is followed by the address of the destination client and the originator client.

Following the address information is the data, if the frame is not a token. The CRC frame check sequence data is next which the information that contains the results of a calculation performed by the originator client. The same calculation is performed by the destination client, the results of which are compared to the frame check sequence data to determine if an error has occurred during transmission.

The final two pieces of information in the frame are the **end delimiter** and the **frame status**. The end delimiter signals the end of the frame. The frame status is used to identify whether or not the frame was recognized and copied from the network by the destination client. It also indicates whether or not the destination client was active on the network to receive the frame.

The frame travels around the network to each client until the destination address of the frame is matches a client's network address. Every client receives the frame, then sends it to the next client making each client a repeater on the network.

When there is a match, the destination client copies the frame into temporary memory called a **buffer**, then changes the frame status to received and ships the original frame to the originator client. When the frame returns home, the frame is transformed back into a token and sent to the next client on the ring.

The initial client activated on the network initiates the first token and takes on the responsibility as the network monitor. Monitoring is performed behind the scenes without the user realizing the role of his computer.

Monitoring entails policing the network to assure that only one token in available at a time. It also involves tracking the number of times a frame has traveled across the network. Frames should make only one loop. A frame than begins the journey a second time is trapped by the initial client, which returns the frame to the originator client, marked undeliverable. Upon receiving the frame, the originator client creates and transmits a new token.

Token Ring Hardware

An advantage of a token ring is that each client is recognized automatically when it becomes active on the network. As part of the activation process, the network compares the address of the client with addresses of clients already active on the network. Any conflicts are resolved before the new client joins the network.

Once the network is assured the new client has a unique address, then each active client on the network is notified of the new client. This practically eliminates the chance a frame might be addressed to a client that is unavailable on the network.

Many Token Ring networks in operation today use an intelligent **multi-station access unit** (MAU) which quickly identifies when a previously active client has become deactivated (Figure 4–8). A MAU is a hub where drop cables from clients connect to form the token ring. It is within the MAU where the ring exists and the token is passed to the next client.

The type of connector used to attach a client's network adapter card to the network cable depends on the type of cabling used for the network. Ei-

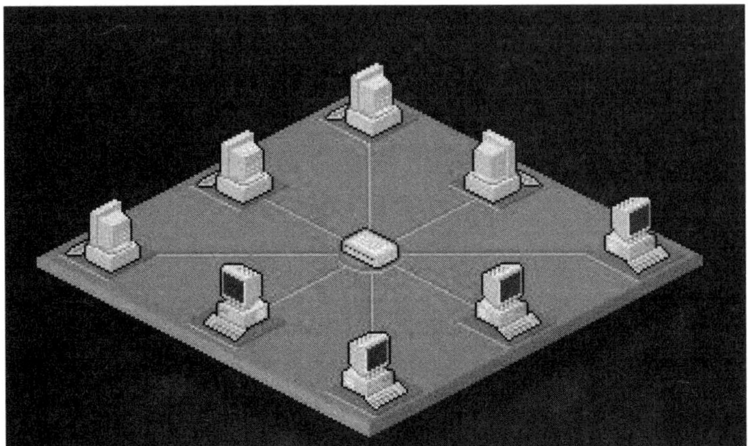

Figure 4–8 *A MAU is a hub used to connect clients to the network.*

ther the RJ-45 (8 wires) or RJ-11 (4 wires) is used if the network is cabled with IBM category type 3 cable. **The Media Interface Connector** (MIC), also known as **IBM category type A**, is used if the networked is cabled with IBM category type 1 or type 2 cable.

A token ring can be extended beyond a single hub by connecting together up to 33 hubs. The maximum number of clients that can be connected to a token ring network is depended upon the type of cabling used in the network and the hub. Shielded cabling can support a maximum of 260 clients and 72 clients if an unshielded cable is in use. The number of clients support by a token ring can be extended beyond the maximum number supportable by the cable by using a more powerful hub.

It is very common for a token ring network to use IBM category type 3 UTP, although types 1 and 2 STP can also be used for the network. The type of cable determines the distance a client can be from the MAU. If UTP cabling is used for the network, then clients must be no more than 148 feet from the MAU. However, the distance can be extended to about 328 feet if STP cabling is used for the link. Each client must be a minimum distance of 8 feet from the MAU.

IBM cabling has slightly different maximum distances between client and MAU depending on the category of cable. A category type 1 cable has a maximum distance of 330 feet while a category type 3 cable has a 150 feet maximum length.

Token ring architecture also specifies the maximum cable length between MAU. Each MAU must be within 500 feet of another MAU if more than one hub is used on the network.

A repeater, which regenerates the network signal, can be used to extend the distance between MAUs to 1,200 feet if IBM category type 3 cable is used and double that distance for type 1 or 2 cable.

A common way in which clients are connected to an MAU is through the use of a **patch panel** and **patch cables**. A patch panel is a device typically housed in a communication closet where drop cables from client are attached. Also attached to the patch panel is one or more MAU.

MCSE 4.3 AppleTalk

AppleTalk is a network architecture specification developed in the 1980s by Apple Computer to enable Macintosh computers to be joined together to form small work groups. It has since been enhanced to adhere to the OSI model, although this network architecture is not widely used in business. This enhancement is know as **AppleTalk Phase2**, which is also known as a LocalTalk network.

The AppleTalk network operating system is a component of the **Macintosh operating system**; it gives each client immediate access to the network. Each client automatically selects its own network address from a range of available addresses built into the system. The address is then transmitted to other clients on the network to determine if the address is already in use by another client. If it isn't, the client saves the address for future use.

AppleTalk uses a bus with **CSMA/CA** as the network access method to connect together a maximum of 32 clients. A typical AppleTalk network uses shielded or unshielded twisted-pair cabling, although fiber-optic cabling can also be used to form the network. Limitations such as the length of the network and number of clients that can be served by the network can be overcome by using vendor software and components.

In addition to using third-party vendor solutions to extend the network, the capacity of an AppleTalk network can be extended by combining small networks into a large network.

The smaller networks are called **zones** (Figure 4–9) and are identified by a unique name. The name of the zone is referenced whenever a client needs to access resources such as a printer server, called a **printer spooler**, located in a different zone. A **printer server** is a client that runs AppleShare software and acts as a gateway between clients on the network and the printer, allowing multiple users to share a printer.

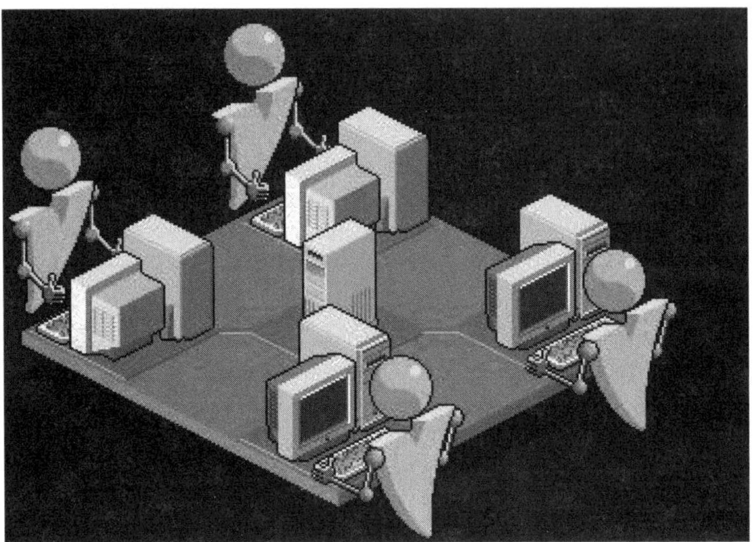

Figure 4–9. *Zones in an AppleTalk network.*

Mac II clients can connect to Ethernet and token-ring networks by using the appropriate network card. The **EtherTalk NB** network adapter card is used with EtherTalk software to enable the Mac II clients to communicate with clients of various manufacturers over an Ethernet. Likewise, the TokenTalk NB network adapter card along with TokenTalk software allows Mac II clients to join a token-ring network.

MCSE 4.4 ArcNet

The most economical network architecture used for workgroups is ArcNet, which was introduced back in the 1980s. ArcNet uses either a star bus or bus topology with a token passing data access method. Transmission is handled using broadband technology at a transmitting rate of 2.5 MBPS. An enhancement called ArcNet Plus improves performance to 20 MBPS.

At the center of the ArcNet network is a hub. The maximum distance between the hub and a client is dependent upon the kind of cable used in the network. For example, 800 feet is the maximum length when an unshielded twisted-pair cable is used. This extends to 2,000 feet when coaxial cable is linked with an active hub (one that regenerates the signal). A **pure bus topology** using coaxial cable can extend no more than 1,000 feet.

Although ArcNet is a token-passing network, the method used to pass the token differs from the token-ring network discussed previously in this

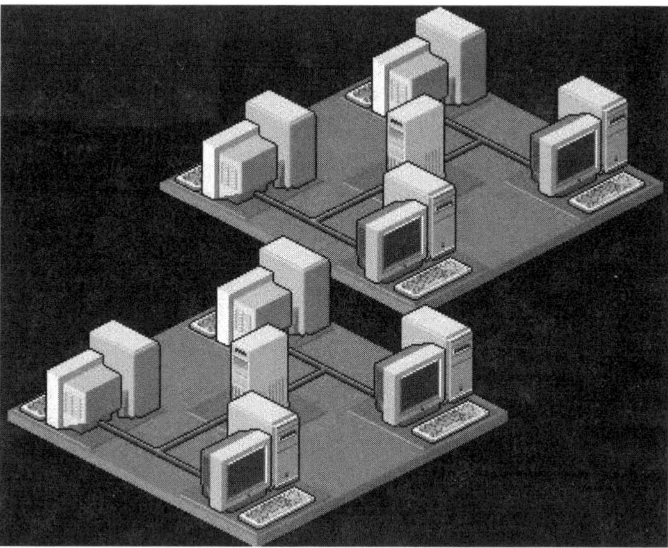

Figure 4–10. *An ArcNet frame.*

chapter. A traditional token-ring network passes the token to the next client on the network. The next client is the closest physical client.

However, clients on an ArcNet network are numbered based on the order in which the client logs onto the network. So, the next client on the network is the client with the next highest number. This means that the next client to receive the token could be physically located at the far end of the network.

ArcNet frames (Figure 4–10) are simple in design when compared with other frames and packets discussed in this chapter. An ArcNet frame contains the destination and originator's address, then 508 bytes of data. However, a frame used with ArcNet Plus can contain 4,096 bytes of data.

■ Summary

Network architecture is a specification as to which network components can be used together to produce reliable data transmissions across a network. Components include protocols, topologies, and networking standards.

There are four well-known network architectures used in commercial networks. These are Ethernet, Token Ring, AppleTalk, and ArcNet. Ethernet and Token Ring are the more popular network architectures.

Ethernet is divided into two major categories based on transmission rates. These are called 10 MBPS and 100 MBPS. 10 MBPS is found in most current implementations of Ethernet, whereas 100 MBPS is an emerging standard designed for transmitting imaging data.

The Ethernet 10 MBPS category is composed of four subcategories. These are: 10BaseT; 10Base2; 10Base5; and 10BaseFL. The names of the subcategories help to define the architecture.

The *10* refers to the data transmission rate of 10 MBPS. *Base* indicates that baseband technology is used to transmit the signal. The *T* denotes that twisted-pair cable is used. The *2* indicates that the network length can be twice as long as 10BaseT because thinnet coaxial cable is used on the network. The *5* means the network length if five times that of a 10BaseT network because thicknet coaxial cable links components on the network. *FL* signifies that fiber optics are used in the network.

An Ethernet network can be divided into segments consisting of a smaller network. Additional segments can be added to the network if network performance degrades because of heavy transmission traffic. Clients can easily be moved from a busy segment to a less active segment.

Ethernet Topology	Cable	Max. Len between Client/Hub	Min. Len	Max. Clients	Max. Segment Len	Max. Clients/ Segment	Max. Network Len
10BaseT	Twisted Pair	328 ft	8 ft	1,024	328 ft	NA	NA
10Base2	Thinnet	656 ft	20 in	1,024	607 ft	30	3,035 ft
10Base5	Thicknet	16,400 ft	8 ft	1,024	1640 ft	100	8,200 ft
10BaseFL	Fiber Optics	16,400 ft	8 ft	1,024	1640 ft	100	32,800 ft

Token-Ring architecture uses a star-wired ring topology, which can transmit data at a rate of either 4 MBPS or 16 MBPS depending on the network adapter cards that are used by clients.

Network access is made available through the use of a token, which is created by the initial clients that become active on the network. The token is then passed to the next physically closest client on the network. A client that receives the token is the only client permitted to transmit data on the network.

Data travels in the form of frame and is received by every client on the network. When a client receives the frame, the destination address of the frame is compared with the client's address. If a match occurs, the frame is copied into the client's buffer and the frame is also marked as received, then transmitted to the originator client. If the addresses do not match, the client sends the frame to the next client.

The token-ring architecture automatically recognizes clients when they become active on the network and resolves conflicts in network addresses before the new client receives a token. Likewise, **multistation access** units (MAUs) are used as the hub, which also automatically detects when a client is deactivated. Up to 33 MAU can be used in a network.

Token-Ring Cabling	Max. Hubs	Max. Clients per Hub	Max. Distance between Client and Hub	Min. Distance between Client and Hub	Max. Client on Network
Twisted-Pair Unshielded	33	8	148 ft	8 ft	72
Twisted-Pair Shielded	33	8	328 ft	8 ft	260

AppleTalk, not widely used in business, uses a bus with CSMA/CA as the network access method to connect together a maximum of 32 clients using shielded or unshielded twisted-pair cabling (or fiber-optic cabling).

The network can be extended by combining small networks (called zones) into a large network. Clients can reference the name of the zones to access resources located on the other smaller network.

Mac II clients can connect to Ethernet and token-ring networks by using the appropriate network adapter card.

ArcNet, introduced in the 1980s, is an economical network architecture used for work groups. It uses either a star bus or bus topology with a token-passing data access method and has a transmission rate of 2.5 MBPS. ArcNet Plus, an enhancement to ArcNet, has a rate of 20 MBPS.

Cabling	Max. Len. between Client and Hub
Unshielded–Twisted Pair	800 ft.
Coaxial	1,000 (bus topology)
	2,000 (star topology using an active hub)

▲ Chapter Review Questions

▲ Fill in the Blanks

1. *____________ is a topology that has a transmission rate of 10 MBPS, uses baseband technology, and twisted-pair cable.*

2. *Ethernet can be ____________ as a way to reduce data transmission on the network.*

3. *The first client active on a token-ring network __________.*

4. *____________ is the common hub used in a token-ring network.*

5. *____________ can extend the distance between hubs on a token-ring network.*

▲ True/False

1. *(T/F) Mac II clients can only connect to AppleTalk networks.*

2. *(T/F) The FL in 10BaseFL stands for frequent link connections.*

3. *(T/F) Ethernet cannot exceed transmission rates of 10 MBPS.*

4. *(T/F) Thicknet cabling increases the distances of an Ethernet network over a 10BaseT topology.*

5. *(T/F) Ethernet clients use the CSMA/CD network access method.*

6. *(T/F) NFS, which was developed by Sun Microsystems, makes a remote file system appear as if it was part of the local file system.*

7. *(T/F) Fiber Optics is a less expensive backbone than thicknet.*

8. *(T/F) 100VG-AnyLAN network has a maximum distance between a client and the hub of 420 feet.*

9. *(T/F) 10Base2 can have an overall network length of no more than 3,035 feet and contain a maximum of 1,024 nodes.*

10. *(T/F) IP uses logical network addresses to handle addressing, switching, routing selection, and connection services.*

11. *(T/F) The server Message Block does not provide peer-to-peer communication between the server software on a file server and the redirector on a client and.*

12. *(T/F) The Token ring system checks for duplicate addresses when a new computer comes on line.*

13. *(T/F) DLC is a sub-layer of the Application Layer of the OSI Reference Model.*

▲ Multiple Choice

1. *(MCQ) What is the maximum amount of data that can be transmitted in a single Ethernet frame?*

A. 48 bytes

B. 2.4 bytes

C. 1,500 bytes

D. 1,200 bytes

E. None of the above.

2. *(MCQ) How can an AppleTalk network be enlarged?*
   A. Create smaller networks called zones, then connect together the zones.
   B. Use an intelligent transponder on the network.
   C. Combine AppleTalk with the Ethernet architecture.
   D. Increase the speed of the network adapter card in clients.
   E. Use thicknet cabling.
3. *(MCQ) A client on an ArcNet network passes a token to:*
   A. The next physically closest client on the network.
   B. The client assigned the next highest number on the network.
   C. The repeater.
   D. The client with the fastest network adapter card.
   E. The client in the next zone.
4. *(MCQ) The VG in the name 100VG-AnyLAN implies:*
   A. Video grade.
   B. Voice grade.
   C. Vector gradient Transmissions.
   D. Fiber-optics trade transmissions.
   E. None of the above.
5. *(MCQ) What is the network access method used in an AppleTalk network?*
   A. CSMA/TD.
   B. AppleTalk proprietary network access method.
   C. CSMA/CD.
   D. Token Ring.
   E. CSMA/CA.
6. *What Apple Talk Protocol works at the Presentation Layer?*
   A. Printer Access Protocol
   B. Zone Information Protocol
   C. PPS
   D. Apple Talk Filing Protocol
   E. PSP

▲ Open Ended

Explain the 5–4–3 thinnet rule.

How are address conflicts avoided in a Token-ring network?

Identify the components of an Ethernet frame.

What are the disadvantages of using 10Base5 over 10BaseT?

Explain how frames are transmitted in an Ethernet network?

FIVE

The Operating and System Operations

▲Chapter Syllabus

MCSE 5.1 The Network Operating System

MCSE 5.2 Network Applications

MCSE 5.3 Computer Networks and Vendors

A network is very similar to a computer in that a computer is a box of switches until the operating system software is loaded. The operating system brings the computer to life. And so is the case of a network. The network consists of cables, network cards, and other components that you learned about in previous chapters. It is the network operating system that enables data to be transferred over these components. The network operating system is software that assures reliable data transfer and handles a host of other functions and gives a network administrator tools to manage the network. In this chapter, you'll explore the network operating system and find out how it works. You'll also learn how to use features of the operating system to optimize your network's performance.

MCSE 5.1 The Network Operating System

A computer is a box containing switches etched into chips. It does nothing until the operating system loads into memory. Operating systems such as DOS and UNIX are a set of programs that manage the flow of instructions and data in the computer.

The **operating system** handles saving and reading files on a disk, storing and retrieving data in memory, displaying information on the screen, and sending information to a printer. Every action taken by your computer is managed by the operating system.

A **network operating system** (NOS) Figure 5–1 is similar to the operating system running on your computer. However, the network operating system manages the flow of data across the network and enables clients attached to the network to access network resources such as files and printers.

Network operating systems can be divided into two categories: an added-on network operating system and an inclusive networking operating system.

Added-on network operating systems are found in mature network operating systems such as MS LAN Manager and were purchased separately from the client's operating system. Therefore, the network operating system had to add to the client's operating system. For example, a client was likely to be running DOS, but could not link to a network unless MS LAN Manager was installed on the client.

Figure 5–1. *A network operating system manages the network and access to network resources.*

Newer operating systems such as Windows NT integrated the network operating system. There is no additional software required to link the client to the network.

Clients attaching to a network must be able to handle several tasks at the same time. This is called **multitasking** (Figure 5–2) and requires a multitasking operating system.

For example, the operating system should be able to handle incoming network traffic without disrupting the user, who might be working with a spreadsheet or word processing program.

Every computer has a **central processing unit** (CPU), which is the chip that handles the processing of instructions and data for the computer. The user tells the operating system which application program to run (i.e., MS Word), then the operating system sends the first instruction of the program to the CPU for processing. The process continues until the CPU executes the final instruction.

However, during this time, requests to process instructions from other programs could be received by the operating system. This would be the case if you printed a document from Word, then wanted to use a spreadsheet while the document is printing.

The CPU, with some exceptions, can process only one task at a time, which is determined by the operating system. However, in a multitasking

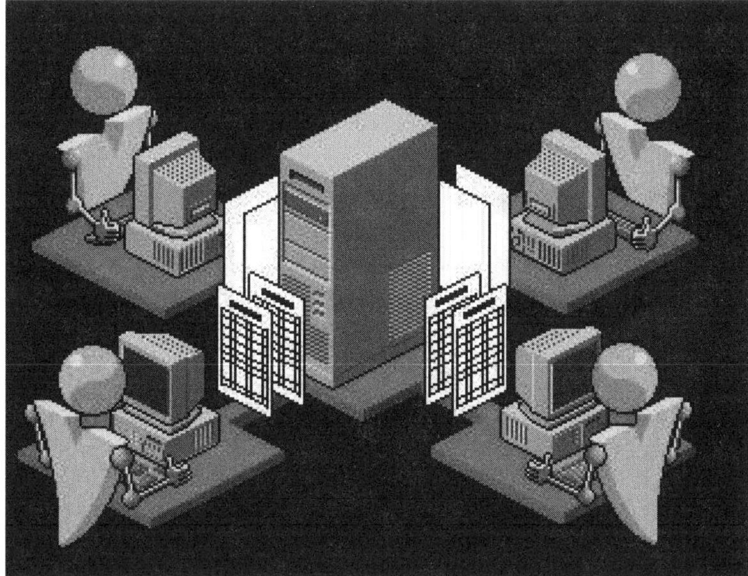

Figure 5–2. *A. multitasking operating system is able to process several tasks at the same time.*

operating system, the CPU must be able to suspend its current task, process any waiting tasks and return to the original task at the exact point it was suspended. This is also controlled by the operating system and happens in microseconds without the user realizing that more than one task is occurring.

There are two ways in which a multitasking operating system manages multitasks. These are preemptive and nonpreemptive. Preemptive multitasking allows the operating system to determine when the CPU stops processing an application temporarily to process a higher priority task. The application being processed (i.e., Word) cannot override the decision.

The **nonpreemptive multitasking**, sometimes called co-operative multitasking, approach is where a request is made to the application being processed to give up the CPU temporarily so that another task can be processed. No other task can be performed until the current task relinquish control of the process.

The NetBIOS Scheme

Each computer on a NetBIOS network is given a unique NetBIOS name when the network software is activated or when the operating system is installed on the computer. The NetBIOS name consists of 15 characters and a 16th character that is used to provide system information.

A computer's NetBIOS name is broadcast on to the network when a computer is powered up. The name uniquely identifies the computer to other computers on the network. If the name isn't unique, then the user or network administrator must change the computer's NetBIOS name.

All the NetBIOS names assigned to Windows NT or Windows 95 can be displayed by entering nbtstat -n at the command prompt. A word of caution: TCP/IP must be the network protocol used on your computer to run this command.

The NetBIOS name is an alias for the computer's hardware address. The association between the NetBIOS name and the address is contained in the local name cache. A computer wishing to connect to another network computer references the local name cache for the hardware address of the destination computer before attempting to create a session with that computer.

However, the destination computer's NetBIOS name may not be in the local name cache. In this case, NetBIOS sends a connectionless broadcast across the network searching for the computer. A session is established once the destination computer responds to the broadcast with its hardware address.

A different technique is employed on networks that use TCP/IP. In this case, NetBIOS uses the NetBIOS Over TCP/IP (NBT) protocol to encapsulate the request in a TCP/IP packet.

TCP/IP poses a problem when the network contains several network segments. Network segments are connected together using routers. Routers drop broadcast packets, therefore the NetBIOS method of broadcasting packets for name resolution wouldn't be successful.

NetBIOS follows six steps to resolve names on a TCP/IP network. These are:

1. Search the NetBIOS name cache
2. Search the WINS server
3. Issue a NetBIOS broadcast
4. Search the LMHOSTS file.
5. Search the HOSTS file.
6. Search the DNS Server

Windows NT contains the Windows Internet Name System (WINS) which resolves NetBIOS names to its corresponding IP address. Each computer configured to use WINS supplies the computer's NetBIOS name and IP address to the WINS server when the computer comes on line.

The WINS server stores the data in the WINS database. This information is replicated to other WINS servers in a large LAN. The WINS server is referenced by NetBIOS when there is a need to resolve a NetBIOS name. WINS enables computers to retrieve the name and network address of computers on other network segments other than its own segment.

Before WINS, NetBIOS names and hardware addresses were stored in the LMHOSTS file or the HOSTS file. Each is a text file maintained manually by the administrator. These files may exist in some networks and are searched by NetBIOS if the name is not located in the local name cache, WINS, and from a broadcast. The last place NetBIOS searches for the destination computer's IP address is in the Domain Name System DNS.

Networking Operating System and Clients

A network operating system is divided into two parts. These are the client software and the server software. The **client software** is installed on each client's hard driver, whereas the server software is installed only on the server (Figure 5–3). Collectively, the client software and the server software provide a secured way for clients to access resources on the network.

The client software uses a network operating system program called a **redirector** to send a client's request for network resources out over the network. The job of the redirector, also known as requester or shell on some networks, is to monitor resource requests within a client's computer, then redirect those requesting network services to the network. All requests from the redirector are processed by the server software.

Figure 5–3. *A computer that is linked to a network is called a client; computers shared among clients are called servers.*

The most common request from a client is to access a file located on a network file server. This is sometimes referred to as a network drive, which can be shared among clients on the network. Adding a shared resource (Drive) is called **mounting**.

A **drive designator**, which can be different for each client on a network, identifies each resource on the network. This is similar to the C: drive used to designate a hard disk connected to a client.

Resources are assigned a **drive designator** by using the File Manager (NT) to connect to the network resource. Once the resource is identified and assigned a designator, applications running on the client can access the resource by specifying the designator, such as F:.

The redirector can also redirect the normal flow of information within a client to a next resource without specifying the designator. An example is when a client wants to use a network printer rather than a local printer connected to the client. A **local resource** such as a printer is directly connected to a client. A **network resource** such as a network printer is connected to the network.

A printer is identified by a symbol that represents the port where the printer is connected. You recognize these indicators as COM1, COM2, LPT1, and LPT2. The port is assigned to a printer when the printer is installed. However, the redirector can redirect data going to a specific port and send it across the network, such as to a network printer.

Networking Operating System and Servers

Every client and server contains both client software and server software as part of the Windows NT operating system. However, the server software typically operates only on the server connected to the network and client software runs only on the client's stand-alone machine. Server software coordinates access to network resources by receiving requests from a client's redirector, then provides the redirector with the requested resource (Figure 5–4).

Server software also has the responsibility to limit access to resources to only those clients that have the right to access the resource in a particular way.

For example, an application running on a client's computer may ask the requestor for a particular file located on a network file server. However, the server software will only grant access if the client has permission to access the file. In the case of a file, permissions could be either *read permission* or *write permission*. A client needs read permission to see the file and write permission to change and save the file.

The third job of server software is to administer the network itself. This includes granting user access to the network. There can be any number of

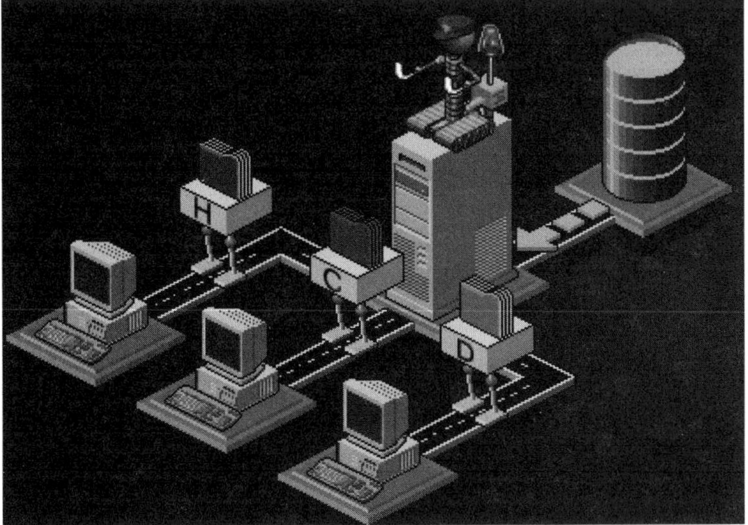

Figure 5–4. *A redirector receives requests from clients, then provides the requested resource if the client has permission to use the resource.*

users, each of which has a unique login to the network and can use any client to access the network.

When a user logs into the network, the requester sends the user's login ID and password to the server software, which compares it against its database of known users. If there is a match, the user is granted access to the network; otherwise, access is denied and the user is unable to log in to the network.

A network administrator is responsible for using server software to manage users. The administrator can create new users, grant or remove specific privileges, and remove users from the network.

Installing and Setting Up Server Software

Although server software is supplied with many newer operating systems, it must still be installed on the server and configured for a particular network. The installation process itself is an automatic process, similar to the installation of all software. The setup or install program handles the installation.

As with other software install programs, you will be prompted for information during the installation. This section will present the questions typically asked by the setup or install program.

One of the first questions that will be asked is for the server name and the name of the segment where the server will reside. As discussed throughout earlier chapters, large computer networks are composed of smaller networks called segments. Each segment contains clients and one or more servers. Each segment is identified by a specific name called a **work-group name** or a **domain name** (Figure 5–5). Both the server name and the domain name are needed to reference the server on the network.

There can be many servers connected to the network. Each server can have a different role in network operations. For example, a server can be used to store applications that are shared among clients on the network like Word or Excel. This is called an applications server.

Another server can be used to store nonapplication files, such as spreadsheets and word processing documents. This server is called a **file server**. A very common server on large networks is a **print server**, sometimes called a **print spooler**, which is used to temporarily store files until they are sent to a printer.

At least one server on a domain is designated as the **primary domain controller** (PDC). A PDC, usually the first server installed on the network has the task of administrating the server's domain. It is the PDC server's job to enforce network security, store information about the domain and information about network users. This is called the master copy of the domain information.

Figure 5–5. *As part of the setup, you'll be asked to enter the work-group name or the domain name.*

Computer networks that must be operational without interruption will have two servers on a domain. One is the PDC and the other is the backup domain controller (BDC) although only the PDC is required. The BDC takes over the network administration chores if the PDC becomes inactive. It can also act in the capacity of a stand-alone server, such as an application, file, or print server.

When the server software is installed, you must designate the role of the server on the domain. Depending on the network, your choices will be PDC, BDC, or stand-alone server.

Network Card Installation

A network server is like other clients on the network, in that it too needs a network card before the server can connect to the network. The network card is a circuit board that is placed in an expansion slot on the motherboard of the server and is connected to the network cable.

The network card must be configured to the appropriate protocol of the network. This is done during the installation of the server software. The most common protocol used in computer networks is TCP/IP, which is the protocol used for the Internet and for intranets. Intranets are proprietary versions of the Internet, where access is restricted to clients on the organization's network. Table 5–1 contains the steps necessary to select TCP/IP as the network protocol for the server.

After selecting the TCP/IP protocol, you must provide three other pieces of information before the server is configured for the network. This is referred to as configuring the TCP/IP protocol and can be performed automatically or manually.

You'll need to identify the IP address of the server, the networks subnet mask, and the default gateway.

The IP address identifies the server as the TCP/IP host. A host is a client on the network. The address consists of two parts. These are the network ID and the host ID. The network ID is used to identify all the hosts on the same network and the host ID specifies a particular host. Each IP address must be a unique 32-bit value that consists of four sets of digits, each separated by a period (e.g., 145.133.6.132).

A portion of the IP address identifies the network and another portion identifies the host. The subnet mask identifies the network ID portion of the IP address, which is used by hosts to determine if the target address is on the same network as the originator client or on a remote network. A typical subnet mask looks like 255.255.0.0.

The default gateway specifies the router to be used whenever the IP address cannot be found on the local network. The default gateway is optional. If there is no remote network connected via a router, then there is no need for setting the default gateway. If there is a remote network connected and the default gateway isn't set, then only clients on the local network can receive data packets.

Some server software, such as the Microsoft NT Server, has the ability to use dynamic host configuration protocol (DHCP) server to automatically set the TCP/IP parameters. The DHCP server, if available on the network, can be requested to automatically configure the TCP/IP parameters by checking the DHCP server check box when selecting TCP/IP as the network protocol.

Table 5–1 *Selecting the TCP/IP Protocol for the Server*

Select the Protocols tab.
Select the Add option.
Select TCP/IP protocol.

The same process can be done manually if a DHCP server is unavailable by entering the IP address, subnet mask, and default gateway when installing TCP/IP.

Whenever a client wants to transmit information to another client on the network or to a network resource such as a printer, the client needs to specify the destination IP address. Unfortunately, the IP address isn't easy to remember. A solution to this problem is to associate a name with an IP address, then use the name to address data packets.

Windows NT contains software that makes this possible. It is called Windows Internet Name Service (WINS), which stores the NetBIOS name of clients with the related IP address. This is called registering the computer's name and the IP address that occurs when Windows NT starts. WINS then inserts the computer name in the data packet into the correct IP address.

Installing and Setting Up Network Administrative Software

Administrative software used to run a network is called network services, which is delimited as *services* for short. Many of the network services required to properly administer the network are automatically installed as part of the network operating system. However, those network services that are not automatically installed can be manually installed.

In networks such as Microsoft NT, there is a network control panel that displays the Network dialog box. The Network dialog box contains five categories of options each displayed on its own tab (Figure 5–6). These are Identification, Services, Protocols, Adapters, and Bindings.

The Services tab of the Network dialog box lists the installed administrative applications. You can add a new service by clicking the Add button that displays the Select Network Service dialog box containing available services that can be installed.

Some new services can be installed directly from the server's hard disk; others not available on the hard disk will require an installation disk or CD. In such cases, it requires you to select the "Have Disk" button to list services on the disk or CD. Double-click the name of the service and it will be installed. You can have the service automatically started when the service is booted by following the steps in Table 5–2.

The Services dialog box also identifies which services are currently running by placing Started beneath the Status column. You can stop a service currently running by highlighting the service and clicking the Stop button. A similar process is used to start the service, except the Start button is clicked.

Network components such as the network card must be bound to services needed by the component. This process is called **binding**, the most common of which is binding a protocol to a network card.

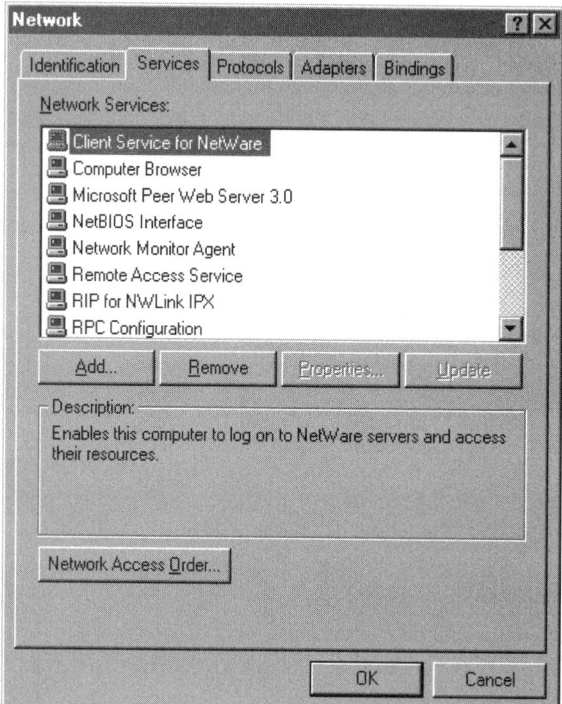

Figure 5–6. *The Network dialog box contains five categories of network options, each displayed on a separate tab.*

The Bindings tab of the Network dialog box contains the list of current bindings. The order on the binding list, called the **binding order**, plays a critical role in the operation of the network. A component such as the network card can be bound to more than one service (i.e., more than one protocol).

Binding occurs each time a client or server connects to the network. In order to reduce the time required to connect to the network, the protocol used the most should be at the top of the binding list. This is called **connect time.**

A binding can be disabled by highlighting the binding, then clicking the Disable button. This removes it from the list. The same process is used to enable the binding, except the Enabled button is clicked.

Table 5–2 *Starting Services Automatically When the Server Is Booted*

Select the Windows NT Server Control Panel.
Select Services to display the Services dialog box.
Highlight the service you want to automatically start.
Select the Startup button. The Startup status is changed from manual to automatic.

You can change the binding order by highlighting the binding you want to move on the list, then clicking on either the MoveUp or MoveDown button. The binding will then automatically be repositioned on the list.

Installing a Network Printer, Fax, and Modem

Whenever you want to print a document, you select File/Print, then choose the name of the printer you want to print to. However, little thought is given to the location of the printer, other than the distance we must walk to it.

The name of the printer that appears in the Print dialog box is associated within the computer to a port such as LPT1 or COM1, which traditionally connects the printer directly to the computer through the paralell port. As we have learned previously in this chapter, the network redirector can intercept information sent to a printer portion identifier and redirect the information to a printer connected to the network.

Network printers are connected to the network through a server called a print server. All documents to be printed on the network printer are sent from the client over the network to the print server.

The print server temporarily stores the incoming documents in memory called a **Simultaneous Peripheral Operation on Line** (SPOOL), which is also known as a spooler. However, heavy demand for the use of the printer can easily exceed the memory allocated to the spooler. When this occurs, documents that can't fit on the spooler are temporarily stored on the server's hard disk.

Each print job is logged in a queue called a **print queue**. This is similar to the line at the grocery store. As a print job comes to the top of the print queue, the file server sends the document from the spooler to the printer. A subsequent print job then moves up in the queue. If there are documents temporarily stored on the server's hard disk, they are moved into the spooler.

Network printers can be connected to a file server using a printer cable similar to how printers are directly connected to clients. However, there are additional steps required to complete the installation or a printer can have its own network card.

Each printer requires a printer driver. The printer driver is the software that handles communications between the file server and the printer. Many printer drivers are distributed as part of the operating system. Some are automatically loaded using the Plug and Play feature. Other printer drivers must be loaded from a disk or CD using the Print Manager and the Add Printer Wizard (Figure 5–7).

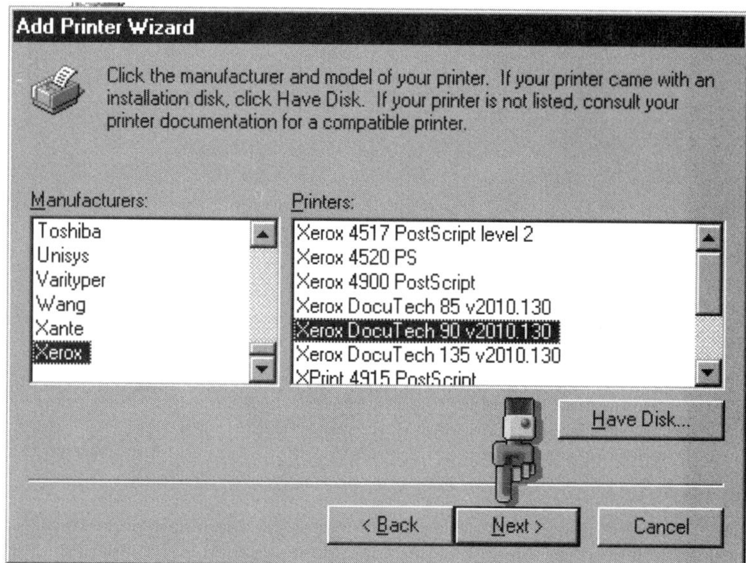

Figure 5–7. *The Add Printer Wizard lists all the printer drivers that come with the operating system software.*

The Wizard walks you through the installation steps, which include selecting the driver, naming the printer server to which the printer is connected, assigning a name to the printer, and making the printer a shared printer.

Once the printer is installed, the server must connect to the printer using the Print Manager setup utility. Connection is made by first finding and double-clicking the name of the print server on the shared printer list in the Connect to Printer dialog box. Names of printers available on the printer will appear in the dialog box. You can connect to the printer by double-clicking on the printer's name.

Maintaining a Network Printer

The person responsible for the network is the network administrator. The network administrator must make sure users have proper access to network resources such as the network printer (Figure 5–8). Access not only means the right to print a document using the printer, but also the right to manipulate the printer queue.

As previously mentioned in this chapter, documents sent to the network printer arrive at the print server, where they are temporarily stored and queued until the document is sent to the printer.

The network administrator can grant a user permission to change jobs in the print queue. The permissions depend on which network operating

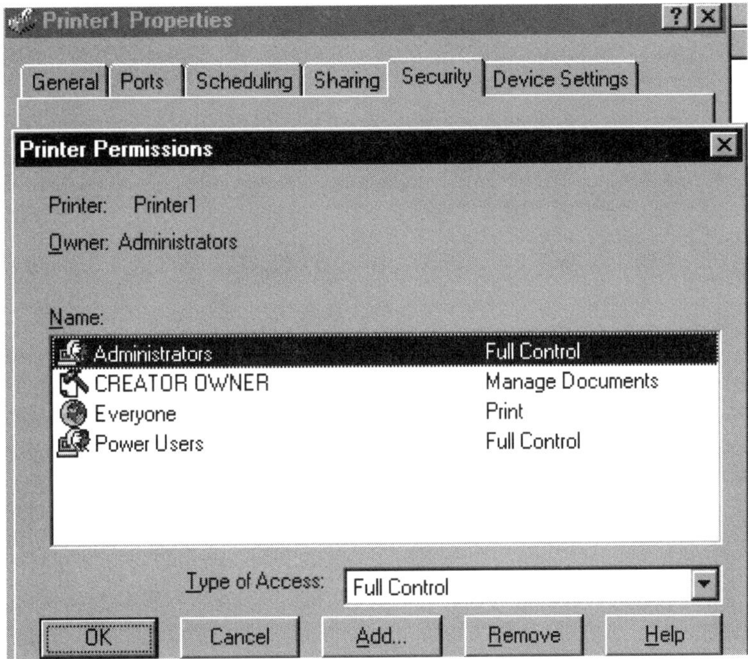

Figure 5–8. *The Printer Properties dialog box Security tab is used to create, modify, or delete permissions for use of the printer.*

system is in use. Most operating systems allow every user to review the print queue and delete their own print jobs from the queue.

Typically, the network administrator has the right to delete any print job from the queue and rearrange jobs on the queue. These rights can also be assigned to any user, assuming the assignment is permitted by the network operating system.

Windows NT Server Print Manager is the network utility used to assign permissions to the printer. Permissions are identified by the type of account that is set using the Printer Permissions tab of the Windows NT Server Print Manager.

Installing a Network Fax Modem

A fax machine is an integral part of any business and with the creation of the fax modem, every client can have his or her own built-in fax machine. While this might be desirable by many users, it could create an unnecessary cost to the organization. The organization must acquire a fax modem for each client and provide him or her with an analog telephone line.

An alternative to individual fax modems is to create a fax server. A fax server is a computer on the network that contains one or more fax modems.

Its job is to receive documents to be faxed from clients on the network, then send those documents to the fax modem, which is similar to the operation of a print server.

A fax server also monitors fax modems for incoming documents. It receives the document from outside the network, then forwards the document to designated clients on the network. This is called routing the fax.

Routing is a major concern when setting up a fax server because incoming faxes don't contain the network address of the client destined to receive the fax. It is up to the fax server to deliver the fax to the proper client.

There are a number of solutions to this problem. Some of the better solutions are T.30 subaddressing, Novell embedded systems technology (NEST), transmission station identification (TSI), or direct inward dialing (DID). All of these follow the same basic concept.

The person sending the fax uses a telephone number that is unique within the organization or contains the extension of the client. The fax server uses this number to uniquely identify the client, then transmits the fax to the client's network address.

T.30 subaddressing, TSI, and NEST require the sender to include a client's telephone extension. DID is a trunk line provided by the telephone company that enables the organization to receive calls from multiple telephone numbers. For example, an organization might be assigned a block of telephone numbers from 555–8000 to 555–8999. Anyone calling a telephone number within the range is directed to the organization's trunk line.

Software used to run the organization's private branch exchange (PBX) system identifies the client by the last three, four or five digits of the incoming telephone number. PBX is the private telephone system that is used within an organization.

There are other less desirable options available to process incoming faxes from the fax server. One such option is manual routing, in which someone reads the recipient's name on the fax, then forwards it to the client.

Another method is to use **optical character recognition** (OCR) or **Intelligent character recognition** (ICR). These are software utilities that convert the graphic file containing the faxed document into a text file. The text file is then searched to identify the client. However, this conversion process is not perfect. On the average, only 80 to 90 percent of the document is converted accurately.

MCSE 5.2 Network Applications

Throughout this book, you've learned about components of a computer network that enable clients to communicate with each other over cables as well as over the air waves. An important component of every network is the network operating system, which consists of a group of software that manages communication over the network.

The first part of this chapter discussed the network operating system. However, there is another kind of software that allows clients to do something more than communicate with each other. This is called network application software.

Application software consists of word processing programs, spreadsheet programs, and customized programs that automate operations within an organization. One could very well mention an endless list of programs. Many of these applications are stand-alone, which means that they run on a single computer although the data files used by the programs might reside on a network file server.

Many applications today are network applications, which means that the software is designed to interact with the network rather than to work within a single client environment.

There are many kinds of network applications that help clients on the network improve the flow of regular communications. These applications are categorized as **GroupWare** because they assist work groups to communicate among members of the group.

Two of the most useful network applications are email and a scheduler, which are likely to be provided with the network operating system. Email software such as Microsoft Exchange is beginning to replace printed mail. A scheduler such as Microsoft Schedule tracks the schedule of each member of the work group. Each schedule is stored on the file server and can be referenced by members of the group.

Email

Electronic mail (email) is likely the most widely used network application in every organization, since this application enables anyone who has a network login to send and receive mail without the need for interoffice mail. It's fast, efficient, and saves time.

Most of us take email for granted. However, there are specific functionality requirements that every email application must provide to network users. These are: the delivery of incoming mail; return receipt when messages are delivered; a user interface that signals when a message is delivered as well as providing the tools to read and write messages.

Email applications also need to have a facility to easily respond to an incoming message. Users expect to press a key on the keyboard or click a button using a mouse, then begin typing the reply. The application automatically generates the destination address using the information from incoming message.

In addition to sending the text of the email message, email applications allow users to attach other documents in the form of a file called an **attach-**

ment to the message. These can include word processing documents, spreadsheets, and graphic files. Practically any kind of file can be attached to an email message and transferred to another user.

Email services used by an organization are provided as a component of the network. This enables any user with a login and mailbox on the network to communicate with any other user on the network.

However, an additional expense is incurred if members of the organization need to send email outside of the firm. Many organizations have a direct connection to the Internet that enables email to be sent and received from around the world. Some organizations subscribe to email services offered by AT&T, MCI, Microsoft, and other service providers sometimes referred to as ISP.

Email applications must follow three industry standards to assure compatibility with other email applications and operating systems. These standards are X.400, X.500, and SMTP. Each of these standards corresponds to the application layer of the OSI model.

The **Comite Consultati Internationale de Telegraphie et Telephonie** (CCITT) created the **X.400** standard to enable email applications to be independent of the operating system and independent of computers. Within the standards, the CCITT defined access protocols, conversion rules, user interfaces, syntax, and how to encode information within the message. It also established how messages are dated and time-stamped, how priorities are set for processing messages, and how return receipts function.

X.400 is divided into three general areas. These are **User Agent** (UA), **Message Transfer Agent** (MTA), and **Message Transfer System** (MTS). These areas specify rules for routing messages over the network to the proper mailbox, how to identify users, the size of and the format of messages such as having an address, subject, return address, and how to return receipts.

The UA is the application software used to access email services. This is what most of us identify as the email application because we use the UA to read our messages and create and send new email messages.

The UA communicates with the **Message Handling Service** (MHS) (Figure 5–9), which translates email messages so that the message can be read by other types UA on the network and throughout the world, if the email message is sent over the Internet.

The MTA is similar to the MHS, except the MTA is defined in the X.400 standard and the MHS is a de facto standard initiated by Novell. The MTA also translates messages. The MTS actually handles the email transfer.

Email can also be transferred between computers using the Simple Mail Transfer Protocol (SMTP), which provides the rules governing message transfer. These rules are part of the TCP/IP protocol stack.

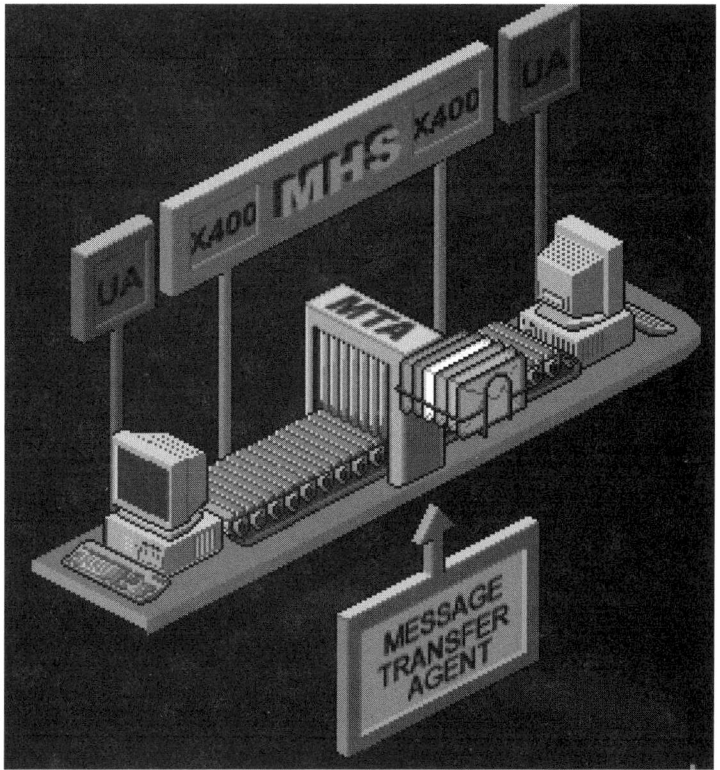

Figure 5–9. *The UA sends email to the MHS, which forwards or temporarily stores the mail using the X.400 protocol.*

SMTP enables email programs to send and receive messages, create and display messages, print messages, and stores email addresses in a manner similar to a telephone book.

All this is possible because SMTP contains the guidelines for handshaking between computers and how messages are to be transmitted.

The X.500 standard specifies the directory structure on the email server, which helps clients on a remote network locate users and a local network.

For example, consider a client that wants to find a user that is located on a different network. Information about the user is contained in a particular set of directories on the remote network; this can be searched as long as the client knows the directory structure on the remote network.

In addition to specifying directory services, the X.500 specification provides guidelines for creating a name service containing names and addresses of users on the network.

While these protocols should reduce the likelihood of incompatibility between email systems, there could be occasions when differences in email systems prevent the exchange of messages. Simply speaking, both email systems speak a different language. Incompatibility problems can be overcome by using a gateway that translates email message formats into the format required by a particular email system. Gateways are included as part of most popular email systems, such as cc:Mail and Microsoft Exchange.

Stand-Alone versus Network Applications

Computer applications typically fall into two general categories based on where the application resides. These are called stand-alone applications and network applications.

A stand-alone application is the category most familiar to every computer user, since these are the programs installed on your computer's hardrive. Stand-alone applications do not require any network resources and typically cannot be shared with other clients on the network, although data files produced by stand-alone applications are commonly shared using network resources. A network application is a program that resides on the network and can be used by any network client.

For example, a word processing program such as Microsoft Word can be either a stand-alone application or a network application. As a stand-alone application, the program is installed on a computer's hard drive and only that computer can run the application.

However as a network application, Microsoft Word can be used by a specific number of clients on the network at the sametime. The actual number depends on the licensing agreement the organization has with the manufacturer. The network application typically resides on an application server.

Network applications are best suited for organizations that have many clients requiring the same application, since the network application is more economical and easier to maintain than a stand-alone application.

For example, everyone on the network receives the same version of the application from the same source and only one copy of the application must be maintained. Table 5–3 lists the procedures that should be followed when installing a network application.

MCSE 5.3 Computer Networks and Vendors

Computer networks are discussed with the same uniformity as Word, Excel, and Access in that we tend to think of a computer network as a cohesive product manufactured by a single manufacturer.

Table 5-3 *Procedures for Installing Network Applications*

1. Create a separate, shared directory for each network application on the application server.
2. Install the network application to the application server.
3. Keep a record of all network applications. Include the serial and version numbers of all applications, installation procedures, installation of upgrades, and a list of users that are allowed to access the network application.

When you purchase a copy of Word, you assume the spelling checker and thesaurus will work flawlessly with every Word document—and you'll be correct in your assumption.

However, the same is not necessarily true about a computer network. You probably realize that various vendors manufacture hardware components of a network, yet all work together because manufacturers adhered to the network standards discussed throughout this book.

A computer network can also run software created by different vendors, such as networking software, client operating systems, and redirectors.

These differences can cause havoc for a network administrator, since it is the administrator's job to make sure network resources are available to all clients regardless of the operating system and software the client is using.

Problems between a computer network and clients arise when the software they run is unable to communicate with each other even though the software adheres to the OSI model.

There are two approaches a network administrator can take to resolve such conflicts. These are to modify the software on the network, called the server solution, or modify the software at the client's end, called the client solution.

The server solution requires the network administrator to install additional software, called services on the server, to translate software running on a client and the network operating system.

A different service is required for each kind of software running on network clients. The service receives requests from client software for network recourses. Before processing the request, the service translates the request into a form readable by the network operating system.

Likewise, transmissions sent to the client are translated from the network operating system back to the form required by the client's software.

The client solution requires that more than one redirector be installed on the client. A redirector intercepts requests for network resources, then interacts with the network operating system to fulfill the request.

Therefore, the redirector must be able to translate the form required by the network operating system and the form required by the software of the client. For each kind of network operating system the client uses, an appropriate redirector must be installed.

The thought of installing multiple services or redirectors may seem overwhelming at first but it isn't because there are basically three common network and client operating system providers. These are Microsoft, Novell, and Apple Computer. Therefore, services or redirectors are limited to three choices.

Each of these firms provides services or redirectors to enable all three clients and services to communicate with each other. Table 5–4 lists the software/hardware required to connect clients to networks.

Client/Servers

The term client is used throughout the book to refer to a computer that is connected to the network and requests a network resource from a server through the network operating system. This is similar to the business model, where a client requests service from a business owner.

Typical requests by clients on a network are to execute an applications program stored on the network application server; to copy files stored on a network file server; or to send/receive faxes.

These requests all have the same characteristics. That is, the client asks for a file to be transferred. Processing of the file is handled by the client and not by a network resource. This is commonly called the **file server model,**

Table 5–4 *Software/Hardware Requirements for Mixing and Matching Clients with Networks*

Connect Windows NT Client to NetWare Network: Install NWLink (the IPX/SPX protocol) and Client Service for NetWare (CSNW) (the NetWare requestor. A requestor is the same as a redirector).
Connect Windows NT Server to NetWare Network: Install NWLink and Gateway Service for NetWare (GSNW).
Connect Windows 95 Client to NetWare Network: Install NWLink and MS Client for NetWare Networks for NetWare. Microsoft Service for NetWare Directory Services (NDS) can also be used for Microsoft clients to connect to NetWare.
Connect Macintosh Client to Windows NT Network: Install Windows NT Services For Macintosh on the server and AppleTalk on the Macintosh.
Connect MS DOS Client to AppleTalk Network: Install AppleShare Personal Computer Software and LocalTalk Personal Computer Card (Firmware on the card handles communication between the client and network).

where the server receives requests to transfer files and not to process the files (Figure 5–10) Files can be transferred both ways and an exact copy of the whole file is transferred.

The file server model was the first model used for computer networks and is still used today. However, enhancements made in database technology have provided an alternative model called the **client/server model**. The client/server model requires the server to process requests for information rather than simply transferring a file to a client.

In the client/server model, the client makes a request to the server for information such as sales for last Monday. A database server running a database management system receives the request. The database management system, such as Sybase and Oracle, searches its database files, then sends the client just the information the client had requested. Thus, instead of transferring the complete sales file (as in the case in a file server model) only the specific data is sent.

The client/server model makes network operations more efficient than the file server model, because less information is transferred across the network. For example, instead of 365 days of sales information, only 1 day is sent. Also the server is doing some of the processing on it's CPU.

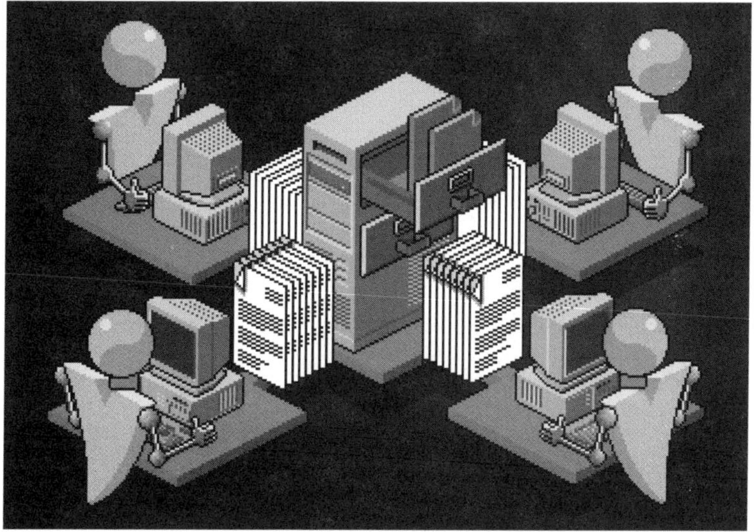

Figure 5–10. *A file server model uses a server as a depository of a file. The server does not process files stored on the server.*

Clients and Requests

There are two components in the client/server model. The clients, referred to as the front end, which communicates or interacts with the user through a program interface with the user. The server referred to as backend, which processes requests from the client and transfers the data back to the client.

Software running on the client is used by the user to formulate a request for information through the use of a data inquiry screen. A data inquiry screen is unique with each application and contains data input fields called search keys.

The user enters values relating to the information he needs by using the search keys, then signals the software (i.e., by clicking the OK button) to retrieve the data. The software then formulates the request using the Structure Query Language (SQL). SQL has become the standard language used to request information from database management systems.

In addition to using the data inquiry screen, a user can directly write requests for information into the database request using SQL. The file containing the SQL request is then submitted to the database management system and is processed in the same manner as if the data inquiry screen generated the SQL request.

When the server returns the requested data to the client, software running on the client is responsible for further processing the information. This might include displaying the information on the screen, in a printed report, or incorporating the data with other information already at the client.

Besides recalling information from the server, software running on the client is also used to maintain the database. It can insert new information into the database, update existing information, and delete unwanted information. Each task is performed by an SQL request that is sent to the server.

Server and Requests

The server component of the client/server model is responsible for processing requests from multiple clients and maintaining the integrity of the data stored in the database.

A request from a client is constructed of SQL statements, which are stored in a file. The file is transferred to the server component for processing. An SBL statement tells the server to do something, such as send me the first and last name data. Another statement typically follows in the file that tells the server where to find the data (i.e., which database to use). Still another statement provides the search criteria. There are statements also for inserting, updating, and deleting data. Database management software on the server reads and follows the directions of the SQL statements in the request (Figure 5–11).

The client/server model greatly reduces the traffic over the network. No longer do clients receive large files and instead clients receive just the information needed to meet the needs of the user.

However, eliminating the need to transmit the same frequent user requests can reduce network traffic further. The code for a request that is made often, such as for the current inventory level, can be stored on the server as part of the database. These stored requests are called stored procedures. A client can ask by name for a particular stored procedure to be run by the database management system.

Besides reducing network traffic, stored procedures also ensure control over requests since a stored procedure need only be created once, whereas an SQL request must be created each time a client requires information from the server.

The Client/Server Database

A database management system is designed to respond to multiple requests within a reasonable time frame, but requests can be delayed because the server component of the client/server model is the central point for requests, which can become a bottleneck on the network. If two requests require the same resources (i.e., data), the second request must wait until the first request is finished being processed.

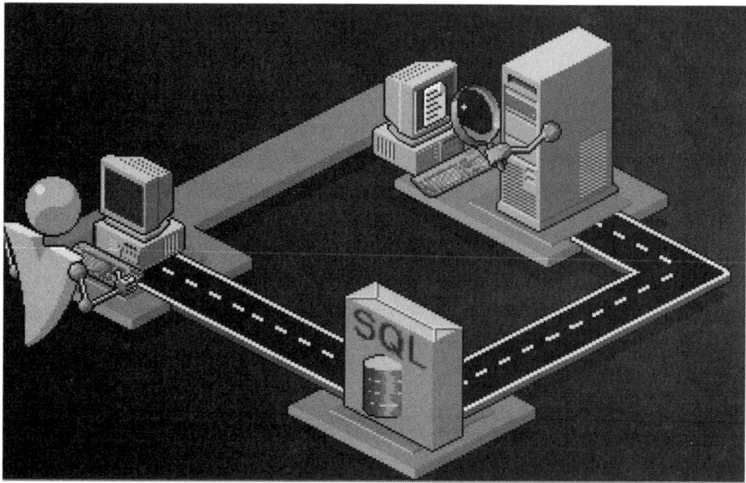

Figure 5–11. *A client sends an SQL request to the SQL server, which searches the necessary databases before responding to the client's request.*

A database management system is unable to accurately determine the maximum time required for processing a request, because each database and each request is unique. The processing of a request is dependent on the design of the database, which is unique to every application, and the way in which the SQL statements are created. An improperly formed request can delay processing, cause an error, and dampen the effectiveness of any database management system.

Steps can be taken to improve processing requests by properly configuring the server components of the client/server model.

Organizations typically use a single server client/server configuration which as the name implies contains a single database server on the network. One server fulfils all requests for data from clients, and is responsible for managing the data stored on the server. If bottlenecks occur, technicians, such as database administrators and programmers, can either redesign the database and/or rewrite SQL requests to improve performance.

However, when these techniques fail, then a multiserver client/server configuration should be considered. In a multiserver client/server configuration, there is more than one database server, each containing the same data. Therefore, the high volume of requests can be divided among servers, so that each client realizes a reasonable response time.

Although there is an improvement in response time, there is a drawback. In this configuration, databases must be synchronized. Changes in data on one server must be replicated on the other servers, otherwise the integrity of the data is questionable. Database management systems support multiserver configurations and provide an automatic method for synchronizing databases.

Another variation on the multiserver client/server configuration is called the data warehouse configuration. Like the multiserver client/server configuration, a data warehouse configuration has more than one server. One server contains all the data. This data warehouse server is sometimes referred to as the main server.

The most requested data is replicated from the data warehouse server to other database servers on the network, sometimes called intermediate servers.

Clients request data from an intermediate server. If the data isn't available on the intermediate server, then the server requests the data from the data warehouse server.

■ Summary

A network operating system manages the flow of data across the network and enables clients attached to the network to access network resources such as files and printers. Network operating systems can be divided into two categories: an added-on network operating system and an inclusive networking operating system. An added-on network operating system such as DOS is added as a separate component to the client's operating system. An inclusive networking operating system is included with the computer's operating system such as NT.

A networking operating system must be capable of multitasking in order to handle requests from multiple clients at the same time. A multitasking operating system manages multitasks by using the preemptive or nonpreemptive methods. Preemptive multitasking requires the operating system to determine when the CPU stops processing an application temporarily to process a higher priority task. The nonpreemptive multitasking approach is where a request is made to the application using the CPU to give up the CPU temporarily so that another application request can be processed.

A network operating system is divided into client software and the server software. The client software is installed on each client's disk driver, whereas the server software is installed only on the server.

The client software uses a redirector program, also known as requester or shell, to request network resources. A redirector monitors resource requests within a client's computer, then redirects those requests to the network.

Server software has three major roles: coordinate access to network resources by receiving requests from a redirector; provide the redirector with the requested resource; and limit access to resources to clients that have the right to access the resource.

Server software must be installed on the server. Installation processes require network specific information to be entered into the setup or install program. These include the server name and the segment name where the server resides, which are known as either the work group or a domain name.

More than one server can be connected to the network, each having a different role in network operations. These include an applications server to store applications; a file server to store data and nonapplication files; and a print server (known as a print spooler), which is used to temporarily store files until they are sent to the printer.

Every domain must have at least one server know as the primary domain controller (PDC). The PDC administers the server's domain; it enforces network security, and stores information about the domain and network users. A second server can be added to the network, known as the backup domain controller (BDC), which takes over network administration if the PDC becomes inactive.

Both servers and clients must run the same protocol, the most common of which is the TCP/IP protocol. Three pieces of information are necessary to configure the protocol: the IP address, which is the network address of the client or server; the subnet mask, which identifies the network ID portion of the IP address; and the default gateway, which specifies the router to be used whenever the IP address cannot be found on the local network. Some network software uses the dynamic host configuration protocol (DHCP) to automatically set the TCP/IP parameters.

Network addresses are associated with names called NetBIOS to make it easier for users to reference the address. This is called registering the computer's name and occurs when Windows NT starts. The Windows Internet Name Service (WINS) is the program that stores the NetBIOS name of clients with the related IP address and manages the lookup process.

Administrative software used to run a network is called network services (or services for short).

In networks such as Microsoft NT, there is a network control panel that displays the Network dialog box, which is used to install or modify services.

A variety of services are available on a network. Two of the most common are a print server and a fax-modem server. Printer servers provide a link to network printers. A fax-modem server provides a connection to network fax-modems.

Network applications consist of any application that clients can run over the network, for instance, common applications such as Word, Excel, and email. Email is an application that enables users to send and maintain messages over the network or Internet.

A network can be created using components from various network manufacturers. Any interoperability conflicts are resolved through the installation of software and/or network adapter cards.

Networks are frequently used to exchange data from a network database to clients. There are two methods used to exchange data: copying the complete database file to the client or using a client/server model. In the client/server model, a client requests information using SQL from a server, which runs a database management system. The database management system searches the database and sends the client just the information requested. The client/server model reduces the network traffic, because only a portion of the database is copied to the client.

▲ Chapter Review Questions

▲ Fill in the Blanks

1. ______________ *describes how a network operating system handles more than one operation at the same time.*

2. *The server on a segment that controls networking operations is called ________________.*

3. *______________ is the method used to link network services to the network adapter card device drivers.*

4. *TCP/IP installation requires the following information ______, ______, ________.*

5. *____________ is the language used to create requests for data by clients.*

▲ True/False

1. *(T/F) X.400 Protocols set standards for using a network printer.*

2. *(T/F) Apple computers and personal computers can communicate using the same network.*

3. *(T/F) Data warehouse is a server that distributes data to other database servers.*

4. *(T/F) A database management system copies files to network clients.*

5. *(T/F) The dynamic host configuration protocol (DHCP) automatically sets the TCP/IP parameters.*

6. *(T/F) NetWare based on Xerox network System contains the IPX/SPX protocol suite and is a server-centric architecture.*

▲ Multiple Choice

1. *The category of a network operating system that is not included as part of the client's operating system is called?*

A. Stand-alone system

B. MS-DOS

C. Added-on network operating system

D. Stand-alone network operating system

E. None of the above

2. *What is the purpose of the subnet mask?*

A. Interprets requests between the operating system and the network card driver

B. Routes email messages across the Internet

C. Combines multivendor networks

D. Identifies the address of the server

E. Identifies the network ID portion of the IP address

3. *A network application means?*

A. An application that uses the telephone network to exchange data

B. File transfer

C. Client/server databases

D. The software is designed to interact with the network rather than work with a single client.

E. Applications that store data on a network server

4. *What is a search key?*

A. Input fields on a data inquiry screen used by the client to search a database for requested information

B. Input fields on a data inquiry screen used by the database management system to search a database for requested information

C. Security information required by the network operating system

D. Information used to locate an IP address

E. Input fields used to install TCP/IP

5. *What is the memory used by the print server to temporarily store the incoming documents?*

A. Simultaneous Peripheral Operation On Line

B. Print router

C. Documents are not stored in memory

D. CSMA/CA

E. VREM

6. *The ________name consists of 16 characters. The first 15 characters refer to the computer's network name and the 16th character provides system information.*

A. OS

B. IP Address

C. DOS

D. NetBIOS

E. NetDOS

7. *A ______ server is a central repository for data.*
   - A. Mail
   - B. Printer
   - C. File
   - D. Fax
   - E. Application

▲ Open Ended

What are the problems of routing incoming faxes over a network?

How are requests processed in the client/server model?

What configurations are available to avoid bottlenecks in the client/server model?

How would you connect a Macintosh Client to Windows NT Network?

What is the role of a redirector?

SIX

Network Management

▲Chapter Syllabus

By now from reading previous chapters in this book you realize that sophisticated network operations take place out of sight. For example, in the client/server model, the information we enter into the screen is converted into an SQL request sent to the server. The server reads the request, searches for the data, and then transmits a copy of the data to our computer, where it is displayed for our review.

Except for installation of network software, humans seem not to be involved in network operations. Software on both the client and the server side function flawlessly.

However true this is, computer networks must be managed to assure networking and data integrity. Someone must manage network operations and be available during those times when the network fails to operate properly. Throughout this chapter, you'll learn how to manage a computer network.

MCSE 6.1 Network Administration

The term used to describe network management is **network administration** and the technician who performs the administrative duties is called the **network administrator.** It is the network administrator's job to make sure that the network operates flawlessly—and if it doesn't, the network administrator must correct any problems.

There are five categories of responsibility for the network administrator. These are: user administration; resource management; configuration management; performance management; and network maintenance.

User administration involves creating and maintaining user accounts and managing access to network resources such as files and printers. A user account refers to information regarding each user who has permission to access the network. Information includes user ID, password, and access rights to specific network resources.

Resource management requires the network administrator to install and maintain network resources, such as fax-modems, printers, servers, files and programs stored on the server. For example, the network administrator must install and update network applications such as email.

Configuration management relates to the topology of the network. The network administrator is the key person involved in the design and configuration of the network. He or she is the one to set up protocol.

Performance management is an on-going job for the network administrator; it requires constant monitoring of network activity to determine reasons for inadequate network response times. And when performance problems exist, it is the responsibility of the network administrator to resolve those issues.

Network maintenance is similar to performance management, but deals with physical network problems with cabling, network adapter cards, and networking software.

User Administration

A user account is information the network operating system requires to permit a user's access to network resources. A user is a person who can log onto a network client. Any network client can be used, since all user account information used by the network operating system during the log in process is stored on the central server of the domain. User specific information is stored in an **account profile** sometimes called a **user profile.**

The network administrator uses utilities available on the network operating system to create new user accounts. The **User Manager for Domains** is

Table 6–1 *Steps Required to Create a New User Account*

Click Start
Click Administrative Tools (Common)
Click User Manager for Domains.
Click User from the menu bar.
Enter user account information.
Click Add

the utility used to create new user accounts on a Windows NT network. Table 6–1 illustrates the steps required to create a new user account.

The *New User* dialog box is displayed when User is selected from the menu bar and is used to enter all the necessary information to set up a new user account on the network (Figure 6–1).

Every user account must be identified by a unique username, which is also known as the user ID or login name. This is the name that the user will enter along with the password whenever they log onto the network. There are a couple of things to remember when selecting a username. In windows NT usernames are not case sensitive, therefore upper and lower case characters are treated the same. Usernames can be up to 20 characters long and can be almost any combination of alpha-numeric characters except those listed in Table 6–1.

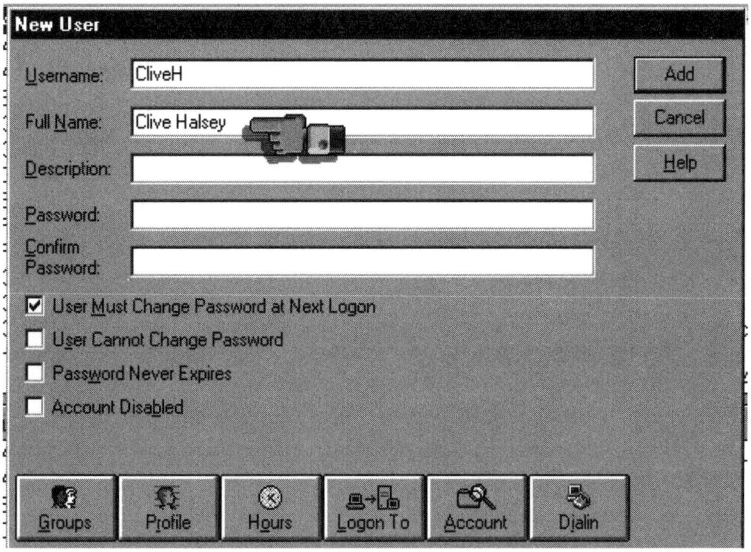

Figure 6–1. *The New User dialog box is used to create a new user account on the network.*

Table 6–2 *Characters That Cannot Be Used to Create a Username*

"	:	=	?
\	;	,	<
/	|	+	>

In addition to the username, each new user account should relate the username to the user's real name. Including the user's Full Name and Description on the New User dialog box makes the relationship.

In addition to a unique username every user on the system needs a password. The password is a secret word or phrase that only the user knows. By requiring a password windows NT is making sure that the person logging in is really who they say they are. It is the network administrator also sets up the initial password for the new user. Up to fourteen upper or lowercase characters can be used for the password. No spaces are allowed. However, unlike the username, Windows NT treats passwords as case-sensitive, which forces the user to enter the proper upper and lowercase combinations.

There are four parameters displayed as check boxes on the New User dialog box that are used to provide network security. The first three are used to manage the password and the last enables the network administrator to disable the account, which prevents the user from logging into the network.

The password parameters force the user to change the password at the next login; prevents the user from changing the password; and prevents the password from ever expiring.

Typically, network administrators require a new user to change the password at least during the next login. This ensures that only the user knows the password associated with his/her username. The network administrator can always reset the password if the user forgets it. A reset password is actually a new password created by the network administrator, which is changed by the user at the next login. Users can change their passwords at any time.

Some network administrators prefer to have total control over passwords and check the second parameter, thus preventing the user from changing the password. In this case at least two users know the password associated with every username. These are the user and the network administrator. There is nothing preventing the network administrator from logging in as the user.

The third password parameter enables the network administrator to require the user to change the password on a regular basis. If *Password Never Expires* is left unchecked, then the password will expire in time. If checked, the password will never expire. This could pose a network security issue, because this gives those wishing to break into the network a greater opportunity to learn a user's password.

Modifying an Existing Account

Any account setting can be changed or the account can be deleted by using the User Manager for Domain. Follow steps 1 through 3 in Table 6–1 to display the User Manager screen. The User Manager screen contains a list of user accounts (top) and a list of group accounts (bottom) (Figure 6–2).

Information about any account can be displayed by first highlighting the account, then select User from the menu bar and Properties to display the User Properties dialog box or double click the account. This dialog box is identical to the New User dialog box. Properties can be modified the same way the initial properties were set when the account was created.

An account can be deleted from the network by highlighting the account in the User manager dialog box, then pressing the delete key and confirming your desire to delete the account. **A word of caution**. A deleted account cannot be reestablished. That is, information about the account's permissions and rights are no longer stored on the network. All association between the deleted username and the account no longer exists. Therefore, the username can be reused.

Disabling versus Deleting an Account

Anyone who knows a username and password can have the same access to the network as the rightful owner of the account. This can cause a breech in network security if the username and password fall into the wrong hands. Although the network administrator can require the password to be changed

User Policies Options Help

Username	Full Name	Description
AdeleW	Adele Williams	Programmer
Administrator		Built-in account for administering the computer/domain
AlexS	Alex Sato	Personnel Officer
BarretM	Barret McDermid	Programmer
GeoffreyW	Geoffrey Wilson	Technical Communicator
GillB	Gill Browne	Project Leader
Guest		Built-in account for guest access to the computer/domain
IUSR_LCSERVER	Internet Guest Account	Internet Server Anonymous Access
JonesJ		
KelvinP	Kelvin Paulo	Systems Analyst
LeslieK	Leslie Katang	Networking Consultant
LisaN	Lisa Nettleton	Programmer

Groups	Description
Account Operators	Members can administer domain user and group accounts
Administrators	Members can fully administer the computer/domain
Backup Operators	Members can bypass file security to back up files
Domain Admins	Designated adminaistrators of the domain
Domain Guests	All domain guests
Domain Users	All Domain Users
Guests	Users granted guest access to the computer/domain
Print Operators	Members can administer domain printers

Figure 6–2. *The User Manager screen is used to modify existing accounts.*

at frequent intervals, this still does not give adequate protection while the existing password is active.

Whenever a breech of network security is suspected, the network administrator has two choices to protect the system against an unauthorized user. These are to disable the user account or delete the user account. The decision which to use is dependent upon the situation and your company's security policies.

Many organizations disable a user's account at the first suspicion of a breech of network security. An account can be disabled by modifying the account using the User Properties dialog box. Access will be denied the next time someone attempts to access the network using the username and password.

The user account can easily be reactivated by unselecting the Account Disabled property on the User Properties dialog box. The network administrator does not need to reestablish permissions and recreate settings for the account. However, if suspicions prove to be true, then the account is typically deleted from the network.

The same process is followed whenever a potential breech of network security exists, such as when an employee is terminated or transferred to a different part of the organization. In such cases, the employee's account is disabled even before the employee is told of his/her change in status within the organization.

Types of Accounts

There are several kinds of accounts available on a typical network, all of which are user accounts, but each having different characteristics. These are the network administrator's account, guest account, regular user account, and group accounts. Accounts with the same specified characteristics are called a **group**.

The **network administrator's account**, also known as the Supervisor account on Novell networks, has access to the network utilities such as the user manager for domain which is used to manage the network The username and password associated with this account can create, modify, and disable any account on the network. It is also used to start and configure the network operating system.

The network administrator's account is automatically created when the network operating system is installed, giving the network administrator full control over network operations.

A **guest account** is used to give a user temporary access to the network. Windows NT Server automatically disables this account after the session.

However, the network administrator can reactivate the account or create another guest account for the user.

A **regular user account** provides general network access to a user, as restricted by the network administrator. Most user accounts fall within this account type.

A **group account** is an account used to identify two or more regular user accounts and used to grant specific permission to a group of users. For example, all users in the East Coast sales region could be members in the East Coast Sales group account. Each of them also has a regular user account. Each member of the group has the same rights as other members of the group.

Mastering Group Accounts

Although each user on the network is unique, some of them have similar characteristics, such as being within the same work group or at the same level in the organization's management. This relationship can be recognized on the network by forming a group account, then assigning these users to the group account. Users can belong to more than one group.

A group account not only recognizes relationships within an organization, but also serves as a useful network management tool. Every account is granted rights to resources that are typically stored in the account's profile. An account profile is a file that contains settings and restrictions that are acted upon each time a user logs into the network.

Many of these settings and restrictions pertain to a group of accounts rather than being a single user account. Therefore, settings and restrictions are typically assigned to the group account's profile rather than the profile of each user in the group. Each group member inherits the settings, rights, and restrictions of the group.

For example, it is common for members of a work group (Figure 6–3) to use the network printer located within the work area of the group. The printer connection can be associated with the group's account rather than individual accounts. If the group switches to a different printer, then the network administrator need only change the setting in the group account profile—not in the profile of each group member.

Category of Groups

There are four categories of groups available in Windows NT. Most other networks have similar groups. These are local groups, global groups, system groups, and built-in groups. **Local groups** are the most common type of group setup by the network administrator. Within this category are users

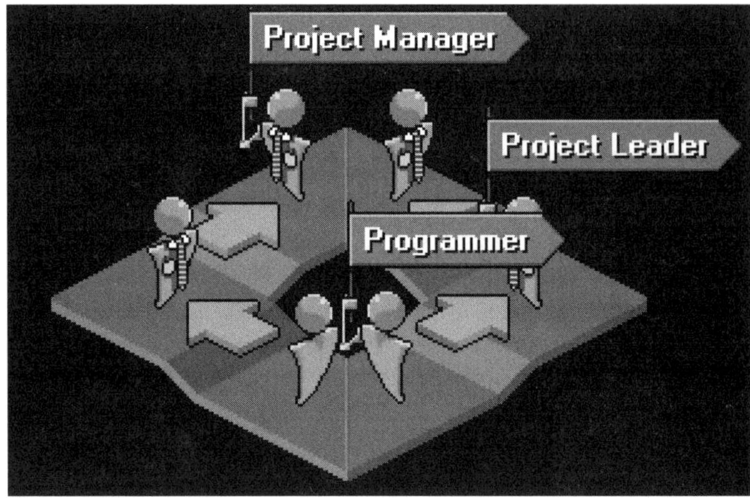

Figure 6–3. *Clients that work on the same task should be organized into a network group.*

who work together or who have similar responsibilities or need access to similar resources within an organization.

Members of a local group can be any user on the network and any global group, although a local group cannot contact another local group.

A **global group** consists of users who belong to the same domain. The user account for those users belonging to a global group must reside on the domain's primary domain controller (PDC) server.

Only user accounts within the domain are permitted to be members of a global group. Global and local groups from other domains are prohibited from joining a global group.

A **system group** contains all network users and the group is created automatically by the network operating system. The network administrator cannot modify members to this group, except to delete the username from the network.

The **built-in group** categories consist of the **network administrator group**, a **server operator group**, a **print operator group**, a **backup operator group**, and **an account operator group**.

Each of these groups is used to grant limited administrator access to a user. For example, the network administrator can assign duties to maintain printers, accounts, and perform backup operations by assigning a technician's user ID to an appropriate built-in group. The technician accesses as a regular user of the network and has access to a right reserved for the network administrator.

Create a Group

Following the steps shown in Table 6–3 can create a new local group. Information required to set up the new group is entered into the New Local Group dialog box (Figure 6–4).

There are three pieces of information that you need to supply. First is the Group Name. The Group Name has similar restrictions as the username, in that the group name must be unique and cannot be the same as any other group nor the same as any username. Also, the name cannot be more than 20 characters nor use any characters listed in Table 6–2.

The description information should contain a few words to describe the purpose of the group. This information does not have any of the restrictions of the group name.

The Members box contains all the usernames that are assigned to the group. None are shown when the group is created. However, usernames can be assigned to the group by clicking Add. A list of usernames is displayed. Double-click on the name to assign the name to the group. All usernames you want added to the group must already exist in domain.

MCSE 6.2 Network Performance

The **network administrator** has the responsibility of insuring that the network always operates efficiently. This can be a simple task when a small network is involved. However, networks of 30 or more users can require a sizable effort to assure that the network flows uninterrupted.

Day-to-day operations of the network must be consistently monitored using a variety of techniques, from simple observations to using sophisticated utilities that capture network performance data and present it in a readable form to the network administrator.

Network performance declines dramatically when network traffic increases and bottlenecks in the network begin to appear. A **bottleneck** is any device on the network that impedes network performance. These can be the

Table 6–3 *Steps Required to Create a New Local Group*

Click Start
Click Administrative Tools (Common)
Click User Manager for Domains
Click New Local Group from the menu bar
Enter group information
Click Add to add user accounts to the group
Click OK to create the new local group

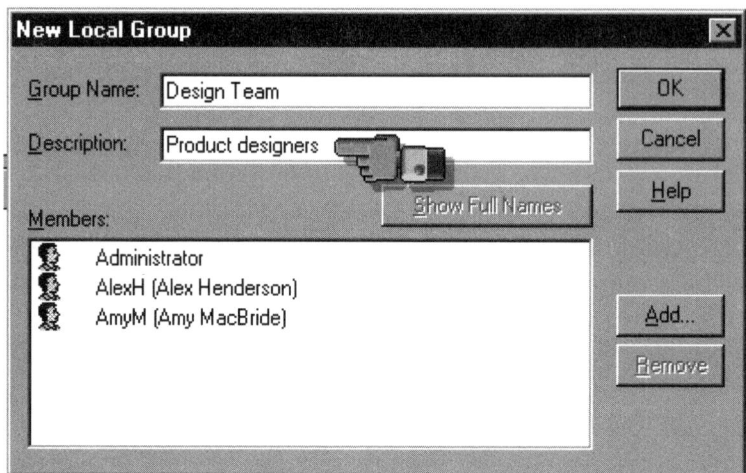

Figure 6–4. *The New Local Group dialog box is used to create a new local group.*

CPU of the server or of clients; the speed of disk drives; and speed of network adapter cards among other devices.

Bottlenecks first become apparent when a user complains about a change in the performance of the network. A complaint is a symptom of an underlying network problem that is likely to spread to many users.

The network administrator must determine the source of the problem, then take corrective action. This could include reconfiguring network components, a DNS problem, cable problem, mis-routing or the outright replacement of components.

Performance Monitoring

Network operating systems such as Windows NT come with utilities that enable the network administrator to monitor activities on the network. A network performance monitor records certain performance criteria in both real-time and in batch mode. **Real-time monitoring** is where performance criteria are updated on a monitor display as the activities occur. **Batch mode** stores those activities in a file that can be analyzed at any time.

The Windows NT utility that monitors the network is called the **Performance Monitor**. It tracks the performance criteria of the CPU, memory, hard disks, and network operations. The most valuable feature of the Performance Monitor is its ability to react to network problems without the utility being constantly reviewed by a technician.

For example, if the Performance Monitor detects a network problem, then it can send a pager message to a technician and, if necessary, automatically execute a program that could rectify the problem.

Network problems can be detected before complaints are received from the user if the network administrator establishes normal performance criteria for the network. This is called a **baseline**.

You can create a baseline for a network by running the performance monitor when the network is operating problem-free. The performance monitor collects performance criteria, which serve as the baseline for network performance. This becomes the acceptable performance criterion.

Daily performance can be compared to the baseline to determine if the network is performing at an acceptable level. Criteria outside the baseline can signal a potential trouble spot, which can be immediately addressed by the network administrator.

Performance criteria should be saved regularly and later used to determine if trends are developing in network activity. A **trend** is a series of data representing a performance measurement of the network that moves in the same direction.

For example, a performance monitor may report the number of data packets transferred during the day. By comparing each day's totals, the network administrator may recognize a trend indicating a steady increase of traffic along a segment of the network.

Windows NT also provides another monitoring tool called the **Network Monitor** that monitors data packet flow, for instance, a data stream. Table 6–4 illustrates the steps needed to install and run the network monitor (Figure 6–5).

Table 6–4 *Steps for Installing and Starting the Windows NT Network Monitor*

Click Start
Click Settings
Click Control Panel
Click the Network Icon
Click Services
Click Add
Click and copy the Network Monitor files
Shut down and restart your computer
Click Start
Click Programs
Click Administrative Tools (common)
Click Network Monitor

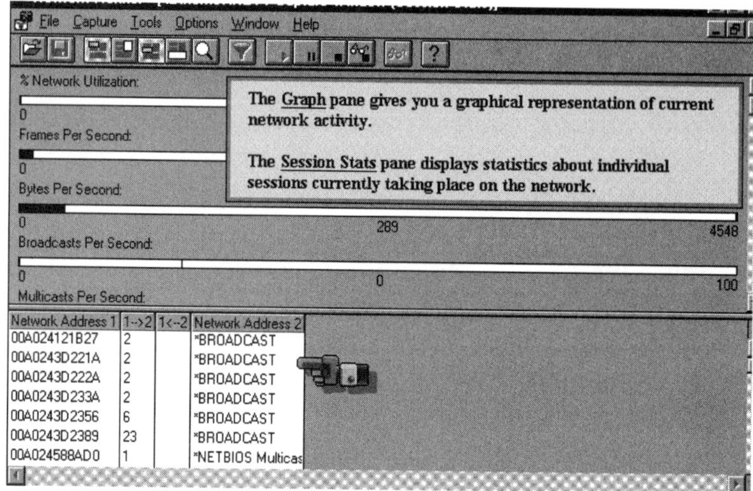

Figure 6–5. *The Network Monitor is used to track network usage.*

Nearly all network management utilities, such as performance monitors and network monitors, adhere to the **Simple Network Management Protocol** (SNMP).

At the heart of SNMP is the use of special programs called agents that capture network data and store them in a **management information base** (MIB). An **agent** is installed on each device that is to be monitored by the network administrator such as clients, hubs, routers, and bridges.

Another program polls the agents regularly and copies their MIB to the network server. Data in the MIBs is analyzed and presented on-screen or in printed reports to the network administrator.

Network performance monitoring is just one of the many responsibilities of a network administrator. Network administrators must also install and troubleshoot application software; maintain an inventory of network components; and create a history of network activity among other tasks.

Microsoft provides a **System Management Server** (SMS) utility as a tool for network management. SMS offers a collection of enhanced utilities that manages inventory, distributes programs to clients; monitors network operations; and enables the network administrator to take over any client or server from any location on the network.

MCSE 6.3 Network Security

Computer networks expose an organization to the possibility that people with clandestine motives, such as a disgruntled employee who wants to corrupt network resources, will infiltrate the network. Therefore, it is critical that measures be taken to protect resources by using network security measures.

The best way to prevent network security violations is to create a plan that addresses theft and destruction of network resources. A **network policy** must prevent security violations, yet still be viable so as not to hinder authorized users access to network resources.

Network Security Policy

A network security plan must establish a clear set of rules that specifies security measures to be taken on the network. These rules are known as the network security policy. These rules provide guidelines for protecting network resources. The policy must examine all facets where the network is vulnerable to invasion and inadvertent destruction.

There is no blanket network security policy that will meet the needs of every organization. For example, a defense contractor typically requires extraordinary network security measures that are not required by a small real estate firm.

Even within the same organization, certain resources require greater protection than other resources. Take, for example, the payroll file that contains the organization's payroll records. The payroll file is a network resource that needs more sophisticated protection methods than a network printer, which is also a network resource.

Degrees of security for network resources are referred to as levels of security. A network security policy should specify the levels of security for each network resource.

A typical network security policy (Figure 6–6) will use permissions assigned to a user account or a group of accounts as the mechanism for enforcing security levels. For example, a user needs to enter a username and a password before being granted access to a particular network resource. Permission to use the resource is associated with the username by the network administrator.

Another level of network security involves physical access to network components such as cables and servers. The network security policy should classify cables according to the data that flows across the cable. Those cables carrying sensitive data must be placed in a restricted area.

Information carried by the cable can be copied from the network using one of two techniques. The first is a tap, wherein someone secretly connects a device to such a computer to the cable and copies data flowing across the cable to a hard disk for later analysis.

Another technique is to listen into the transmission using sophisticated electronic devices without physically connecting to the cable. This is made

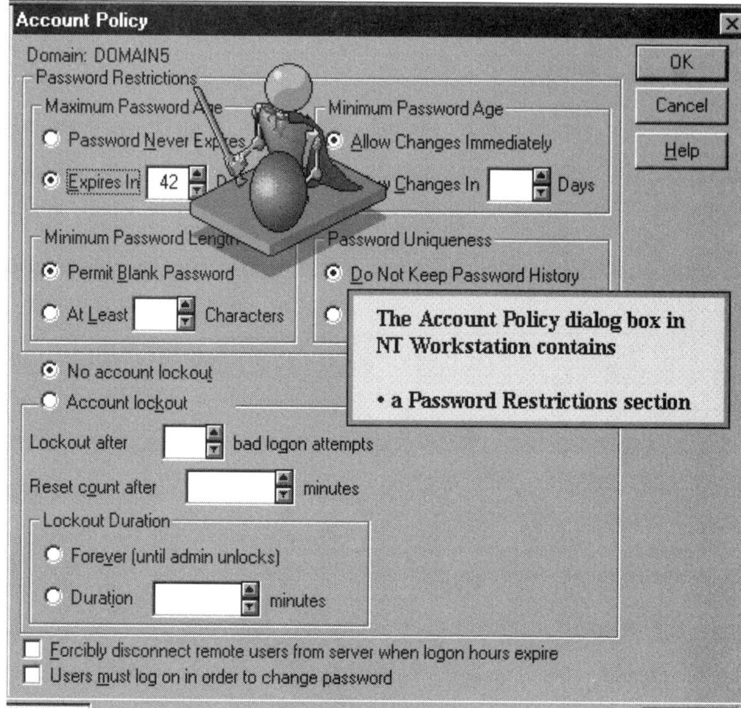

Figure 6–6. *The Account Policy dialog box is used to set an access security policy for the network.*

possible because of the radio transmission properties of copper cable. Cables emit electronic signals, which carry data transmitted over the cable.

Therefore, all places where sensitive cables are stored, called a cable run, should be in a secured area and inaccessible to unauthorized personnel.

Servers too must be located in an area where they will be protected from danger, which includes accidents such as leaks or fire. The best way to secure a server is to place the server in a locked room or closet.

Security Measures

The network administrator is typically responsible for establishing the network security policy for the organization. There are several security measures that are commonly found in a security policy. These are auditing network traffic, data encryption, and running specialized software such as a virus protection program.

Auditing network traffic entails recording each network event into a log. These events include identifying when users access specific network resources; when a user is connected to the network; and other similar activities. Entries can be reviewed and analyzed to determine suspicious patterns or help in an investigation into a breach of security (Figure 6–7).

Data encryption involves encoding information transmitted over the network, making it unreadable to those who intercept the data. Each client that transmits data on the network has an encryption algorithm that is typically contained on the network adapter card.

Likewise, each client has a key used to decipher the data. The weakness is that the key must be transmitted to the destination address and therefore becomes exposed to potential interception from clandestine personnel.

Virus detection software is a critical security measure required by every network. A virus is a small program created to cause problems on a network or on a computer's disk. Problems can be a simple annoyance such as writing an inappropriate message on the screen or more serious trouble such as the corruption of application files.

Virus detection software attempts to detect known viruses before the virus is copied to the network. Some virus protection software also repairs damage caused by a virus.

Viruses typically infect a network when someone loads a program, data file, or email that contains a virus on to a client or network server. The virus then has the opportunity to spread and do its damage.

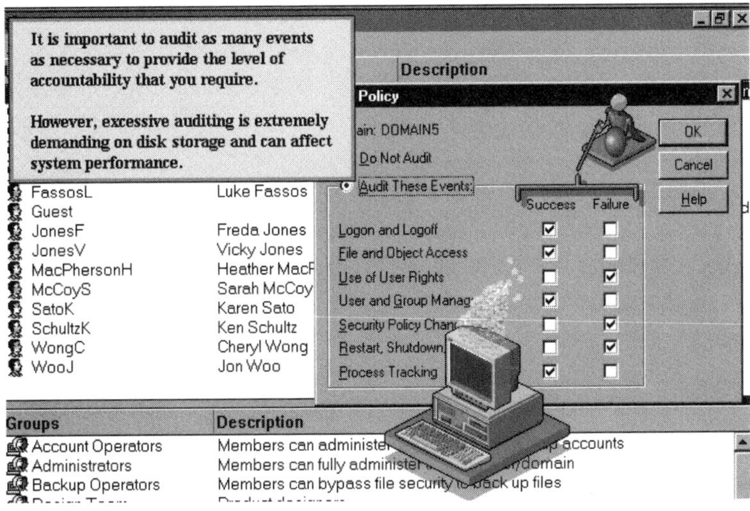

Figure 6–7. *The Audit Policy dialog box is used to set the auditing policy for the network. However, an intense audit can have a performance impact on the network.*

However, some organizations are eliminating this possibility by replacing personal computers with diskless computers. A diskless computer does not contain any disk drives, which prevents a user from loading software on to the firm's computers and from copying the organization's data from the network.

A **diskless computer** only operates on a network because the network adapter card contains a chip called a ROM boot chip. When the diskless computer is turned on, the ROM boot chip requests the client operating system be downloaded from the server, after which the diskless computer functions like a personal computer on the network.

Security check list

Passwords

- Don't write down password
- Change often
- Don't use dictionary words
- Don't use part of your name

General

- Lock doors and cables
- Rename the administrator account
- Use the NTFS file system
- Restrict access to the registry
- Disable floppy drives
- Set power on password protection

Security Guidelines

A network security policy must conform to the needs of the organizations. Some situations require tighter security than others. It is the responsibility of the network administrator to assess the network security needs, then tailor a policy that will protect the organization.

There are two network security techniques that have proven successful and should be considered as part of any network security policy. These are password-protected shares, also known as share level security and access permissions, which is known as user level security for access permissions. The term share refers to a shared resource such as a file or a server or access to printers.

Password-protected shares and access permissions typically are blended to restrict use of resources. Password-protected shares require that all network resources be accessed after someone has entered the correct password. Passwords are typically entered when the user logs on to the network. However, it is common for additional passwords to be attached to access restricted resources such as confidential files.

Access permissions provide user level access restrictions to a particular functionality. For example, a user may have no access, read access, write access, delete access, execute, or full access to a file. These are called access permissions and are typically associated with the username and password.

Network administrators typically grant access permissions in the form of a group permission rather than individual permissions. A group is a collection of usernames that are associated with a group name. Members of a group have something in common, such as working performing similar tasks. Access permissions are usually assigned to the group. Thus, everyone in the group has the same access permissions.

MCSE 6.4 Data Recovery

The most important organizational asset that is exposed to danger on a computer network is data. Data are facts used to run the organization, such as customer, inventory, and accounting information. Without secure and reliable data, an organization could cease to function.

Data can be compromised in a number of ways, including hardware failure, vandalism by a disgruntled employee, by a virus, or by a natural disaster. Every organization, including the most secured sectors of the government, has the same risk in losing data.

You learned about common ways to secure your network and prevent the loss of data in the previous section. However, can your data be recovered if data integrity is breached? This section shows you some common techniques that can be used to restore lost data by us, backups, fault tolerant systems, and UPS.

Data Backup

Whenever there is a question about the integrity of data, the network administrator should attempt to find the cause of the problem and replace the data. Replacing the data is the first task that must be performed, since this information keeps the organization operational. There are two ways in which data can be replaced: by recreating the data or by copying the data from another source.

Recreating the data is the least desirable choice, since it is time-consuming; could introduce data errors; and may be impossible to do in many cases.

Copying data, which is called **restoring data**, is the most desirable choice, since restored data is exactly the same data that was on the server before the data problem occurred.

However, before data can be restored, the original data must have been copied to tape, CD, or disk. This is known as **data backup** (Figure 6–8). The

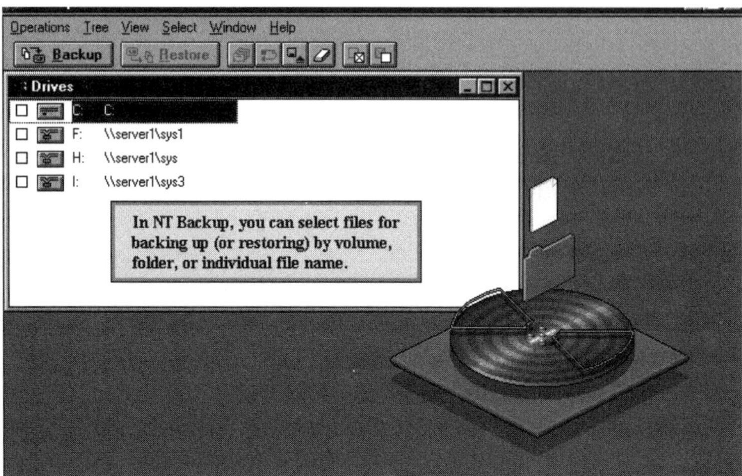

Figure 6–8. *The Windows NT backup dialog box is used to back up and restore specific drives.*

most common data backup method used on computer networks is the tape backup, where data and other files such as programs stored on a server are copied to a tape on a regular schedule.

Data Backup Plan

The network administrator is responsible for creating a backup plan which assures that the organization can easily recover data if data security is breached. The network administrator must determine which data or files are at risk and the size of those files. This information is used to create the backup schedule and is used in the selection of the backup method and equipment. When assessing the risk factor for each type of data or file, the network administrator must answer these questions:

Can the organization function without this data or file?

How long can the organization function without access to this data or file?

The answer to the first question determines whether or not the data needs to be backed up. If the answer is yes, then the data is included in the backup process. The answer to the second question helps decide the schedule of the backup and the equipment used for the backup.

For many organizations, a nightly backup is sufficient protection. The worst case scenario is that the organization loses the current day's activity, which can be recreated once the prior day's data is restored.

If loss of a day's data can't be tolerated, then a more frequent backup schedule must be introduced. This may require a fault-tolerance-data-recovery system, discussed later in this chapter.

Equipment used for the backup must reliably copy the data from the server to a tape, CD, or disk within the time frame allotted for the backup process. As a general rule, the backup medium (i.e., tape) must have more than enough room to back up all the data. The backup must also be able to check and correct for data transmission errors during the backup process.

Data deemed mission critical (i.e., the organization cannot function without it) can be further categorized as those requiring more frequent backup than others.

For example, some data may need to be backed up hourly; this would be the case for new orders. Other data, such as employee files, can be updated daily. Still others, such as program files, can be backed up monthly or when they have been changed.

These categories help to formulate which backup method will be used in the backup plan. There are three methods used for backing up data and files on a network. These are differential backup or incremental backup, copy, and full backup.

A **differential backup**, also known as **incremental backup** or daily backup, is used to backup selected files when the content of a file has changed. The backup system reviews the date and time of the file, which indicates the last time the file was updated and compares it with the file. If they differ, then the backup system copies the file, otherwise the file is not backed up. Files that are backed up are not marked as backed up.

A **copy backup** is used to backup selected files. Files that are backed up are not marked as backed up. A full backup copies all the files on a server regardless of whether they changed or not since the last backup.

The choice of backup methods is important to the efficiency of the backup schedule and the capacity of the backup medium. For example, a full backup takes longer and requires the most storage capacity. The differential backup requires less time and less space because fewer files are backed up. The copy method entails the least amount of time and space, because only one or a small selection of files is backed up. You also need to consider how long the restore can take and how many tapes you will have to refer to after a complete disk loss.

Backup Maintenance

A critical aspect of every backup plan is the method used to maintain backup copies of data. There are three areas that must be addressed by the network administrator. These are identifying the backed up data, storage, and retrieval.

Every backup must clearly identify the data, date and time of the backup, storage location, backup method, and who performed the backup.

This information should be clearly written on the backup media, and also in a backup log. A **backup log** is a listing of pertinent information about each backup and should be stored electronically and in printed form. Many network administrators enter log information into a file (i.e., Word, Excel, or some proprietary program), then immediately print out a copy of the log.

Backup copies should be stored both on and off site. That is, a few weeks of backups should be on site, so the information can be restored quickly. Another copy of all backups should be sent to an **off-site facility** designed to protect tapes, CDs, and disks. More than two sets of backups should be made for extraordinarily sensitive data, which should be stored at two or more off-site locations.

Information from either on- or off-site locations must be retrieved and restored within a reasonable time. For example, a few hours is reasonable for accounts receivable data, whereas a shorter time frame is reasonable for Wall Street security transaction data.

A network administrator should perform periodic scheduled, and thorough tests to determine the actual length of time that is required to restore backup data and the quality of the backups. The tests will reveal the organization's readiness to recover from a data disaster.

Fault-Tolerant Data Recovery

There is a time lag between when data integrity occurs and when a copy of the data is restored. The lag time can be less than an hour for many organizations if the backup data is available on site and several hours if the backup is kept off site.

However, even a minute's delay is unacceptable for some applications, such as a stock exchange trading system. Therefore, special considerations must be taken by the network administrator to address these needs.

Nearly instantaneous data recovery is possible if a fault-tolerant backup-recovery system is employed on the network. Fault-tolerant means that if a problem occurs, the operation continues unaffected.

For example, a stock exchange records hundreds of security transactions a minute. A failure of data files for even a minute can have serious financial repercussions. However, a fault tolerant system enables a security exchange to recover almost instantaneously from any breakdown.

A **fault-tolerant system** replicates changes to data immediately following a data change in the file. This is called **redundancy**. The replicated data is physically stored in a different location on the network, such as a different server called a replication server. If an application cannot access data from the primary data file, it automatically accesses the data from the replication server.

The Fault-Tolerant Technique

Fault-tolerance systems adhere to the **redundant arrays of inexpensive disks** (RAIDs) standard that is divided into seven categories called **levels.** Some fault tolerance systems such as Windows NT Server support some, but not all, levels. RAID describes how data is to be stored on a group of disks called a **disk array** (Figure 6–9). Each in the array disk is a seperate hard disk with its own disk controller.

Level 0, the first of the levels, specifies the technique used to divide data. This is called **disk stripping**, which distributes 64K blocks of data evenly among the disks at the same time. This distribution method is called **interleaving.**

There are two significant advantages of disk stripping. First, each disk in the array can process the transfer of data rather quickly, because each has its own disk controller. Also, disk stripping makes better use of disk space,

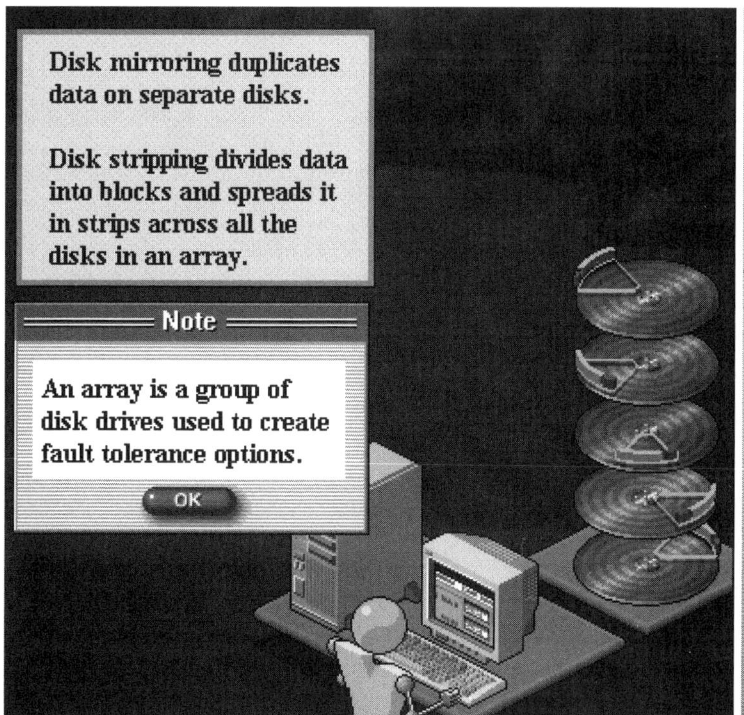

Figure 6–9. *A disk array spreads the data across disks in the disk array.*

because it creates a large partition from several smaller partitions. However, a major drawback of disk stripping is that if a partition fails all the data stored in the partition is lost. There is no fault tolerance.

Level 1, called **disk mirroring**, requires data to be copied to the disk array intact. The entire partition of the primary storage device (i.e., the hard disk) is duplicated on a separate partition in the disk array. The technique is called **disk duplexing**.

Level 2, called **disk stripping with error correction code** (EEC), is similar to level 0, but the software transferring the data must employ an error correction scheme to determine if errors occurred in the transfer.

Level 3, known with error correction code as **parity**, is the same as level 2, except parity is used as the error-checking technique. Data is represented as a serious of 0s and 1s. Parity specifies that there must be either an even or odd number of 1s in the data. This is called even or odd parity. If parity is even and an odd number of 1s is received, then a data error is assumed and a request is made for the data to be retransmitted.

Level 4, called **disk stripping with large blocks**, is the same as disk stripping, except each large piece of data, called **blocks**, are stored on each disk in the disk array. This technique is not suited for transactional processing such as an order entry system.

Level 5, known as **stripping with parity**, is the most common method used by fault tolerance systems. Data and parity information are stored on different disks. The parity information and data stored on the other disks are used to reconstruct data if a disk in the array fails.

Level 10, called a **mirrored drive array**, replicates data stored on one disk of the array to another disk of the array.

Another common fault-tolerance technique is called **sector sparing** used on SCSI devices (Figure 6–10). Sector sparing is contained within some operating systems, such as Windows NT Server, and automatically relocates data stored in a bad sector to a good sector on the same disk when the bad sector is detected during normal input/output operations.

Uninterrupted Power Supply

Implementing a fault-tolerant system, scheduled backup procedures, and a good data security policy will not eliminate the Achilles heal of every computer network—electrical power. Both clients and servers and other network resources are disabled during an electrical failure.

There isn't a way to prevent power outages or predict when they will occur. However, the network administrator can keep the network operating during these times by using an **uninterrupted power supply** (UPS).

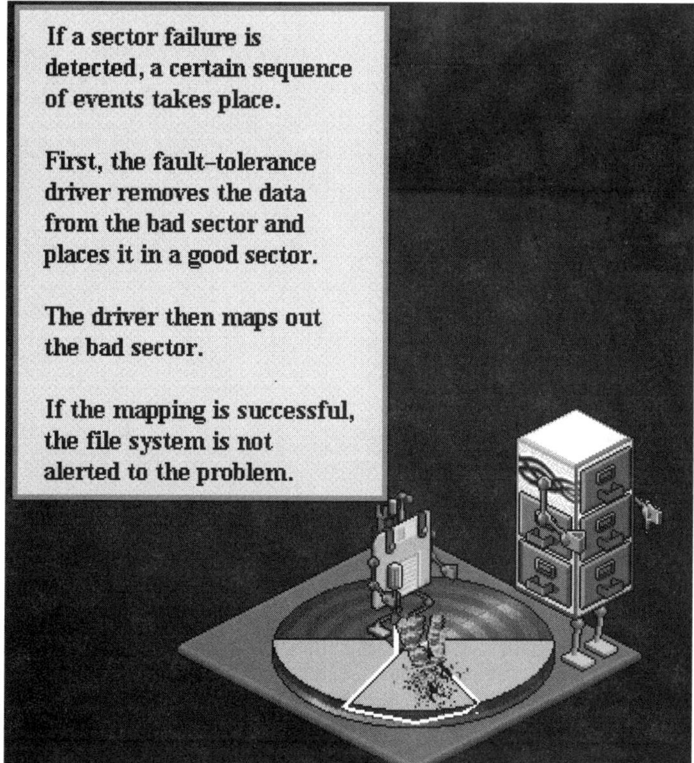

If a sector failure is detected, a certain sequence of events takes place.
First, the fault-tolerance driver removes the data from the bad sector and places it in a good sector.
The driver then maps out the bad sector.
If the mapping is successful, the file system is not alerted to the problem.

Figure 6–10. *Sector sparing is a technique for automatically relocating data stored in a bad sector.*

There are two kinds of UPS used in industry. These are battery powered and generator powered. Both supply electricity to clients, servers, and network resources during power outages.

Battery-powered UPS offer power for a limited time period. This is usually enough time for the network administrator to notify users that power has been lost. Users can then save their work and shut down their computers safely.

Likewise, the network administrator will shut down servers and other network resources. Battery-powered UPSs are not designed to power network operations for the duration of the power outage.

Generator-powered UPSs use an electrical generator to provide power for network operations until power is restored. Smaller organizations use gasoline engines to generate power, whereas large organizations, such as Wall Street firms, use jet engines. The generator power can continue until the generator runs out of fuel.

When choosing a UPS, the network administrator must determine the electrical requirements of clients and network resources. The UPS must provide more electricity than the amount required to power the clients and network.

Furthermore, the UPS should activate automatically and alert the network administrator of power events. It should also have software that automatically initiates a safe shutdown. A **power event** could be the loss of power, the restoring of power, and if the UPS is about to stop providing power, such as when a battery is low or there is lower fuel for the generator.

■ Summary

The task of managing a computer network is called network administration and is performed by the network administrator. The network administrator is responsible for user administration, resource management, configuration management, performance management, and network maintenance.

A user is a person who has the presence to log onto the network using a client. The user is identified to the network using a username and a password. These plus other information unique to the user, called a user profile, is referred to as a user account.

The network operating system contains the utility programs that enables the network administrator to create, modify, and delete a user account. The User Manager for Domain is such a utility for Windows NT Server.

There are several kinds of accounts available on a typical network, all of which are user accounts, but each having different characteristics. These are the network administrator's account, guest account, regular user accounts, and group accounts. An account with network administrator's privileges allows the user complete access to all network resources, whereas a guest account grants limited access to the network for one session. A regular user account is used to perform all but administrative tasks on the network. A group account is used to associate two or more regular user accounts that have similar access needs, such as the use of the same network files.

There are four categories of groups available in Windows NT, other networks have similar groups. These are local groups; global groups; system groups; and built-in groups. A local group contains accounts of users that work on the same project. Global groups are users that belong to the same domain. A systems group are users that belong to the same network. Built-in groups typically consist of users that have some network administrative responsibilities.

A critical role of the network administrator is to monitor the performance of network operations in order to assure that information is transmitted efficiently. As additional clients are connected to the network, there is a tendency for bottlenecks to develop. A bottleneck is a network device that impedes the flow of data on the network. It is the job of the network administrator to remove bottlenecks.

The network administrator uses a network operating system tool called a performance monitor to observe the flow of data along the network. Once the network is operating smoothly, the network administrator should make note of various measurements reported by the performance monitor. This creates a baseline of data that is used to compare to daily performance readings. The closer the measurements are to the baseline, then the closer the network will perform without problems.

Nearly all network performance monitors adhere to the Simple Network Management Protocol (SNMP). SNMP is a standard that requires the use of agents to capture network data and store them in a management information base (MIB). An agent is installed on each device that is to be monitored by the network administrator such as clients, hubs, routers, and bridges. Another program polls the agents regularly and copies their MIB to the network server. Data in the MIBs is analyzed and presented on-screen or in printed reports to the network administrator.

The network administrator is also responsible for network security, which involves protecting network hardware, software, and data stored on network servers. The network administrator must establish a network security policy that sets rules for how network resources are accessed and protected.

There are several security measures that are commonly found in a security policy. These are auditing network traffic, data encryption, and running specialized software such as a virus protection program.

Auditing network traffic involves tracking every user's network activity to determine if someone is a threat to network security. Data encryption is a method used to encode data transmitted on the network. This inhibits an unauthorized person that taps into the network for easily reading the data. Virus software acts as a roadblock, preventing the invasion of programs that are designed to corrupt network operations and resources.

Some network administrators install diskless computers to eliminate the chances of virus infiltration and the unauthorized copying of programs and data from the network. A diskless computer does not contain any disk drives and is activated using a ROM boot chip that loads the operating system from the network server to the diskless computer.

The first line of network security is restricting network access to only authorized users. There are two network security techniques that have proven successful in this area. These are password-protected shares, also known as share level security and access permissions which is known as user-level security. The term share refers to a shared resource, such as a file or a server.

Password-protected share requires a user to enter the correct password for a particular resource before access is granted. On the other hand, access permissions restrict access to a network resource based upon the user profile. For example, there are several types of permissions that can be granted to use a file. A user may be granted full permission or read-only permissions based upon the user's need to access the file.

The network administrator must provide a way to restore any data or program on the network server that becomes corrupted. This task is called data recovery. However, before data can be restored, it must be backed up. Backup refers to the task of making a copy of the data. There are three methods used for backing up data files on a network. These are: differential backup; copy; and full backup.

Differential backup is where a file or program is copied only if it has changed since the last time a backup was taken. If it hasn't changed, then no backup is taken. The copy method is where individual files or programs are selected for backup. If a file or program isn't selected, then it isn't backed up. A full backup is where every file and program on the server is copied regardless if it has changed since the last backup.

Backups must occur on a regular schedule, typically at the end of the day. However, data can be backed up and restored nearly instantaneously by using a fault-tolerant backup-recovery system. Fault-tolerant means that if a problem occurs, the operation continues unaffected. In a fault-tolerant backup-recovery system, data is maintained on at least two separate disk drives on two servers) that are accessible on the network. If the file fails on one drive, the network switches to the copy of the file, thus allowing the user to keep working.

Another threat to network operations is a power outage. The network administrator must keep the network operating at least temporary during these times to allow for safe shutdown by using an uninterrupted power supply (UPS). There are two kinds of UPS used in industry. These are battery-powered and generator-powered. Both supply electricity to clients, servers, and network resources.

Battery-powered supplies power for a limited time; a time only sufficient for users to save their work and shut down their computers properly. Generator-powered supplies a continual flow of electrical power until normal power is restored.

▲ Chapter Review Questions

▲ Fill in the Blanks

1. ______________ *account are commonly used to assign permissions to a set of users.*

2. __________ __________ *system allows network operations to continue uninterrupted if a data file becomes corrupted.*

3. ______________ *is a term given to any network device that slows the flow of data across the network.*

4. *Software that can infect and destroy network resources is called a ________.*

5. ____________ *is the device that supplies power to the network during a poweroutage.*

▲ True/False

1. *(T/F) RAID is a utility used to change an individual account to a group account.*

2. *(T/F) The network administrator creates the initial password for every account.*

3. *(T/F) A network performance monitor is used by the network administrator to spot trouble on the network.*

4. *(T/F) All clients on the network must contain a disk drive.*

5. *(T/F) A network administrator can delegate some responsibilities to other administrators by granting limited permissions to network resources.*

6. *(T/F) A tape backup system is not a good method to use to recover from a failure in a network file server.*

7. *(T/F) A group account is used to assign the same permissions to more than one user.*

8. *(T/F) Once a network is installed and is operating with adequate performance, the network administrator should measure network performance to create a baseline.*

▲ Multiple Choice

1. *What is the name of the program that runs on a client to gather network information?*

A. SNMP

B. ROM on the network interface card

C. Agent

D. Duplex

E. No such program exists

2. *Copper network cables should be secured because …*

A. Stray electrical signals can disrupt transmissions.

B. Airborne viruses can penetrate the coating around the cable.
C. Cables are costly and expensive to run throughout the building.
D. Network connectors are frequently stolen.
E. Someone can tap into the cable or copy data because signals traveling along the cable can leak out the cable as radio waves.

3. *Which of the following isn't a valid permission?*
   A. Delete
   B. No access
   C. Execute
   D. Dead-locked
   E. Read

4. *What is a backup log?*
   A. A common name given to the cable that serves as the backbone for the network.
   B. A paper notebook that contains a record of all tapes, CDs, and disks used to back up files on the server.
   C. The tape, CD, or disk that contains backed up files.
   D. The name associated with the computer used to back up files.
   E. The name of the file that starts the backup process.

5. *What is the term used to describe copying data stored on a bad sector to a good sector?*
   A. Sector sparing
   B. Sector clustering
   C. Disk mirroring
   D. SCSI
   E. Block stripping

▲ Open Ended

Describe how permissions are used to protect network resources?
Describe how a diskless computer operates on a network?
What network components would cause a bottleneck?
What information do you need to create a user account?
Describe how groups play a role in network security?

SEVEN

Wide Area Networks

▲Chapter Syllabus

- MCSE 7.1 Modems, a Simple WAN
- MCSE 7.2 Large Networks
- MCSE 7.3 Expanding to a WAN
- MCSE 7.4 WAN and Data Transmission

It isn't long after an organization sets up a peer-to-peer network that management begins to see the advantage of sharing data among a group of workers. Peer-to-peer networks soon grow into a network encompassing several work groups, then several floors of workers in the same building.

Networking technology does not limit an organization to data communications within the walls of a building. The same information that can be transmitted to a colleague to a floor below can also be sent to the regional office location on the other side of the globe.

Computer networks that focus on data exchange within a building are called a **local area network** (LAN), which has been the topic of most of the chapters in this book. A network that extends beyond a building is called a **wide area network** (WAN), which is also known as a large network.

A WAN uses similar yet different technology than those used in a LAN. This chapter takes a close look at WAN technology.

Modems, a Simple WAN

A LAN becomes a WAN when data can be transferred to another computer or network located outside the walls of the building. There are several transmission techniques that can be used, but the simplest is with a modem and a telephone line.

A **modem**, also known as **data communications equipment** (DEC), is a device that translates a digital signal produced by a computer into the analog signal required to transmit the signal across the telephone line. A modem also translates incoming analog signals into digital signals for the computer to process.

Data is represented within a computer in binary format as 0s and 1s. A **binary value** can be encoded into an electronic signal (digital signal) by changing the voltage of the signal such as from zero voltage (0) to a predetermined voltage (1). This forms a **square wave** (Figure 7–1). The height of the wave represents the voltage of the signal, for example, the higher the wave, the higher the voltage.

In an **analog signal,** various voltages are used that form a variable wave (Figure 7–1). Analog signals are used for telephone transmission. As someone speaks into the telephone, the transmitter in the handset fluctuates the voltage of the telephone signal. These fluctuations contain the encoded voice message that is then decoded by the receiver in the handset at the other end.

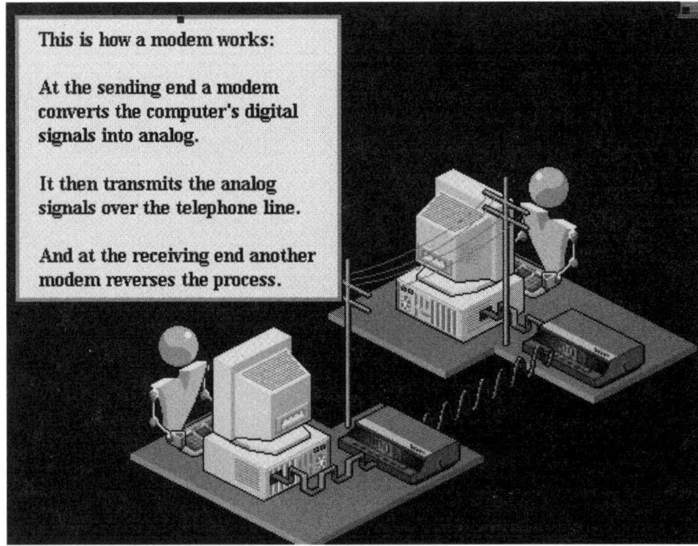

Figure 7–1. *Digital signals are translated to an analog signal, then are transmitted over a telephone line using a modem.*

The translation from digital to analog is called modulating the signal and the translation from analog to digital is called demodulating. The term modem is derived from the first few letters of each of these terms (Mo Dem).

There are two kinds of modems: internal modems and external modems. An **internal modem** is a modem contained on a card inserted into the computer. The power to run the card is supplied by the computer. The modem card is connected to a telephone line using a twisted-pair cable and an RJ-11C connector.

An **external modem** is a device that connects to the telephone line in the same way as an internal model; however, the external modem must connect to the computer's serial port using an RS-232 connection. An external power source is required to operate an external modem.

The **Internal Telecommunications Union** (ITU), a French-based organization, established standards known as the **V series** for modem manufacturers. These standards enable modems designed by different manufacturers to communicate with each other.

The V series standards is specified with the letter V followed by a decimal value such as V.22 (Figure 7–2). V.22 is the standard transmitting a 1,000-word letter in 25 seconds.

These standards are revised occasionally and revisions are noted using either bis or terbo following the name of the standard. Bis refers to the sec-

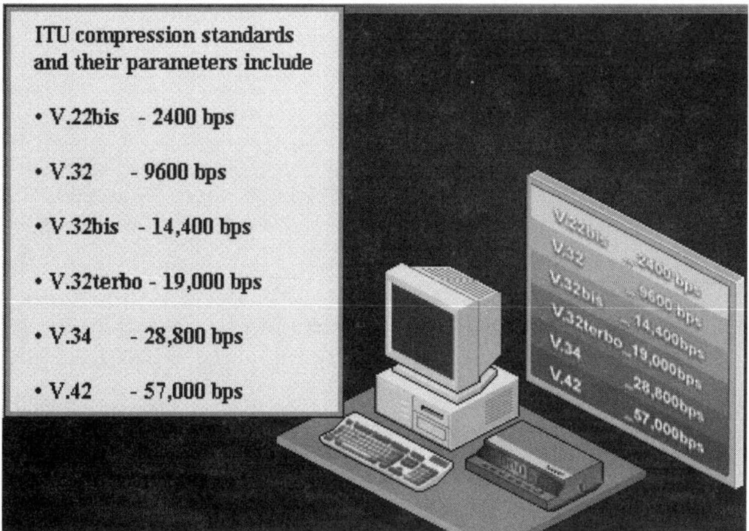

Figure 7–2. *The ITU established standards for modem manufacturers. Each standard refers to a specific BPS rating.*

ond and terbo the third. Therefore, the second revision of the V.22 standard is called V.22bis and the third revision is V.22terbo.

Although there are specific modem standards followed by modem manufacturers, the industry commonly classifies modems based on baud rate.

Baud refers to the speed of the oscillation of the sound wave on which a bit of data is carried over the phone line. The **baud rate** is defined as the speed in which a bit of data can be transmitted. A modem having a baud rate of 300 BPS means 300 bits can be transmitted by the modem per second. BPS stands for bits per second.

Transmission techniques changed during the mid-1980s with the introduction of data compression and data encoding. Data compression refers to a technique of reducing the number of bits it takes to represent the data. Data encoding means a group of bits can be represented as a code symbol that uses fewer bits.

Data compression and data encoding obscure the one-to-one relationship between the number of bits used to represent data and the number of bits transmitted using the modem. For example, 28,800 baud implies 28,800 bits per second can be transmitted. However, the actual amount can be up to four times greater when both data compression and encoding are used.

The latest standard for modems is V.42, which has a rating of 57,600 baud and is compatible with modems that meet previous standards. When connection is made between the modems, the modems automatically agree on the baud rate to use for the transmission. The baud rate is always the highest baud rate available on both modems. So an older modem using lower V standards such as V.34 (28,800) baud will transmit and receive data at that rate although the other modem is built to the V.42 standard.

Transmission Modes

Modems communicate using one of two data transmission modes. These are **asynchronous**, also known as **async** or **synchronous**, commonly called **sync**. In asynchronous mode, data that is being transmitted is divided into groups. Each group consists of one or more bytes. Consider a byte the equivalent to a character on the keyboard and containing eight bits.

Each group of data is transmitted separately from other groups, which is similar to **data packets** on a network (Figure 7–2). At the beginning of a group is a special marker called a **start bit** that signals the receiving modem that a new group of data follows. At the end of the group is another special marker called a **stop bit** which it indicates the end of the group to the receiving modem.

Each group also contains a parity bit that is used by the receiving modem to determine if an error in transmission has occurred. Before transmission begins, communication software at both the sending and receiving modems agree that parity will be either even or odd. **Even parity** means that each group of data will have an even number of 1s. **Odd parity** means there will be an odd number of 1s in each group.

You can imagine that some groups will have an even number of 1s and others an odd number. The only way to assure each group complies with the even or odd parity rule is to insert another bit in the group. This bit is called the parity bit and is set by the communication software to either a 1 or a 0 depending on the parity rule and the number of 1s in the group.

For example, assume even parity is used and the group of data being transmitted has five 1s making it an odd number of 1s. The communications software will make the parity bit 1, making the group comply with the even parity rule. However, if group has four 1s, then the parity bit is set to 0, since the group already meets the even parity requirements.

As each group is received, the modem and communications software checks the parity of the group. If an error is detected, a request is made to resend the data, otherwise a request to send the next group is sent.

Retransmission of data due to transmission errors detracts from the speed at which information can be transmitted using a modem. The baud rate indicates the transmission speeds also called channel speeds. Generally, the higher the baud rate the faster the rate of data transmission. However, both modems must be operating at the same baud rate and no transmission errors can occur if the full impact of the baud rate is to be realized.

Throughput is a better way to measure data transmission using asynchronous communication. **Throughput** refers to the amount of data successfully transmitted to another computer. Retransmission errors are reflected in throughput, but not in the baud rate.

In an effort to reduce transmission errors, the Microcom corporation developed a new communications protocol called Microcom Network Protocol (MNP). Transmissions using MNP tend to have a higher throughput than those that don't use MNP. MNP improves error control and a data compression standard called ***classes***, the latest of which is class 5.

Synchronous mode communication transmits data in a single stream called a frame rather than in groups that require start and stop bits as in asynchronous mode. Both the sending and receiving computers are synchronized for the transmission.

There are three common protocols used for synchronous mode. These are **synchronous mode data-link control** (SDLC); **high-level data-link control** (HDLC), and **binary synchronous communications protocol** (bisync).

MCSE 7.2 Large Networks

Nearly every WAN is an expansion of a larger LAN. As discussed throughout the previous chapters, networks begin in many cases as a peer-to-peer network where instead of network resources, clients share each others' resources.

Peer-to-peer networks naturally progress to a LAN, where clients are connected together using cables and the network is under the control of the network operating system. At least one server exists on each LAN to manage network resources such as files and printers.

Every LAN has restrictions based on the number of clients that can be connected to the network and limits in the distance the network can cover within a building. These limitations are overcome by dividing the LAN into segments. A **segment** is similar to a branch of a tree, where branches are attached together to a trunk. The **trunk** in a LAN is called the backbone. Clients connect to a segment. If that segment becomes congested, then the network administrator moves the client to a less busy segment.

However, there is a physical limit to the number of clients per segment and a limit of segments on a network. It is at this stage when the network administrator must reconfigure the current network to create a large network.

A large network contains many independent LANs connected to each other. The most direct way to create a large network is to make each LAN segment into its own LAN. A segment has all the components required to convert a LAN such as the cabling, servers, network operating system, and clients. For each new LAN the network operating system and client accounts need to be reconfigured to reflect the new configuration.

Reconfiguring LAN segments into LANs leaves the organization with a fragment networking system, since clients on one LAN cannot communicate with clients on a different LAN. LANs within the organization must be connected to form a large network sometimes called a **logical network**.

Expansion Components

LANs can be connected to each other by using one of five expansion components. These are: bridges; routers; brouters; gateways; and repeaters.

A **bridge** (Figure 7–3) A bridge is a device that can connect segments of a single LAN together or several seperate LANs together. Each segment or LAN is connected to a separate port on the bridge. All packets flow through the bridge, where they are forwarded to the proper port. This enables the bridge to reduce the amount of network traffic across segments of a LAN.

A key feature of a bridge is its capability to create its own routing table by monitoring the flow of packets across the network. A routing table associates network addresses (the MAC address) with a port on the bridge.

When the bridge receives a packet, the bridge searches the routing table for the originator's address. If the address is not on the routing table,

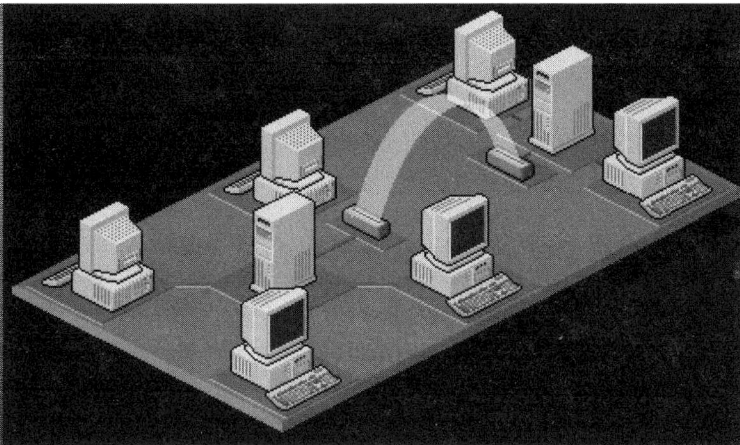

Figure 7–3. *A bridge uses a routing table to forward packets between segments or networks.*

then the bridge appends the address and the address's port to routing table for future reference.

Next, the bridge compares the destination address of the packet with addresses in the routing table. If there is a match, the bridge regenerates the signal to extend the distance the signal can travel and forwards the packet to the port that corresponds to the destination address. If there isn't a match, then the packet is forwarded to all the ports. This is **call-forward broadcasting**. This can lead to increased data traffic called a **broadcast storm**.

Only one address on one of the ports will recognize the destination address as its own and accept the packet. The bridge notes the ports that accepted the packet, then appends the destination address and the corresponding port to the routing table.

The network administrator can configure the bridge's routing table to restrict the segments or LANs that can receive packets. This is known as **segmenting network traffic**.

A bridge is protocol and is physical-media insensitive. That is, a bridge can connect different kinds of networks (i.e., Token Ring, Ethernet), different protocols, and different physical media (i.e., fiber optics and twisted pair). This is possible because a bridge works at the data-link layer of the OSI model and is not involved with protocols or the physical connectivity of devices.

A large network can use a remote bridge to connect distant LANs together. A distant LAN is a LAN that is located in a different building. A remote bridge is one that connects the distant LAN through the use of a modem and a telephone line or lease line. At the other end of the telephone line is another modem and another remote bridge that connects to the distant LAN.

The modems are treated as normal ports on each bridge. That is, packets with unknown ports or with the modem port are forwarded to the modem and over the telephone line to the remote bridge. The packet is then forwarded to the designated port or to all the ports on the remote bridge if the port is unknown.

Modems used to bridge distant LANs must use synchronous communication, otherwise the flow of packets across the remote bridge can become a bottleneck in the network.

Routers and Brouters

A bridge does not always use the best path to forward a packet, because the bridge at times needs to broadcast the packet to all ports. A device that is more robust than a bridge, yet fulfills the same functionality is a **router**.

A router (Figure 7–4) forwards packets using the best possible network path, because the router has more information about the network than does a bridge. This is because a router works at the network layer of the OSI model as compared to a bridge that works at the data-link layer.

A router uses a routing table that stores more information than the routing table used in a bridge. A router's routing table contains network numbers instead of MAC addresses. It also contains all the paths between the router and addresses on the network and has information that identifies the most efficient way to send packets to any network address. Routers are also good at filtering network traffic and isolating segments.

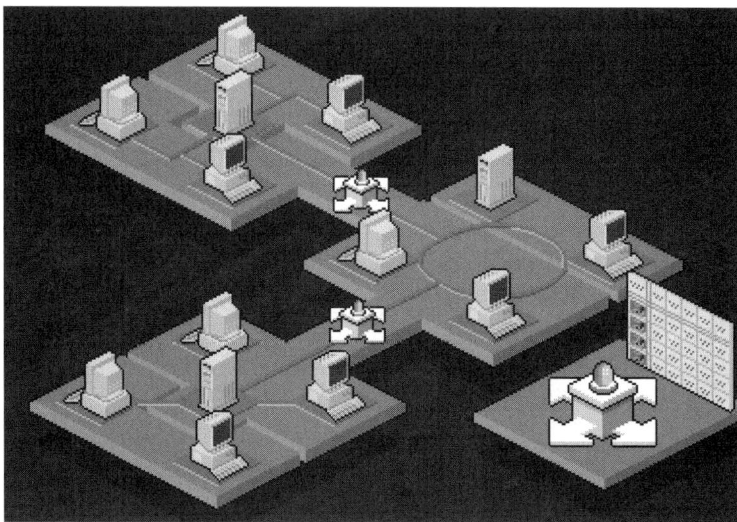

Figure 7–4. *A router identifies the shortest path to a designation router by using a router table.*

Each network has a router that communicates with clients on that network or to another network's router. The routing table used by a router contains at least three pieces of information. These are: the **destination router**; the **adjacent router**; and the **number of hops required to reach the destination router**.

Each row of the router table contains a path to the destination router. The path is the adjacent router and the length of the path is indicated by the value in the hops column. There can be more than one path for each destination router, each of which would have its own row in the router table.

The length of the path is recorded as a number of hops. A **hop** is the number of routers the packet must travel to before it reaches the destination router. For example, a hop value might be three routers, which includes the destination router.

The router determines the destination router based on the destination address of the packet. It then uses the table to determine the shortest path (lowest number of hops) to the destination router. The router then forwards the packet to the adjacent router that is associated with the shortest path. If that router is unavailable, then the router locates the next shortest path and sends the packet to the corresponding adjacent router.

The same process occurs within each router when it receives packets from either clients on their own network or from an adjacent router. If the destination address of the packet isn't a client on the router's network, then the router looks for the shortest path to the destination router.

An adjacent router can be unavailable for a number of reasons, such as a hardware malfunction or simply a traffic jam. Routers use routing algorithms to detect a traffic problem and to reroute its packet to a lesser-used path to the destination router. **Open Shortest Path First** (OSPF) is a commonly used routing algorithm. OSPF is one of a group of algorithms called the **link-state algorithms**, which uses the **Dijkstra algorithm** to determine the most efficient path to use when sending a packet to a destination router.

Another method to route a packet is the **Routing Information Protocol** (RIP), which the **distance-vector algorithm** deemed to be less efficient than the link-state algorithm. And the other common routing method is **NetWare Link Services Protocol** (NLSP), which also uses the link-state algorithm. TCP/IP uses both OSPF and RFP. IPX uses both RIP and NLSP. Routers cannot be used with all protocols. For example, the **Local Area Transport Protocol** (LAT) and NetBEUI cannot be used with routers. These are called **nonroutable protocols**.

There are two kinds of routers. These are static routers and dynamic routers. **A static router** requires the network administrator to configure the router and create the routing table. This is more time-consuming to set up than a dynamic router; however, the static router gives the network administrator more control over the routing paths, since it is the network administrator who creates those paths.

A **dynamic router** requires little configuration and automatically creates routing paths once the network administrator creates the first route in the routing table. An advantage of a dynamic router is that the router determines the most efficient secondary path to the destination router automatically.

Organizations that use both routable and nonroutable protocols on their networks can use a brouter to link together LANs. A **brouter** is a combination bridge and router. The brouter functions like a bridge if a nonroutable protocol is used, otherwise it functions like a router. It is more cost effective then having a router and a bridge.

Gateways and Repeaters

Linking a network to various platforms can be a challenge, since each platform has its own protocols and architecture that can become a roadblock to data communication. If the format of the data transmitted over the network is not the same format used by a platform, then the platform is unable to read the data. However, the network administrator can use a gateway to remove this roadblock.

A **gateway** (Figure 7–5) is a device that translates protocols, architectures, languages, and data formats. For example, a data packet transmitted across the network can be translated to the format required for a mainframe environment. The data contained in the packet is stripped from the network data packet (**decapsulating**), then repackaged as required by the mainframe (**encapsulating**).

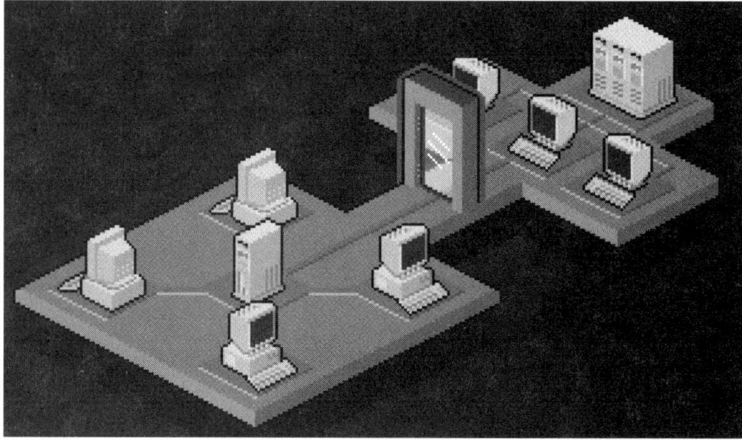

Figure 7–5. *A gateway is used to link disimiliar platforms.*

Unlike other devices on the network, such as the router, a gateway is dedicated to a single type of translation to the translation and can be expensive. For example, only the Windows NT Server to SNA gateway performs the SNA to Windows NT Server translation. This gateway cannot be used for any other type of translation.

A word of caution. Gateways should be installed on a dedicated server, because data translations require a substantial amount of resources. Placing a gateway on a shared server can cause performance degradation between the network and the other client/devices.

A common problem network administrators will see in large networks is the degradation of transmissions over the network. This is called attenuation. As discussed in previous chapters, each network topology has a limit as to the distance a signal can travel along the network. Beyond this distance, the signal becomes weak and is unrecognizable by clients and network resources.

A way to overcome this limitation is to install a repeater on the network. A **repeater** receives the network signal, then transmits a stronger signal across the network. This is called **regeneration**. A repeater must be used with the same LAN protocol and the same access method, although a repeater can be used to connect unlike cables such as a fiber optic and twisted pair.

MCSE 7.3 Expanding to a WAN

Organizations that have more than one office typically find themselves needing extend their computer network to include all offices so that data and network resources can be shared throughout the whole firm.

A large LAN can be expanded to include networks in other offices by using a remote bridge that was discussed earlier in this chapter. The remote bridge connects two LANs using dedicated modem and telephone lines. This is the first step to transforming a large LAN into a WAN.

LANs have a tendency to gradually evolve from a simple peer-to-peer network into a WAN; it often occurs in a patchwork way without careful planning. For example, a remote bridge, modem, and telephone line is a quick fix to link two distant LANs. But, is this the most economical choice? Are there more efficient methods of accomplishing the same objective? This section explores the technology available for WANs.

Networks and Lines

Nearly every organization required to transmit data over long distances uses the Public **Switched Telephone Network** (PSTN)—for instance, a telephone company (Figure 7–6). There are several firms that provide access to the

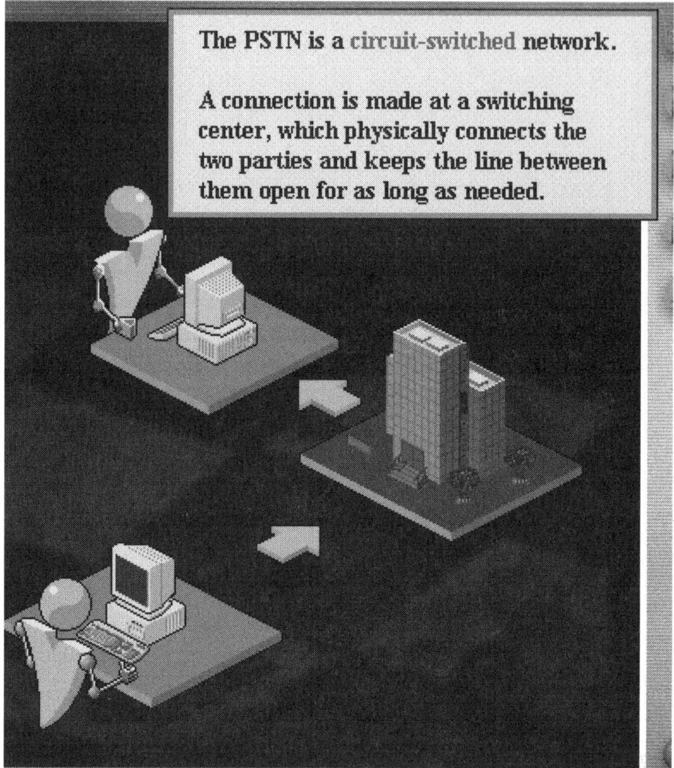

The PSTN is a circuit-switched network.
A connection is made at a switching center, which physically connects the two parties and keeps the line between them open for as long as needed.

Figure 7–6. *A PSTN is a physical connection between two clients using a common carrier.*

global telephone network where data, voice, or video can be transmitted practically anywhere in the world.

PSTNs offer transmission services in the form of a line. Lines are categorized as analog or digital, dialup or dedicated, and by the quality of the line called conditioning.

Analog or digital refers to the method used to transmit the information. Analog is the most common technology used in PSTN, although carriers are moving toward digital technology as demand for fast, reliable data transfer increases.

A **dialup line** is the standard telephone line where a telephone number is used to connect to the remote location. A dialup line is shared. That is, once the connection is broken, such as when you hang up the telephone, the line can be used by another subscriber to the PSTN.

In contrast, a **dedicated line**, also known as a **lease line**, is used to connect two fixed locations, such as a client to a customer. No telephone number is required because the line connection is never terminated at the end of a transmission. The line is also not shared by other subscribers.

The decision to choose a dialup or dedicated line is based on economics. Dedicated incurs monthly charge. Dialup is on a per call basis. If a connection is made infrequently to multiple remote locations, then the dialup line is generally the approach taken by many organizations. This is true in the case of an end-of-day transfer of sales data from a remote location to the home office.

However, a dedicated line is likely to be a more efficient choice if data is exchanged constantly between two locations, as is the case when security transactions are transmitted every minute during the trading day from a remote office of a security firm to a centralized data center.

The third category used to describe lines refers to its **quality** or **conditioning.** The line condition refers to the reliability of the network connection. Although PSTN refers to a line, there is a network of lines and switches used to transmit information between remote locations. This is known as a circuit-switched network. The quality of the transmission (i.e., the amount of interference on the line) is dependent upon the condition of each circuit on the network. PSTN assures the reliability of a line based upon the condition of the line required by the organization.

A type **designator** and a **conditioning symbol classify** lines. Table 7–1 lists typical lines that are available from any PSTN provider. An A, C, or D rating designates quality of the line. The C rating is divided into eight levels, the meaning of which is determined by the PSTN provider. Therefore, a network administrator who wants to transmit data using a dialup line would ask the PSTN provider for a Type 5/C4 line. This is a base data line with a C4 quality rating.

Table 7–1 *Dialup Lines Are Classified By the Intended Use of the Line*

Line Type	Purpose
1	Voice
2	Voice with quality control
3	Voice/radio with tone conditioning
4	Slow speed (under 1200 BPS) data applications
5	Data
6	Voice/data using trunk circuits
7	Voice/data using private lines
8	Voice/data using trunks (computers)
9	Voice/video
10	Application relays

Digital Lines

PSTN providers offer another type of transmission method called **Digital Data Services** (DDS). DDS uses digital technology to transfer data in a more secured, faster, and economical way than an analog line.

DDS is a dedicated line that connects two locations, which is very similar to a dedicated analog line. Adds connections called a **dedicated circuit** and can transmit information at up to 56 KBPS in synchronous mode also known as point-to-point asynchronous connections. Unlike an analog line that is affected by line interference, a digital line is capable of transmitting information practically error free.

Information from a computer is transmitted over the LAN to a bridge or router, where a **Channel Service Unit/Data Service Unit** (CSU/DSU) is used to send the signal across the digital line. The CSU/DSU function is similar to how a modem is used on an analog line in that it translates the network signal to the bipolar DDS signal and vice versa.

There are three commonly used types of digital lines. These are T1, T3, and switched 56. The most frequently used digital line is the T1 line. A **T1** line consists of wire pair that are divided into 24 communication channels, each of which can transmit 64 KBP. This is known as the DS-0 (DS-1=1.544 MBPS) rate.

Information is transmitted over T1 line (Figure 7–7) using multiplexing technology, which is also known as muxing. Signals from various trans-

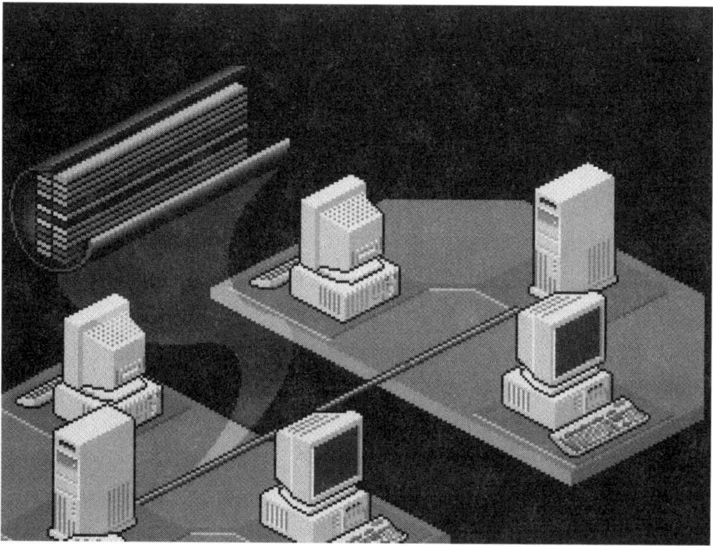

Figure 7–7. *Each of the 24 channels of a T1 line carries 64 MBPS of information.*

mitting devices are received by a device called a **multiplexor** that sends the signal across the T1 line. A multiplexor at the receiving end of the line demultiplexes the signal back into the original signals.

Network administrators whose organizations want the speed and reliability of a T1 line, but do not have the need to use 24 channels, can subscribe to one or more channels. This is known as **Fractional T1** (FT-1) and provides a more economical solution to WAN transmission than acquiring more capacity than is needed.

A **T3** line provides the same features of a T1 line, but three times the data transfer capacity. It is like have three T1 lines. The Switched 56 digital line is part of a circuit switch that consists of other Switched 56 digital lines. A CSU/DSU device on a LAN can dial up any CSU/DSU connected to the Switched 56 digital circuit switch. A **Switched 56 digital line** provides a more economical choice than a dedicated line, because an organization is charged only for transmission. A flat charge is imposed on a dedicated line regardless of usage.

Packet Switching

Dialup and dedicated lines provide a pathway from an organization's large LAN to remote locations. However, at times these connections can be costly, especially if large amounts of information are regularly transmitted to various remote locations.

A more economical method is to use a packet-switching network. A packet-switching network owned by a common carrier such as the Telephone Company, offers fast, reliable data transfer on a needed basis (Figure 7–8).

Packet-switching technology is similar to the way data is transmitted across a LAN, in that information is divided into small data packets. Each data packet contains the destination, source address and data correction information. Packets are reassembled into the information when they reach their destination.

Data packets travel across segments of the public telephone network. These segments are connected together by switches, which is similar to a series of router on a large LAN. Switches read the destination address of a packet, then send the packet to the switch closest to the destination address by referencing a table similar to the router table discussed earlier in this chapter.

Like data transfer in a LAN, transmission errors can occur in a packet-switching network. The switch receiving the packet detects errors, then requests the originating switch to resend the packet.

Virtual circuits are used in most packet-switching networks. We tend to think a circuit is composed of segments of communication lines. However, a virtual circuit uses bandwidth of a line to form the circuit. A **virtual**

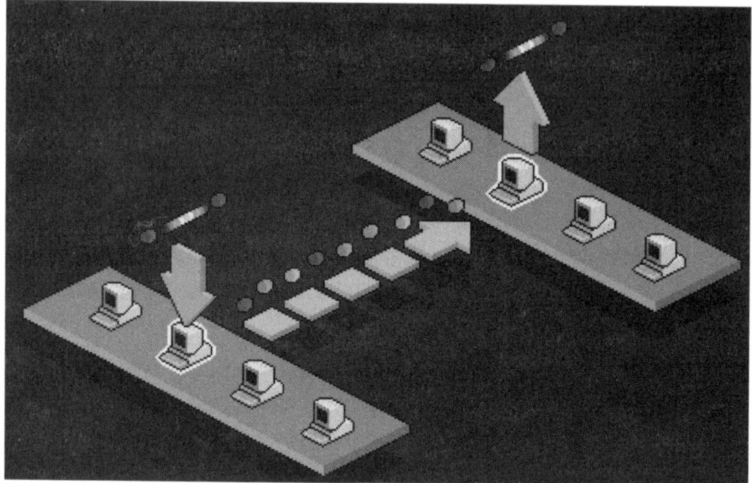

Figure 7–8. *Packet-Switching network transmits information in small packets.*

circuit is a logical connection between two points. All packets follow the same path.

A cable (line) can transmit a range of frequencies, each of which can be used as a communication channel to send or receive data. This is called a **bandwidth**. A virtual circuit uses one of these channels to link two devices and is created after both devices agree on communication parameters which is faster than other options.

A virtual circuit can be temporary or permanent depending on the needs of the organization. A temporary virtual circuit is called **Switched Virtual Circuit** (SVC), which is also called a **point-to-many-point** connection. The connection between the two devices remains active until the transmission is completed.

A **permanent virtual circuit** (PVC), similar to a dedicated line, maintains the connection as long as the two devices are connected to the circuit.

MCSE 7.4 WAN and Data Transmission

Speed and reliability are the two critical factors to consider when deciding on how information from a large LAN is to be transmitted to remote locations using WAN technology. There are six techniques currently available to provide economical data transmission across a global network.

These are X.25 protocols, frame relay; Asynchronous Transfer Mode (ATM); Integrated Services Digital network (ISDN); Switched Multimegabit Data Service (SMDS); Fiber Distributed Data Interface (FDDI); and Synchronous Optical Network (SONET).

X.25 protocol is slow and uses switched circuits to provide the best rate at a particular time. It (Figure 7–9) is used to define how data packets are created and transmitted over a packet-switching network. The X.25 protocol requires strict error checking and retransmission procedures. It uses specifications for the **Data Terminal Equipment/Data Communications Equipment** (DTE/DCE) interface. DTE/DCE manages communication between the X.25 host and the **public data network** (PDN). This includes packet assembly and disassembly, which is also known as **PAD**.

The X.25 protocol was developed for analog networks that experienced more transmission errors than a digital network. With the rapid expansion of digital networks, the X.25 protocol is being replaced with the frame relay protocol.

The frame relay protocol transmits packets faster and more reliably than X.25 because digital transmission enabled technologist to remove the enhanced error checking and other administrative information from packets.

A network that uses the frame relay protocol is called a **frame relay network,** which is a private virtual circuit (PNC) consisting of digital dedicated lines. This is more reliable because the path from the source through digital packet switches to the destination is always the same. There is no opportunity for the data packet to hop to a secondary digital packet switch.

The length of data packets vary, enabling the frame relay network to send more information than an X.25 packet-switching network that uses

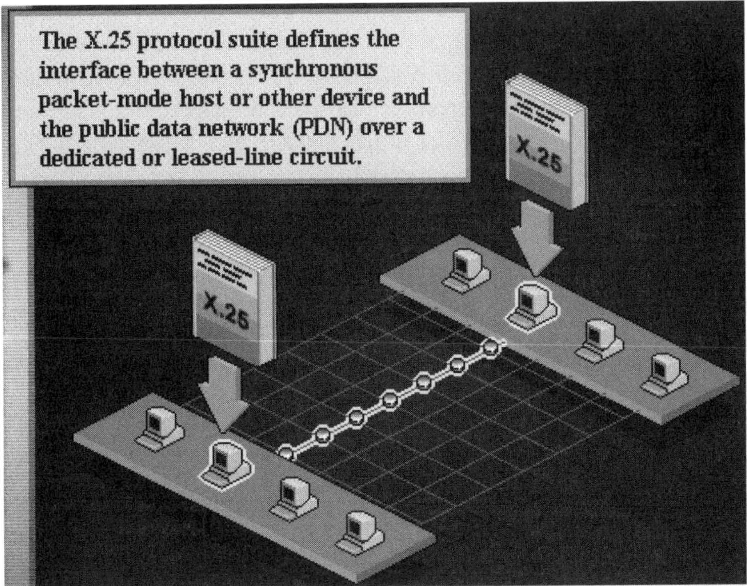

The X.25 protocol suite defines the interface between a synchronous packet-mode host or other device and the public data network (PDN) over a dedicated or leased-line circuit.
X.25
X.25

Figure 7–9. *X.25 is a protocol suite for long distance data transmissions.*

fixed, smaller data packets. You'll recall that smaller data packets are used to reduce the time it takes to resend a data packet if an error is detected. Digital networks reduce the need to resend data packets.

Frame relay networks offers bandwidth on an as-needed basis. That is, during a period of heavy data transmission, the network administrator can ask that the bandwidth of the dedicated line be increased so that more data can flow during the same time period.

ATM and ISDN

Asynchronaus transfer mode (ATM) is an enhancement to the frame relay protocol where all connections are one way and uses a fixed size data packet of 53 bytes to transfer various kinds of information across a WAN. This includes live video, voice, audio, and huge amounts of data (i.e., multi-megabits) all traveling at 155 MBPS, although transmission rates of 622 MBPS are available using fiber optics. ATM supports **Bandwidth Reservation** (QOS) using streamlined data transfer.

Each data packet called a **cell** contains a five-byte address followed by 48 bytes of data. A standard size data packet makes managing data transfer more efficient than when variable-length data packets are used. Bandwidth allocations, buffer sizes, and tweaking network equipment for data processing are made easier because of the standard size data packet.

Although ATM offers a more robust WAN and can also be used for LAN, current network devices such as routers and cabling must be upgraded to take advantage of all of ATM's capabilities.

For example, an ATM switch is called a **multiport device** and can take the role of a hub to transfer data within a network and as a router to transfer data between networks. Furthermore, the ATM switch can serve as a multiplexor enabling more than one client to transmit data at the same time across the network.

Until ATM technology is fully embraced by the corporate community, ISDNs will remain a popular method for WAN communication. **ISDN** is a dialup service using telephone lines that replace the analog-based **public-switched telephone network** (PSTN). However, ISDN does not replace T1 line service and is not like frame relay, where bandwidth can be increased during peak data transfer periods.

There are two types of ISDN service: basic rate ISDN and primary rate ISDN. **Basic rate ISDN** service, also known as **2B+D**, consists of two 64 BPS channels **called B** channels and one 16 KBPS channel called a **D channel**. The D channel is used to carry information that helps to manage the transmission. Network devices use both B channels to send and receive data. The **primary rate ISDN service** divides the ISDN line into 23 B channels and a D channel.

FDDI, SONET, and SMDS

FDDI is a protocol used on token-passing ring networks which can be up to 60 miles (100 km) long and have a maximum of 500 clients; although the length can be extended by using repeaters.

FDDI networks are primarily designed for massive data transfer such as copying distributive databases to remote locations. FDDI is also suited for LANs that use data-transfer intense applications such as in computer-aided design (CAD) and computer-aided manufacturing (CAM).

The token-passing data access method used with FDDI is slightly different than the 802.5 token-passing protocol mentioned in earlier chapters. The 802.5 protocol enables a client that receives the token to transmit a single data packet.

In contrast, the FDDI protocol allows the client to hold the token for a specific amount of time. During that period, the client can transmit as many frames of data as possible before the client releases the token.

An FDDI network is divided into two rings, the primary ring and the secondary ring. The **primary ring** is used for all data transmission, whereas the **secondary ring** is used backup in case the primary ring fails. Each ring can be about 60 miles long and have up to 500 clients.

Clients attached to an FDDI network are divided into two classes; Class A and Class B. **Class A** clients are connected to both rings of the network and can be repointed to the secondary ring if the primary ring is disabled. However, **Class B** clients are connected to one ring and cannot be repointed if the ring fails.

FDDI has a clever way of detecting a malfunctioning client. The technique is called beaconing. Every client on the network listens for a network error, called a **fault**, which is caused by another client on the network.

Once a client detects a fault, it sends an alert called a **beacon** across the network. The next client on the network receives the beacon and retransmits the beacon. This continues until it is the turn of the client who caused the fault to retransmit the beacon. Obviously, it can't because of the error. Therefore, the last client who retransmits the beacon is next to the client that has malfunctioned. Network administrators can immediately locate the troubled client.

Another network protocol creating interest in the corporate community is **synchronous optical network** (SONET). Like FDDI, SONET is designed for use with fiber optics. SONET specifies the **optical carrier** (OC) equivalent to the electrical **synchronous transport signals** (STS). SONET is suited for ATM and the basic rate ISDN service.

A network administrator that requires multimegabit data transfer at a rate of up to 34 MBPS, but is not in the position to use FDDI or SONET, should consider SMDS.

Switched Multimegabit Data Service (SMDS) is a service available from some common carriers that allows an organization to use one line to transfer data to many sites. SMDS is similar to ATM technology, but uses a distributed **queue dual bus** (DQDB) to form an open-ended network ring. SMDS is an economical solution to massive, regular data transfer in a WAN environment.

■ Summary

The most common way to allow a remote location access to a LAN is through the use of a modem. A modem, also known as data communications equipment (DEC), is a device that translates a digital signal produced by a computer into the analog signal needed to transmit the signal across the telephone line. A modem also translates an incoming from analog to digital.

The Internal Telecommunications Union (ITU) established standards known as the V series for modem manufacturers. These standards enable modems designed by different manufacturers to communicate with each other.

Although there are specific modem standards followed by modem manufacturers, the industry commonly classifies modems based on baud rate. The baud rate is defined as the speed in which a bit of data can be transmitted.

Modems communicate using one of two data transmission modes. These are asynchronous, known as async or synchronous, commonly called sync. In asynchronous mode, data that is being transmitted is divided into groups. Each group consists of one or more bytes. Each group of data is transmitted separately from other groups similar to data packets along the network.

Synchronous mode communication transmits data in a single stream called a frame rather than in groups. Both the sending and receiving computers are synchronized for the transmission.

There are three common protocols used for synchronous mode. These are synchronous mode data link control (SDLC), high-level data link control (HDLC), and the binary synchronous communications protocol (bisync).

It is common for a modest LAN to grow into a large network that contains many LANs because organizations realize the benefits of sharing network resources. The most direct way to create a large network is to make each LAN segment its own LAN. A segment has all the components required to create a LAN, such as the cabling, servers, network operating system, and clients. The network operating system and client accounts need to be reconfigured to reflect the new LAN.

LAN, can be joined together by using one of five expansion components. These are bridges, routers, brouters, gateways, and repeaters.

A bridge is a device that connects LANs to a port in the bridge. All packets flow through the bridge, where they are forwarded to the proper port.

A bridge creates its own routing table by monitoring the flow of packets across the network. A routing table associates network addresses with a port.

The bridge searches the routing table for the originator address. If the address is not on the routing table, then the bridge appends the address and the address's port to the routing table for future reference.

Next, the bridge compares the destination address of the packet with addresses in the routing table. If there is a match, the bridge forwards the packet to the port that corresponds to the destination address. If there isn't a match, then the packet is forwarded to all the ports. This is called forward broadcasting.

A large network can use a remote bridge to connect distant LANs together. A remote bridge connects the distant LAN, through the use of a modem and a telephone line.

A bridge does not always use the best path to forward a packet, because the bridge at times needs to broadcast the packet to all ports. A device that is more robust than a bridge, yet fulfills the same functionality, is a router.

A router forwards packets using the best possible network path because the router uses a routing table that stores more information than the routing table used in a bridge.

Each row of the router table contains a path to the destination router. The path is the adjacent router and the length of the path is indicated by the value in the hops column.There can be more than one path for each destination router, each of which would have its own row in the router table.

The length of the path is recorded as a number of hops. A hop is the number of routers the packet must travel to before it reaches the destination router. For example, a hop value might be three routers, which includes the destination router.

The router determines the destination router based on the destination address of the packet. It then looks up the router table to determine the shortest path (lowest number of hops) to the destination router. The router then forwards the packet to the adjacent router that is associated with the shortest path. If that router is unavailable, then the router located the next shortest path and sends the packet to the corresponding adjacent router.

There are two kinds of routers. These are static routers and dynamic routers. A static router requires the network administrator to configure the router and create the routing table.

A dynamic router requires little configuration and automatically creates routing paths once the network administrator creates the first route in the routing table. Organizations that use both routable and nonroutable protocols on their networks can use a brouter to link together LANs. A brouter functions like a bridge if a nonroutable protocol is used, otherwise it functions like a bridge.

Linking a network to various platforms can be a challenge, since each platform has its own protocols and architecture that can be a roadblock to data communication. However, the network administrator can use a gateway to remove this roadblock. A gateway is a device that translates protocols, architectures, languages, and data formats. Unlike other devices on the network such as a router, a gateway is specific to the translation.

Another problem with a large network is the degradation of transmission over the network. The signal will become weak and is unrecognizable by clients and network resources if the length of the network exceeds the limits of the topology. A repeater overcomes this problem. A repeater receives the network signal, then transmits a strong signal across the network. This is called regeneration.

Large networks typically grow into a WAN that joins together remote LANs. Connection to remote sites is made using the Public Switched Telephone Network (PSTN), for example, a telephone company. PSTN offer transmission services in the form of lines that are categorized as analog or digital, dialup or dedicated, and by the quality of the line called conditioning.

Analog or digital refers to the method used to transmit information. A dialup line is the standard telephone line, where a telephone number is used to connect to the remote location. A dedicated line, also known as a lease line, is used to connect two fixed locations such as a client to a customer. No telephone number is required, because the line connection is never terminated at the end of a transmission.

The line condition refers to the reliability of the network connection. The PSTN is a network of lines and switches used to transmit information to the remote location. This is known as a circuit-switched network. The quality of the transmission is dependent upon the condition of each circuit on the network.

A type designator and a conditioning symbol classify lines. An A, C, or D rating designates the quality of the line. The C rating is divided into eight levels, the meaning of which is determined by the PSTN provider.

PSTN providers offer another type of transmission method other than analog called Digital Data Services (DDS). DDS uses digital technology to transfer data in a more secured, faster, and economical way than available with an analog line.

DDS is a dedicated line that connects two locations very similar to a dedicated analog line. This is called a dedicated circuit and can transmit information at up to 56 KBPS in synchronous mode.

There are three commonly used types of digital lines. These are T1, T3, and switched 56. The most frequently used digital line is the T1 line. A T1 line consists of two wires that are divided into 24 communication channels, each of which can transmit 64 KBP.

Information is transmitted over T1 lines using multiplexing technology, which enables signals from various transmitting devices to use the line at the same time. An organization can subscribe to one or more channels of a T1 line. This is known as Fractional T1 (FT-1) and provides a more economical solution to WAN transmission than acquiring more capacity than is needed.

A T3 line provides the same features of a T1 line, but three times the data transfer capacity. The Switched 56 digital line provides a more economical choice than a dedicated line because an organization is charged only for transmission. A flat charge is imposed on a dedicated line regardless of usage.

Dialup and dedicated lines provide a pathway from an organization's large LAN to a remote location. However, at times these connections can be costly, especially if large amounts of information are regularly transmitted to various remote locations.

A more economical method is to use a packet-switching network. A packet-switching network owned by a common carrier such as the Telephone Company, offers fast, reliable data transfer on an as-needed basis.

Packet-switching technology is similar to the way data is transmitted across a LAN, in that information is divided into small data packets. Each data packet contains the destination and source address and data correction information. Packets are reassembled into the information when they reach their destination.

Virtual circuits are used in most packet-switching networks. We tend to think that a circuit is composed of segments of communication lines. However, a virtual circuit uses the bandwidth of a line to form the circuit. A cable (line) can transmit a range of frequencies, each of which can be used as a communication channel to send or receive data. This is called a bandwidth. A virtual circuit uses one of these channels to link two devices and is created after both devices agree on communication parameters.

A virtual circuit can be temporary or permanent, depending on the needs of the organization. A temporary virtual circuit is called a Switched Virtual Circuit (SVC), which is also called a point-to-many-point connection. The connection between the two devices remains active until the transmission is completed. A permanent virtual circuit (PVC), similar to a dedicated line, maintains the connection as long as the two devices are connected to the circuit.

Speed and reliability are the two critical factors to consider when deciding on how information from a large LAN is to be transmitted to remote locations using WAN technology. There are six techniques currently available to provide economical data transmission across a global network.

These are X.25 protocols, frame relay; Asynchronous Transfer Mode (ATM); Integrated Services Digital network (ISDN); Switched Multimegabit Data Service (SMDS); Fiber Distributed Data Interface (FDDI); and Synchronous Optical Network (SONET).

The X.25 protocol is used to define how data packets are created and transmitted over a packet-switching network. With the rapid expansion of digital networks, the X.25 protocol, designed for analog networks, is being replaced with frame relay.

Frame-relay protocol transmits variable size packets faster and more reliably than X.25, because digital transmission enabled a technologist to remove the enhanced error checking and other administrative information from packets.

ATM is an enhancement to the frame-relay protocol and uses a fixed size data packet of 53 bytes to transfer various kinds of information across a WAN. This includes live video, voice, audio, and huge amounts of data (i.e., multimegabits) all traveling at 155 MBPS, although transmission rates of 622 MBPS have been seen using fiber optics.

ATM technology requires the upgrading of most of the network devices currently in use by corporations. It is for this reason that it hasn't been fully embraced by the corporate community. ISDN is a popular method for WAN communications. ISDN is a dialup service using telephone lines that replaces the analog-based public-switched telephone network (PSTN).

There are two types of ISDN service: basic rate ISDN and primary rate ISDN. Basic rate ISDN service, also known as 2B+D, consists of two 64 BPS channels called B channels and one 16 KBPS channel called a D channel. The D channel is used to carry information that helps to manage the transmission. Network devices use both B channels to send and receive data. The primary rate ISDN service divides the ISDN line into 23 B channels and a D channel.

Fiber Distributed Data Interface (FDDI) is a protocol for a token-passing ring network that is up to 60 miles long with a maximum of 500 clients, although the length can be extended by using repeaters. The FDDI protocol allows the client to hold the token a specific amount of time. During that period, the client can transmit as many frames of data as possible before the client releases the token.

An FDDI network is divided into two rings, called the primary ring and the secondary ring. The primary ring is used for all data transmission, whereas the secondary ring is used as a backup in case the primary ring fails.

The FDDI uses beaconing to detect a client who has malfunctioned. Once a client detects an error called a fault, it sends an alert called a beacon across the network. The next client on the network receives the beacon and retransmits the beacon. This continues until it is the turn of the client who caused the fault to retransmit the beacon. Obviously, it can't because of the error. Therefore, the last client who retransmits the beacon is next to the client that has malfunctioned.

Another network protocol creating interest in the corporate community is synchronous optical network (SONET). Like FDDI, SONET is designed for use with fiber optics. SONET specifies the optical carrier (OC) equivalent to the electrical synchronous transport signals (STS). SONET is suited for ATM and the basic rate ISDN service.

Switched Multimegabit Data Service (SMDS) is a service available from some common carriers that allow an organization to use one line to transfer data to many sites. SMDS is similar to ATM technology, but uses a distributed queue dual bus (DQDB) to form an open-ended network ring. SMDS is an economical solution to massive, regular data transfer in a WAN environment.

▲ Chapter Review Questions

▲ Fill in the Blanks

1. _____________ *is a network device that forwards all packets to networks except the network that sent the packet to the device.*

2. _________ *is a network device that uses a table to locate the most efficient path to an address.*

3. *The distance between the address that sent the packet and the destination address is measured in*___________.

4. *A brouter combines the capabilities of a* __________ *and a* _______.

5. ___________ *is the device that makes communication possible between unlike architectures.*

▲ True/False

1. *(T/F) A telephone line is described by type and quality.*
2. *(T/F) A dedicated line can be used to dial up a remote computer.*
3. *(T/F) A T1 has 23 channels.*
4. *(T/F) Signals from various sources can be transmitted at the same time using multiplexing.*
5. *(T/F) All switched virtual circuits are permanent.*
6. *(T/F) X.25 protocol replaces frame relay protocol for network transmission.*
7. *(T/F) Asynchronous Transfer Mode is an enhancement to the frame relay protocol and uses a fixed size data packet of 53 bytes to transfer various kinds of information across a WAN.*
8. *(T/F) Wireless communication can be used to connect a Local Area Network to a Wide Area Network.*

▲ Multiple Choice

1. *What communication standard is replacing the X.25 protocol in packet-switching networks?*
   A. DTE/DCE
   B. PAD
   C. Frame Relay
   D. ISDN
   E. SMDS

2. *What is the major reason ATM technology is not in widespread use?*
   A. Existing network hardware must be upgraded.
   B. ATM boards have not been developed for PCs.
   C. ATM does not conform to the OSI model.
   D. Switcher technology cannot handle ATM transmission speeds.
   E. Fear that ATM technology will soon become obsolete.

3. *How can you extend a network beyond its limited length?*
   A. Use a repeater.
   B. Increase the bandwidth of the cable.
   C. Install a CCITT modem.

D. Increase the baud rate of the modem.

E. Use V.43 bit compression.

4. *What type of communication is received in a timed, controlled fashion?*

   A. Async

   B. Sync

   C. RTM signals

   D. V.32bis signals

   E. V.42bis signals

5. *What device is used to give a remote client access to a network?*

   A. An IP address

   B. A modem

   C. A repeater

   D. CSMA/CD

   E. Logical link controller

6. *A key feature of a _____ is its capacity to create its own routing table by monitoring the flow of packets across the network.*

   A. bridge

   B. router

   C. repeater

   D. gateway

   E. ISDN

7. *A key feature of a _____ is its inability to create its own routing table by monitoring the flow of packets across the network.*

   A. bridge

   B. router

   C. repeater

   D. gateway

   E. ISDN

8. *A _______ functions like a router if a non-routable protocol is used, otherwise it functions like a bridge.*

   A. NVS

   B. brouter

   C. repeater

D. gateway

E. ISDN

9. *A ________ regenerates data recieved on a network.*

A. bridge

B. router

C. repeater

D. gateway

E. ISDN

10. *A ________ is a device that translates protocols, architectures, languages, and data formats between two unlike networks.*

A. bridge

B. router

C. repeater

D. gateway

E. ISDN

11. *________ is a dialup service using telephone lines that replace the analog-based public switched telephone network.*

A. X.25

B. ISDN

C. Frame relay

D. ATM

E. PSTN

▲ Open Ended

1. How is a router table used to find the best path to a destination?
2. What is the difference between a router and a bridge?
3. Describe how FDDI locates a disabled client on the network?
4. What are the advantages of frame relay?
5. What are the advantages and disadvantages of using a dedicated line?

EIGHT

Network Tools and Troubleshooting

▲Chapter Syllabus

MCSE 8.1 Preventing Networking Problems

MCSE 8.2 Monitoring Network Operations

MCSE 8.3 Troubleshooting Network Problems

Throughout this book, you learned that a computer network is comprised of many different hardware and software components, nearly all of which are created by different manufacturers.

Components work well together despite their various origins, because manufacturers adhere to internationally recognized industry standards for data and telecommunications.

Network components are typically purchased separately. That is, a network administrator may decide that a fiber optics backbone is the best choice for the network and twisted pair for clients connections. Likewise, a router may be used to organize smaller LANs into a large LAN; A repeater can be used to boost network signals and extend the technical length of a network topology.

Together, selected components form a network. However well the network functions, the network administrator must monitor network operations regularly for signs of network problems.

There are various kinds of network problems that can occur, including but not limited to breachs of security and temporary or permanent degradation of network response time. Some are easy to detect and fix while others require good detective work. You'll learn about techniques for monitoring the network, planning for trouble, and how to handle network problems when they arise.

MCSE 8.1 Preventing Networking Problems

The old saying, that an ounce of prevention is better than a cure, holds true for computer networks. Although all the planning in the world won't guarantee that the network will keep running forever. A good plan will minimize the impact that a network failure will have on the organization's ability to operate.

It is the responsibility of the network administrator to develop good administrative planning for the network, which will reduce the opportunity for mistakes. The plan must consider network security, standardization procedures, good documentation of all procedures and network topology, backups of network resources, and regular maintenance and upgrading of network components.

The Network Security Plan

Network security involves more than preventing an intruder from accessing network resources. In fact, there are very few accounts of such attacks when compared with the number of people who use networks daily (Figure 8–1).

Of greater concern is the likelihood that someone who has legal access to the network will do something inadvertently to halt network operations such as deleting the client database. This includes network administrators whose mistakes because of access privileges can be irrecoverable.

The best way to reduce the chance of these errors from occurring is to establish and strictly enforce access restrictions. Access restrictions limit network resources that a person can access and specifies how the person can use those resources.

One of the most exposed and most used network-resources is a file server. A file server contains data files that can be shared among network users. Typically, everyone on the network will be able to access the file server. However, each person should be restricted to those directories relevant to their job. Furthermore, it may be advisable to limit a person to a particular file(s) within the directory and grant that person readonly or read/write access to those files as needed.

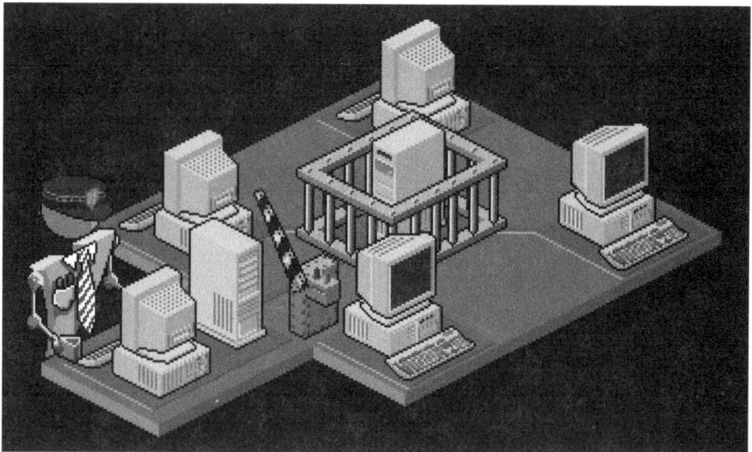

Figure 8–1. *Enforcing the network security policy is the first line of defense against an attack on the network.*

A person who has read-access can view information stored in the file, but is not able to modify or delete the information. Write-access gives a person the ability to change information and inadvertently corrupt the data in the file.

While network software such as Windows NT provides the utilities to limit access to network resources, it is up to the network administrator to institute the access restrictions described in the network plan.

Imposing access restrictions on network users can meet with resistance, especially when some see these limitations as an impairment to a smooth running organization. A network administrator must be careful to strike a balance between network protection and the need to use network resource as a tool for doing business.

A good approach to take is to identify the owner of the network resource, then let the owner decide which users are granted access to the resource. The owner is probably the best person to weigh the business needs against the need for protection.

For example, the owner of a file is in the position to identify which user should see the information stored in the file and whether or not that person has a need to modify the information.

Likewise, the network administrator takes ownership of network resources such as printers, printer servers, and fax/modem servers. In a large organization, the network administrator may want to delegate management of a network resource to an assistant. Only the designee and the network administrator will have access to modify the resource.

Network administrators that adhere to the ownership method of granting access rights typically institute a sign-off procedure whenever anyone requests access to a network resource. In addition to the normal security clearance required to receive a network login, permission must be obtained from the owner of the network resource before access is granted.

This policy gives the resource owner sign-off control over the resource, although physical control to the resource remains with the network administrator. That is, the network administrator can ignore the sign-off policy and grant access to any user to any network resource.

Standardized Procedures and Good Documentation

A computer network can be a hodgepodge of hardware and software (Figure 8–2). Although components work well together, each manufacturer has its own way to connect to the network.

This becomes evident when routers from different manufacturers are used on the same network or each of smaller LANs in the organization use different network operating systems.

These variations make any network more complicated than necessary, because the network administrator must learn how to configure and maintain several different network devices that have the same functionality, such as routers made by different manufacturers. If you have 3 different routers made by 3 different manufacturers then you will probably have 3 extremely different configuration procedures which might involve reading 3 different manuals all to accomplish one function.

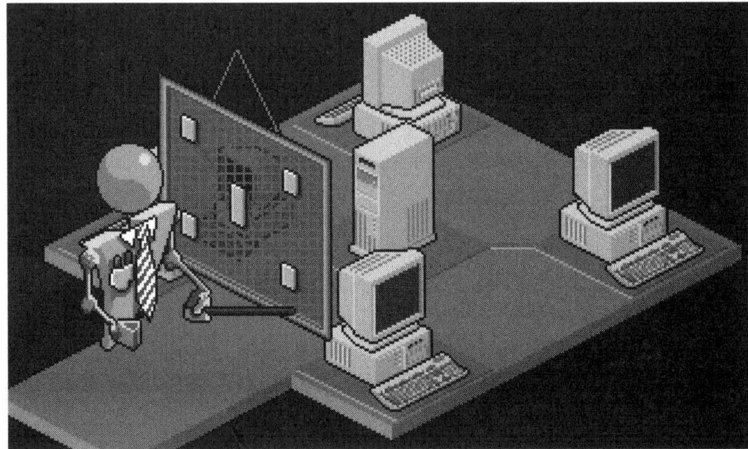

Figure 8–2. *Network documentation should include the location of all network components.*

A better approach is to standardize network components. For example, find the best network operating system for the organization's needs, then plan to use it on all the networks when possible. Likewise, use a router from the same manufacturer when possible.

Standardizing components before the network is installed makes supporting network operations more efficient. Each component has setup and maintenance procedures that can be incorporated into a handbook to help network technicians keep the network running.

Each procedure should be a step-by-step guide that walks a technician through the process. Most of these procedures can be copied from the manufacturer's documentation. However, the network administrator will need to include settings, called configurations, that are relative to the organization, such as locations of network resources.

The combination of standard components and standard procedures simplifies network administration and reduces the operating cost of network support. This becomes evident when an organization loses a network technician.

The network administrator can use the procedure handbook to train another staff person to handle routine tasks until an experienced replacement can be found. In many cases, the staff person permanently fills the position, because 80 percent of what the technician needs to know about the network is found in the procedural handbook. The network administrator can supplement the missing 20 percent.

The procedure handbook should contain more than procedures. It should contain the physical location of network components in the organization. Some network administrators include floor plans of each floor, which identify all the departments that occupy the location, desks, jack locations, type of wiring, and desk numbers. Desk numbers are referenced when a trouble call is received from a user.

Also found in the handbook should be the names and telephone numbers of secondary support staff. These are the people, sometimes manufacturer's reps, who can help the technician resolve problems that are not contained in the procedural handbook along with device configuration information, make and model number.

Backups

A network plan must consider contingencies. What will you do if something catastrophic occurs? All of us hope network operation will continue to run smoothly, but there will be a time when a critical component of the network breaks down and disables the network.

You can't prevent hardware failures, but you can develop a plan to minimize the network downtime when hardware failures occur. The best approach is to have backups available that can immediately take over for the failed component. Backups (Figure 8–3) typically refer to copies of software and data stored on network servers that should be copied to tape or CD regularly, as described in Chapter 7.

Backups can also refer to having duplicate hardware available on site. It is not uncommon for an organization to have drop cables, connectors, hard disk, modems, network adapter cards, and even ready-to-run servers available to go online at a moment's notice. Any network component that could fail and interrupt business should be replicated on site.

For example, what happens if a database server crashes? If there is a back up server on site you can immediately restore the data from the tape backups and very quickly and efficiently replace the crashed server with a working one. Once the replacement server goes online, technicians can concentrate on troubleshooting and repairing the failed server.

Having a sufficient backup plan is costly and may be beyond the economical reality for smaller organizations. For example, it probably isn't economical for an organization that has one server to have a backup server, although software and data files stored on the server should be backed up on tape.

The network administrator should conduct a risk analysis to determine how much of a backup plan is needed by the organization. A risk analysis is a review of network operations and components to assess the chances of failure and the economical cost of those failures. Risk analysis must consider these factors:

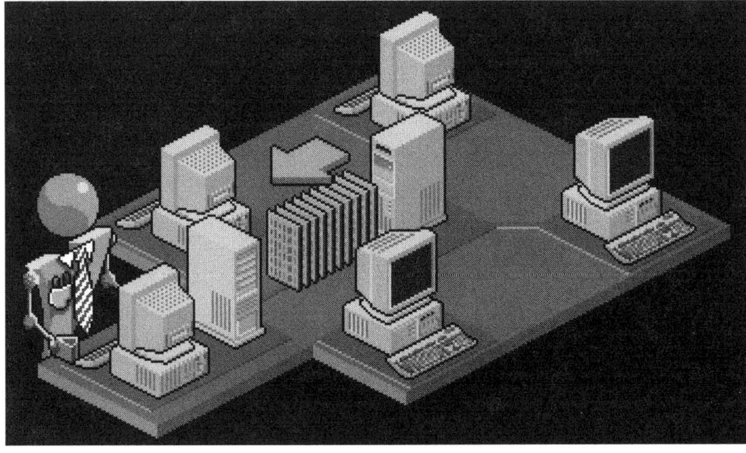

Figure 8–3. *Backup files can be restored whenever files become corrupted, therefore minimizing the network downtime.*

- How much would the organization lose if a particular component (i.e., server) became disabled?
  The network administrator must answer this question in the context of each component and the estimated length of time the network would be unavailable. For example, a five-hour malfunction of the network segment that supports the accounts payable department might have little effect on the organization. In contrast, the organization would be deeply hurt if the telephone sales department's segment were offline for even an hour.
- How soon can the malfunctioned component be replaced?
  An assessment must be made to determine how quickly replacement parts can arrive at the site if they are not stored on the premises. As a general rule, the longer to delivery time, the more the network administrator should consider having a replacement part on hand at all times.
- What is the failure rate of network components?
  No one can predict when a component will break down, but component manufacturers typically have specifications citing their experiences. This is called the component failure rate and is sometimes identified as the number of hours of operation before a failure occurs. The network administrator should consult with the component manufacturer to determine the failure rate of each component. Once known, the network administrator can estimate the time frame when the network component is likely to fail.
- Is it economical for the organization to stock replacement components?
  This isn't an easy question to answer. For example, an organization may invest $20,000 for a backup server that wouldn't be used for years. Yet, the server could be disabled in six months and the backup server becomes a lifesaver. Here's an approach to take when answering this question.

  First, determine how much money the organization would lose per hour if a component in the network fails. For example, practically no economic loss would occurs if a client's drop cable or connectors malfunctions. However, a drop cable connecting a router to a server could have an economical effect on the organization.

  Next, determine how soon a replacement component can be delivered. If your supplier can deliver the component within the hour, then it is unlikely you'll need to have a supply on hand. However, the longer the delivery time, the more money your organization could be losing.

  Finally, determine if the cost of having the replacement component in stock is less than the money the organization would lose. If so, then you should seriously consider stocking those components.

Keep track of replacement components. Make sure they are clearly labeled and store them in an equipment closet in an orderly manner. Make sure boxes containing components are properly labeled and contain all necessary documentation so that a technician can find them in an emergency. Also be sure components are inventoried at least once a month to determine if components should be reordered.

Maintenance and Upgrades

Network planning must include scheduled maintenance of hardware. Maintenance is probably the most overlooked factor involved with keeping a network operational, because the impact of maintaining a network isn't obvious.

For example, removing the buildup of dust inside a router doesn't make the router perform any better than if the dust was allowed to accumulate. However, dust can increase the operating temperature of the router by reducing the cooling area of circuits inside the route. Eventually, the increased heat will take its toll on the router.

A good maintenance schedule will include:

- Making sure all network cable connects are tight. A loose cable can cause intermittent network outage for a client—and a headache when troubleshooting the network.
- Removing dust from the inside of all electronic network components. This includes network components and clients.
- Comparing the in-service time of components with the failure rate of the component. The in-service time is the length of time a component has been connected to the network. You can expect a problem with the component to occur if the in-service time is close to the fail rate.
- Examining the network response time for various network segments. If response time is slowly becoming unacceptable, then plan to reorganize the segment.
- Testing all components to make sure they work correctly. Some network components such as printers or fax-modems may be underutilized by clients and may not be operational. For example, a network may have ten fax-modems, but only four of them are used frequently.

The network administrator should create a network maintenance log that contains the maintenance schedule of network devices, maintenance procedures, and information on when those procedures were performed and who performed them.

You can consider the maintenance log like a patient's hospital chart. The log should detail the status of the component during the maintenance check. This can be compared to previous status reports to determine if a trend is occurring, such as a steady decrease in network response time. The trend frequently points to future troubles that can be avoided before the problem affects network operations.

Maintenance procedures are typically supplied by the component manufacturer and are usually found with the owner's documentation that is supplied with the equipment. Follow these procedures carefully. Not only do they support any warrantee claims you might make to the manufacturer, but they also prevent the device from failing prematurely.

In addition to developing a good maintenance plan, the network administrator should make sure all network devices are upgraded, as required by the equipment or software manufacturer. An upgrade is the replacement of part of the component (Figure 8–4).

Some organizations are skeptical about manufacturer-recommended upgrades, since many of these require the company to pay for the upgrade. Is an upgrade a ploy by manufacturers to make more money or will the upgrade provide more service?

This isn't an easy question to answer. However, upgrades are commonly issued to fix bugs in the product. It is always wise to discuss the difference between the upgrade and your current product with the product's manufacturer before installing the upgrade. This provides a rational for upgrading your network.

A word of caution. An upgrade can cause problems with the network operation. It is mandatory that you backup components before you perform

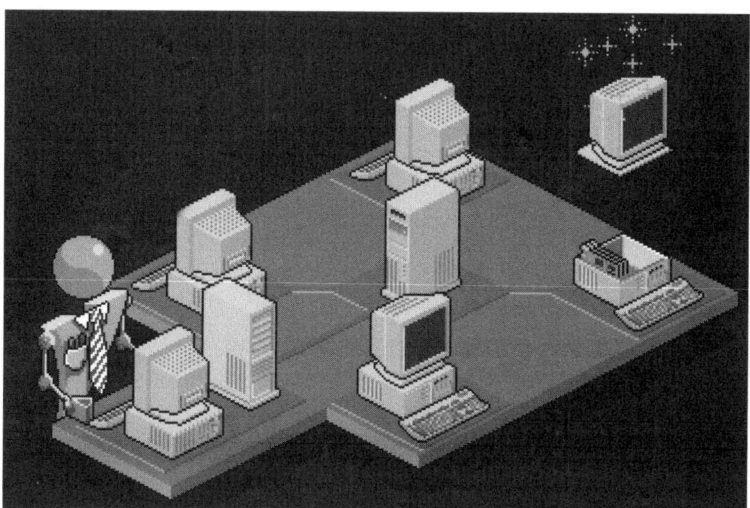

Figure 8–4. *The network administrator must make sure upgrades to network hardware and software are made in a timely fashion.*

the upgrade. All upgrades should be installed and tested on a Friday night. This gives you the weekend to fix any collateral problems that might arise from installing the upgrade.

MCSE 8.2 Monitoring Network Operations

A good network-operating plan needs to be augmented by consistent monitoring of information throughout the network. Monitoring network operations gives the network administrator an insight into how well the network design meets the needs of the organization.

The need for network services changes slowly as network usage grows. As you learned throughout this book, these gradual changes tend to exceed the original design, which can cause degradation of performance.

Monitoring the network regularly enables the network administrator to see clues of forthcoming difficulties so that preemptive action can be taken before users notice a drop in network services.

Many network operating systems provide monitoring software that adheres to the ISO's five network management categories. These are: accounting management; fault management; performance management; security management; and configuration management.

Accounting management monitoring is a utility that tracks the usage of network facilities. For example, the network operating system makes note each time a user logs into the network and uses a network resource.

Fault management monitoring tracks the workings of network components. The monitor then detects components that failed to work and reports problems to the network administrator.

Performance management monitoring tracks the flow of data throughout the network. Typically, the performance management monitor receives and counts all the data packets that flow through the network.

Security management monitoring involves making sure users have proper access to network resources. Configuration management monitoring is used to set the parameters of the network operating system and of network components.

Network performance is the ability of the network to transmit data at a reliable and consistent speed. As demand for network resources increase, traffic across the network also increases and the response time of the network gradually decreases.

It is the job of the network administrator to identify and resolve network performance problems. The network administrator's initial step is to create a baseline measurement of performance when then network is running smoothly. This defines the normal network performance called a **base-**

line. Baseline measurements should be taken using tools like Windows NT Performance Monitor after a network becomes fully operational.

On a regular schedule such as the first Friday of every month from 10 a.m. to 2 p.m., the network administrator should take the same measurements of the network and compare the results to the baseline measurements. Over time, this comparison shows a trend in the network performance.

If the trend indicates degradation in network performance, then the network administrator must identify the cause of the problem, which is called a **bottleneck**. Any network component can be a bottleneck if it impedes the flow of data across the network.

A bottleneck does not necessarily mean a network component has malfunctioned. It could simple mean network traffic patterns have changed or network upgrades have increased transmission speed beyond the capability of the device that is causing the bottleneck.

Network performance measurements compared with a baseline indicate if a network performance problem exists. The next question the network administrator must answer is which component is causing the bottleneck.

Here are the more common sources of network bottlenecks:

CPU speed of a server
Available memory of a server
Network interface cards in a server
A server's disk controller cards.
Routers
Gateways

Tracking Down Bottleneck

It is common that complaint about network performance will stem from users who are connected to the same network segment. Therefore, it is important for the network administrator to gather as much information from persons who complains as possible. For example, you'll need to know the person's location, telephone number, computer name, and a detailed description of why the person believes there is a network problem. Ask detailed question such as "has this ever happened before? "What time did you first notice it?" and "have you moved your computer recently?" Reviewing the locations of all the complaints will tell you which network segment is experiencing a performance problem.

Next, you'll need to review the network maintenance log to determine if any network component has been recently changed. If so, then that component is your first suspect. If not, then you must identify all the network components that are connected to the segment.

Measure network traffic in the segment using a protocol analyzer. This provides you with a real-time analysis of data flow and a snapshot of network components on the segment. You can compare the results of this analysis with baseline measurements to isolate the bottleneck.

If network components seem unlikely suspects based on the results of the protocol analyzer test, then suspect the cabling. Check cables to the NIC card and to the jack first. You can identify cable problems by using A Time-Domain Reflectometer (TDR) or a network analyzer. Compare the results of the cable test with the baseline measurements to determine if the cabling is at fault. If it is, then the cabling needs to be replaced.

Network components and the cabling may not be the source of the problem. In that case, determine if a new application is running on a client or server. A new application could be transmitting an unusual amount of data traffic such as stock ticker application that updates many clients on a segment several times a minute.

Also, don't overlook the possibility that a few users are playing games over the network. A case in point occurred in a major international Wall Street firm. Traders were playing air combat against the sales staff who was located in another building. The entire trading floor network slowed to a snails pace.

If the problem is caused by an application, you can ask users to curtail use of the application, ask the software developer to modify the application, or plan to increase the size of the network to accommodate the application.

However, if software isn't causing the problem, then it might be time to redesign the network. The organization has likely outgrown the original network design as the last resort.

Techniques for Reading a Monitor

Network monitors collect information and count certain activities on the network and relate them to the time the activity occurred. This information can then be displayed in various ways to help the network administrator analyze network operations.

For example, a performance monitor can display the number of data packets traveling across the network per hour as a graph. This enables the network administrator to determine the maximum volume of traffic over the network.

Once a network is installed and has stabilized, the network administrator should run all the monitors to determine a baseline for the network. A baseline consists of statistics that represents acceptable performance and must be stored for future reference (Figure 8–5). Many network-monitoring utilities provide a facility to save network statistics.

Each time the network is measured, the network administrator should compare the results of monitoring to the baseline. This helps to determine if current network activities conform to acceptable levels.

An acceptable level is subjective within an acceptable tolerance range. For example, many users won't complain if there is a couple of seconds of delay in the network response. However, a volume of complaints can be expected if there is a ten second response time.

The network administrator should track the date and time of all user complaints and associate them with network statistics at that moment. This provides the network administrator with an unacceptable level.

Network monitors can be used to forecast trouble before it arises so long as the network administrator establishes a baseline and an unacceptable line. As statistics move closer to the unacceptable line, the network administrator can anticipate trouble and take measures to avoid the problem and reduce the progression toward the unacceptable line.

Windows NT Server and Monitors

Windows NT Server contains a utility called the **Performance Monitor** that is ideal for tracking network operations. The Performance Monitor offers two methods of counting network events; realtime and recorded time. If the events

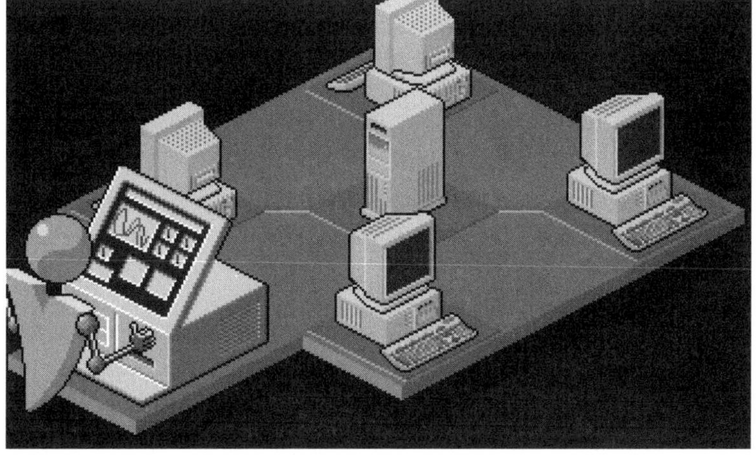

Figure 8–5. *Develop a baseline of key network parameters once the network is stabilized.*

are recorded and counted as they occur, it's called **realtime**. If the events are logged to a file and then analized at a later date, it's called **recorded time**.

From the data captured by the Performance Monitor, the Network Administrator will be able to spot bottlenecks in the network and determine the impact that modifications have on network operations.

Each event, called a **counter**, can be displayed on the screen, saved to a log, or printed in a report. Also, the network administrator can set up a threshold value for each counter. If the value of the counter falls above or below the thresholds then the Performance Monitor sounds an alarm that alerts the network administrator to the problem.

Another useful monitor you'll find with the Windows NT Server is the Network Monitor, which tracks data packets flowing over the network. The Network Monitor copies data packets into a log. Information in the log can be filtered by network address, data packet type, or by any pattern of characters.

MCSE 8.3 Troubleshooting Network Problems

The most important role of a network administrator is to be able to quickly respond to disruptions in network operations. When a network malfunction occurs, the network administrator has two objectives; to locate the trouble and correct the problem.

Typically, a malfunctioning component can be corrected quickly if the network administrator implemented a good network plan, as is discussed earlier in this chapter.

However, locating the troubled component is an ardent task, since there could be hundreds of network connects in a large network, thousands of feet of cable, and many routers, repeaters, and other line devices. Anyone of them could be the culprit and it is the job of the network administrator to track down the problem within the shortest time frame.

In this section, we'll explore some of the proven techniques that are used to troubleshoot a network. Following these methods will reduce troubleshooting to a minimum.

Organize for Fast Reaction to Complaints

The network operations support team must establish a help telephone number that can be called when a user experiences network trouble. The help line needs to be supported by a technician whenever people are working. This typically includes extended business hours and weekends.

Procedures should be created by the network administrator to guide technicians through the process of addressing the user's network problems.

Procedures provide the most efficient way to approach a network problem. Here's what needs to be included in these procedures:

- Identify the caller by login ID and client location. This information helps to pinpoint the network address that is experiencing a problem.
- Identify the problem. The technician needs to be able to interpret the user's complaint into technical terms.
- Replicate the problem if possible. The technician should try to connect to the remote client using software such as Timbuktu, which lets the technician take over a client without having to visit the client's site.
- Determine the severity of the problem. The technician needs to determine how the network malfunction affects the business by questioning the caller.
- Set the priority of the call. Compare the severity of the problems with other outstanding network problems. The most severe problem must be addressed before all others. This is called triage.

Research the Problem

A complaint call reveals the experience encountered by the user. This alone is not sufficient to address the user's network problem. Instead, information gathered from the call provides the network support technician a starting point from which to further explore the situation.

The caller typically makes a passionate plea for help that sometimes is tainted with accusations and condemnation of technicians that run network operations. Somewhere in the midst of the call, the caller gives the network support technician clues, some of which are pertinent to the problem and others that are not related.

It is the job of the network support technician to sort through the information to identify clues that will be helpful in tracking down and fixing the problem. Once the information is elicited from the caller, the network support technician must systematically research the information. Here are a few factors that research should address:

- Has the caller complained about a network problem recently?
  Each call should be recorded in a log, where the nature of the problem is listed along with details of the steps used to attempt to fix the problem. Both successful and unsuccessful steps should be entered into the log. If the caller experienced previous problems, then there is a high probability that the problem wasn't fixed and could be an intermittent problem or the remedy could have caused another problem. An intermittent problem is one that occurs irregularly and is difficult to repli-

cate. The research provided can narrow the scope of the technician's tests and possible solutions.

- Have other callers complained about the same network problem recently?
  A network malfunction typically affects more than one user. The call log can be searched to identify recent callers that have recorded similar problems. This information can help to narrow the network fault to a common device, such as a router. A router, as discussed previously in the book, is the network device that directly connects clients on different networks. Drop lines from clients are connected to a hub, which is connected to another router on the network.
- What network events occurred around the time the user experienced the problem?
  A change in the network or a specific sequence of events could be the cause of a network problem. For example, a new repeater that has been installed on the network or if a router's router table was reconfigured are changes that may or may not have influenced network failure. Likewise, network activities that occur in a certain sequence could cause an intermittent network problem. The network support technician must examine call logs, maintenance records, and, in the case of an intermittent problem, network monitors to determine network changes and patterns. The objective is to collect information. The network support technician who must diagnose and fix the problem will determine whether or not the information has a bearing on the problem.
- Has any network user reported a similar problem in the past?
  Rarely is a network problem unique. Many problems have occurred previously—although not necessarily recently—such as a malfunctioning router or a loose cable connection. Caller, repair, and maintenance records should be reviewed to identify previous occurrence and to learn steps used to solve the problem.

Isolate the Problem

After a complaint is received and researched by a network support technician, the source of the problem must be identified. This is called isolating the problem. Network complaints arise from four general areas of network operations: software, hardware, user-training, or network design.

Software and hardware problems can be located at either the client or the network level. For example, the client requires client-side network software configured to use the proper protocols; a valid network ID and password; a network interface card; and a proper type of cable connection to the router. The network contains the network operating system; routers; repeaters, bridges, fax/modems, printers, servers, related cabling, and other network devices.

Analyzing the information that is known about the problem can help isolate a network problem. Here is a procedure (Figure 8–6) that can help to track down the troubled network component.

- Is the problem located on the client or the network?
  When more than one caller complains about the same problem, the trouble is likely located on the network side rather than the client. An exception to this rule is if new client-side software was recently installed, then the network support technician should suspect a configuration problem with the software installation as the culprit. However, if there is only one reported incident, then the client side is a good place to begin the investigation.
- If the client side is suspected, is the client's address active on the network?
  Network operating systems provide a utility to test if a network address is active. This is called *pinging* the address. If the address is not active, then the network support technician should suspect problems with the client's network interface card, the drop cable connection, the router port to which the client is connected, and possibly the router table. If the address is active, then problems with network software on the client side should be suspected.
- If the network side is suspected, is there commonality among clients who report problems?

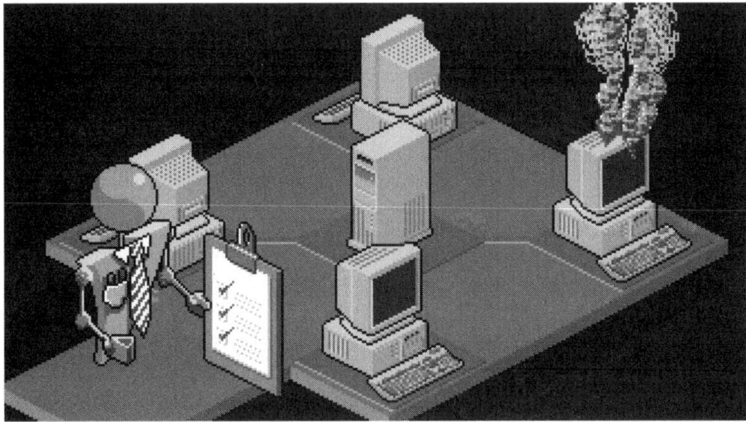

Figure 8–6. *Always follow a procedure for troubleshooting a network problem.*

Typically, there is something in common with users that complain about the same problem at the same time. For example, all of them might be on the same network segment serviced by the same router or other network device. Likewise, they might use the same network printer and be unable to print documents. Refer to the network layout to trace clients to common devices, then examine shared devices, beginning with the first device common to clients.

- If the client side appears to be operating properly, is the user properly trained?
  The network support technician needs to visit the user or remotely connect to the user's computer and ask the user to repeat the steps that lead up to the problem. It will become apparent if the user makes an error. For example, a network operating system may require a user to enter the proper case for a password. The user may have inadvertently activated the cap lock on their keyboard, then complained that they can't log onto the network.
- If the network side appears to be operating properly, is the design of the network causing the problem?
  An organization can easily grow beyond the initial design of the network. This growth can lead to all kinds of problems. For example, users would complain about poor network response time or of intermittent problems on the network.

Troubleshooting Network Devices

Once the network support technician has isolated the problem to one or more network devices, each device must be examined and tested to determine if it is at fault. Manufacturers of many network devices provide guides for troubleshooting their devices. They list step by step procedures which should be followed, starting with the most common problems down to the less common. These include routers, bridges, repeaters, and gateways.

As a general rule, try the simplest solution first to fix the problem. Let's assume one client cannot communicate with the network and you've pinged the address to find the address is not active. Examine the cable connection before replacing the network adapter card or conducting more sophisticated tests on the network.

Network support technicians should use the most efficient technique for locating a malfunctioning network device. Sometimes this involves swapping a device known to work with one that is suspected of causing the problem. This technique is at times faster than using sophisticated test equipment to locate the problem.

However, network components such as the backbone cable cannot be easily replaced and therefore test equipment is required to determine if the component is working properly. There are a number of common test equipments used to track down network problems. These include Time-Domain Reflectometers (TDRs); oscilloscopes; a digital voltmeter (DVM); protocol analyzers; and a cable tester.

TDR (Figure 8–7) is a tool used to test cables. It does this by sending a sonar signal across a network cable, then analyzes the strength of the returned signal to determine the condition of the cable.

Typically, a TDR is used with an oscilloscope to display the voltage of the pulse. The oscilloscope shows voltage over time in a graphical form on the oscilloscope screen. This enables the network support technician to see the decay of the signal as the signal is reflected back to the TDR. The TDR and the oscilloscope are mainly used during the installation of network cables, although they can be a necessary tool when identifing a problem with an existing cable.

A **DVM** is another tool commonly used by a network support technician to determine the flow of current through a cable and other network devices. The DVM measures both the voltage of the signal and the resistance of a device. Think of voltage as the force of the signal over the cable and resistance as the force pushing against the signal by the cable.

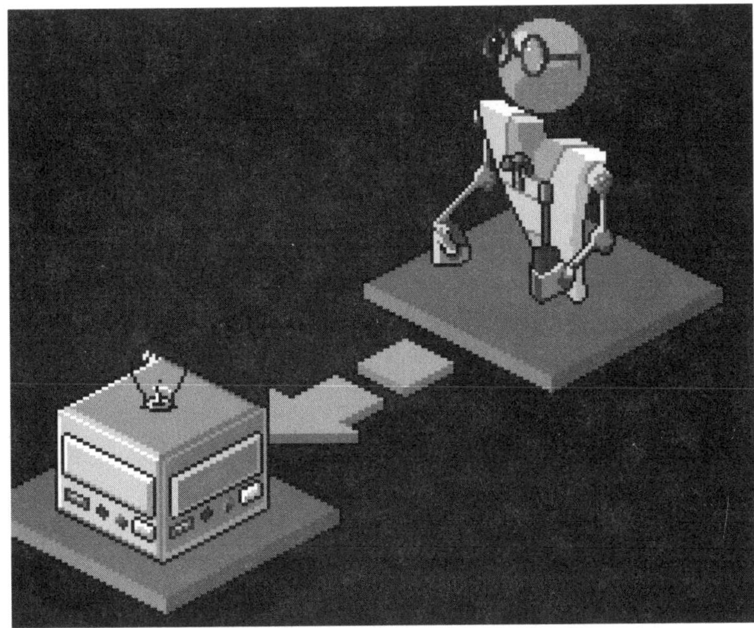

Figure 8–7. *A TDR helps to identify a bad cable using a sonar signal.*

Although a DVM is used primarily to determine if a signal can flow across a cable, it can also be used to search for malfunctions within a network device, such as a router or network interface card. However, it is rarely used in this manner.

The TDR, the oscilloscope, and the DVM are tools used to measure hardware components of the network, but these devices do not give the network support technician any insight into the local components such as data packets.

A **protocol analyzer** and an **advanced cable tester** are used to measure network traffic. This includes counting data packets that are transmitted, counting the number of collisions that occur, counting the number of resent data packets, and measuring the traffic flow across various segments of the network.

Network traffic can radically increase when a network interface card, hub or other network device malfunctions. These devices can saturate the network with broadcast packets called a broadcast storm.

Broadcast storms impede the flow of normal network traffic. When this occurs, network administrators typically receive complaints of poor network performance from users. The protocol analyzer is used to track down the malfunctioning component, which is then replaced.

However, the network administrator can reduce the impact of a broadcast storm by employing routable network protocols and routers on the network. Routers automatically drop broadcast packets.

Therefore, the malfunctioning network device won't be able to broadcast erroneous packets to network segments linked by a router.

■ Summary

The network administrator must develop a good network operating plan to reduce the opportunity for mistakes, mistakes that could disrupt network operations. The plan must consider network security, standardizing procedures, good documentation of those procedures and the network topology, backups of network resources and their locations, and regular maintenance and upgrading of network components.

Network disruptions typically occur when someone that has access permission to the network does something inadvertently to halt network operations. This includes the network support technicians, whose mistakes can be irrecoverable.

The best way to reduce these errors is to establish and strictly enforce access restrictions. Access restrictions limit network resources a person can share and how the person uses those resources.

While network software provides the utilities to limit access to network resources, it is up to the network administrator to implement the access restrictions defined in the network plan.

Granting access to a network resource begins by identifying the owner of the network resource, then letting the owner decide which users can have access to the resource. The owner is probably the best person to weigh the business needs against the need for protection. When someone requests access to a network resource, permission must be obtained from the owner of the network resource before access is granted.

The network administrator should develop a handbook that contains setup and maintenance procedures for every network component. Each procedure should be a step-by-step guide that walks a technician through a process. Most of these procedures can be copied from the manufacturer's documentation.

The handbook should contain the physical location of network components, configurations, floor plans that identify departments, and desk and desk numbers used to identify a user when a trouble call is received.

The handbook should also contain the names and telephone numbers of secondary support staff. These are the people, sometimes manufacturer's reps, who can help the technician resolve problems that are not contained in procedures.

You can't prevent hardware failures, but you can develop a plan to minimize the network downtime when hardware failures occur. And the best approach is to have backups available that can immediately take over for the failed component.

Backups refer to duplicate software and hardware available on site. It is not at all uncommon for an organization to have drop cables, connectors, hard disks, modems, network adapter cards, and even a configured server available to go online at a moment's notice.

A backup plan is costly and may be beyond the economical reality of smaller organizations. The network administrator should conduct a risk analysis to determine how much of a backup plan is needed by the organization. A risk analysis is a review of network operations and components to assess the chances of failure and the economical cost of those failures. Risk analysis must consider these factors:

- How much would the organization lose if a particular component (i.e., a server) became disabled?
- How soon can the malfunctioning component be replaced?
- What is the failure rate of network components?
- Is it economical for the organization to stock replacement components?

Network planning must include scheduled maintenance of hardware. This will extend the mean time between failures of network components. The maintenance schedule of network devices, maintenance procedures, and information when those procedures were performed and who performed them should be kept in a maintenance log.

Network operations must be consistently monitored to give the network administrator an insight into how well the network design meets the needs of the organization. The network administrator should look for clues of forthcoming difficulties so that preemptive action can be taken before users notice a drop in network services.

Network monitors collect and count certain activities on the network and relate them to the time the activity occurred. The information can then be displayed in various ways to help the network administrator analyze network operations.

Once a network is installed and has stabilized, the network administrator should run all the monitors to determine a baseline for the network. A baseline consists of statistics that represent acceptable performance and must be stored for future reference. Network performance is compared to the baseline to determine if the network is operating efficiently. If not, then adjustments can be made to the network to bring network operations closer to the baseline.

Windows NT Server contains a utility called the Performance Monitor that is ideal for tracking network events. The Performance Monitor tracks network performance in real and recorded time.

Each event is called a counter and can be displayed on the screen, saved to a log, or printed in a report. Also, the network administrator can set up a threshold value for each counter. If the value of the counter falls above or below the threshold values, then the Performance Monitor should sound an alarm that alerts the network administrator to the problem.

Another useful monitor you'll find with the Windows NT Server is the Network Monitor, which tracks data packets flowing over the network. The Network Monitor copies data packets into a log. Information in the log can be filtered by network address, data packet type, or by any pattern of characters.

▲ Chapter Review Questions

▲ Fill in the Blanks

1. ____________________________ *limit network resources a person can share and how a person uses those resources*

2. *Network downtime caused by a failure of a network device can be minimized by using a ________________________.*

3. *__________ is a review of network operations and components to assess the chances of failure and the economical cost of those failures.*

4. *_______________ is the number hours of operation before a device is expected to fail.*

5. *_________________ reduces the likelihood that a network device will break down.*

▲ True/False

1. *(T/F) Network monitors collect and count certain activities on the network and relate them to the time the activity occurred.*

2. *(T/F) From the data captured by the Performance Monitor, the Network Administrator is able to find missing users on the network.*

3. *(T/F) Delivery time of replacement network components should not be considered as part of the network plan.*

4. *(T/F) TDR is a tool used to track down a bad cable by sending a sonar signal across a network cable.*

5. *(T/F) A protocol analyzer and an advanced cable tester are used to measure cable length.*

6. *(T/F) The network administrator can reduce the impact of a broadcast storm by employing routable network protocols and routers on the network.*

7. *(T/F) Combining the current performance level with the baseline performance level will indicate if there is a performance problem.*

8. *(T/F) A performance monitor is used to measure trends in a network.*

9. *(T/F) A cable malfunction to a network card can be identified by using the Time-Domain Reflectometer (TDR)*

▲ Multiple Choice

1. *What is the term used to identify the source of a malfunction on the network?*

A. Frame Analysis

B. Isolating

C. The spy inspector

D. Sonar the network
E. Backing up the system

2. *An event tracked by the performance monitor is called?*
A. Counter
B. Internal check
C. Event modulation
D. Access right
E. Access restriction

3. *What is the term used to describe measurement of the acceptable level of network performance?*
A. Baseline
B. The performance monitor
C. The oscilloscope
D. The specification ratio
E. The 5.3 ISS protocol

4. *What term is used to describe the settings of network devices?*
A. Configuration
B. Sync set
C. RTT adjustments
D. Baseline setting
E. Tweaking the network

5. *What protects the network from users or network staff from making inadvertent mistakes that could cause a network disruption?*
A. Network security plan
B. Background checks of employees
C. Testing potential employees before they are hired
D. System tracking
E. The network controller

6. *The cause of a network problem is called a* _______.
A. bad zone
B. network failure
C. STV error

D. STP error
E. bottleneck

▲ Open Ended

1. How would you use a network monitor to determine if there is a degradation in network performance?
2. What procedures would you use to respond to a complaint from a network user?
3. Describe the ISO's five network management categories?
4. How would you determine if a network malfunction is critical to the organization's operation?
5. How would you go about creating a handbook for network support technicians?

APPENDIX A

Hands-On Tasks

Administrative Issues

Facts You Should Know About User Accounts

- A user account consists of all the information that identifies the user to the network operating system.
- The network administrator can set up more than one account for a user, as long as there is a different user name for each account.
- The network administrator should maintain two accounts: one as an ordinary user and the other as the network administrator.
- The network administrator account should be used only when the network administrator's ordinary user account does not have rights to perform the necessary task, such as creating a new user or new group.
- New user accounts are created using the User Manager, which can be started from the Start button or from the command button. MUSRMGR starts the User Manager for NT Workstation and USRMGR for NT Server.

- Two accounts are automatically created when NT is installed. These are the network administrator's account and a guest account. Both are permanent accounts and cannot be deleted.
- The network administrator account has complete network authority.
- A guest account gives temporary access to the network to a user. The guest can change settings, but the settings are not saved.
- A guest account is disabled when NT is installed. The network administrator must enable the account explicitly before it can be used to log on to the network.
- A new account can be explicitly created, although the preferred approach is to create then copy a model account.
- A new account only requires a user name. A password is not required. However, if a password is entered, then the network administrator must also enter the same password into the Confirm Password field.
- Every user account has a home folder in \USER\DEFAULT on the local drive that is the default location used to save files. This is also the folder used when the user selects the command prompt.

Creating a New User Account

Click Start (Figure A–1)
Click Programs
Click Administrative Tools
Click User Manager for Domains
Select User from the menu bar
Select New User from the submenu to display the New User dialog box (Figure A–2)
Enter user information into the New User dialog box (Figure A–2)
Click Add
Highlight the user name in the User Account screen
Select User from the menu bar (you can also just double click on the user you want to edit)
Select Properties from the submenu to display the user properties box which looks like the New user dialog box
Click the Profile button to create the user's profile to display the User Environment Properties dialog box (Figure A–3)
Click OK

Disabling a User Account

Click Start
Click Programs

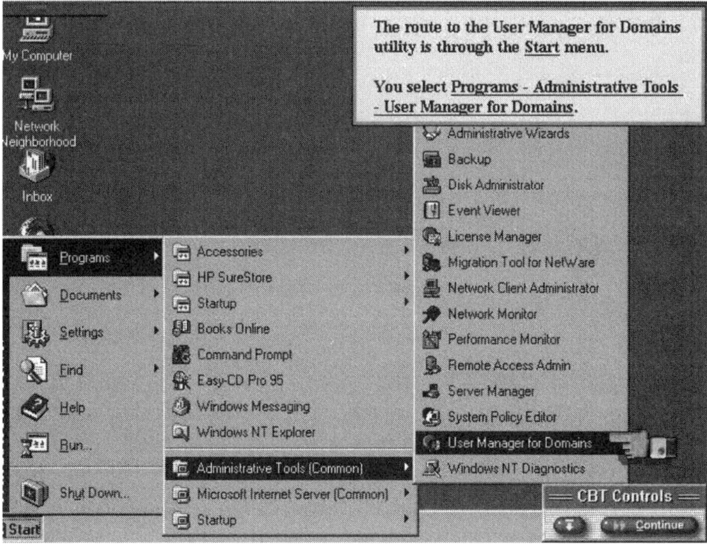

Figure A–1. *Open the User Manager for Domains screen.*

Click Administrative Tools
Click User Manager for Domains
Highlight the user account name in the User Account screen
Select User from the menu bar

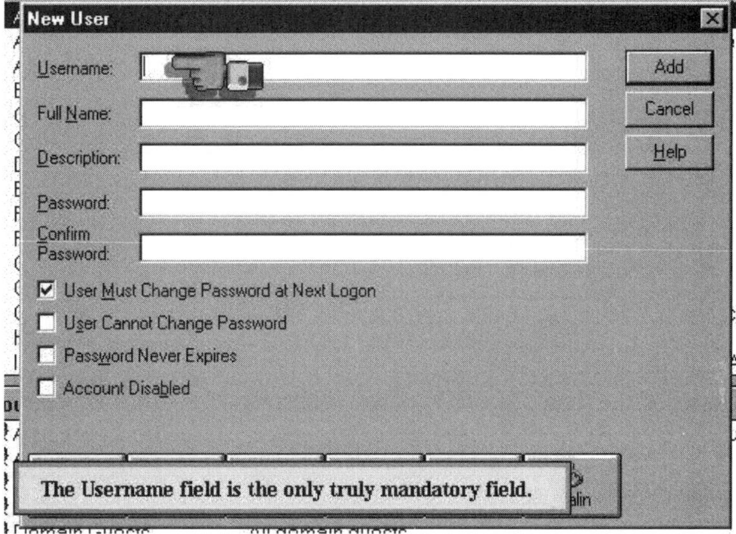

Figure A–2. *Enter information about the user into the New User dialog box.*

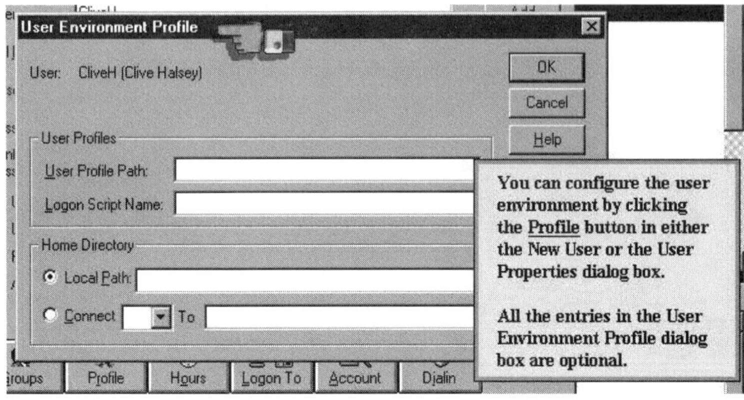

Figure A–3. *Enter the user profile properties in the User Environment Properties dialog box.*

Select Properties from the submenu to display the User Properties dialog box
Click the Account Disabled check box (Figure A–4)
Click OK

Figure A–4. *Click the Account Disabled checkbox to disable an account.*

Deleting an Account

Click Start
Click Programs
Click Administrative Tools
Click User Manager for Domains
Highlight the user account name in the User Account screen
Select User from the menu bar
Select Delete from the submenu (Figure A–5)
Click OK in response to the warning message to remind you that the account access is forever deleted
Click Yes to confirm that you want to delete the account

Copying an Account

Click Start
Click Programs
Click Administrative Tools
Click User Manager for Domains
Highlight the user account name in the User Account screen
Select User from the menu bar
Select Copy from the submenu
Enter user information into the Copy dialog box (Figure A–6)
Click Add to create the new account

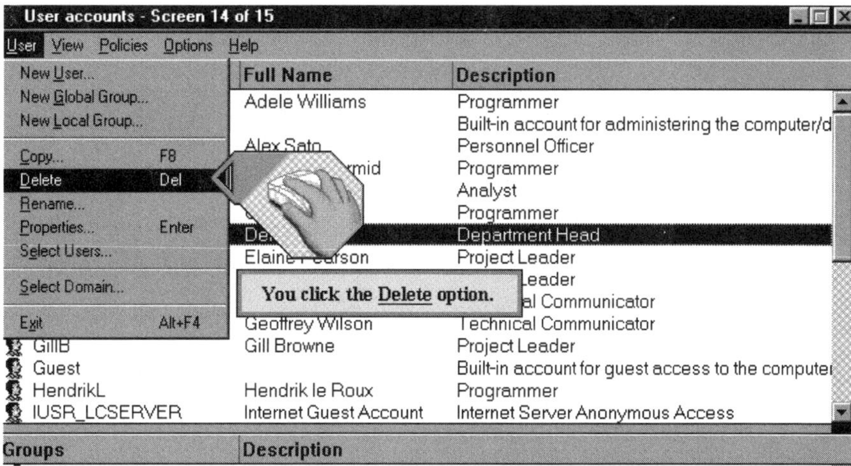

Figure A–5. *After highlighting the account you want to delete, then select delete from the User submenu.*

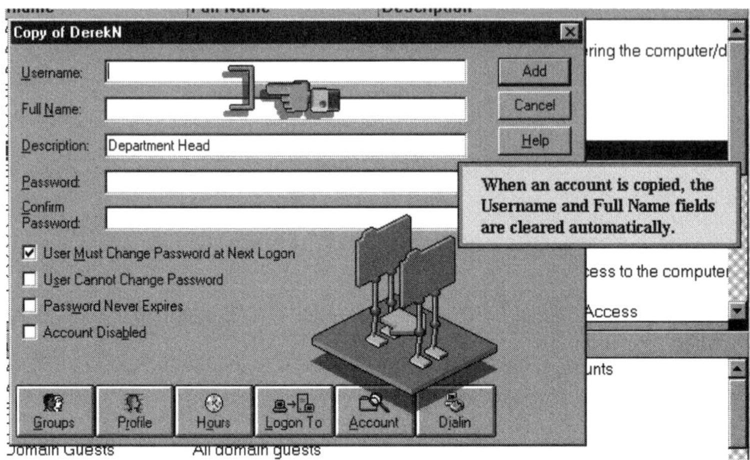

Figure A–6. *The user name fields are automatically erased in the copy of the account.*

Renaming an Account

Click Start
Click Programs
Click Administrative Tools
Click User Manager for Domains
Highlight the user account name in the User Account screen
Select User from the menu bar
Select Rename from the submenu
Enter new name for the user is the Rename dialog box (Figure A–7)
Click OK

Facts You Should Know About Group Accounts

- A group account is used to refer to or manage multiple user accounts.
- Permissions for network resources are typically assigned to a group account instead of individual user accounts.
- User accounts assigned to a group account inherit all the permissions granted to the group account.
- A user account can be a member of multiple group accounts.
- There is no limit to the number of group accounts that can be created in NT.
- There are two kinds of groups: local and global.
- A local group can only use the workstation where they are created.

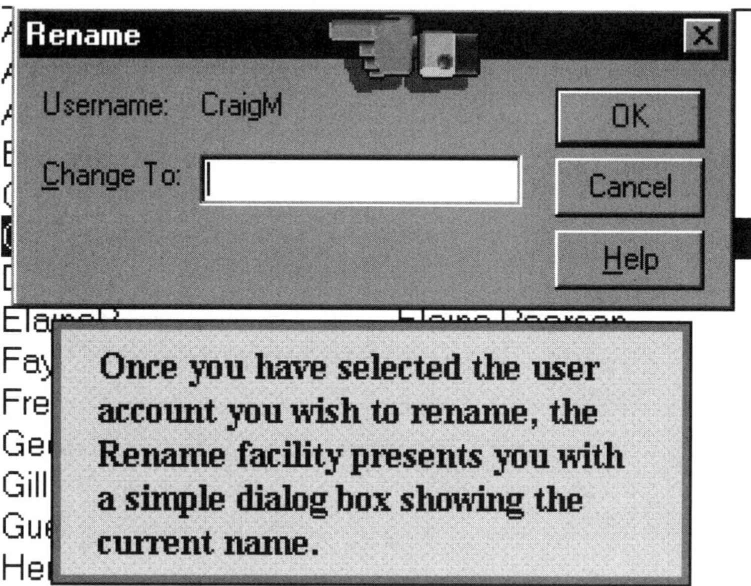

Figure A–7. *Enter the new name of the account in the Rename dialog box.*

- A local group can contain a global group from the same domain.
- A global group can contain local user accounts, but not local groups, global groups, and user accounts from other domains.
- Default user accounts are created when NT is installed. These include: Power User Group, Backup Operators Group, User Group, Domain User Group, Administrators Group, and Replicator Group.
- A group can be created by copying an existing group or by explicitly creating the group.
- When a group is copied, the new group receives the description and membership from the copied group. All permissions, rights, and built-in abilities must be explicitly added to the new group.

Creating a New Group

Click Start
Click Programs
Click Administrative Tools
Click User Manager for Domains Select User from the menu bar
Select New Local Group from the submenu
Enter information about the new group in the New Local Group dialog box (Figure A–8)

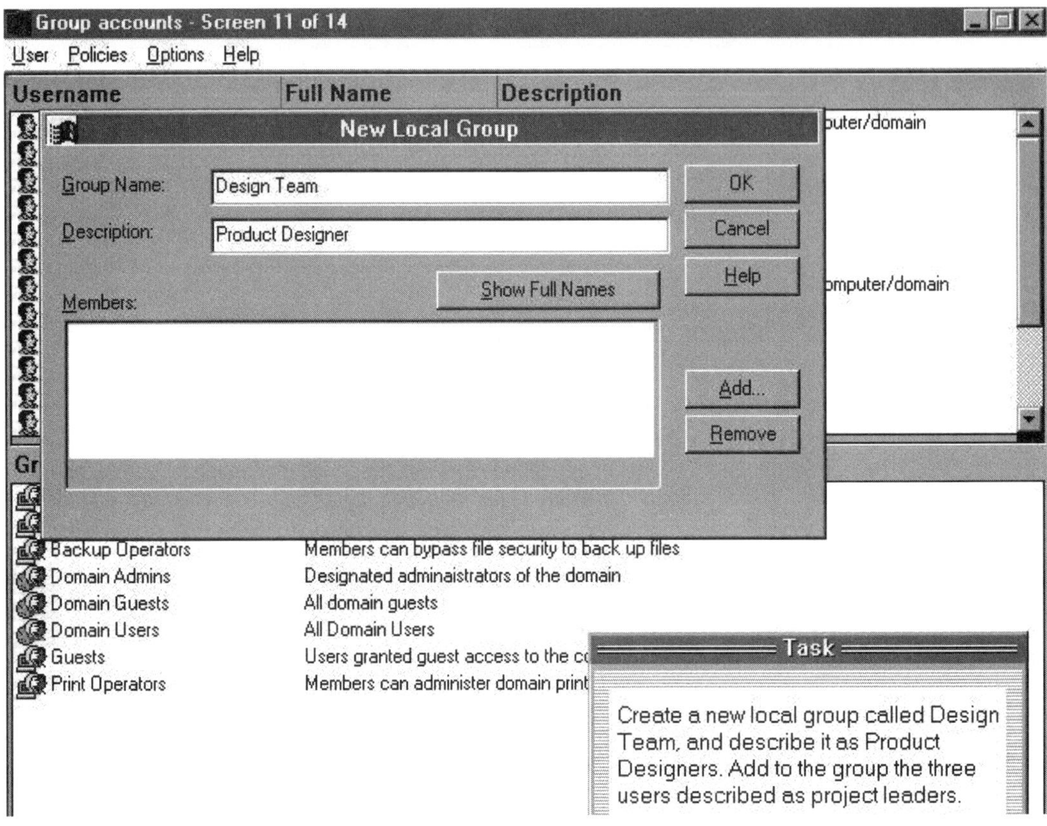

Figure A–8. *Enter the group information in the New Local Group dialog box.*

Click Add
Highlight the users to be added to the group (Figure A–9); remember to hold down Ctrl to select more than one user from the user list
Click Add
Click OK to close the Add User and Group dialog box
Click OK to close the New Local Group dialog box

Delete a Group

Click Start
Click Programs
Click Administrative Tools
Click User Manager for Domains
Highlight the name of the group you want to delete (Figure A–10)
Select User from the menu

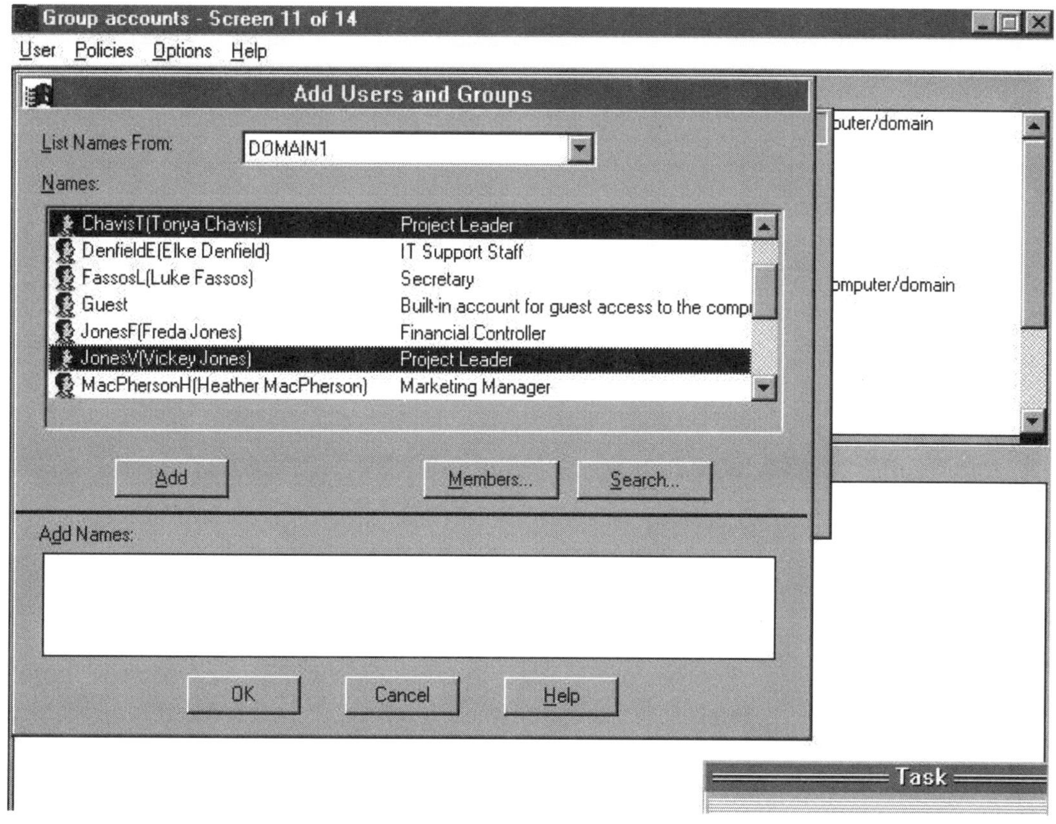

Figure A–9. *Highlight users that you want to join the new group.*

Select Delete from the submenu
Click OK when the warning message appears; this warning message reminds you that the group is forever deleted
Click Yes to confirm that you want to delete the group

Remove a User from a Group

Click Start
Click Programs
Click Administrative Tools
Click User Manager for Domains
Highlight the name of the group you want to use
Press Enter to display the Local Group Properties dialog box notice that the Remove button is now selectable.
Highlight the user you want to remove (Figure A–11)
Click Remove

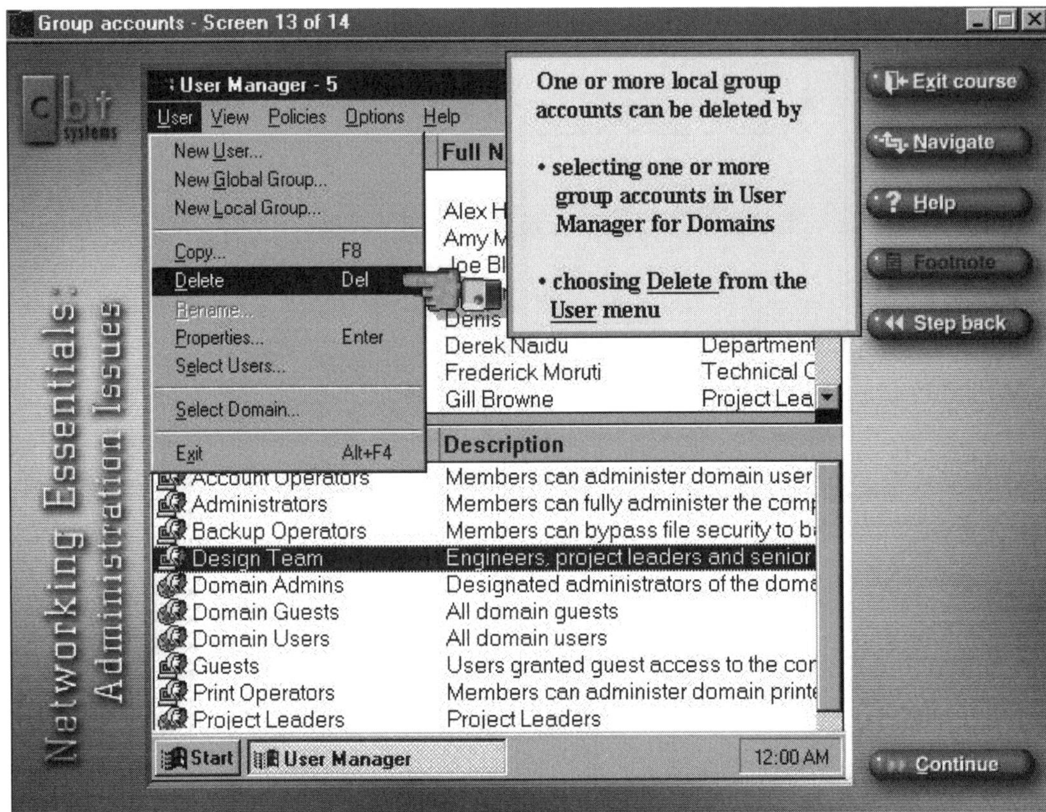

Figure A–10. *Highlight the group you want to delete, then select delete.*

Facts You Should Know About Performance Optimization

- Poor performance occurs when a device slows down the flow of the network. This is referred to as a bottleneck.
- Devices that can cause bottlenecks include the CPU, memory, network cards, disk controllers, network media (cables), and data bus.
- The Performance Monitor is used to track the CPU, hard disks, memory, network utilization, and the whole network both in real time and recorded time. In addition, the Performance Monitor can start another program or alert the network administrator when a performance problem occurs.
- Clients can run a program called an agent, which captures network traffic received by the client and stores the data in a Management In-

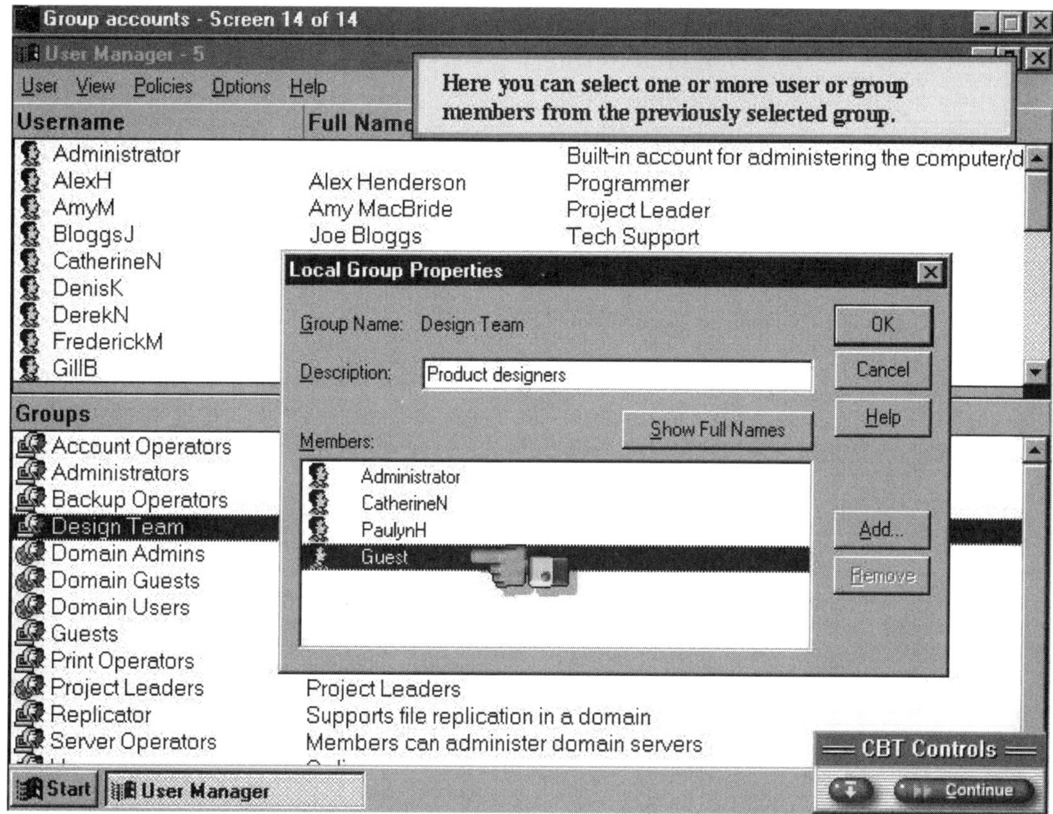

Figure A–11. *Highlight the user you want to remove, then click OK.*

formation Base (MIB). This data is collected by the Performance Monitor for analysis.

- The Microsoft Systems Management Service (SMS) helps to manage the network by inventorying network hardware and software, distributing and installing software, and troubleshooting network hardware and software programs.
- Performance Optimization is designed to maximize network performance of the processor power, physical RAM, and hard-disk space by balancing the use of network resources by setting priorities for resources.
- First, identify bottlenecks using the Performance Monitor. Every physical component on the network can be a bottleneck.

- If memory is a bottleneck, then modify virtual memory.
- Virtual memory is a method of extending RAM by using a hard disk.
- When a request for memory exceeds RAM, data is moved from RAM to the virtual memory paging file on the disk. This process is called paging or paged memory.
- Paged memory is divided into Page Frames, each of which holds various pages of code or data.
- The NT Memory Manager manages storing and retrieving pages from Page Frames.
- The size of a page is platform dependent, where MIPS Intel and PowerPC 4KB and DEC ALPHA platforms have 8KB pages.
- Paged memory refers both to RAM and Page files that are Pages stored on a hard disk.
- Both the physical memory and Page files are treated as an array of pages.
- The Virtual Memory Manager translates from virtual memory to physical memory addresses.
- NT can use more than one processor installed; however, the Multitasking Model must be upgraded to the Multiprocessing Model.
- NT Workstations can use two processors and NT Server can use four processors.
- There are two categories of multiprocessing systems. Asymmetric Multiprocessing (ASMP), which assigns specific tasks to each processor and Symmetric Multiprocessing (SMP).
- NT is an SMP operating system that balances the process load among all the processors.
- A process is a unit of labor such as a program that consists of one or more subprocesses called a thread.
- Threads can be scheduled for execution on different processors.
- A process begins with a normal priority, called the base priority, and can be increased or decreased by two levels.
- Threads inherit the base priority of its process.

Change the Size of the Virtual Memory Paging File

Click Start
Click Settings
Control Panel

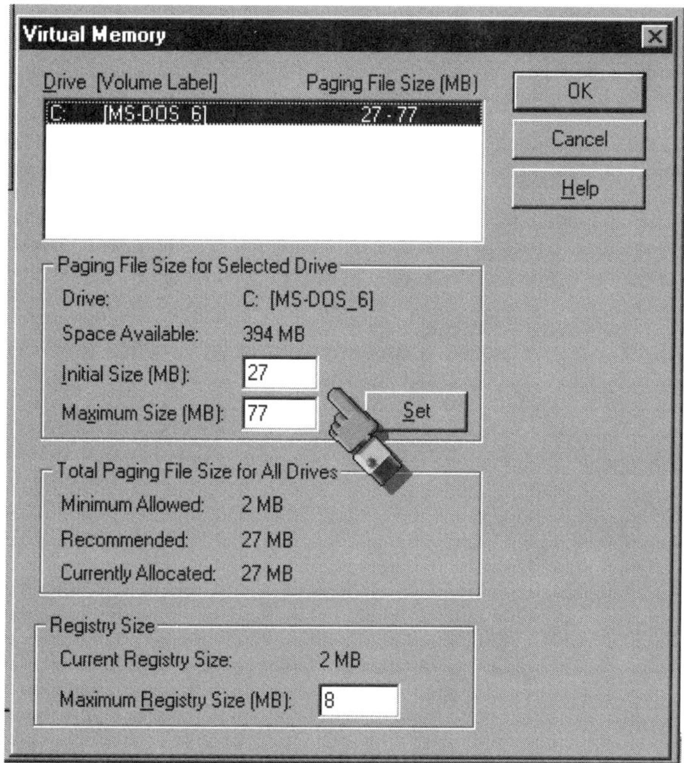

Figure A–12. *Enter the minimum and maximum size of the page file.*

Double-Click System to display the System Properties dialog box
Click the Performance tab
Click the Change button to display the Virtual Memory dialog box (Figure A–12)
Highlight the drive of the page file you want to change
Enter the new Minimum and Maximum size of the page file for the selected drive
Click the Set button
Click OK

Change the Performance of a Foreground Process

Click Start
Click Settings
Click Control Panel
Double-Click System to display the System Properties dialog box

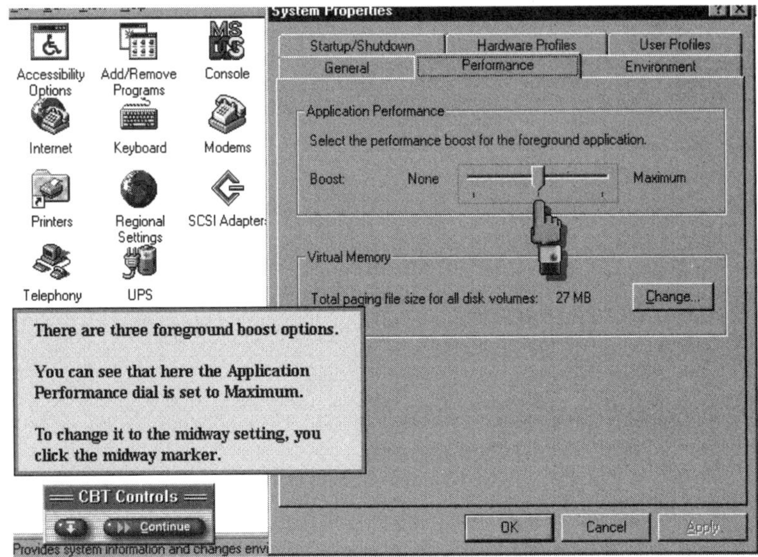

Figure A–13. *Adjust the slider to increase or reduce the performance of the foreground process.*

Click the Performance tab
Adjust the performance slider (Figure A–13)
Click OK
A message will appear asking you if you want to restart your computer
Click Yes

Create a Stripe Set

Click Start
Click Program
Click Administrative Tools
Click Disk Administrator
Hold down Ctrl, point and click on the other areas of the hard disk to use for the stripe set (Figure A–14)
Click Partition on the menu bar
Click Create Stripe Set from the submenu
Enter the size of the stripe set you want to create (Figure A–15)
Click OK
Click Partition on the menu bar
Click Commit Changes Now from the submenu
Click OK when the message asking if you want to save changes now is displayed

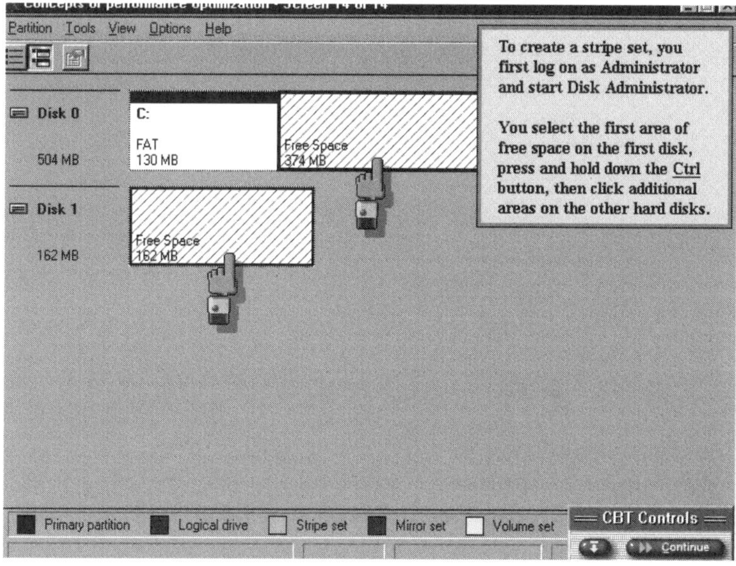

Figure A–14. *Select the areas of the hard disk you want to use for the stripe set.*

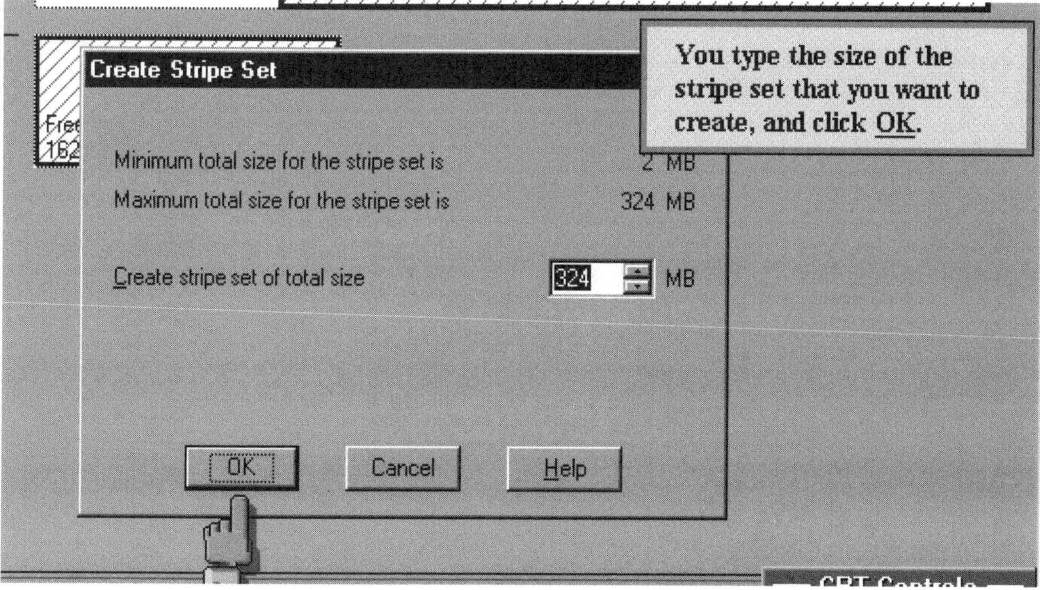

Figure A–15. *Enter the size of the stripe set you want to create.*

Click OK when the message reminding you to update the emergency repair disk is displayed
Click Yes when prompted to restart your computer
Log in as Administrator
Click Start
Click Program
Click Administrative Tools
Click Disk Administrator
Click Tools from the menu bar
Click Format from the submenu to format the drive

Starting the Performance Monitor

Click Start
Click Program
Click Administrative Tools
Click Performance Monitor to display the performance monitor
Click Edit on the menu bar
Click Add to Chart on the submenu to display the Add Chart dialog box
Select the Object type (Figure A–16)
Select the Counter you want to track (Figure A–17)
Click Add
Click Done to monitor the object (Figure A–18)

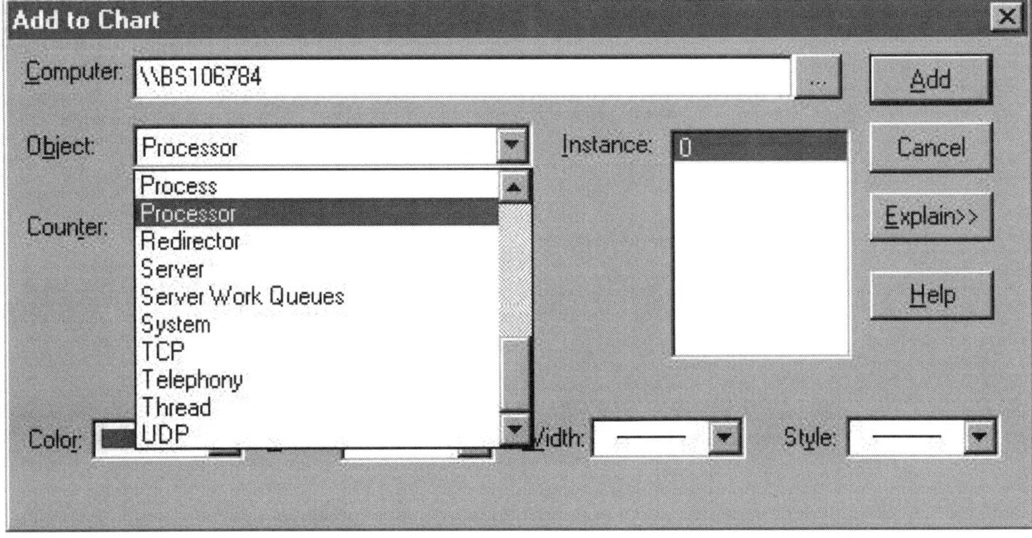

Figure A–16. *Select the object that you want to monitor.*

Add to Chart
Computer: \\BS106784
Add
Object: Processor
Instance: 0
Cancel
Counter:
% DPC Time
% Interrupt Time
% Privileged Time
% Processor Time
% User Time
APC Bypasses/sec
Explain>>
Help
Color:
Scale: Default
Width:
Style:

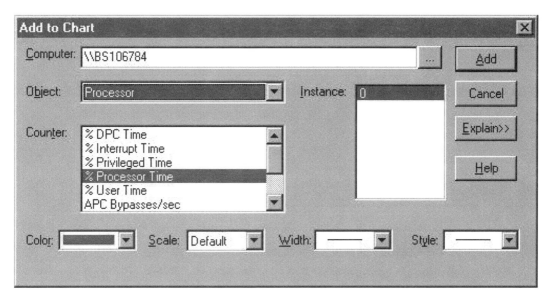

Figure A–17. *Select the counter you want to track.*

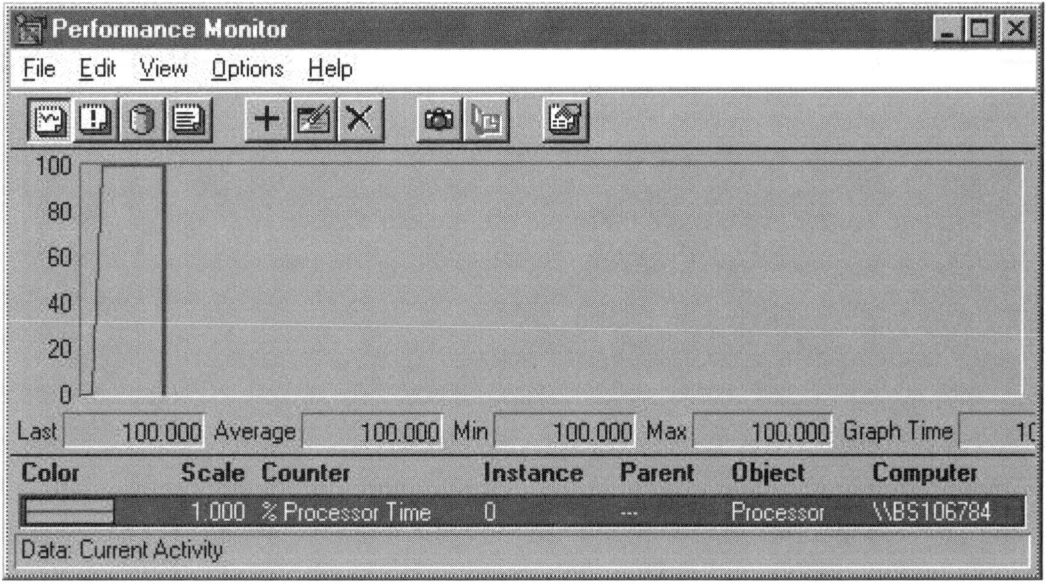

Figure A–18. *The performance monitor provides real-time statistics of the object.*

Set the Performance Monitor Alert

Click Start
Click Program
Click Administrative Tools
Click Performance Monitor to display the performance monitor
Click View on the menu bar
Click Alert on the submenu
Click Edit on the menu bar
Click Add To Alert on the submenu to display the Add Alert dialog box
Select the Object type
Select the Counter you want to track
Enter the value of the alert in the Alert If text box (Figure A–19)
Click Add
Click Done to display the Performance Monitor again showing the alert log (Figure A–20)

Determine If There Are Too Many Network Errors

Click Start
Click Program
Click Administrative Tools

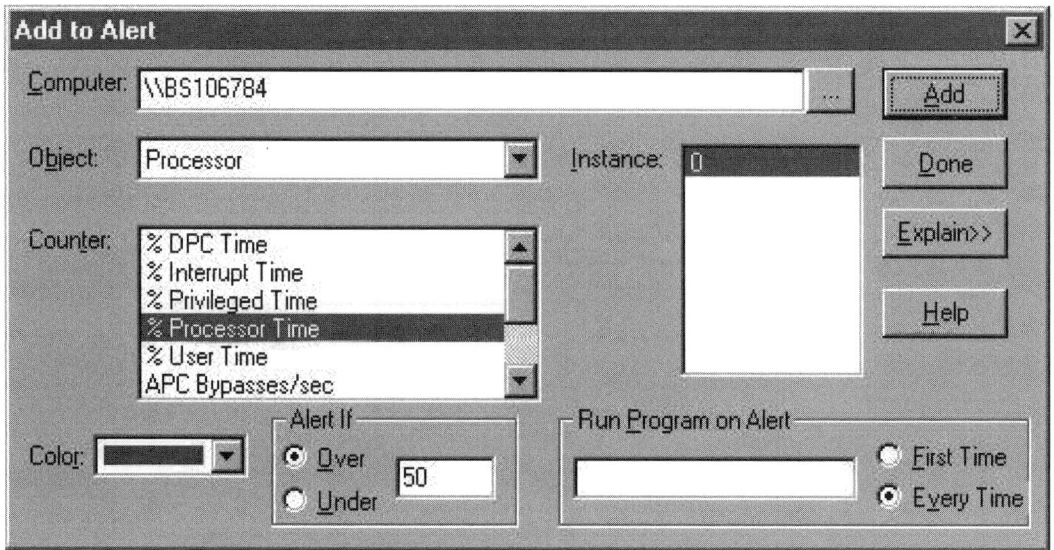

Figure A–19. *Sound the alert if the count is over 50.*

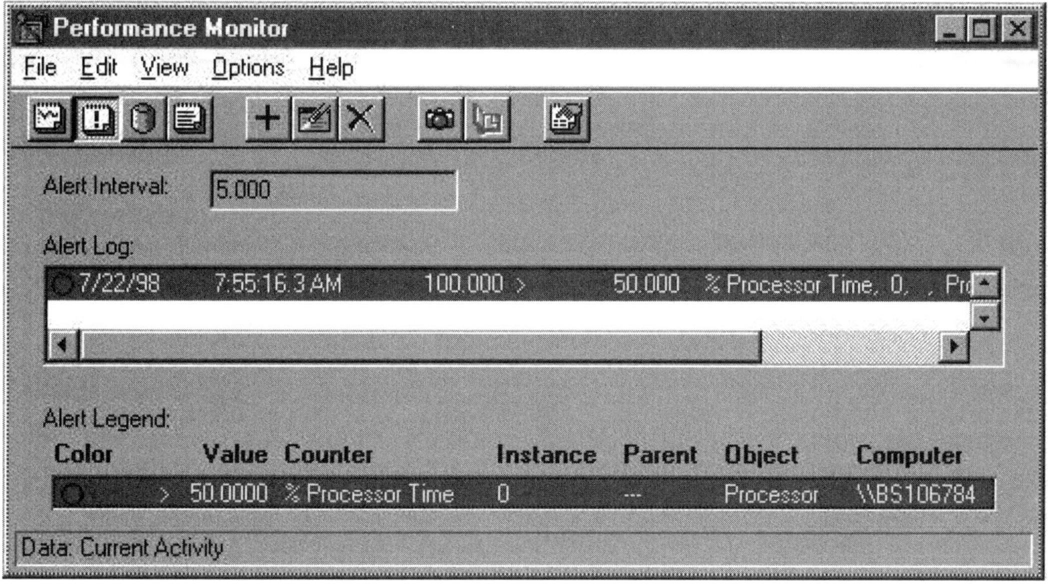

Figure A–20. *The Performance Monitor showing the alert log.*

Click Performance Monitor to display the performance monitor
Click Edit on the menu bar
Click Add to Chart on the submenu to display the Add Chart dialog box
Select the Object type as Redirector
Select the Counter to Network Errors/sec (Figure A–21)
Click Add
Click Done
Compare results to baseline for Network Errors/sec

Determine If Client's Requests Are Rejected Due to Shortage of Work Items

Click Start
Click Program
Click Administrative Tools
Click Performance Monitor to display the performance monitor
Click Edit on the menu bar
Click Add To Chart on the submenu to display the Add Chart dialog box
Select the Object type as Server

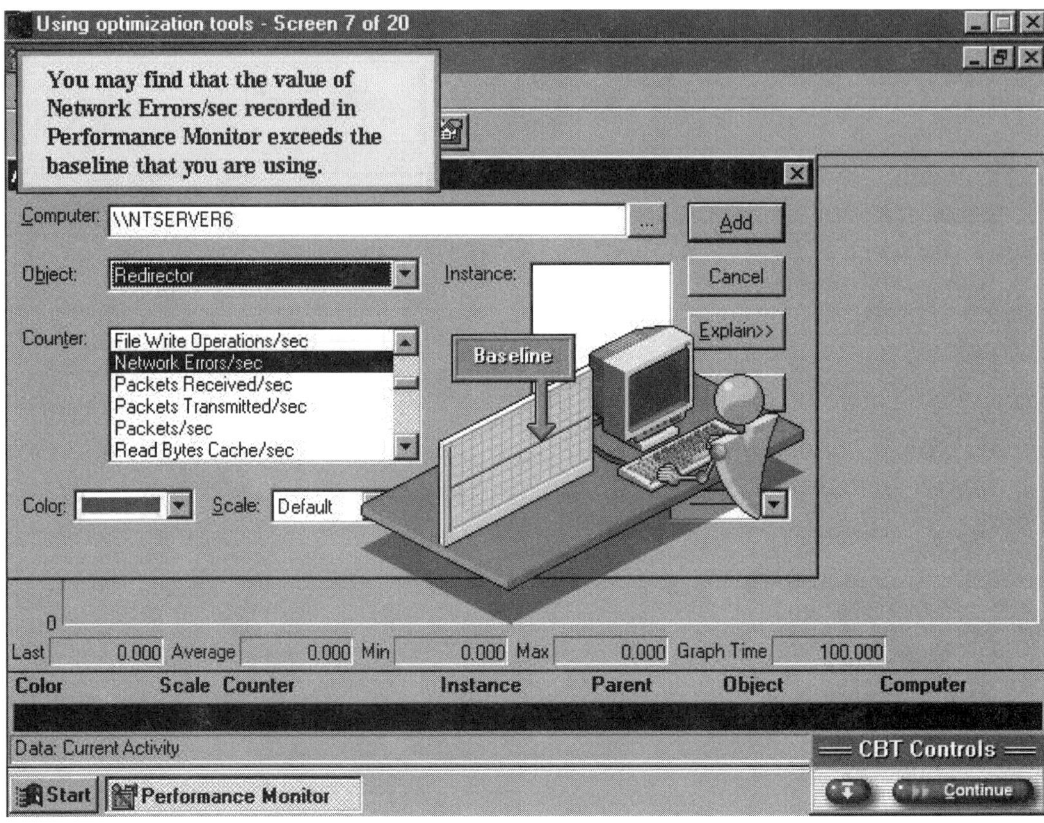

Figure A–21. *Set the Object to Redirector and Counter to Network Errors/sec.*

Select the Counter to Work Item Shortage (Figure A–22)
Click Add
Click Done
Compare results to baseline for Network Errors/sec

Determine If the NT Server Is Short of Memory

Click Start
Click Program
Click Administrative Tools
Click Performance Monitor to display the performance monitor
Click Edit on the menu bar
Click Add to Chart on the submenu to display the Add Chart dialog box
Select the Object type as Server

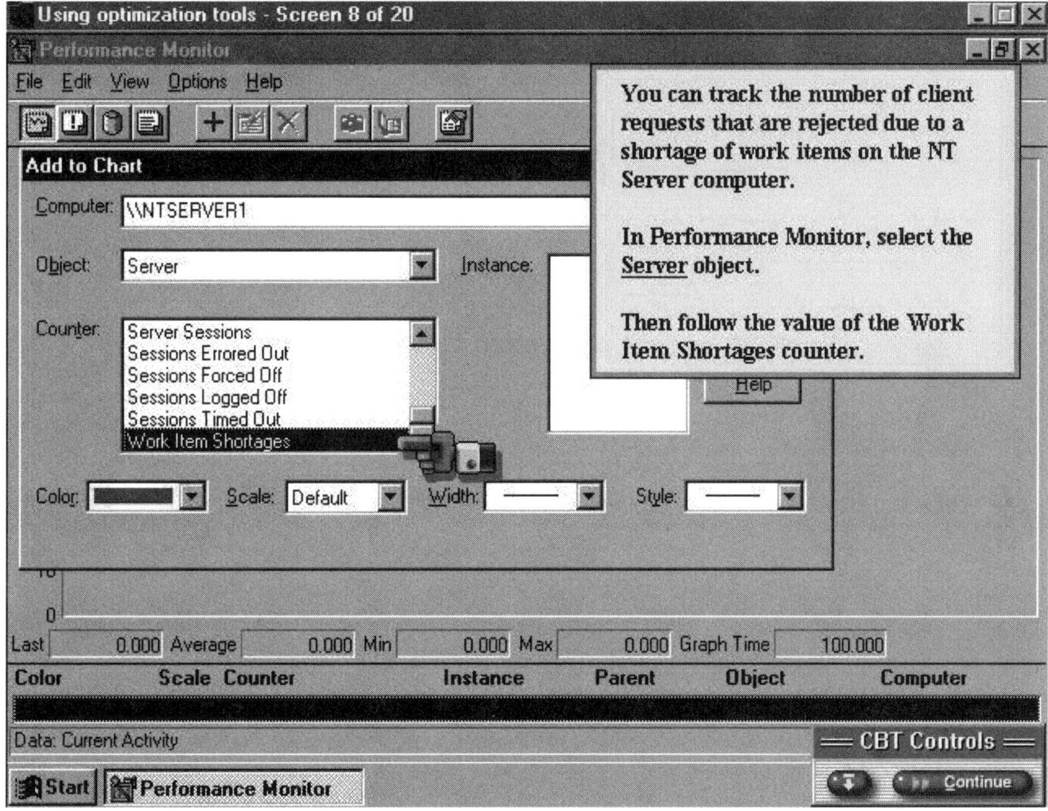

Figure A–22. *Set the Object to Server and Counter to Work Item Shortage.*

Select the Counter to Pool Nonpaged Failure (Figure 9–23)
Click Add
Click Done
A large value indicates insufficient memory

Determine If the NT Server Is Short of Memory and/or The Paging File Is Operating at Full Capacity

Click Start
Click Program
Click Administrative Tools
Click Performance Monitor to display the performance monitor
Click Edit on the menu bar
Click Add to Chart on the submenu to display the Add Chart dialog box

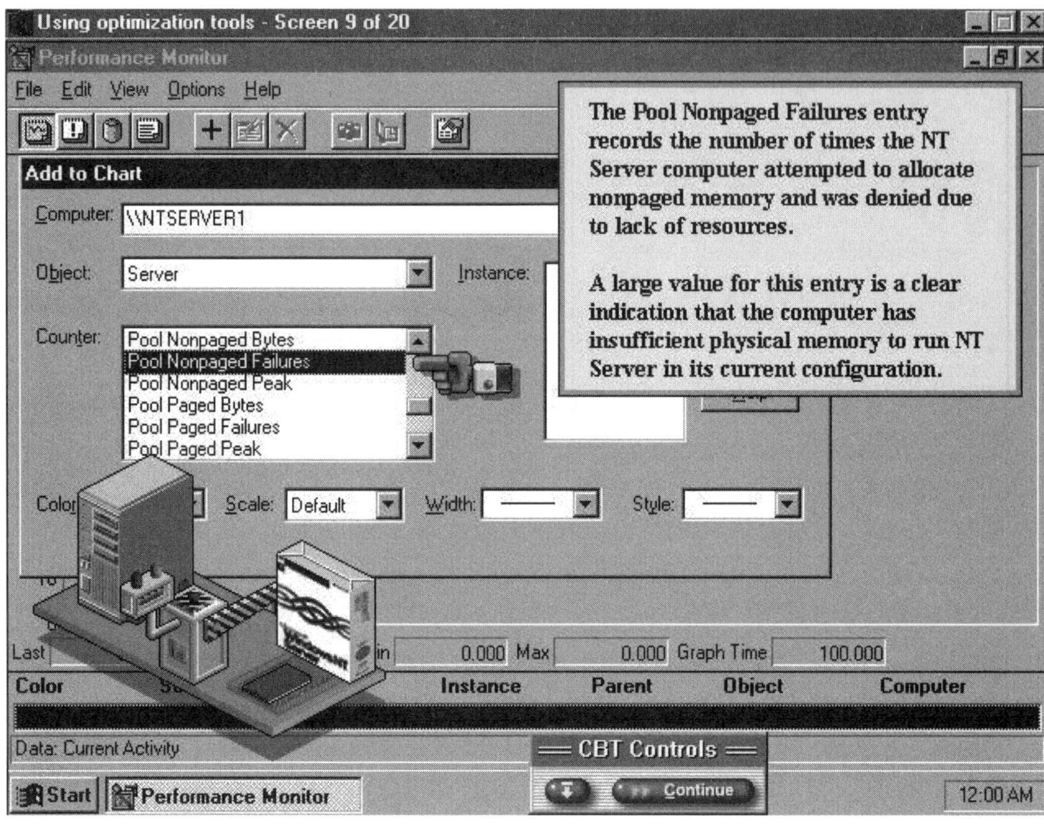

Figure A–23. *A large value indicates insufficient memory.*

Select the Object type as Server
Select the Counter to Pool Page Failures (Figure A–24)
Click Add
Click Done
A large value indicates insufficient memory and/or the paging file is operating at full capacity

Determine If a Remote Server Bottleneck Is Causing a Memory Problem on the NT Server

Click Start
Click Program
Click Administrative Tools
Click Performance Monitor to display the performance monitor
Click Edit on the menu bar

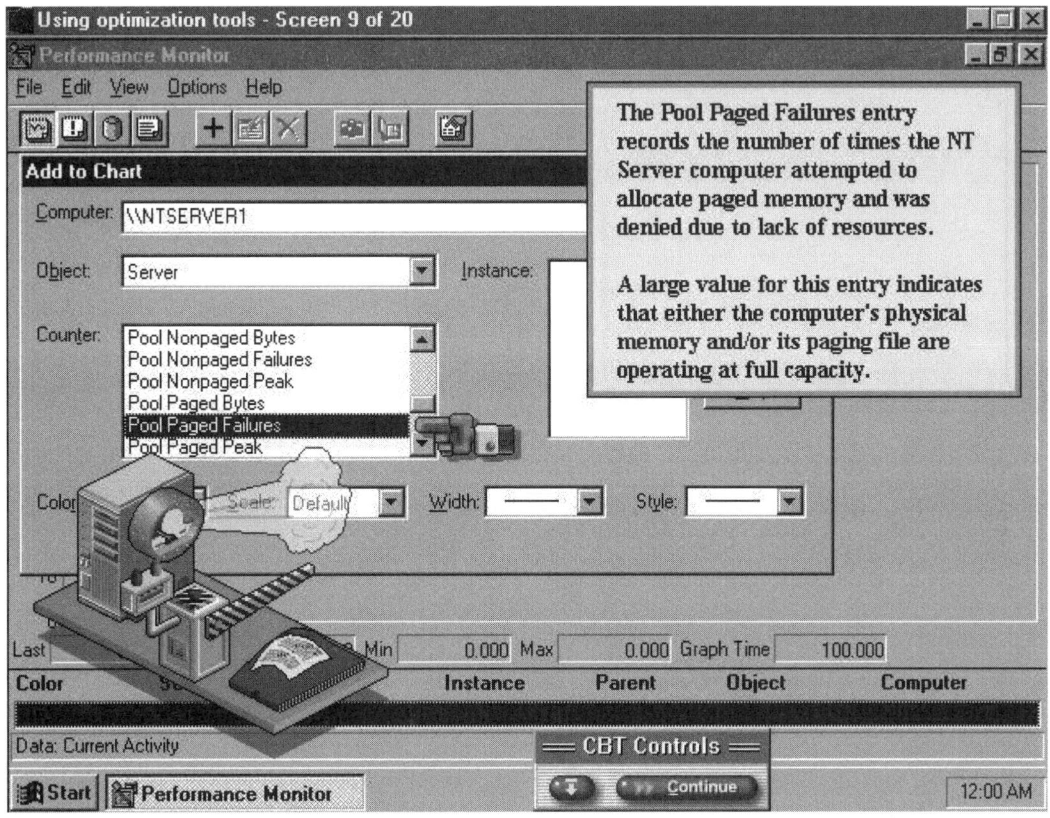

Figure A–24. *A large value indicates insufficient memory and/or the paging file is operating at full capacity.*

Click Add to Chart on the submenu to display the Add Chart dialog box
Select the Object type as Redirector
Select the Counter to Writes Denied/sec and Read Denied/sec (Figure A–25)
Click Add
Click Done
A large value indicates a bottleneck with a remote server
Optimize the amount of memory the NT server allocates for itself
Click Start
Click Settings
Click Control Panel
Click Network to display the Network dialog box
Click Services tab

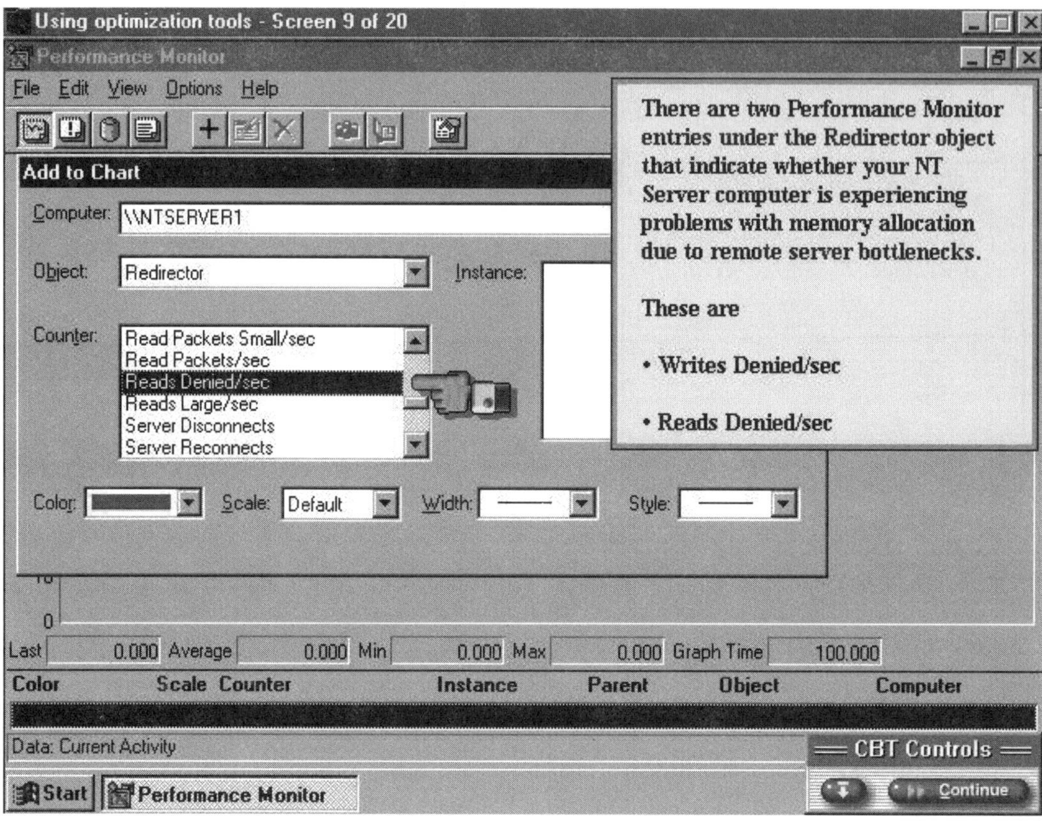

Figure A–25. *A large value indicates insufficient memory.*

Click the appropriate optimization selection (Figure A–26)

Network Troubleshooting

Structured Troubleshooting

- Assess the impact of the problem to the rest of the network.
- Collect information to help you isolate the problem.
- Compare the network baseline with the current network performance.
- Review the network and try to find obvious causes of the problem.
- Determine if the problem has occurred before and if there is a record of its solution.
- Question users why they think there is a network problem.
- Investigate user's comments further.

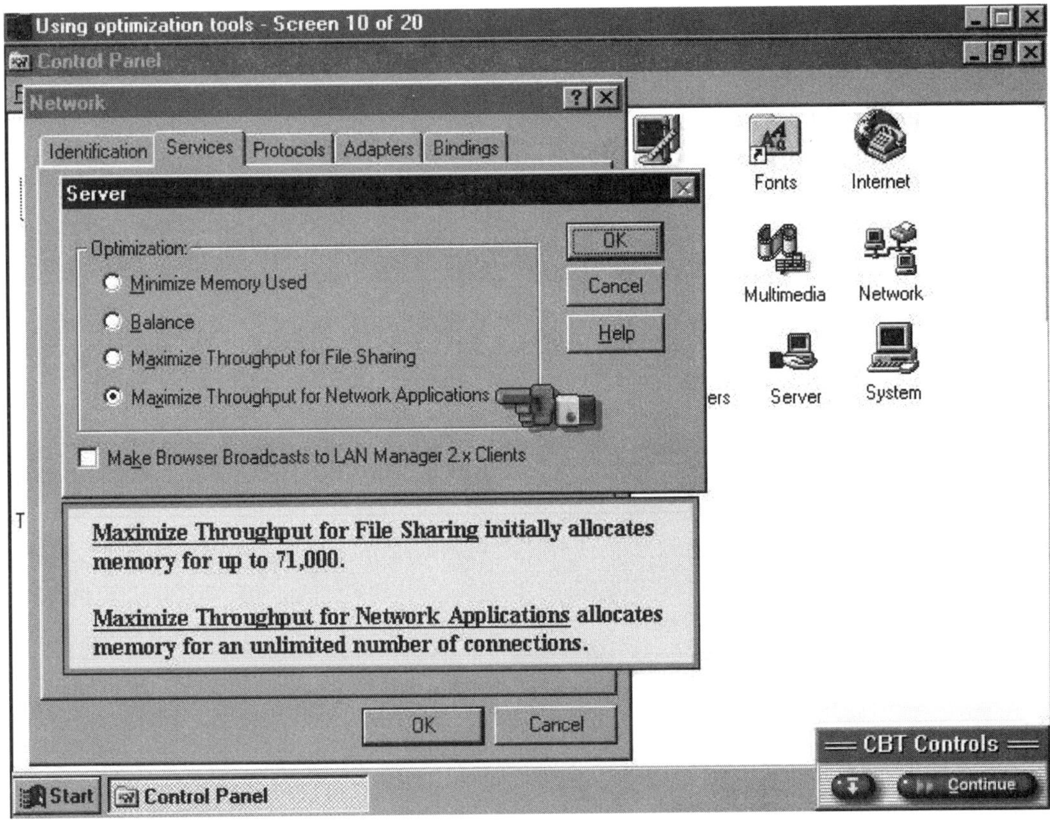

Figure A–26. *Maximum Throughput for Network Applications allows for unlimited connections.*

- How many computers are affected by the problem?
- Is the problem related to a group of computers.
- Was there a recent upgrade to the network or to the computer?
- Is this an intermittent problem or consistent problem?
- Is the problem with a new user or new equipment?
- Has the equipment been moved recently?
- Is it isolated to a vendor's product?
- Has the user or a technician tried to fix the problem?
- Was the network or the computer reconfigured?
- Questions 8 through 16 will help you isolate the problem.
- If not, then mentally divide the net into segments to narrow your investigation.

- Examine each network component in the segment. Be sure to include: network adapter cards, hubs, repeaters, routers, bridges, gateways, cables, connections, services, and protocols.
- Create a list of possible causes and sort them in the most probable order.
- Investigate each cause on your list.
- If you still haven't found the problem after exhausting the list, then consult with other technicians within your organization or at the equipment manufacturer.

Starting the Event Viewer

Click Start
Click Program
Click Administrative Tools
Click Event View to display the Event Viewer
Graphic symbols represent events
Red Error Symbol signifies a problem such as loss of data
Yellow Exclamation is a warning that indicates a future problem such as low disk space
Blue Lower Case i indicates a successful operation
Lock indicates a successful security access

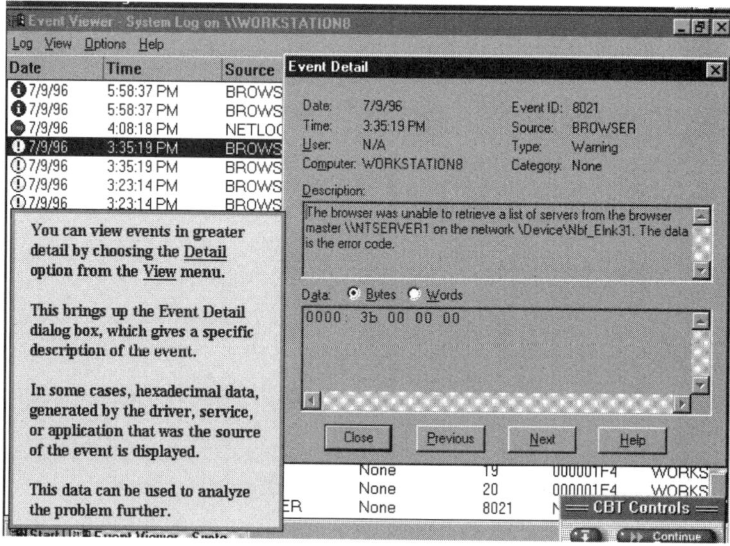

Figure A–27. *The Event Viewer is used to track network events.*

Key indicates a failed security access
Click OK to close the Event Viewer

View the Event Detail

Click Start
Click Program
Click Administrative Tools
Click Event View to display the Event Viewer
Highlight the event you want to examine in detail
Click View from the menu bar
Click Detail from the submenu to display the Event Detail screen
You can also just double click on the event
Click OK after reviewing the event details

View the Event Viewer Log File

Click Start
Click Program
Click Administrative Tools
Click Event View to display the Event Viewer
Click Log from the menu bar
Click the log you want to view from the submenu
Click OK after reviewing the log

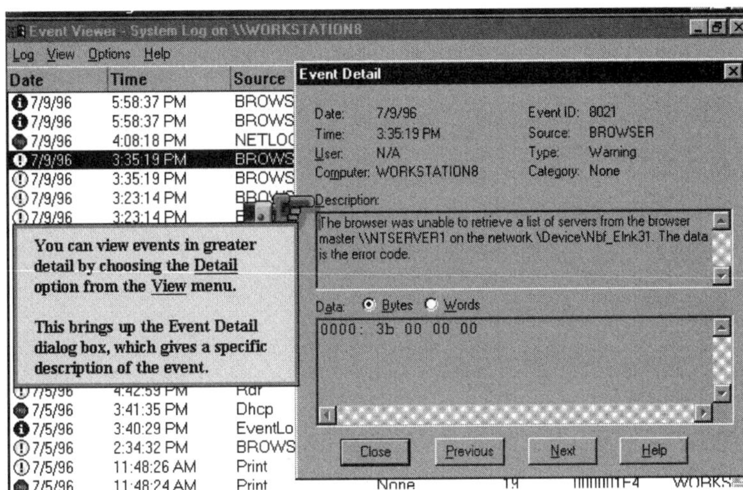

Figure A–28. *The Event Detail screen enables you to explore the details of an event.*

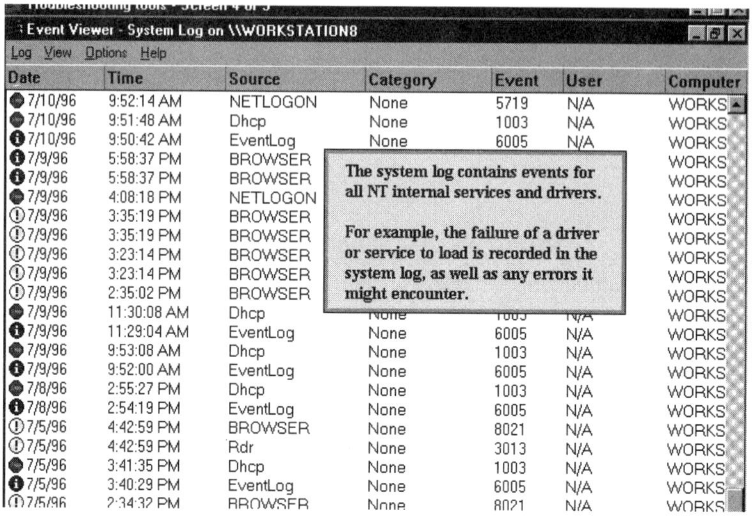

Event Viewer - System Log on \\WORKSTATION8

Log View Options Help

Date	Time	Source	Category	Event	User	Computer
7/10/96	9:52:14 AM	NETLOGON	None	5719	N/A	WORKS
7/10/96	9:51:48 AM	Dhcp	None	1003	N/A	WORKS
7/10/96	9:50:42 AM	EventLog	None	6005	N/A	WORKS
7/9/96	5:58:37 PM	BROWSER				WORKS
7/9/96	5:58:37 PM	BROWSER				WORKS
7/9/96	4:08:18 PM	NETLOGON				WORKS
7/9/96	3:35:19 PM	BROWSER				WORKS
7/9/96	3:35:19 PM	BROWSER				WORKS
7/9/96	3:23:14 PM	BROWSER				WORKS
7/9/96	3:23:14 PM	BROWSER				WORKS
7/9/96	2:35:02 PM	BROWSER				WORKS
7/9/96	11:30:08 AM	Dhcp				WORKS
7/9/96	11:29:04 AM	EventLog	None	6005	N/A	WORKS
7/9/96	9:53:08 AM	Dhcp	None	1003	N/A	WORKS
7/9/96	9:52:00 AM	EventLog	None	6005	N/A	WORKS
7/8/96	2:55:27 PM	Dhcp	None	1003	N/A	WORKS
7/8/96	2:54:19 PM	EventLog	None	6005	N/A	WORKS
7/5/96	4:42:59 PM	BROWSER	None	8021	N/A	WORKS
7/5/96	4:42:59 PM	Rdr	None	3013	N/A	WORKS
7/5/96	3:41:35 PM	Dhcp	None	1003	N/A	WORKS
7/5/96	3:40:29 PM	EventLog	None	6005	N/A	WORKS
7/5/96	2:34:32 PM	BROWSER	None	8021	N/A	WORKS

The system log contains events for all NT internal services and drivers.

For example, the failure of a driver or service to load is recorded in the system log, as well as any errors it might encounter.

Figure A–29. *The System Event log is one of three logs you can examine.*

Change the Size of the Event Log (Figure A–30)

Click Start
Click Program
Click Administrative Tools
Click Event View to display the Event Viewer
Click Log from the menu bar
Click the log setting from the submenu
Select the name of the log you want to modify
Change the size of the log; changes are in 64K increments
Select if you want to manually delete the log; have NT deleted it as needed; or specify the maximum number of days to store events in the log
Click OK

View a Log File on Another Computer within Your Workgroup or Domain

Click Start
Click Program
Click Administrative Tools

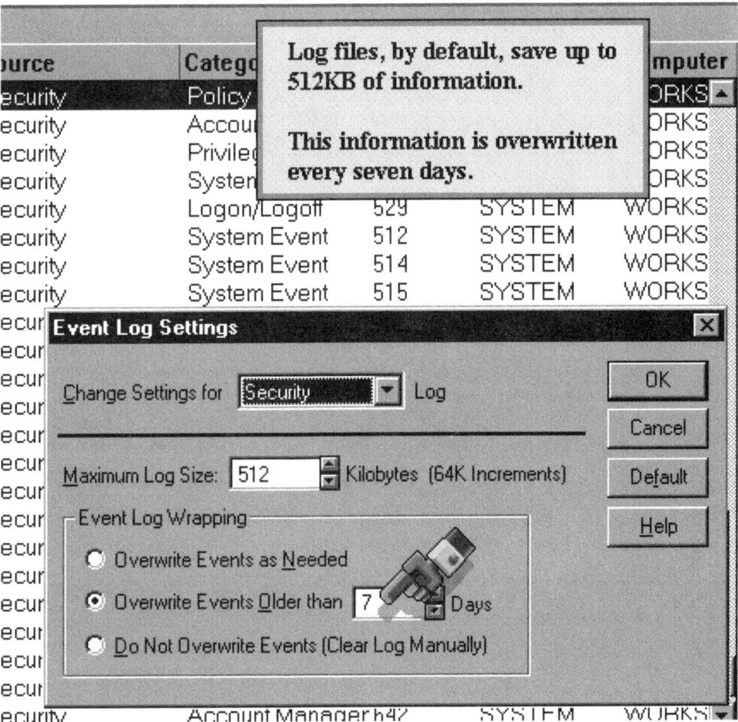

Figure A–30. *The Log Setting screen is used to modify the default settings for all logs.*

Click Event View to display the Event Viewer
Click Log from the menu bar
Click to select the computer
Click OK after reviewing the log

Sorting Events in the Event Viewer

Click Start
Click Program
Click Administrative Tools
Click Event View to display the Event Viewer
Click View from the menu bar
Click the way you want to sort events: Newest First; Older First: Filter Events; Find Event

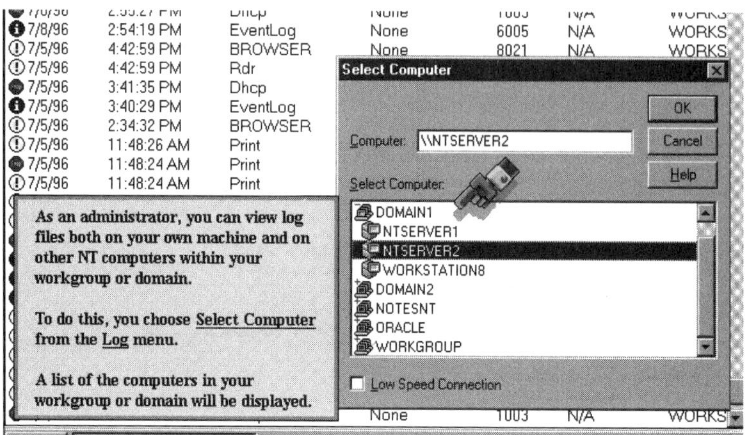

Figure A–31. *Select the computer whose log you want to view.*

Facts You Should Know About the Windows NT Diagnostics Utility

- The Version tab displays the build number, registered owner, and version number.
- The System tab describes the CPU.
- The Display tab displays information about the network adapter card and drivers.

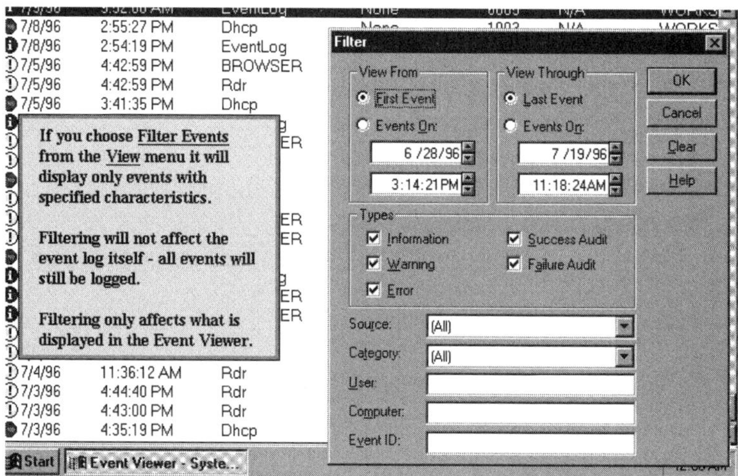

Figure A–32. *The Filter Event screen is used to hide those events you don't want to see.*

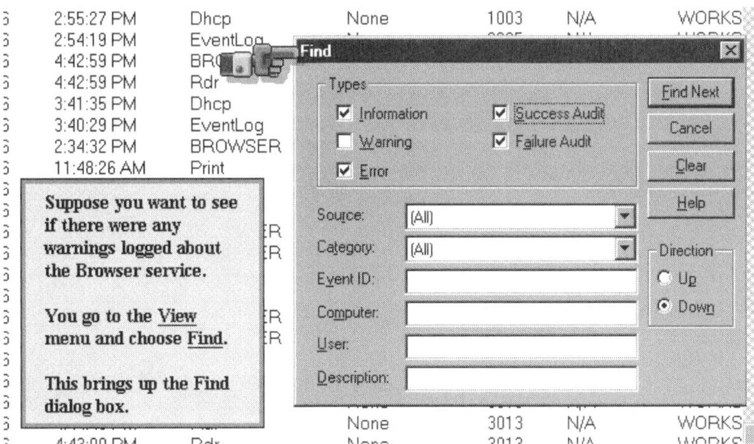

Figure A–33. *The Find screen is used to locate a specific event.*

- The Drives tab list drives by category such as floppy and other removal drives, local hard drives, CD ROM drives, and network-connected drives.
- The Memory tab list information about the physical memory, kernel memory, and the Page file.
- The Services tab display a list of all the services and whether or not the service is running or stopped.
- The Resource tab lists information about devices on the computer such as the interrupt for the device (IRQ button); port address used by the device (I/O Port button); the use of direct memory and related channel by a device (DMA button); memory area reserved for devices (Memory button); and list all devices (Device button).
- The Environment tab displays process, system, and user-environment variables.
- The Network tab lists network-related configuration information such as the domain name, log on server, and transport protocols.

Display Windows NT Diagnostics Utility

Click Start
Click Program
Click Administrative Tools

Click Windows NT Diagnostics to display the Windows NT Diagnostics Utility

Display Information About Drives

Click Start
Click Program
Click Administrative Tools
Click Windows NT Diagnostics to display the Windows NT Diagnostics Utility
Click Drive tab
Double click the category of drive to see the list of drives within that category (Figure A–35)

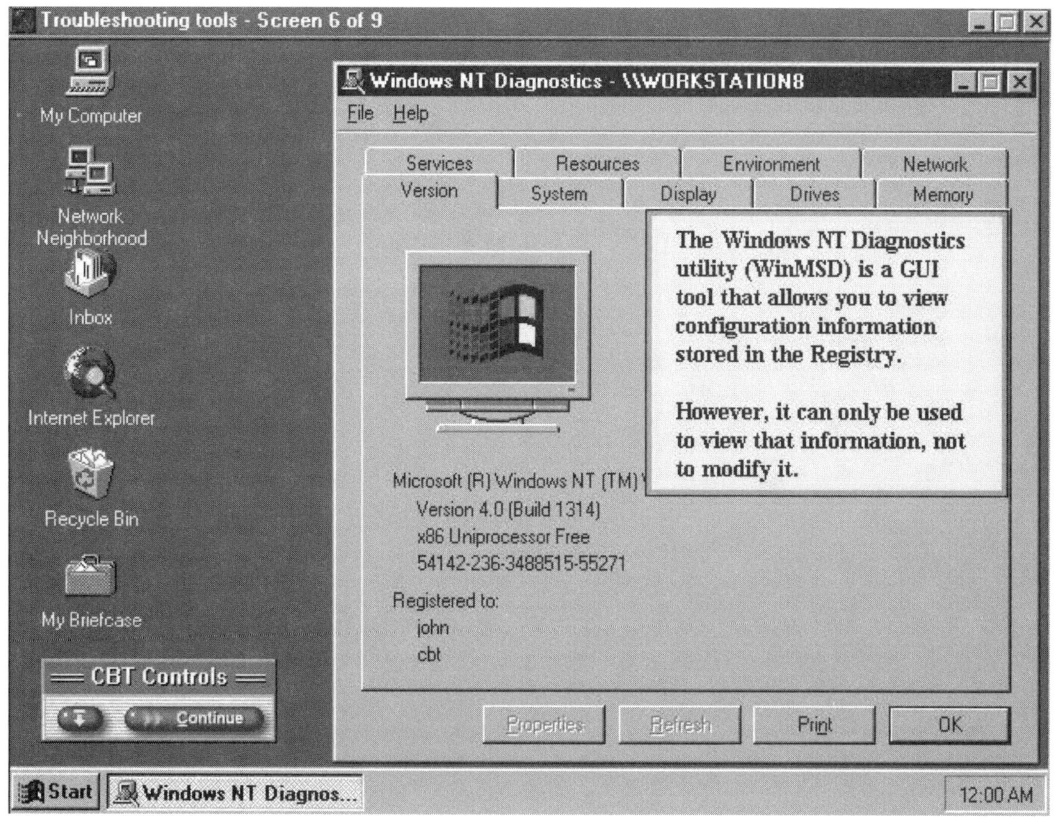

Figure A–34. *The Windows NT Diagnostics Utility provides valuable information that helps you track down network problems.*

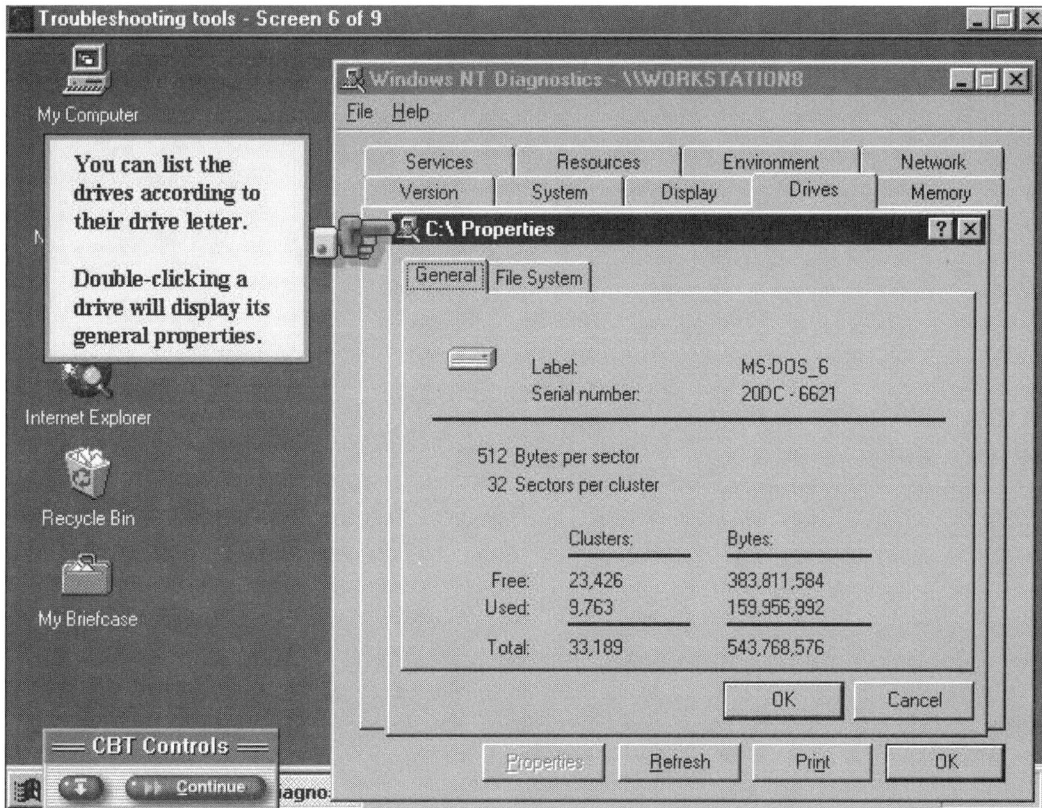

Figure A–35. *Drive Properties contains general information under the General tab and detailed information in the Detail tab.*

Click the Drives By Letter button to see a list of drives listed according to their drive letter

Double click the name of the drive to see the properties of the drive

Display the Properties of a Service

Click Start

Click Program

Click Administrative Tools

Click Windows NT Diagnostics to display the Windows NT Diagnostics Utility (Figure A–36)

Click Services tab

Double click the service to see the properties of any service

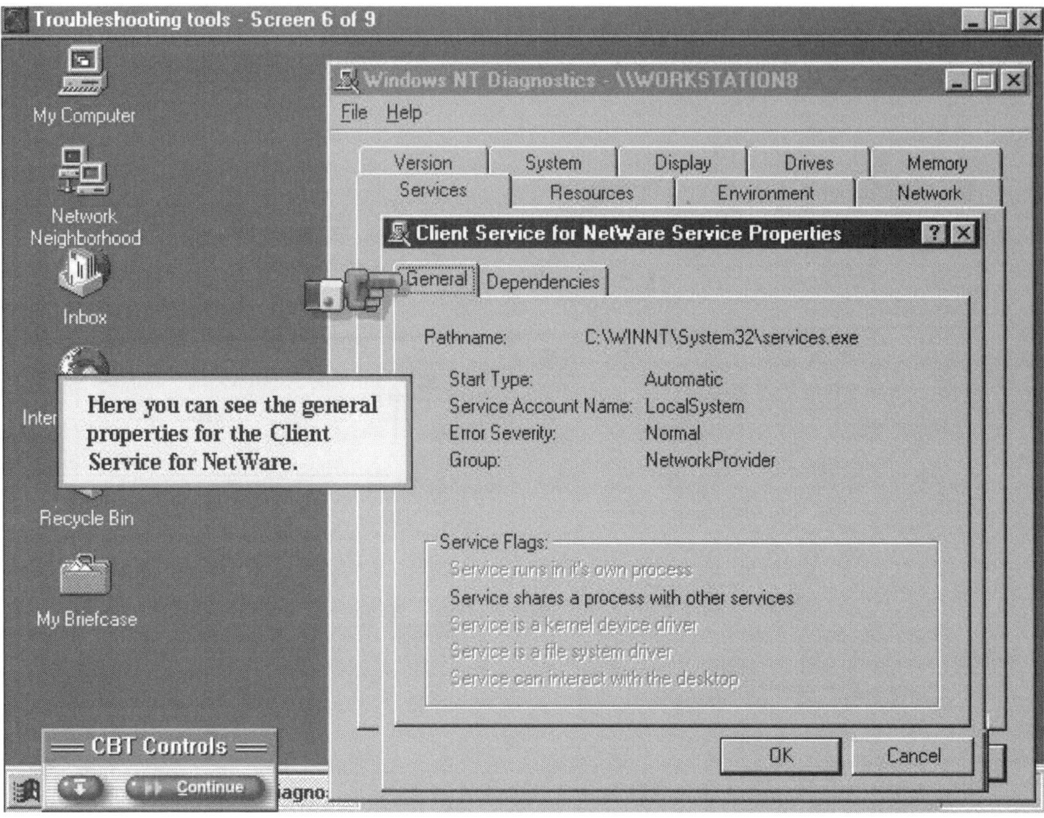

Figure A–36. *The Device button lists the devices that are stopped or running and the Properties button displays a list of devices.*

Information You Should Know About the Recovery of the System

- If a stop error occurs, the program called savedump.exe writes the content of memory to the page file and marks the error part of the file with a stamp.
- The marked part of the Page file is copied to the file specified in the "Write debugging information to" checkbox in the Startup/Shutdown tab of the Systems Properties screen. This occurs automatically when NT is restarted.
- The winddb.exe program can be used to debug the system.
- The Page file must be as large as the physical memory in the system.
- The Page file must reside on the same partition where NT is installed.

- If you leave "Overwrite any existing file" unchecked, then new debugging information won't be created if a stop error occurs.
- Checking the "Automatically Reboot" check box will allow the system to come back online quickly without having to manually restart the system.

Configure the Recovery of the System

Click Start
Click Settings
Click Control Panel
Double-click the System icon to display the System Properties screen
Click the Startup/Shutdown tab (Figure A–37)
Click the appropriate settings in the Recovery section
Click OK

Information You Should Know About Troubleshooting the Network

- Cabling is the most common cause of network failure.
- Isolate whether or not the problem is caused by the cable by disconnecting the computer having the problem from the network and connecting

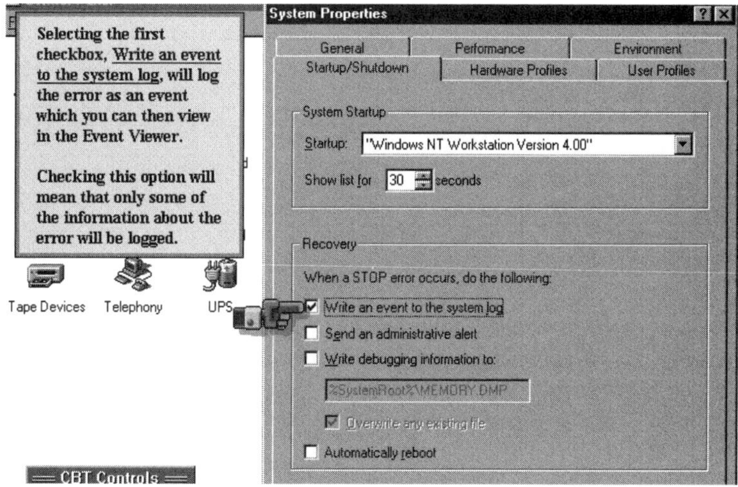

Figure A–37. *Windows NT will automatically record a stop event in the Event Log when you check the appropriate item in the Startup/Shutdown tab.*

a portable PC to the network. If the portable PC sees the network, then there isn't a cable problem. Assume the problem lies with the computer.

- If the problem is with the cable, scan the cable for obvious problems: cable connection, condition of the cable, the length of the cable, termination of the cable, is there a source of interference, does the cable conform to the network specifications.
- If the cable appears to be properly connected, then disconnect the computer from the network in the midpoint of the network. Connect a terminator to one side of the network. If the network remains operational, the repeat the process on the other side of the network. The side that is not operating contains the problem. Repeat this process until you discover the segment of cable that is a fault.
- The network adapter card can also cause a network problem.
- Determine if the problem is permanent or intermittent.
- If the problem is permanent, make sure the cable is plugged into the correct interface on the network adapter card; check that the settings of the network adapter card match the settings of the network software; make sure the speed of the network adapter card is at the same speed as the network; make sure the correct network adapter card is being used.
- If the answers are yes, you've identified the problem and correct it.
- If the answers are no, then suspect the network adapter card and replace it.
- Intermittent problems are caused by: setting conflicts between network adapter cards (I/O Port Address, Interrupt, memory) which require replacement of the network adapter card; faulty driver software which requires replacement or upgrade; and duplicate network address found by using a Protocol Analyzer.

Change a Duplicate Address

Click Start
Click Settings
Click Control Panel
Double click the Network Icon to display the Network dialog box
Select the Protocols tab (Figure A–38)
Highlight the TCP/IP protocol
Click the Properties button
Enter the new IP address
Click Ok

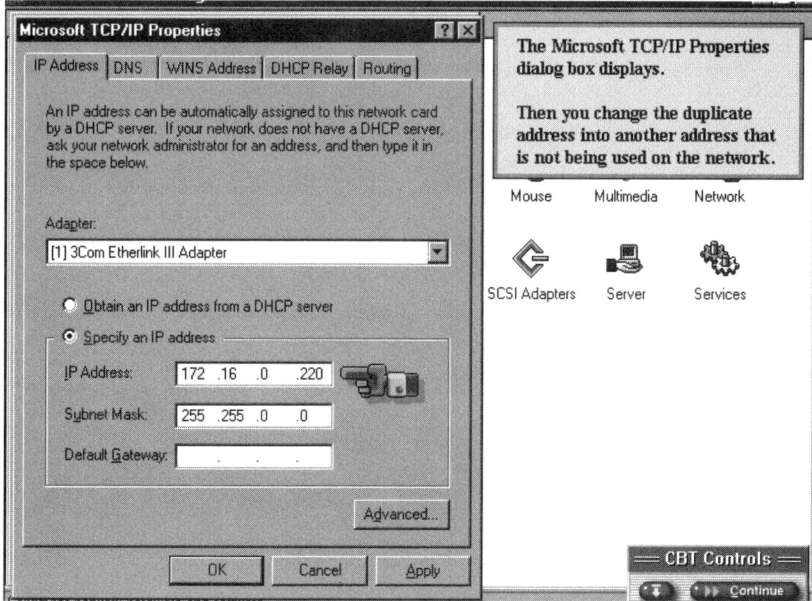

Figure A–38. *Change the existing duplicate IP address to a new IP address.*

Information You Need About Restoring Files

- Create an emergency repair disk when NT is installed.
- An emergency repair disk is used to restore corrupt files, missing files, and registry files.
- An emergency repair disk can only be used to correct a problem on the computer that created the emergency repair disk.
- In addition to the emergency repair disk, NT uses the emergency repair folder located at \winnt_root\repair.
- The Repair Disk utility allows the network administrator to update the emergency repair folder or disk and create a new emergency repair disk.
- When the emergency repair folder is updated, NT prompts you to create a new emergency repair disk.
- The emergency repair disk contains: setup.log that is used for verifying files installed in the system; config.nt and autoexec.nt used to intialize the NT virtual DOS Machine (NTVDM); a number of hives from the register such as system._, sam._ (security accounts manager), security._, softwae._, and default._.

NT Fails to Boot or Function Properly

Turn off the computer
Insert the NT Setup boot disk (disk 1) into drive A
Turn on the computer
Replace disk 1 with NT Setup disk 2 when prompted
Press Enter
Press R to initiate the emergency repair process
Select “Inspect Registry Files”
Unselect “Inspect Startup Environment,” “Verify Windows NT System Files,” “Inspect Boot Sector”
Select “Continue (Perform Selected Tasks)”
Press Enter
Press Enter
Replace disk 2 with NT Setup disk 3 when prompted
Press Enter
Press Enter
Press Enter
Replace disk 3 with the emergency repair disk when prompted
Press Enter
Remove the emergency repair disk
Press Enter to restart the computer

Create an NT Boot Disk

Double-click on MyComputer
Insert a disk in drive A
Single click the 3 1/2 Floppy [A:] icon (Figure A-39)
Select File from the menu bar
Select Format from the submenu to display the Format screen. Make sure you make a bootable disk.
Check Quick Format
Click the Start button
Click OK
Click OK when formatting is completed
Click the Close button
Double click C: icon on MyComputer to display the Explorer
Click C: on the tree section
If this is an Intel computer, highlight ntldr, boot.ini, ntbootdd.sys
If this is an RSIC computer, highlight osloader.exe, hal.dll, jzsetup.exe
Drag the file to A:

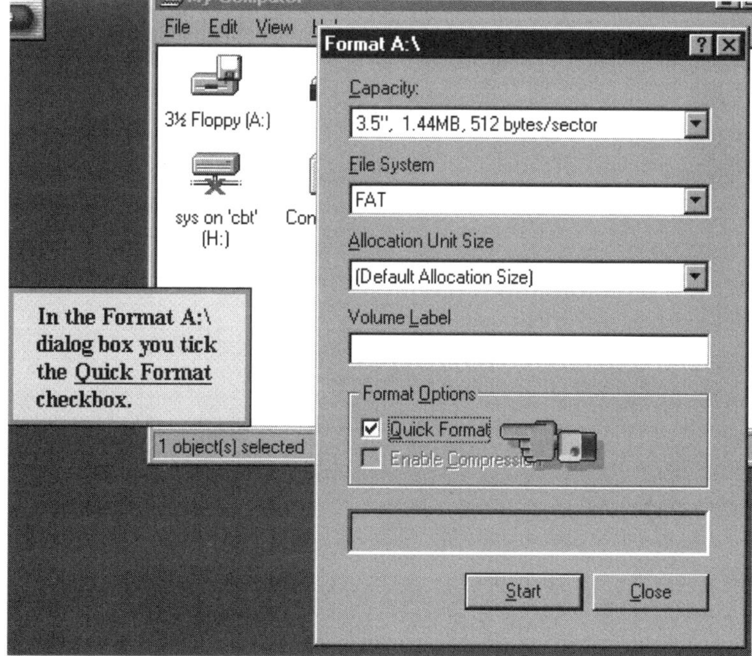

Figure A–39. *Check the Quick Format check-box before formatting the disk.*

Note: You can also use the Repair Disk Utility to create an NT Book disk

How to Configure Uninterrupted Power Supply (UPS)

Click Start
Click Settings
Click Control Panel
Double click on the UPS icon to display the UPS dialog box
Select the serial port where the USP is connected
Click the check box so a signal is sent when the regular power supply fails
Click the check box to send a warning when the UPS battery is low
Click the check box to send a signal when the UPS is turned off
Enter the name of the command file that will be run when the UPS is activated; the command file will have 30 minutes to complete all its tasks
Enter the expected life of the battery and the amount of time it takes for the UPS battery to recharge
Click OK

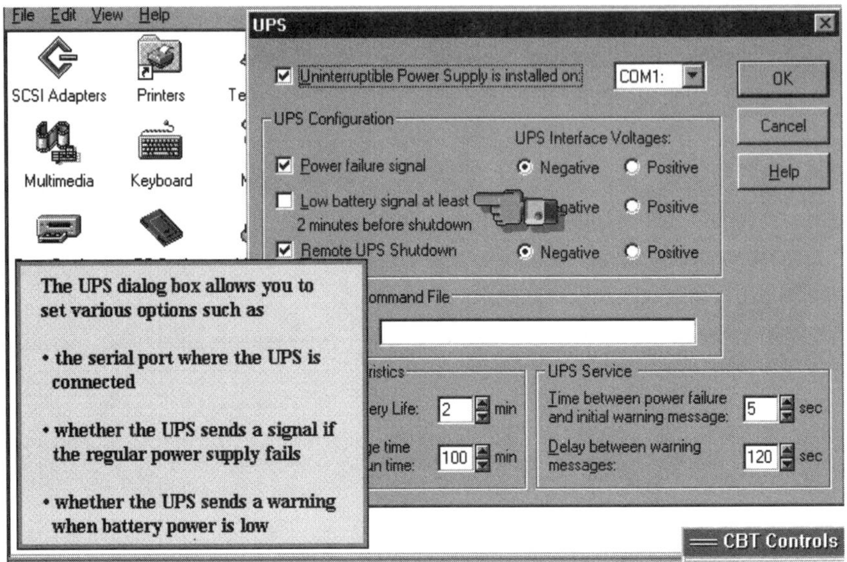

Figure A–40. *The UPS dialog box is used to configure the UPS.*

Data Integrity

How to Back Up Files

Click Start
Click Programs
Click Administrative Tools
Click Backup to display the backup graphical interface
Highlight the drive you want to backup
Click Select from the menu bar
Click Check from the submenu (Figure A–41)
Double-click the drive in the backup graphical interface to display a list of files on that drive
Highlight the files you want to backup. (Figure A–42)
Click the Backup button to display the Backup Information dialog box
Change backup specifications if necessary. (Figure A–43)
Click OK to begin the backup; the Backup Status dialog box shows the status of the backup. (Figure A–44)
Click the Control menu
Click Close from the submenu

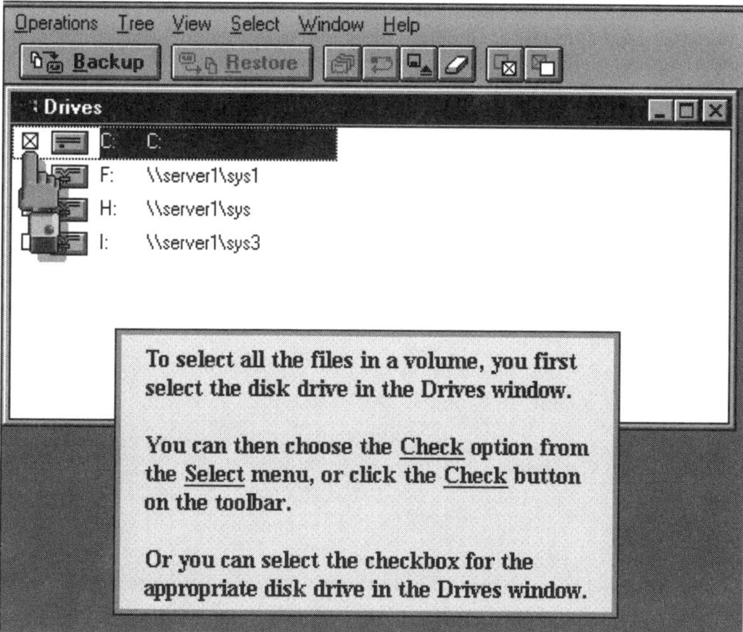

Figure A–41. *Check the drive you want to back up using the backup graphical interface.*

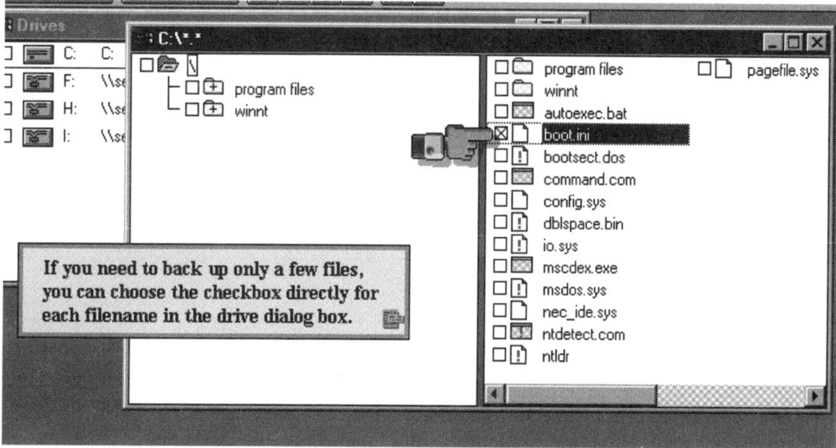

Figure A–42. *Highlight the files you want to back up.*

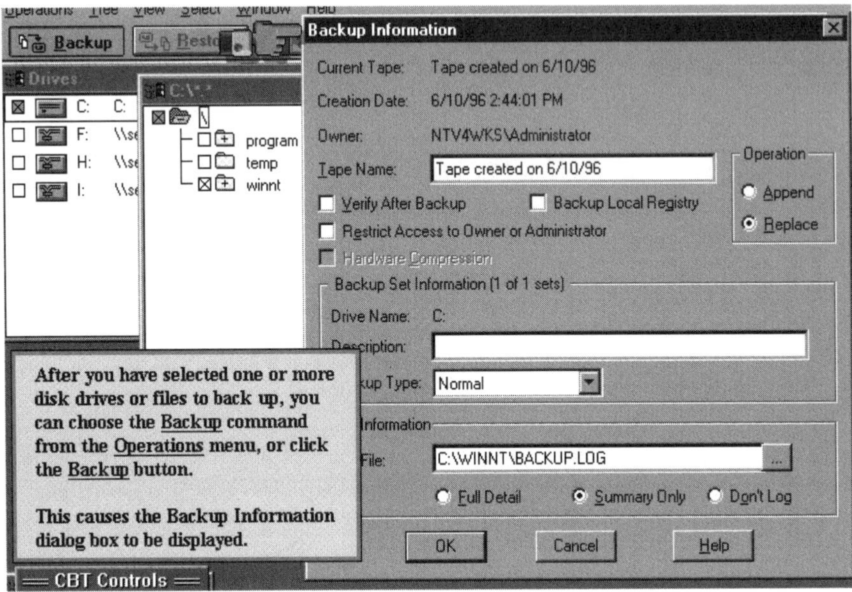

Figure A–43. *Change backup specifications if necessary.*

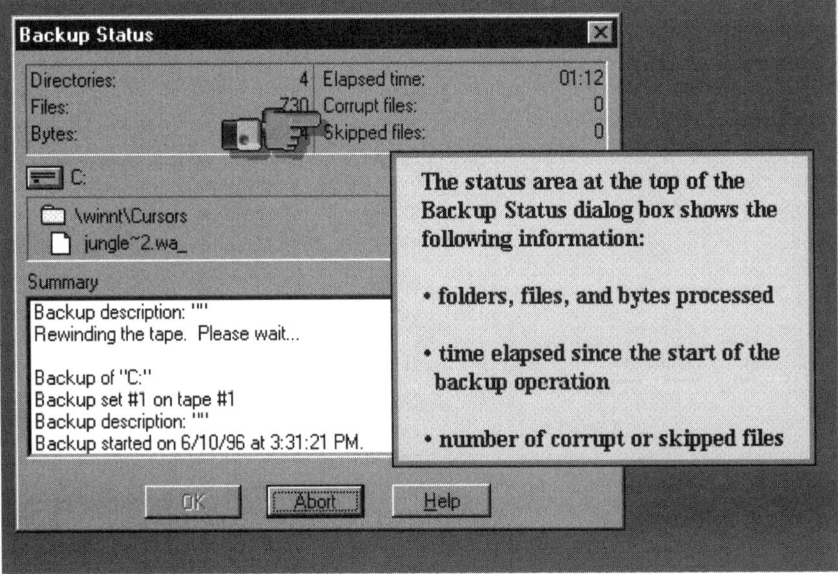

Figure A–44. *Backup Status dialog box keeps you informed of the status of the backup.*

How to Restore Files from a Backup Tape

Click Start
Click Programs
Click Administrative Tools
Click Backup to display the backup graphical interface
Select the Tapes window (Figure A–45)
Insert the tape to be restored into the tape drive
Select Operations from the menu bar
Select Catalog from the submenu to see a complete list of backup sets on the tape
Highlight the backup set you want to examine
Select Operations from the menu bar
Select Catalog from the submenu to see a complete list of files contained in the backup set
Highlight the files you want to restore. (Figure A–46)
Click the Restore button
Change the specification in the Restore dialog box if necessary (Figure A–47)
Click OK to begin the restoration; the Restoration Status dialog box shows the status of the backup
Click the Control menu
Click Close from the submenu

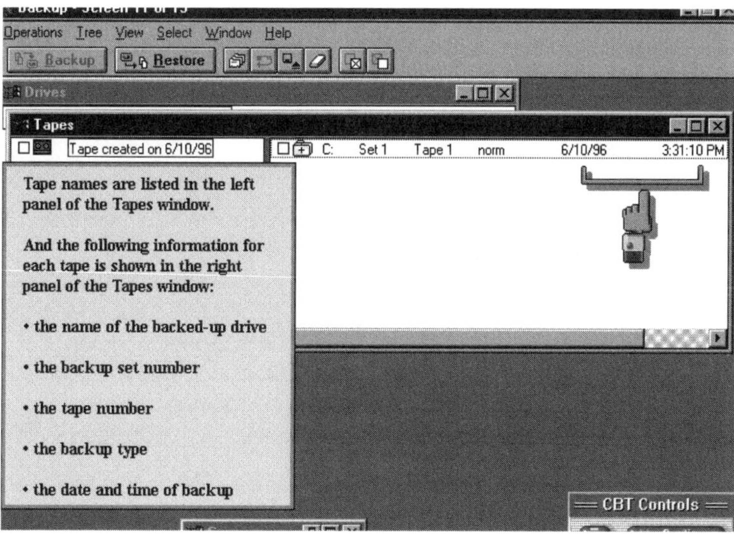

Figure A–45. *Highlight the tape that contains the backup files.*

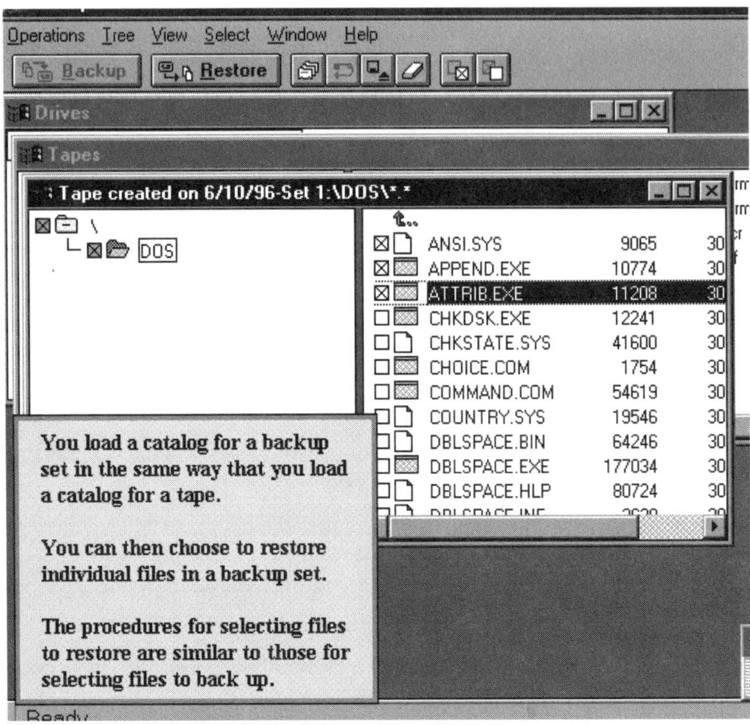

Figure A–46. *Highlight the files you want to restore.*

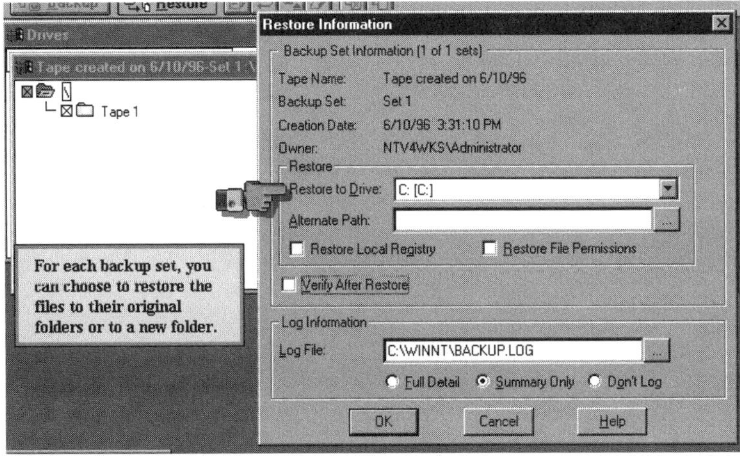

Figure A–47. *Change specification in the Restore dialog box if necessary.*

How to Check if the NT Fault Tolerance Driver Fixed a Sector Failure

Click Start
Click Program
Click Administrative Tools
Click Event View to display the Event Viewer
Highlight the fault tolerance event you want to examine in detail
Click View from the menu bar
Click Detail from the submenu to display the Event Detail screen
Click OK after reviewing the event details

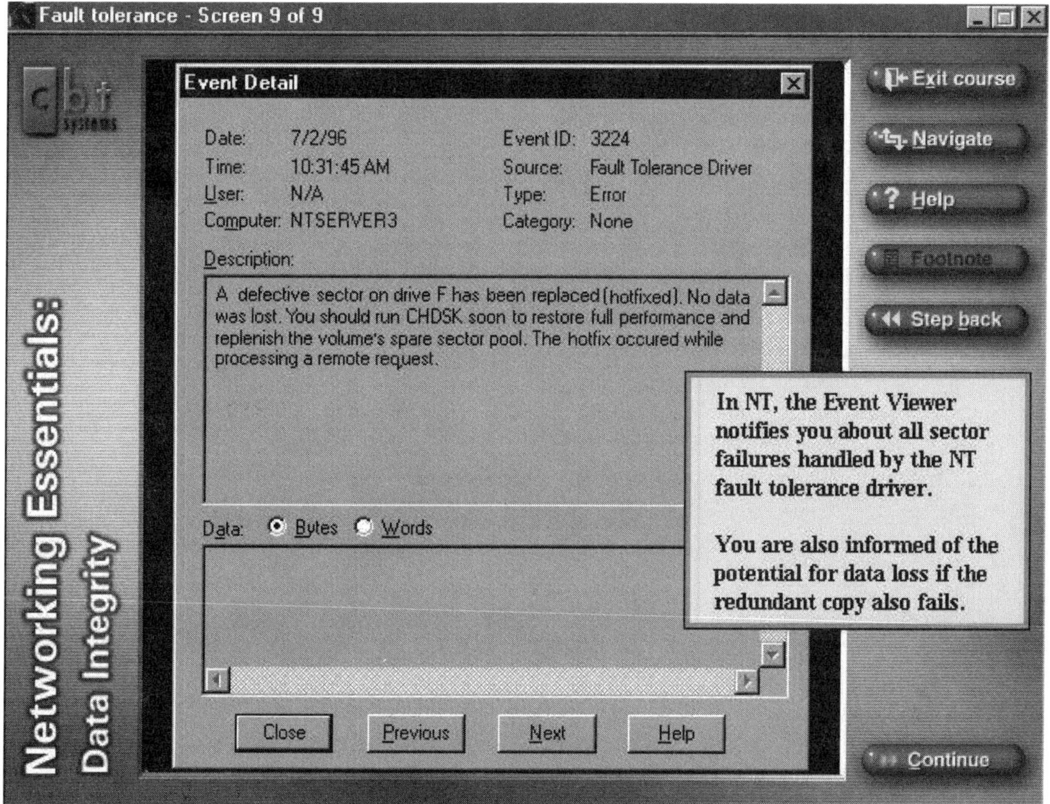

Figure A–48. *The Event Monitor can be used to see the details of the fault tolerance driver event.*

Information You Should Know About Recovering from a Mirror Set Failure

- The physical disk of mirror or stripe set is called a member.
- When a member fails, all I/O is redirected to the remaining members of the fault-tolerance volume by the fault-tolerance driver.
- You can repair the mirror set by breaking the mirror set relationship so the remaining good partition becomes a separate volume.

How to Repair a Mirror Set

Click Start
Click Programs
Click Administrative Tools

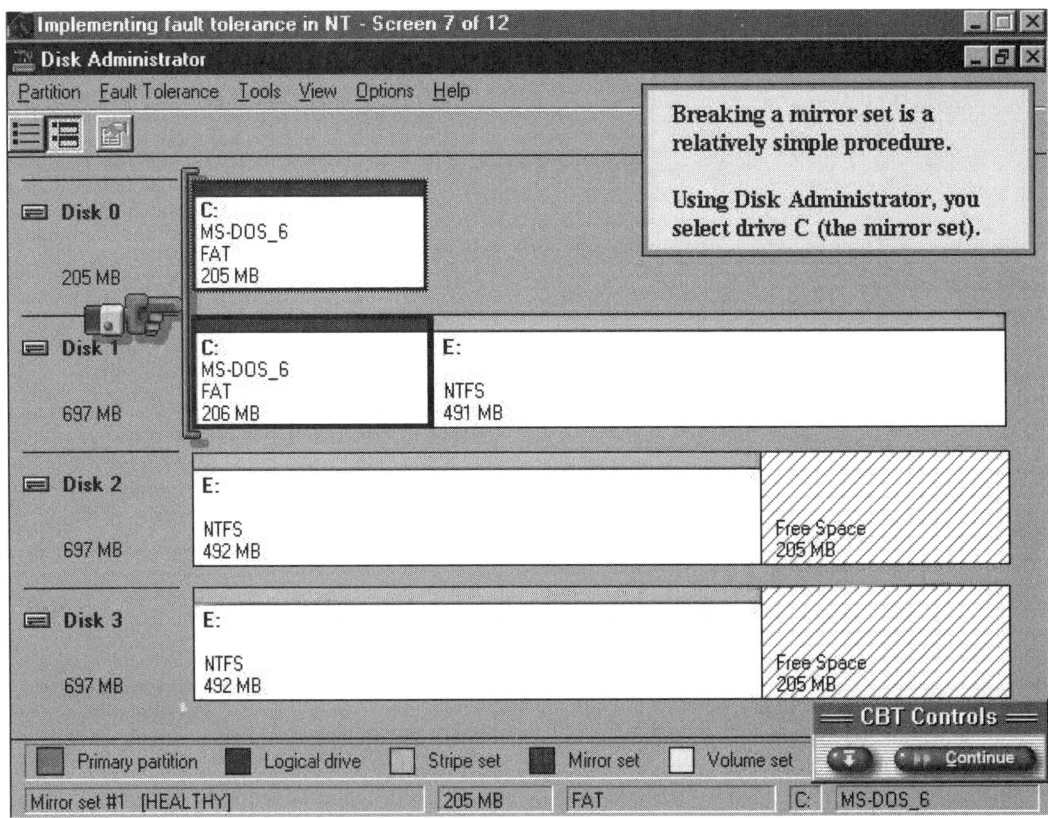

Figure A–49. *Select drive C assuming this is the mirror set you need to repair.*

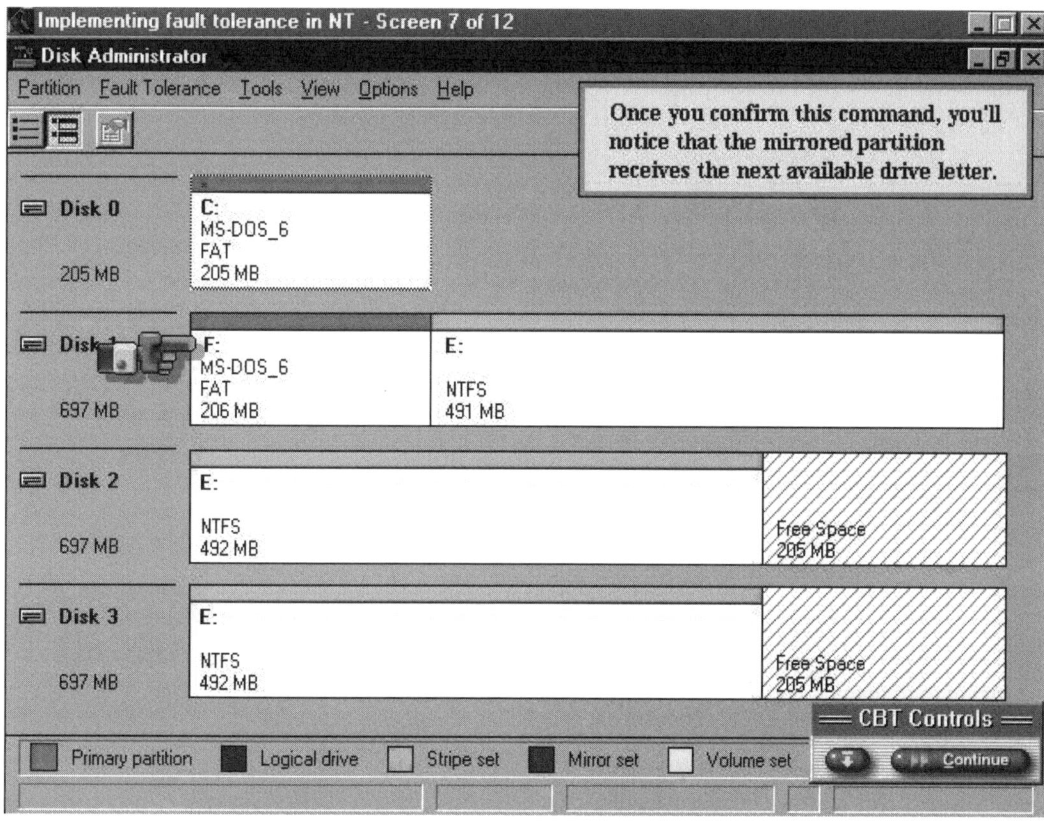

Figure A–50. *The mirrored partition receives the next available drive letter.*

Click Disk Administrator
Select drive C assuming this is the mirror set you need to repair
Select Fault Tolerance from the menu bar
Select Break Mirror from the submenu
Click OK to confirm and the mirrored partition to receive the next available drive letter (Figure A–50)
Select Partition from the menu bar
Select Commit Changes Now from the submenu
Click OK to acknowledge the message reminding you to update the emergency repair disk
Select Partition from the menu bar
Select Exit from the submenu
Select Start
Select Program

Select Windows Explorer. Notice drive F is the exact duplication of drive C (Figure A–51); this assumes that drive C contained the mirrored set needing repair and that F was the next available drive letter

How to Regenerate Data from a Filed Stripe Set Member

Click Start
Click Programs
Click Administrative Tools
Click Disk Administrator
Select the stripe set
Select the new area of free space on a different hard disk; this must be the same size as or large than the stripe set member that failed
Click Fault Tolerance from the menu
Click Regenerate from the submenu (Figure A–52)

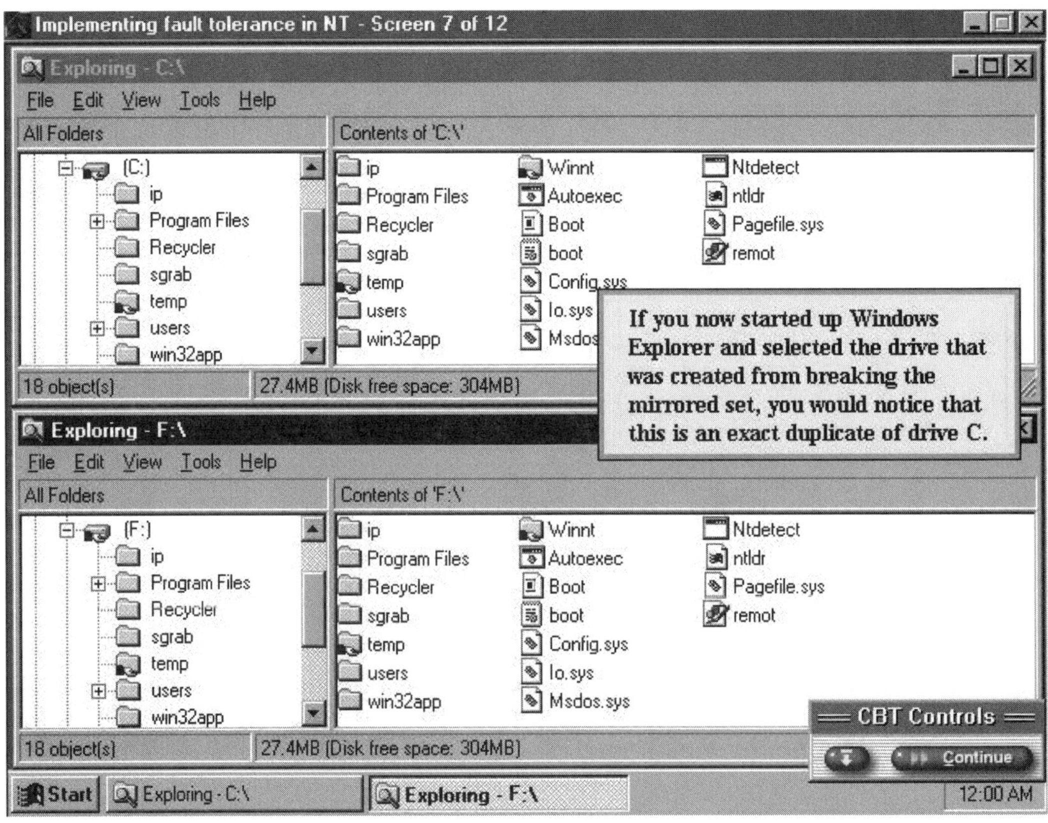

Figure A–51. *Notice the content of the new drive (F) matches the content of the old drive (C).*

Figure A–52. *Select Regenerate, then restart the computer.*

Restart the computer; the fault tolerance driver will read the information from the stripes on the other members, then recreate the data of the missing member that will be written to the new member

Create an NT Fault-Tolerant Boot Disk

Double click on MyComputer
Insert a disk in drive A
Single click the 3 1/2″ Floppy [A:] icon
Select File from the menu bar
Select Format from the submenu to display the Format screen
Check Quick Format
Click the Start button
Click OK
Click OK when formatting is completed

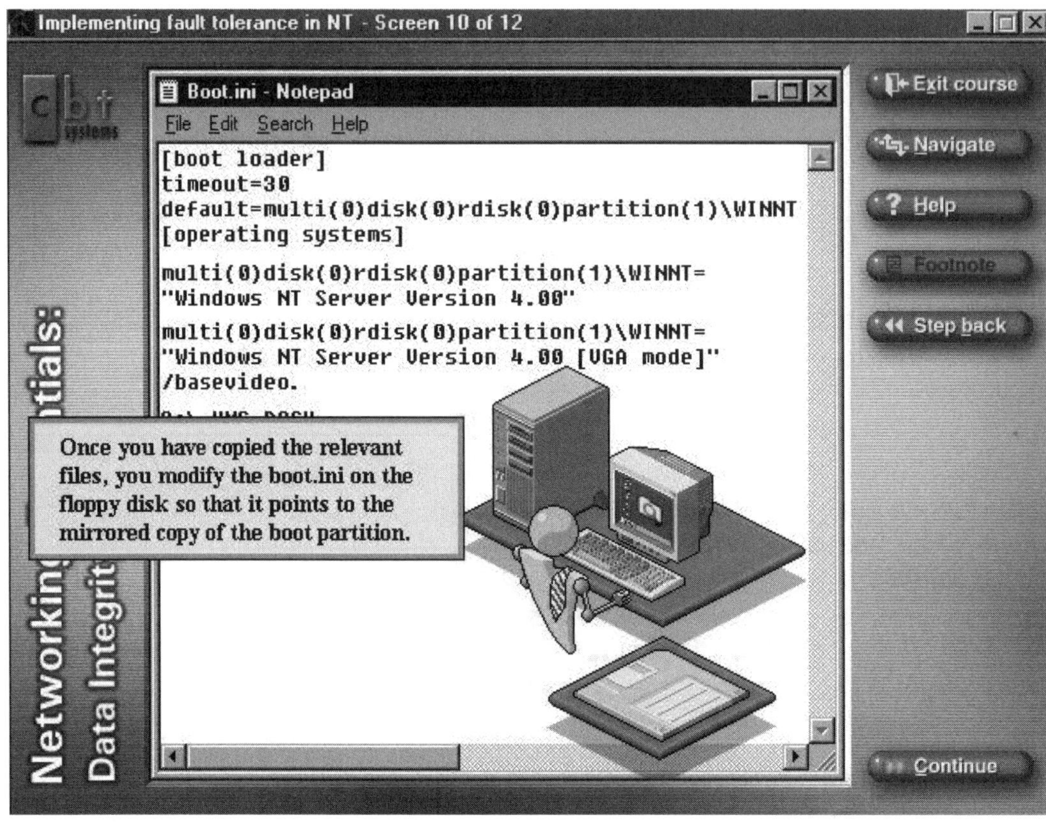

Figure A–53. *Modify the boot.ini file on the floppy disk to mirror the copy of the boot partition.*

Click the Close button
Double-click C: icon on MyComputer to display the Explorer
Click C: on the tree section
If this is an Intel computer, highlight ntldr, boot.ini, ntbootdd.sys, nt-detect.com
If this is an RSIC computer, highlight osloader.exe, and hal.dll
Drag the file to A:
Modify the boot.ini file on the floppy disk to point to the mirrored copy of the boot partition
Boot from the fault-tolerant disk when a physical disk on the server fails

How to Make a Backup Copy of the Registry

Click Start
Click Program

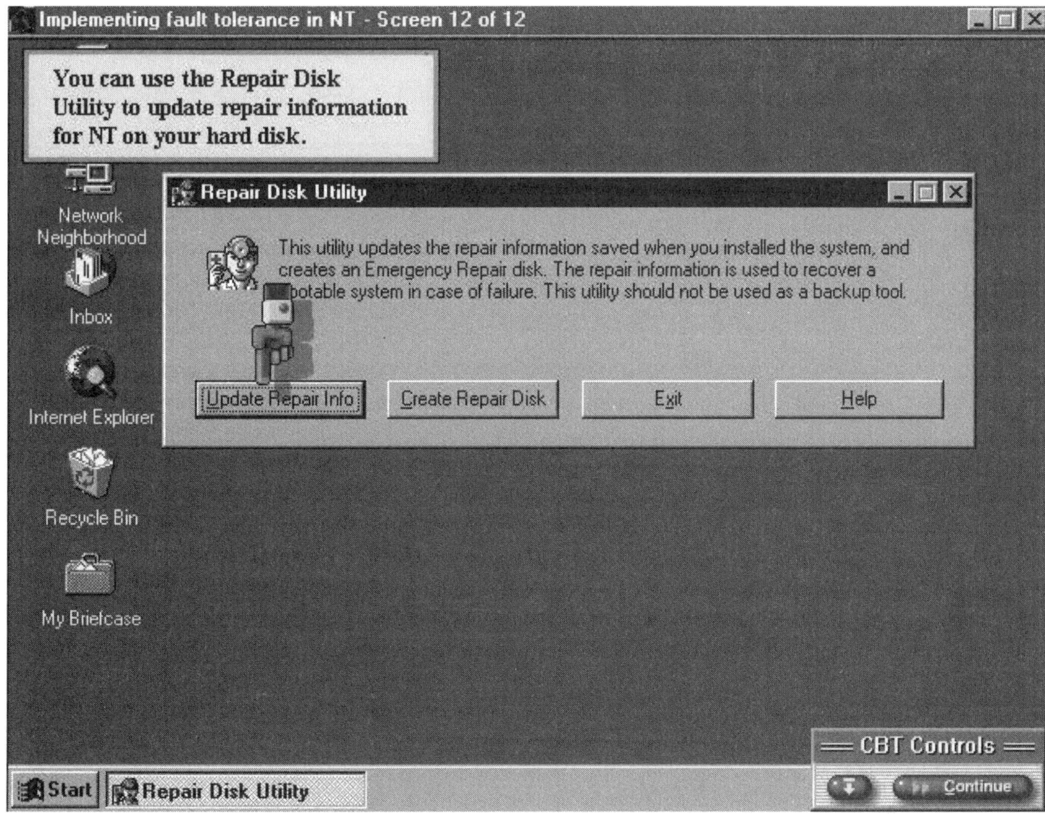

Figure A–54. *Use Repair Disk Utility to copy the registry. The standard NT copy method will not work because the registry file is locked.*

Click Administrative Tools
Click Rdisk to display the Repair Disk Utility (Figure A–54)
Insert a floppy disk
Click Create A Repair Disk; the registry and other necessary files will be copied to the floppy disk

Data Security

Information You Should Know About Account Policy

- Account policy controls the way passwords must be used.
- Changes to the account policy affect each user at the next login

- Passwords can be set to expire in a specified number of days or never expire.
- A user can be set up to change the password immediately or wait a specified number of day.
- A password can be a specified size or not required at all.
- A user can be required to use a different password by having NT remember the last specified number of passwords or can reuse old passwords.
- The account can be locked after a specified number of bad attempts to login or can try an endless number of times to login.
- A user can change a password by pressing Ctrl + Alt + Delete keys, then click Change Password.
- The built-in administrator's account cannot be locked out.

How to Set the Password Policy

Click Start
Click Program
Administrative Tools
Click User Manager
Click Policies from the menu bar
Click Account from the submenu to display the Account Policy dialog box (Figure 9–55)
Select policy features
Click OK

Information You Should Know About User Rights Policy

- A right authorizes a user to perform a certain action on the system.
- Permissions apply to specific objects.
- An object is a network device such as a printer.
- Rights apply to the system as a whole.
- A permission is a rule associated with an object that regulates the user who accesses the object.
- Rights can override a permission.
- Special rights called advance rights can be granted to programmers who write NT applications, but not granted to typical users or groups.
- The easiest way to assign a right to a user is to assign the user to a group that already has the right.

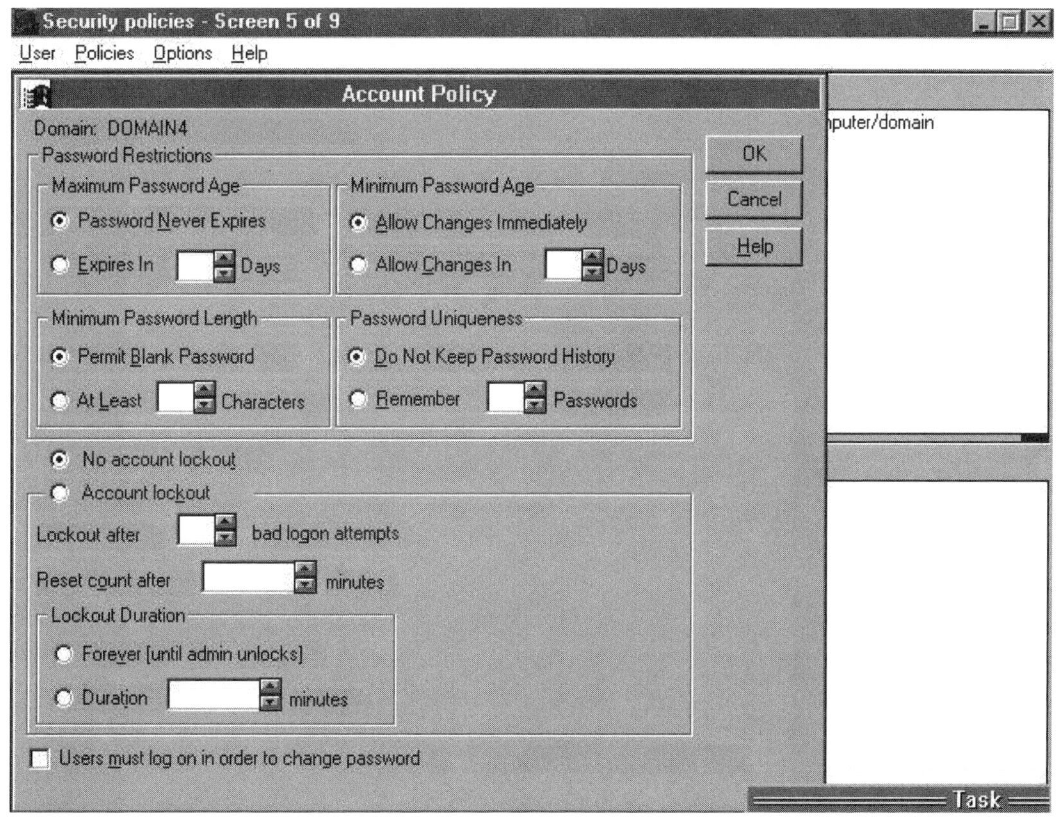

Figure A–55. *Enter the features you want to include in the account policy.*

How to Add a Right

Click Start
Click Program
Click Administrative Tools
Click User Manager
Select Policies from the menu bar
Select User Rights from the sub menu to display the User Rights Policy dialog box (Figure A–56)
Select the right you want to assign from the Rights drop-down list box
Click the Add button to add a user to the right to display the Add User and Group dialog box
Double click on the name of the users in the Add User and Group dialog box
Click OK
Click OK

How to Remove a Right

Click Start
Click Program
Click Administrative Tools
Click User Manager
Select Policies from the menu bar
Select User Rights from the submenu to display the User Rights Policy dialog box (Figure A–56)
Select the right you want to assign from the Rights drop-down list box
Highlight the user you want to remove
Click the Remove button
Click OK

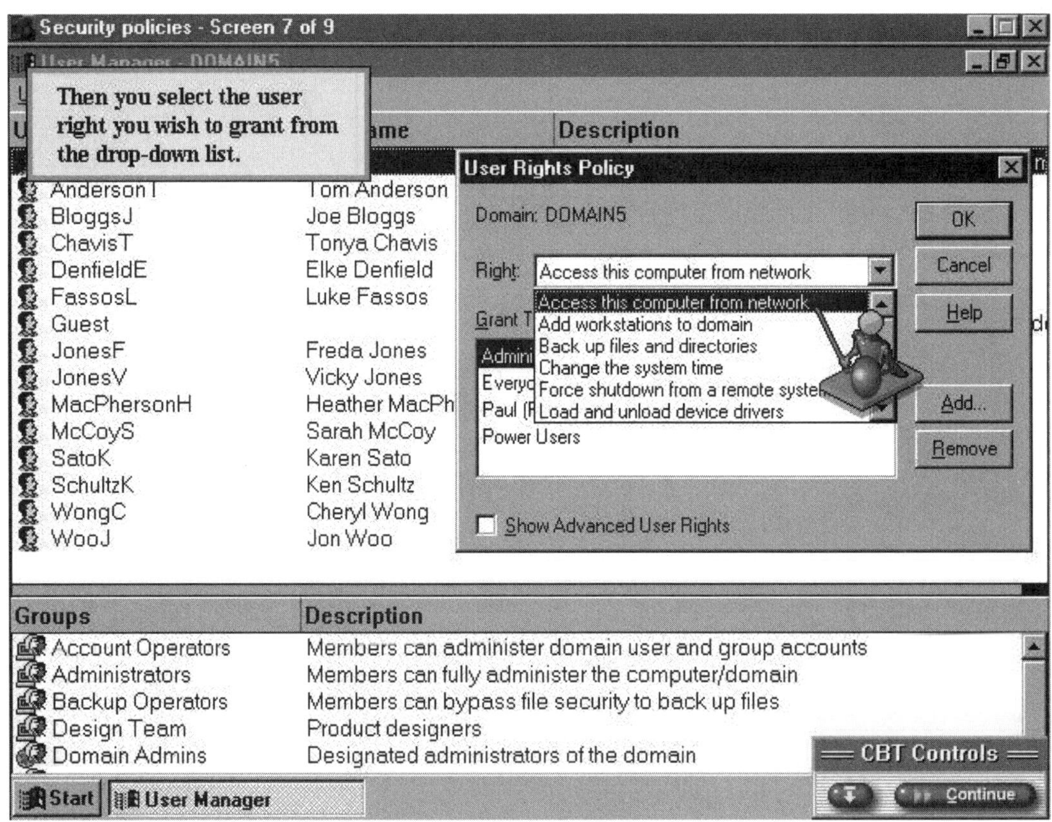

Figure A–56. *Set all rights in the User Rights Policy dialog box.*

How to Add Advance Rights

Click Start
Click Program
Click Administrative Tools
Click User Manager
Select Policies from the menu bar
Select User Rights from the submenu to display the User Rights Policy dialog box (Figure A–56)
Check the Show Advanced User Rights; this adds additional rights to the Rights drop-down list box
Select the right you want to assign from the Rights drop-down list box
Click the Add button to add a user to the right to display the Add User and Group dialog box
Double click on the name of the users in the Add User and Group dialog box
Click OK
Click OK

How to Create an Audit Policy

Click Start
Click Program
Click Administrative Tools
Click User Manager
Select Policies from the menu bar
Select Audit from the sub menu to display the Audit Policy dialog box (Figure A–57)
Check the appropriate features you want to include in the audit policy
Click OK

Information You Need to Know to Set Rights

- A folder is a container object that can contain other objects such as subfolders and files.
- You can set rights to a folder or to objects contained in the folder.
- Letters shown in Table A–1 identify rights.
- By default, everyone is granted full control of objects.
- The owner of the object can assign rights to the object.
- When an object is copied, the permission of the object is not copied to the new object.

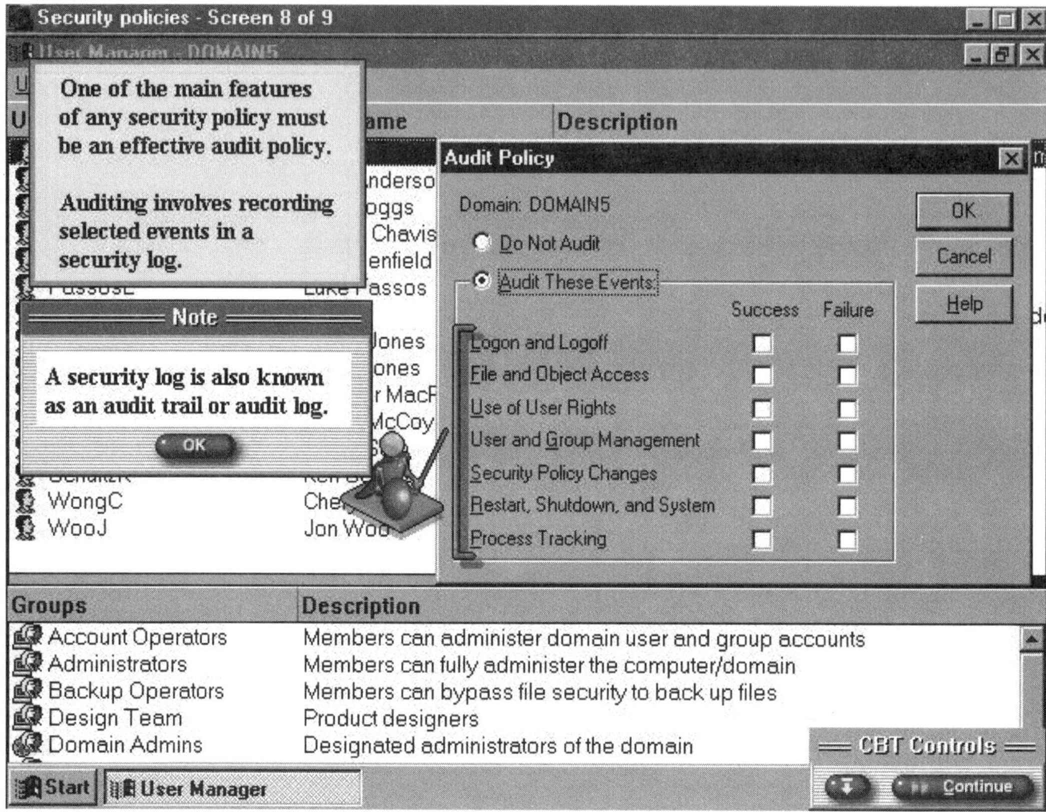

Figure A–57. *Check the appropriate features of the audit policy.*

Table A–1 *Rights and Their Symbols*

Letter Symbol	Right
R	Read
X	Execute
W	Write
D	Delete
P	Change file permissions.
O	Take ownership of object
List	Read and Write
Add	Execute and Write
Add and Read	Read, Execute, and Write

- When an object is moved, all permissions of the object are retained.
- You need permission to read the original file and permission to add files to the target folder when you copy an object.
- You need delete and write permissions to an object to move it and you need permission to add files to the target folder.

How to Set Permission to a File

Click Start
Click Program
Click Windows NT Explorer
Highlight the folder for which you want to set permissions
Select File from the menu bar
Select Properties from the submenu to display the Properties dialog box (Figure A–58)

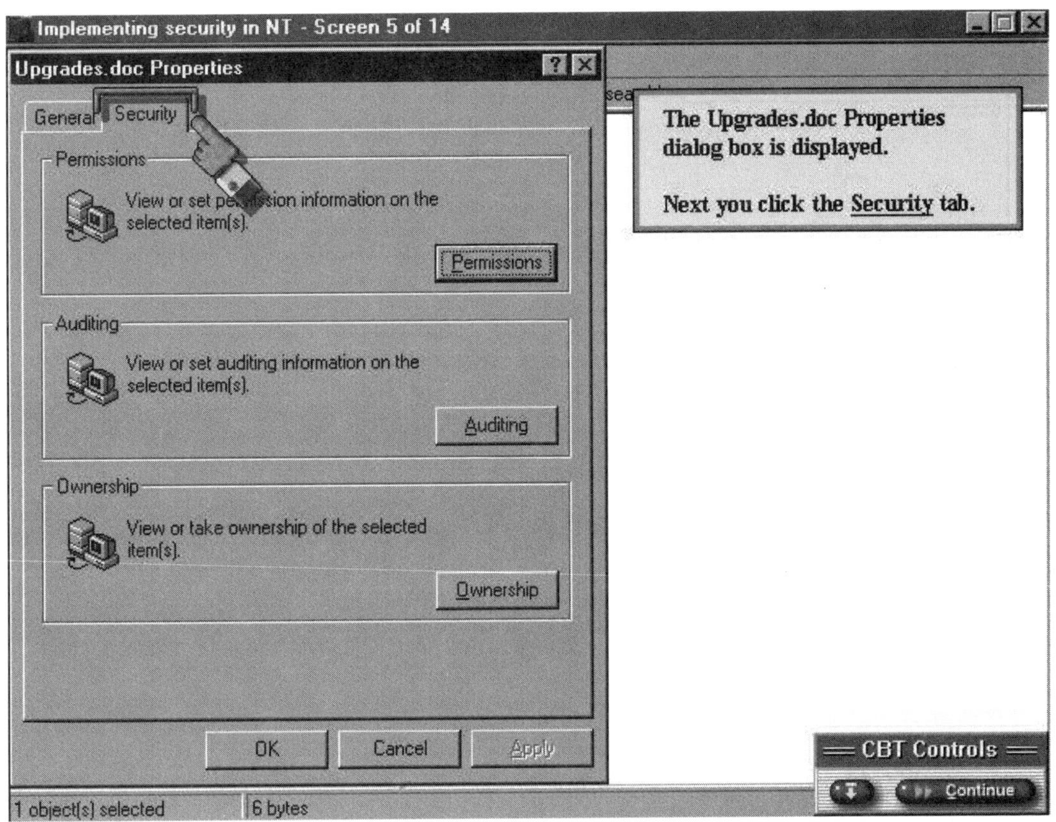

Figure A–58. *Select the properties from the object by using the Properties dialog box.*

Select the sharing tab
Click the Permission button to display the File Permissions dialog box
Click the Add button
Highlight and click the user or group name you want to access the object (Figure A–59)
Click OK
Select the type of access you want to grant.
Click Special Access to display the Special Access dialog box (Figure A–60)
Check the permissions you want to grant
Click OK
Click OK

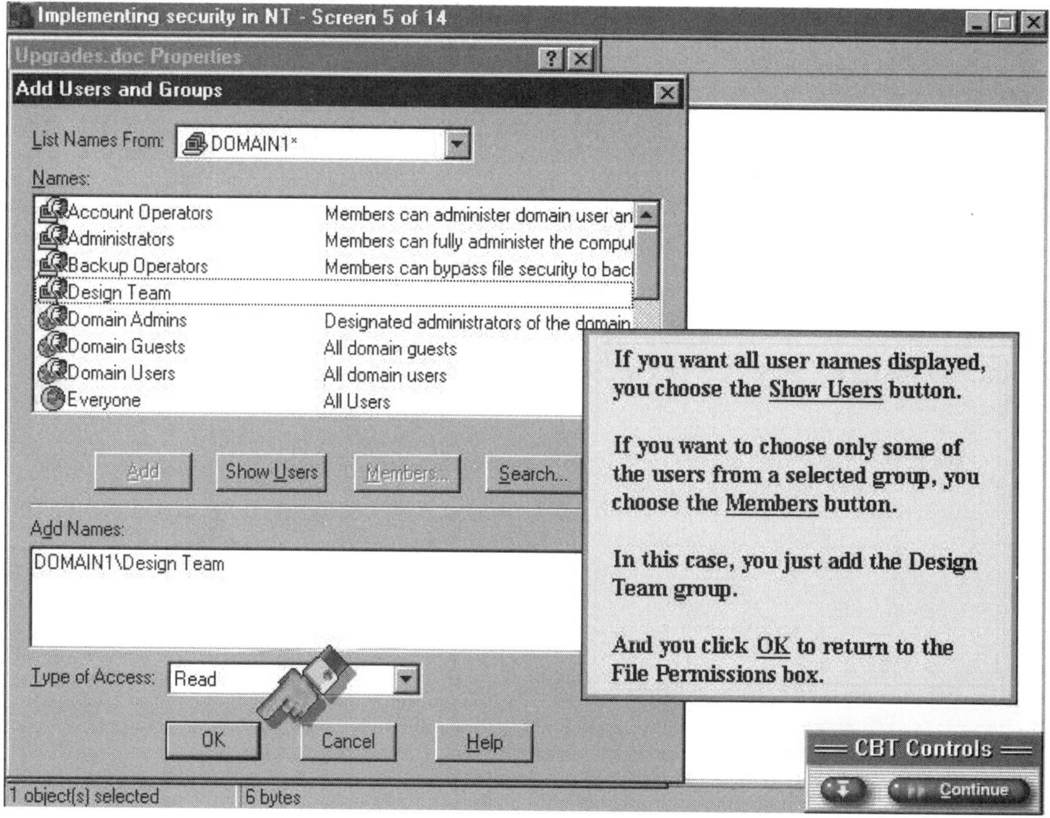

Figure A–59. *Highlight and click the user or group who will have permission to access the object.*

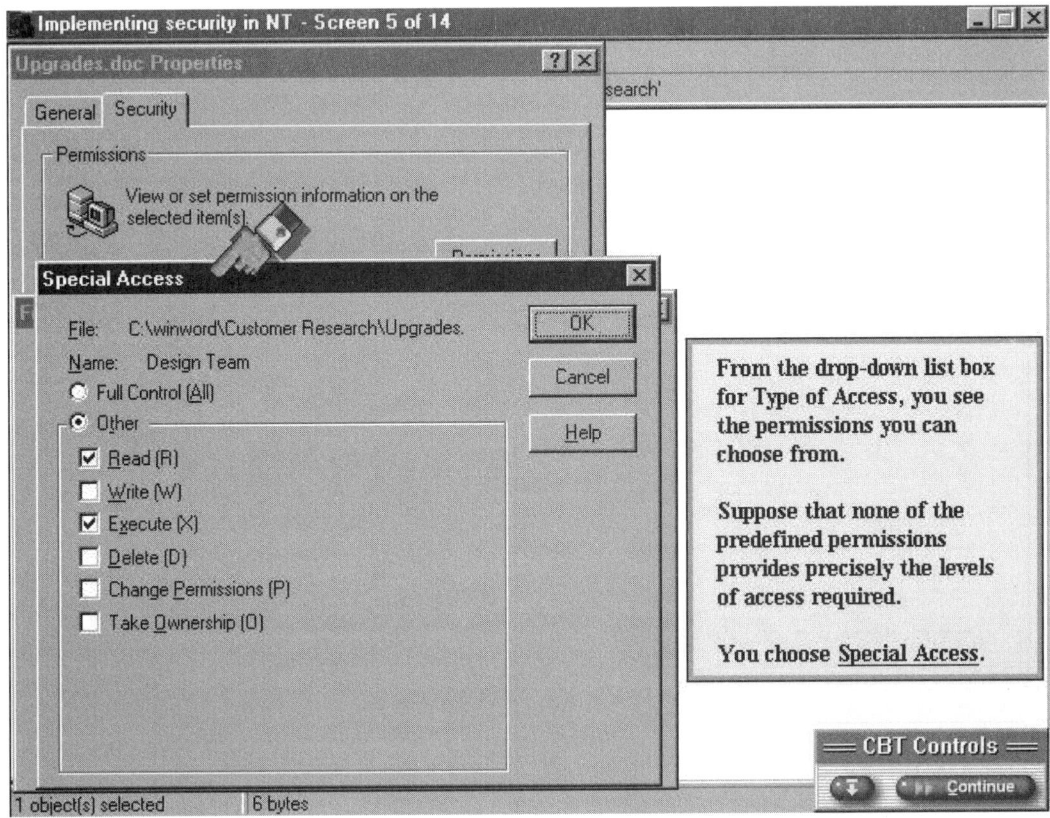

Figure A–60. *Check the permissions you want to grant to the object.*

How to Delete a Permission to a File

Click Start
Click Program
Click Windows NT Explorer
Highlight the file for which you want to set permissions
Select File from the menu bar
Select Properties from the submenu to display the Properties dialog box (Figure A–58)
Select the Security tab
Click the Permission button to display the File Permissions dialog box
Highlight the permission you want to delete
Click the Remove button
Click OK

How to Restrict Access to a Folder

Click Start
Click Program
Click Windows NT Explorer
Highlight the folder for which you want to restrict access
Click File from the menu
Click Properties from the submenu to display the Properties dialog box
Select the Security tab
Click the Permission button to display the Directory Permissions dialog box
Select Special Directory Access from the Type of Access drop-down list box (Figure A–61); this sets the access type for the folder and subfolders
Select Special File Access from the type of Access drop-down list box; This specifies the type of access for files contained in the folder

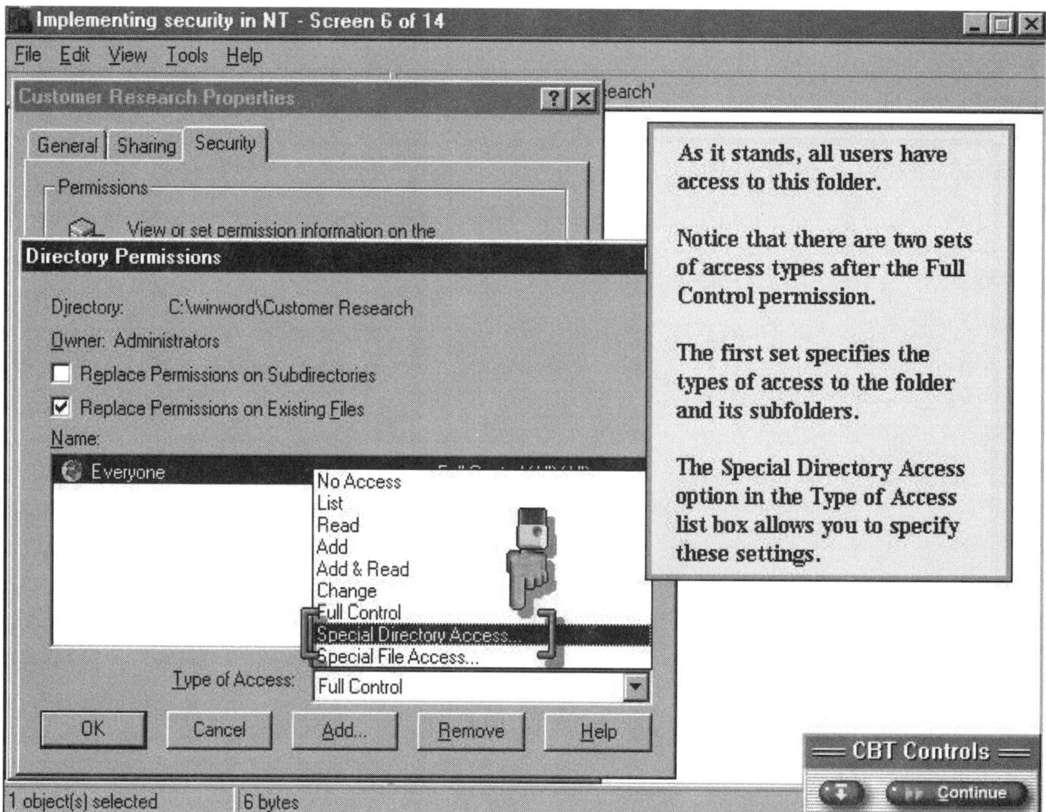

Figure A–61. *Special Directory Access from the Type of Access drop-down list box.*

Check Replace Permissions on Subdirectories
Check Replace Permission on Existing files (Figure A–62)
Click the Remove button to remove the group Everyone from having access to the folder
Click the Add button to display the Add User and Groups dialog box
Double-click on the user or groups you want to grant access to the folder
Click OK
Highlight the name of the user or group whom you gave access to the folder
Select the access rights from the Type Of Access drop-down list for the highlight user or group
Click OK

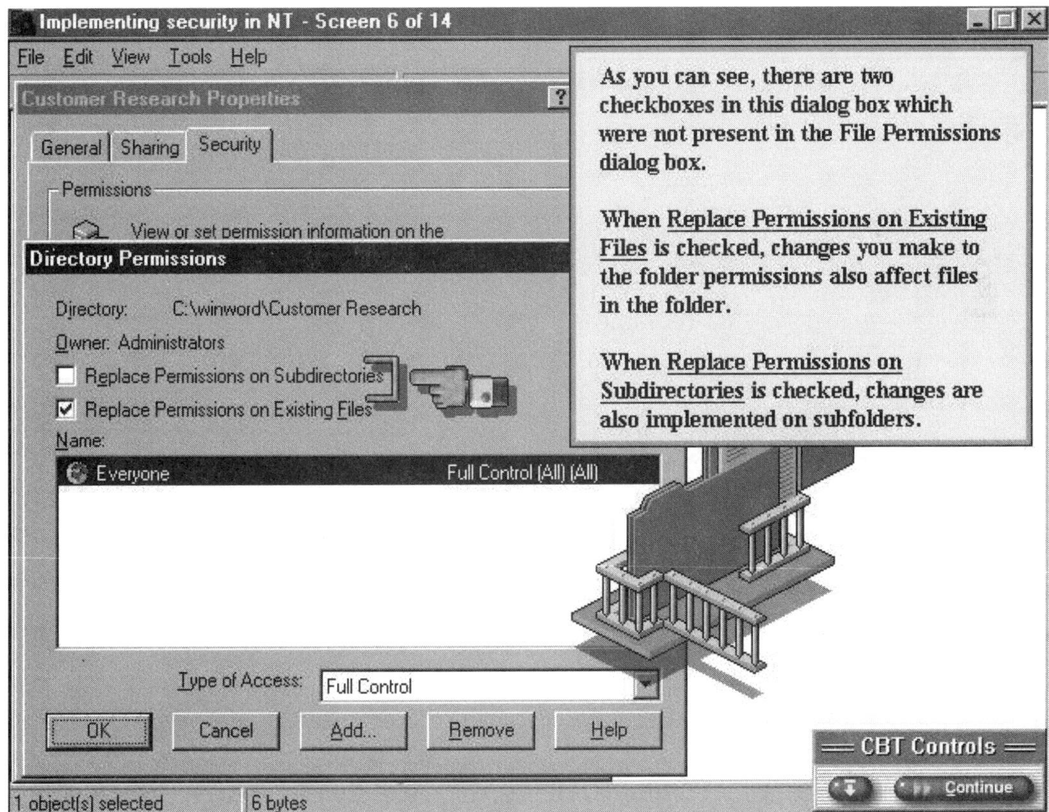

Figure A–62. *Check Replace Permissions on Subdirectories and existing files.*

Information You Should Know About Sharing a Folder with a Remote Computer

- Shared folders are shown on a remote computer within the Neighborhood folder.
- The Remote computer can see subfolders and files within the shared folder.
- Access can be restricted to the folder.
- A maximum of ten users can connect to a shared folder on an NT Workstation.
- An unlimited number of users can connect to a shared folder on an NT Server.
- Only one permission is listed for each user or group.
- You cannot set separate share permissions on files within the shared folder.

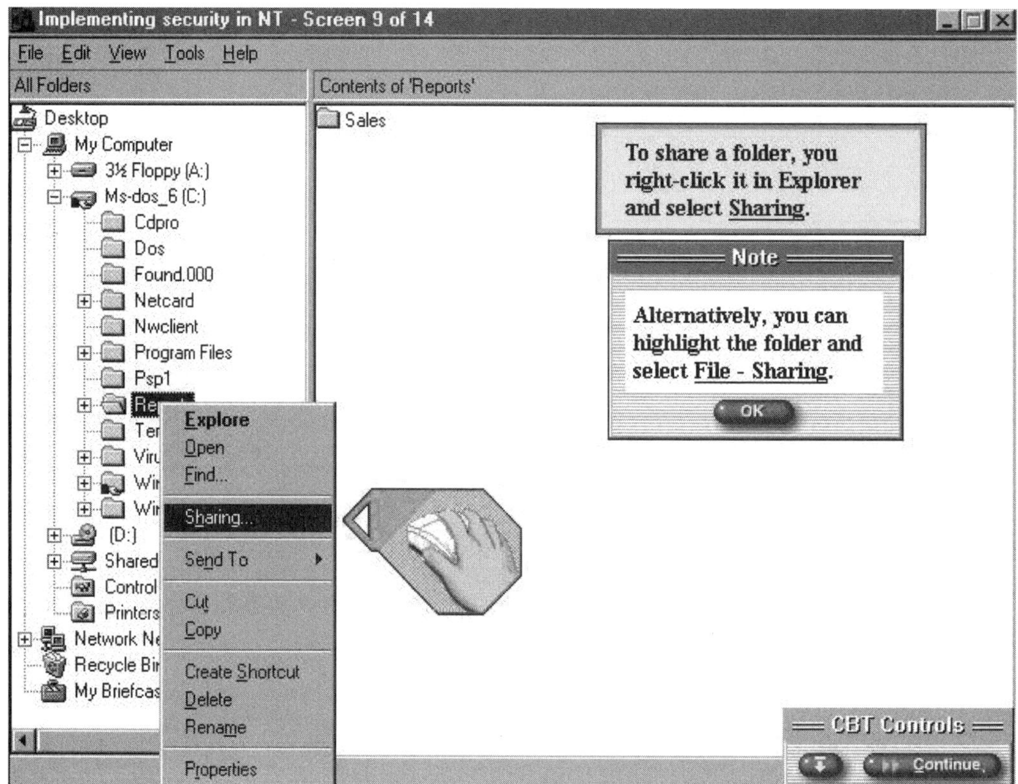

Figure A–63. *The Sharing option enables you to designate a folder to be shared by a remote computer.*

How to Share a Folder with a Remote Computer

Click Start
Click Program
Click Windows NT Explorer
Highlight the folder for which you want to share
Right-click the mouse
Click Sharing (Figure A–63)
Click the Sharing tab
Check the Shared As check box (Figure A–64)
Click the Permission button to see the Permissions dialog box
Click the Add button to display the Add User and Group dialog box
Double-click on the users or groups with whom you want to share the folder
Click OK
Highlight the user or group you want to set access to the folder

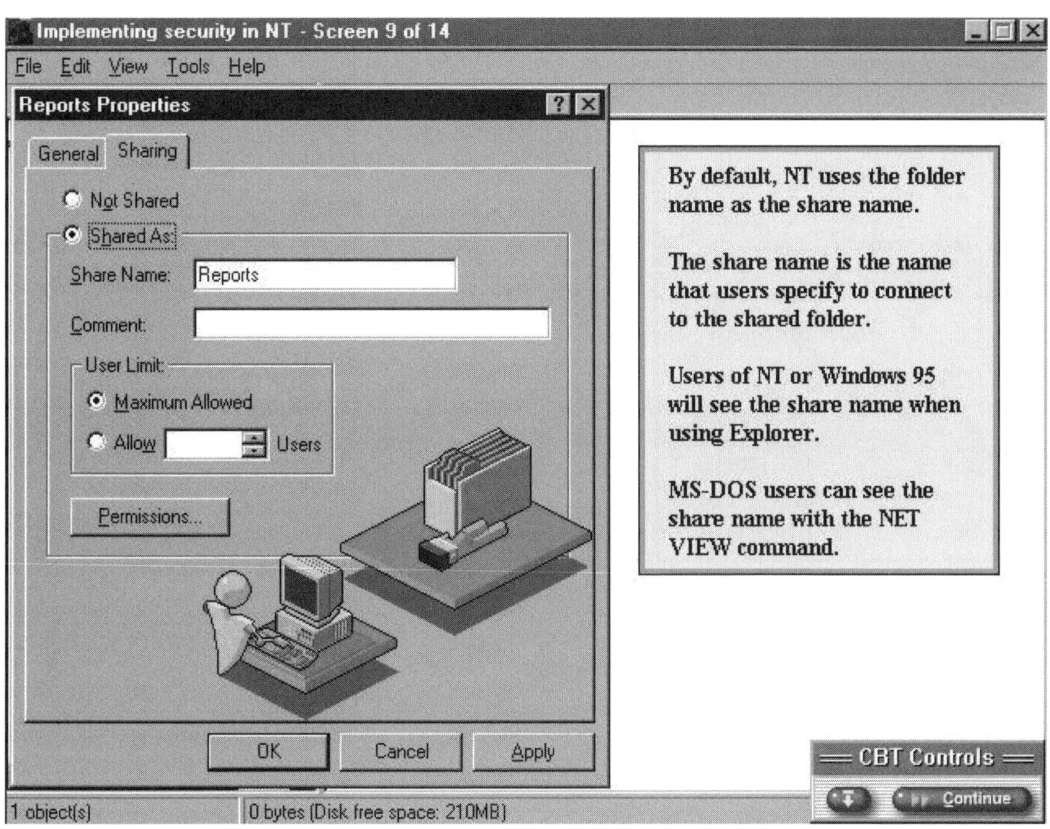

Figure A–64. *Check the Shared As check box to make the folder a shared folder.*

Select the access permission from the Type of Access drop-down list
Click OK

How to Unshare a Folder with a Remote Computer

Click Start
Click Program
Click Windows NT Explorer
Highlight the folder for which you want to share
Right-click the mouse
Click Sharing
Click the Sharing tab
Check the Not Shared radio button
Click OK

Information You Should Know About Ownership of an Object

- You become the owner of an object, such as a folder or file when you create the object.
- The owner of an object has full control over the object.
- Other users can gain ownership of an object.
- You cannot give someone else ownership of your object directly.
- You can grant someone else permission to take ownership of your object.
- A member of the administration group can take ownership of any file or folder object.

How to Take Ownership of an Object

Click Start
Click Program
Click Windows NT Explorer
Highlight the folder to which you want to take ownership
Click File from the menu bar
Click Properties from the submenu to display the Properties dialog box
Click the Sharing tab
Click OK

How to Audit Access to a Folder or File

Click Start
Click Program

Click Administrative Tools
Click User Manager
Select Policies from the menu bar
Select Audit from the submenu
Select File and Object Access from Audit These Events group (Figure A–65) to turn on the audit option
Click OK
Highlight the folder or file in Windows NT Explorer that you want to audit
Click File from the menu bar
Click Properties from the submenu to display the Properties dialog box
Select the Security tab
Click the Auditing button to display the Directory Audit dialog box
Click the Add button to display the Add User and Group dialog box
Double click the user or group you want to audit (Figure A–66)
Click OK

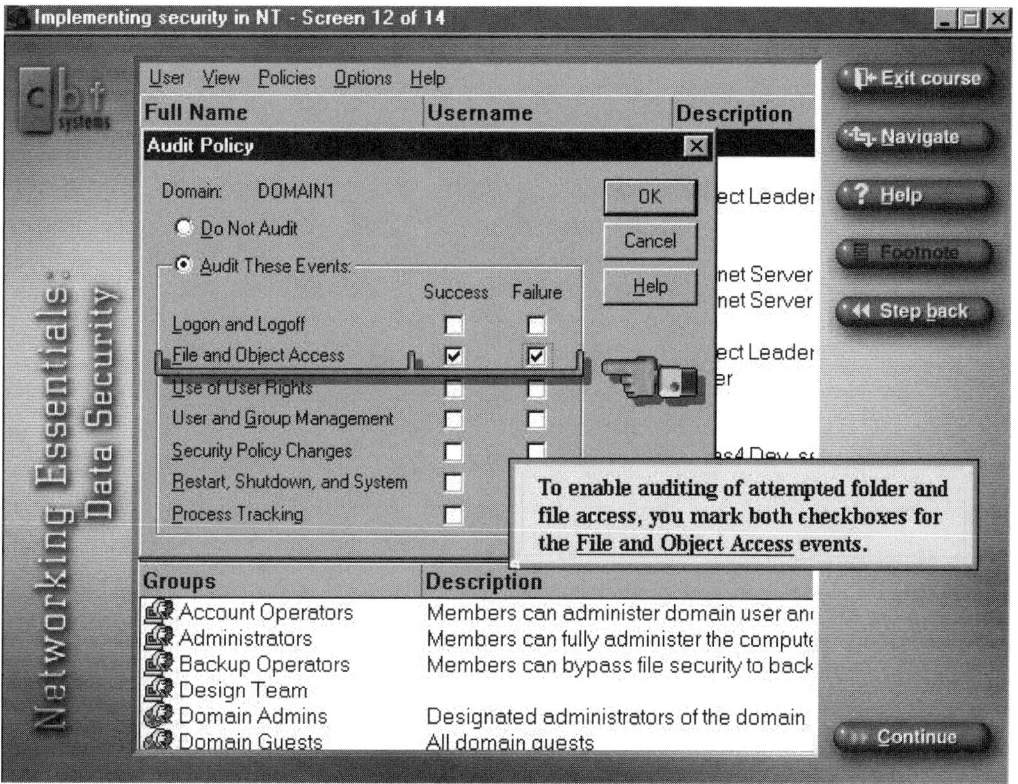

Figure A–65. *Select the file and Object Access from the Audit These Events group.*

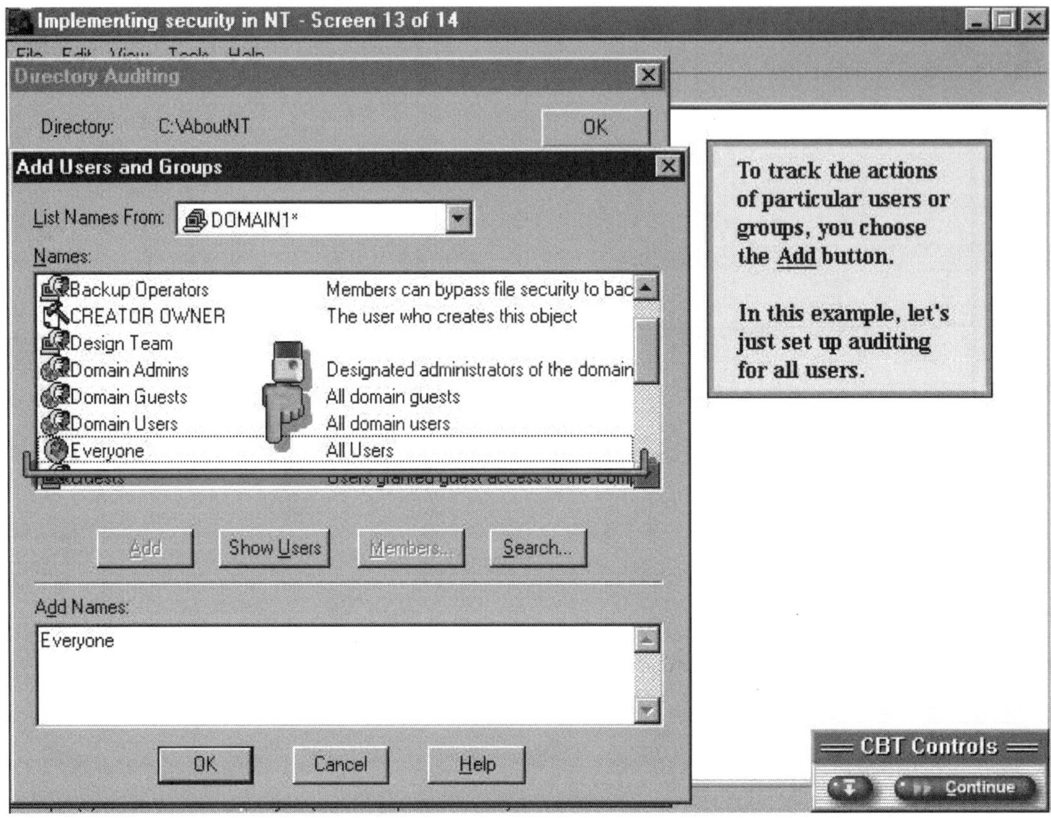

Figure A–66. *Double-click the user or group you want to audit.*

Select the audit events you want to audit (Figure A–67)
Click the Replace Auditing On Existing Files checkbox and the Replace Auditing On Subdirectories check box
Click Ok
Click OK
Use the Event Viewer to see the audit trail

How to Turn Off Auditing Access to a Folder or File by Deactivating the Audit Option

Click Start
Click Program
Click Administrative Tools
Click User Manager
Select Policies from the menu bar

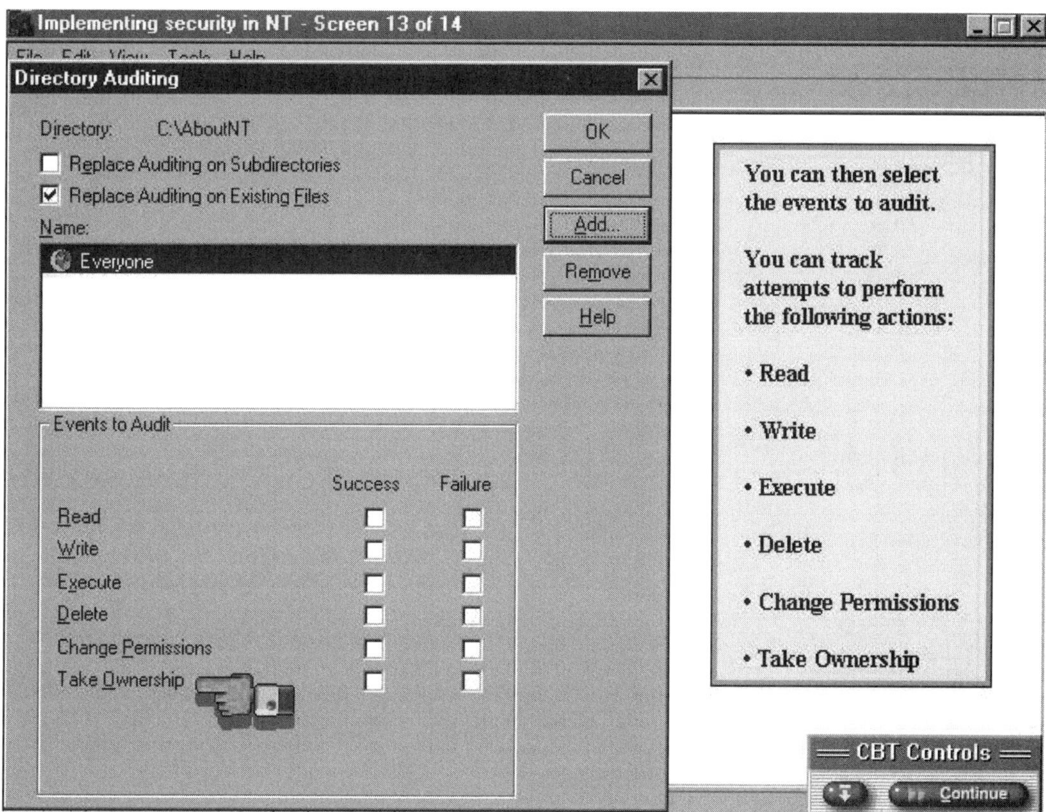

Figure A–67. *Select the audit events you want to audit.*

Select Audit from the submenu
Click Do Not Audit checkbox
Click OK

Network Adapter Card

How to Configure a Network Adapter Card

Insert the Network Adapter card into the computer
Turn on the computer
Click Start
Click Settings
Click Control Panel
Double-click the Network icon to display the Network dialog box

Select the Adapter tab
Click the Add button
Highlight the name of the Network Adapter card you installed (Figure A–68); if the name does not appear, then insert the vendor's installation disk in drive A and click the Have Disk button
Click OK
Verify the Network Adapter card settings (Figure A–69)
Click OK
If your system has more than one hardware bus, then you may be asked to verify the bus type and number; do so, then click OK
You may be asked to copy files from the Windows NT Setup disk (Figure A–70) Insert the Windows NT Setup disk in drive A and click the Continue button
The name of the Network Adapter card will appear in the Adapter tab of the Network dialog box

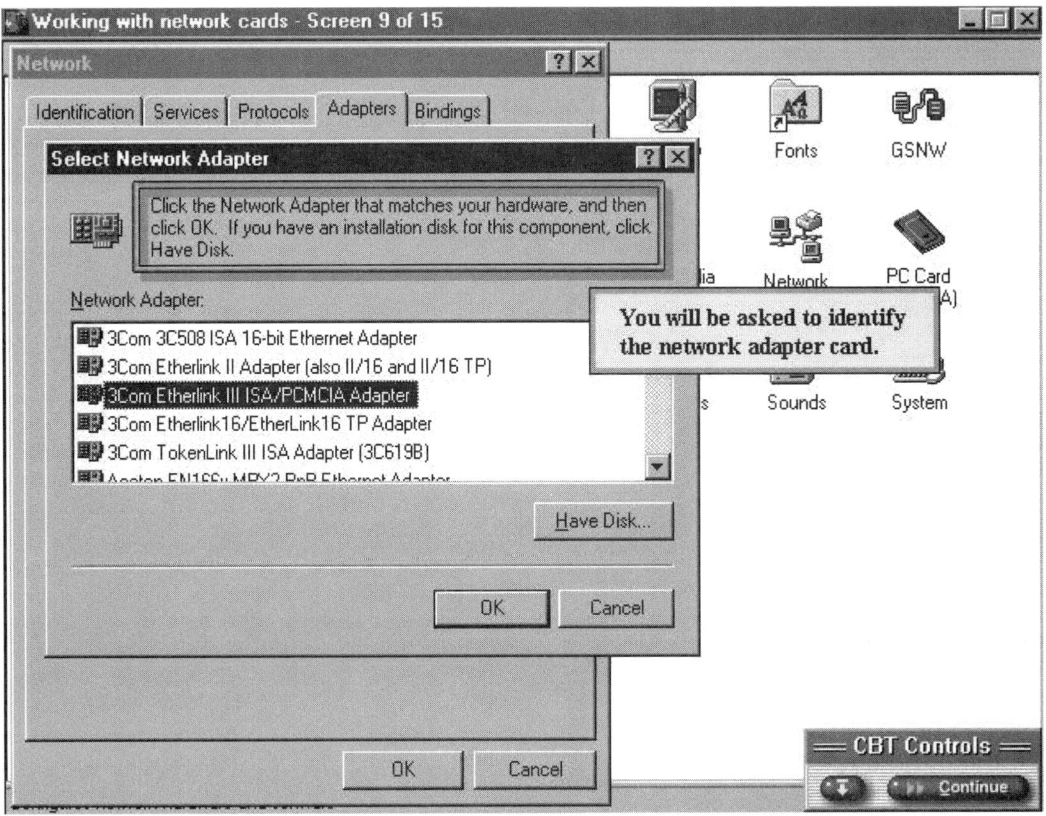

Figure A–68. *Highlight the name of the Network Adapter card you installed.*

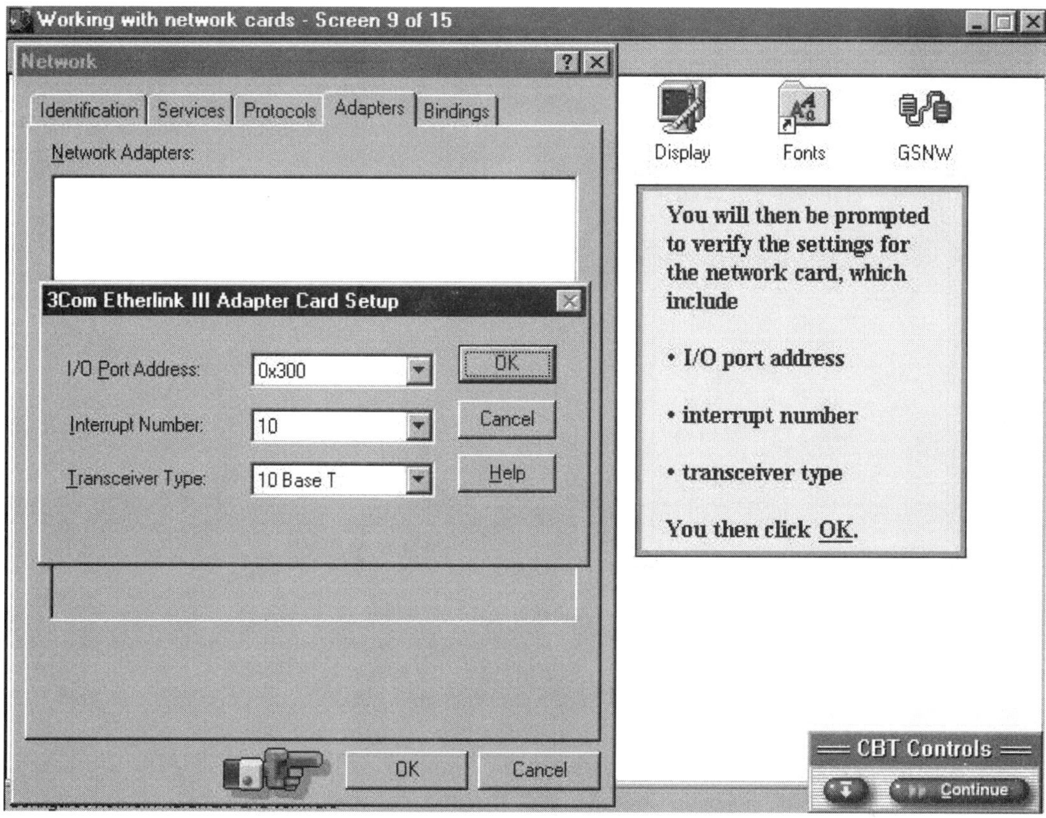

Figure A–69. *Insert the Windows NT Setup disk in drive A when prompted.*

Select the Protocol tab
You don't need to install a protocol if your network uses NetBEUI; if not, then you need to install the appropriate protocols by clicking the Add button
Highlight the protocols you want to install
Click OK
Click the Close button
Click the Yes button when prompted to restart your computer

How to View the Network Adapter Card Configuration Information in the Registry

Click Start
Click Program
Click Administrative Tools
Click Windows NT Diagnostics to display the Windows NT Diagnostics dialog box

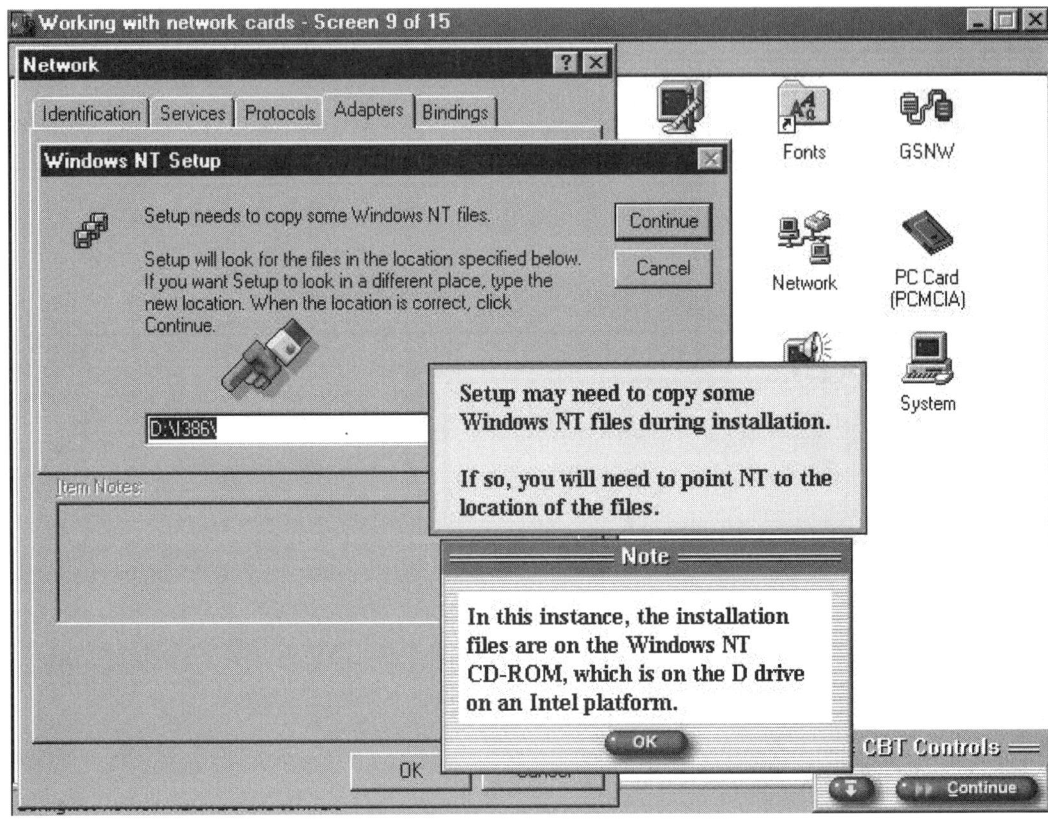

Figure A–70.

Select the Resource tab
Click the Include HAL Resources checkbox (Figure A–71)
Click the various option buttons to view various kinds of information about the Network Adapter card
Click OK

How to Assign a New Interrupt Number to the Network Adapter Card

Insert the Network Adapter card into the computer
Turn on the computer
Click Start
Click Settings
Click Control Panel
Double-click the Network icon to display the Network dialog box
Select the Adapter tab

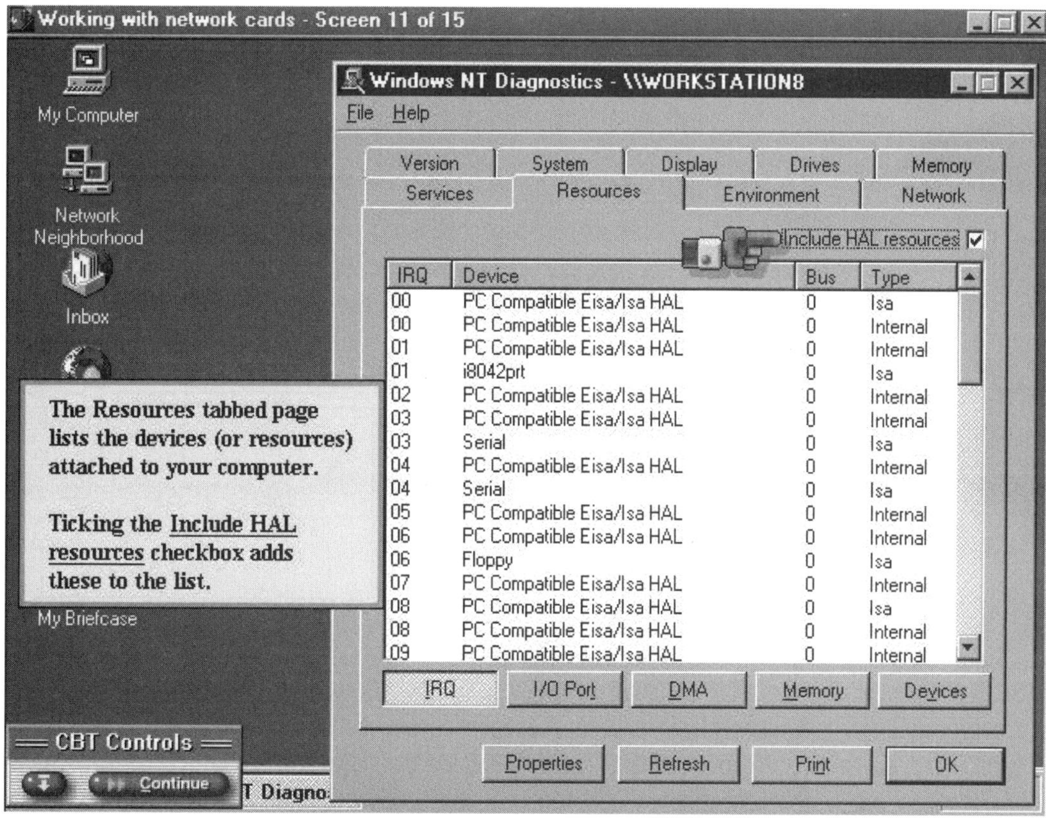

Figure A–71. *Be sure to check the Include HAL Resources checkbox.*

Double-click the name of your Network Adapter card to display the Adapter Card
Setup dialog box
Select an available interrupt
Click OK
Click the Yes button to restart your computer

Network Operating System

Information You Need to Know About Windows NT Server

- The NT Server setup program will detect hardware and software installed on your computer and load and configure the most appropriate drivers.

- The NT Server setup program can be run from a supported or unsupported CD ROM or run over the network. A supported CD ROM is that NT Server contains on its known hardware list. An unsupported CD ROM is one that is not on this list.
- Running the NT Server setup program from an unsupported CD ROM requires three formatted, blank disks if the setup program is run as WINNT /B. Otherwise, floppy disks are not required.
- Running the NT Server setup program over a network must be run from a computer running Windows NT, Windows 95, Windows 98, MS Lan Manager, Novell Netware, Banyan Vines, and Windows for Workgroups. Also the NT Server distribution files must be a shared point.
- You need the following information before running the NT Server Setup program:
  Full details of installed hardware
  Licensing information
  File system, partition, and folder information
  Domain information
  Types of processor(s) running on the computer
  Type of network adapter card and its settings
  The Model of the printer and port used by the printer
  Know if the CD ROM is supported or not
  The name of the computer
  The name of the domain the server is joining or the new domain if one is being created
  Will the server be the primary controller (PDC) or the backup domain controller (BDC)?
- There are two NT setup programs: WINNT.EXE and WINNT32.EXE.
- WINNT.EXE is used when the computer is booted under MS DOS, Windows 95, Windows 98, or installed over a network.
- WINNT32.EXE is used for upgrading the NT operating system.

How to Install NT Server

Insert the Net Server setup CD into the CD ROM
Make the i386 folder on the CD ROM the current folder
Type WINNT at the command prompt and press Enter
Press Enter to accept the suggested path for the installation or type a new path, then press Enter
If the CD ROM is unsupported, you'll be prompted to insert the three floppy disks into drive A; the NT Server setup program will create a set of boot disks

Insert the NT Server boot disk 1 into drive A:
Press Enter when The NT Server setup program will prompt you to restart your computer
Replace disk 1 with disk 2 when prompted and press Enter
Press Enter when prompted and the NT Server setup program will search for mass storage devices
Replace disk 2 with disk 3 when prompted and press Enter
A list of mass storage devices found by the NT Server setup program is displayed (Figure A–72). Press Enter or continue or press S to specify an additional device
Press Enter to accept the list of hardware and software components found by the NT Server setup program
Highlight the disk partition where you want NT Server installed then press Enter (Figure A–73)
Press Enter when asked to confirm your selection of the disk partition
Select basic or exhaustive examination of your hard disk; NT Server setup program will perform either task before continuing with the installation

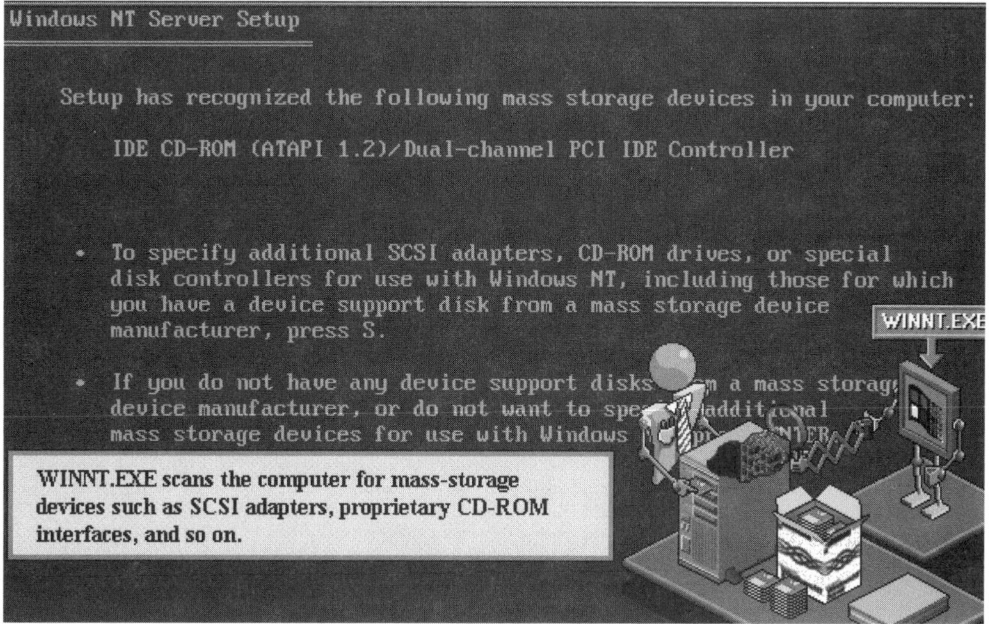

Figure A–72. *A list of mass storage devices are displayed. Press S to include one that might be missing.*

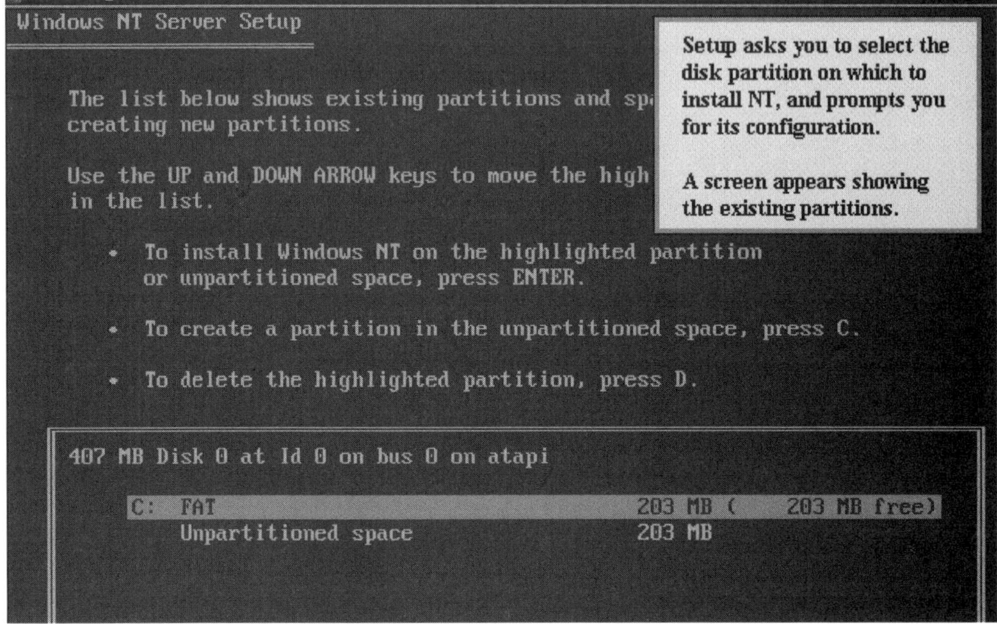

Figure A–73. *Highlight the disk partition where you want NT Server installed. You might be requested to format the partition.*

Remove the floppy disk, then restart the computer when prompted; you'll see this prompt after NT is finished loading the necessary NT Server files onto your computer

Press F8 if you agree to the licensing agreement when the agreement is displayed on the screen

The NT Server setup program runs the NT Server Setup Wizard

Click the Next button

Enter your name and the name of your organization and click the Next button

Select the appropriate licensing mode and click the Next button (Figure A–74)

Enter the name of the computer and click the Next button; the name must be unique and not more than 15 characters long

Select if the server will be the Primary Domain Controller, Backup Domain Controller, or a stand-alone server, then click the Next button

Enter the administrative password that consists of 14 characters or less, then enter it a second time for confirmation; click the Next button

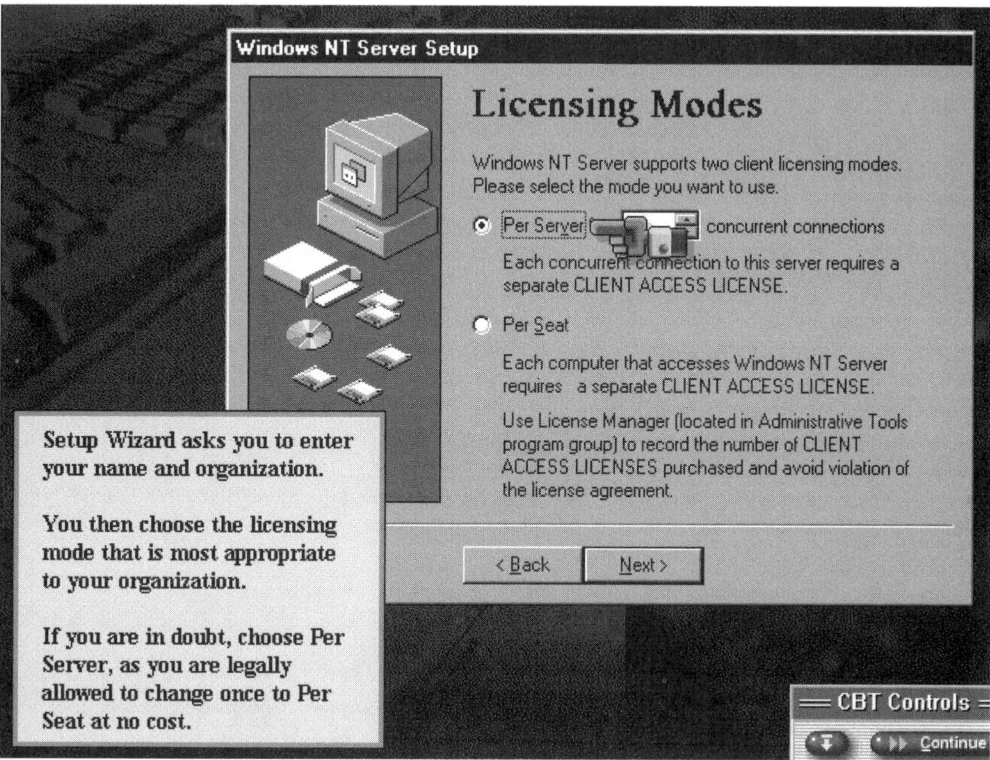

Figure A–74. *Select the appropriate licensing mode.*

Select to create an Emergency Repair Disk then click the Next button
Select the optional components that you want installed (Figure A–75) and click the Next button
Click the Next button to install Windows NT Networking; **caution**: this is your last opportunity to use the Back button to change your previous selections
Select Wired to the network or Remote access to the network, which means the network is accessed using a modem; click the Next button
If the NT Server is going to be used for an Internet or Intranet, then click the checkbox. Click the Next button
Click Start Search to have the wizard search for the Network Adapter card; click the Next button
Click Select from List then click the Next button
Highlight the Network Protocol that is to be used and click the Next button (Figure A–76)

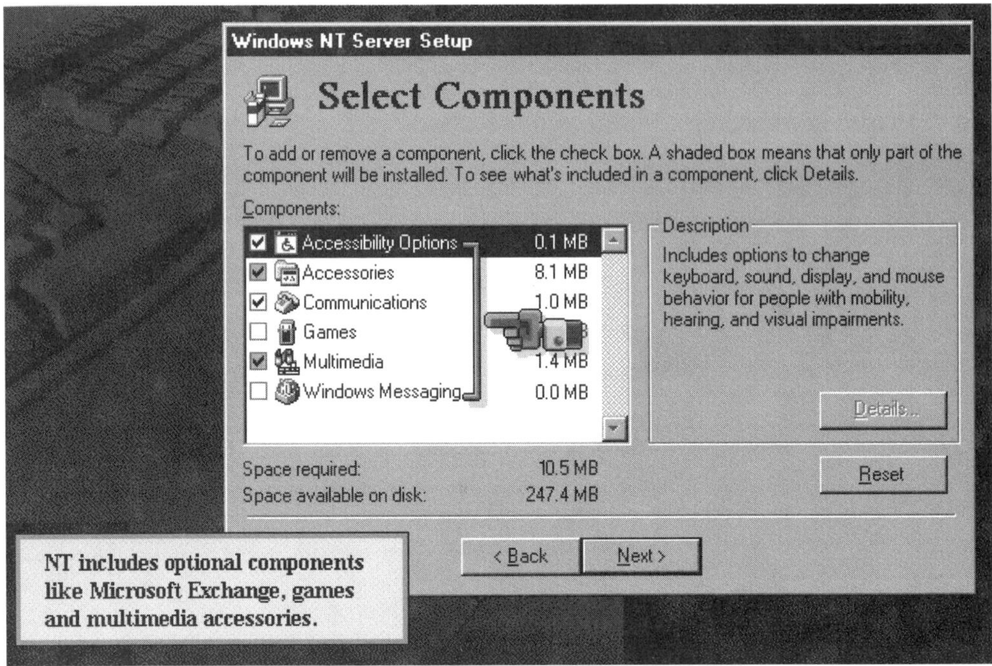

Figure A–75. *Check the optional components that you want installed.*

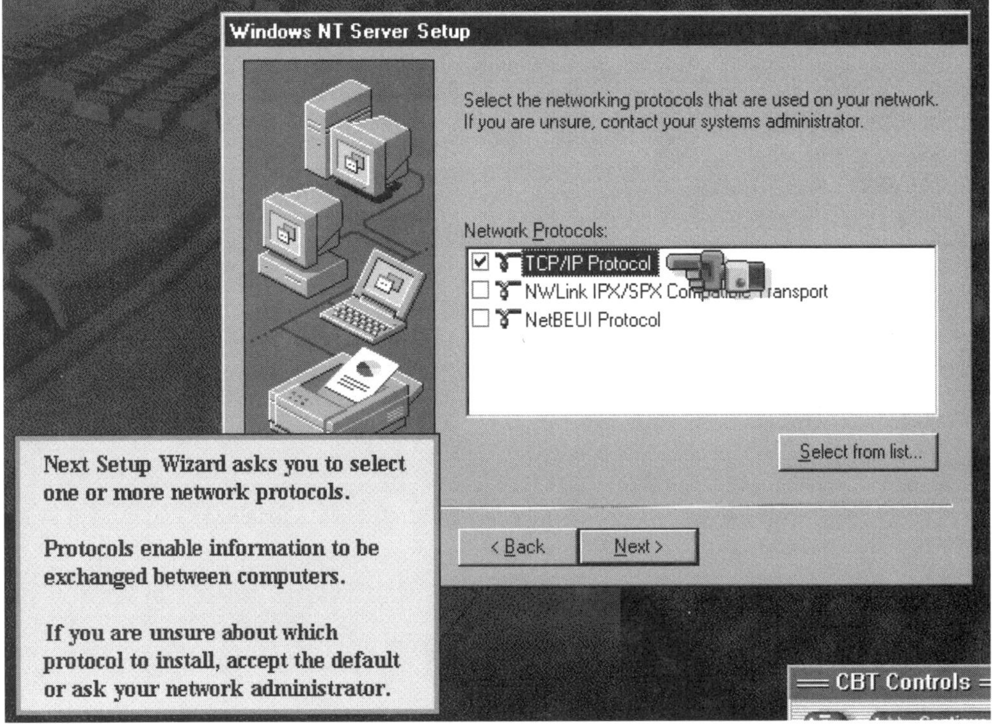

Figure A–76. *Highlight the Network Protocol that NT Server should use on the network.*

Highlight the network services you want to install and click the Next button
Click the Next button to install selected components
Highlight the binding(s), then click the Enabled or Disabled button depending if you want to use them in the installation; click the Next button (Figure A–77)
Enter the name of the domain that the NT server is joining and click the Next button
Click the Finish button
Select the appropriate date, time, and time zone and click the Close button
Configure your video display (if necessary) and click the OK button
Click the Restart icon to restart your computer that will boot under NT Server
Press Ctrl + Alt + Delete, then logon to the server as the administrator

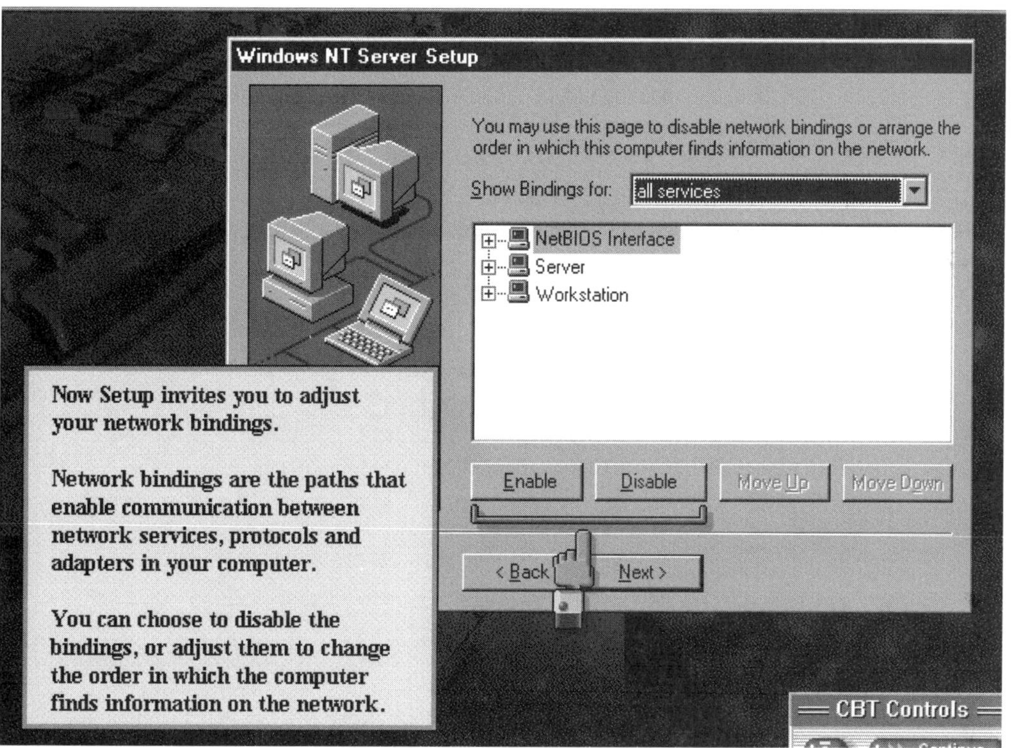

Figure A–77. *Highlight the binding(s), then click the Enabled or Disabled button depending if you want to use the binding in the installation.*

Information You Should Know About Working with Multivendor Networks

- More than one type of operating system is running in a multivendor network. For example, a Windows NT client may need to access resources on a Novell NetWare server.
- The ability of clients and servers running different operating systems to communicate with each other is called interoperability.
- Interoperability is made possible through the use of a redirector.
- A redirector is a component through which a client establishes a connection with a server.
- Client Services for NetWare (CSNW) allows an NT client to connect to a NetWare server.
- Gateway Service for NetWare (GSNW) enables an NT server to connect to NetWare computers in the network.

How to Install Gateway Service for NetWare (GSNW)

Click Start
Click Settings
Click Control Panel
Double-click the Network icon to display the Network dialog box
Select the Services tab
Click the Add button to display the Network Services dialog box
Highlight Gateway (and client) Services for NetWare (Figure A–78)
Click OK
Enter the path of the NT Server distribution files
Click the Continue button to return to the Services tab
Click Yes to restart your computer

How to Install Client Services for NetWare (CSNW)

Click Start
Click Settings
Click Control Panel
Double-click the Network icon to display the Network dialog box
Select the Services tab
Click the Add button to display the Network Services dialog box
Highlight Client Services for NetWare
Click OK
Enter the path of the NT distribution files

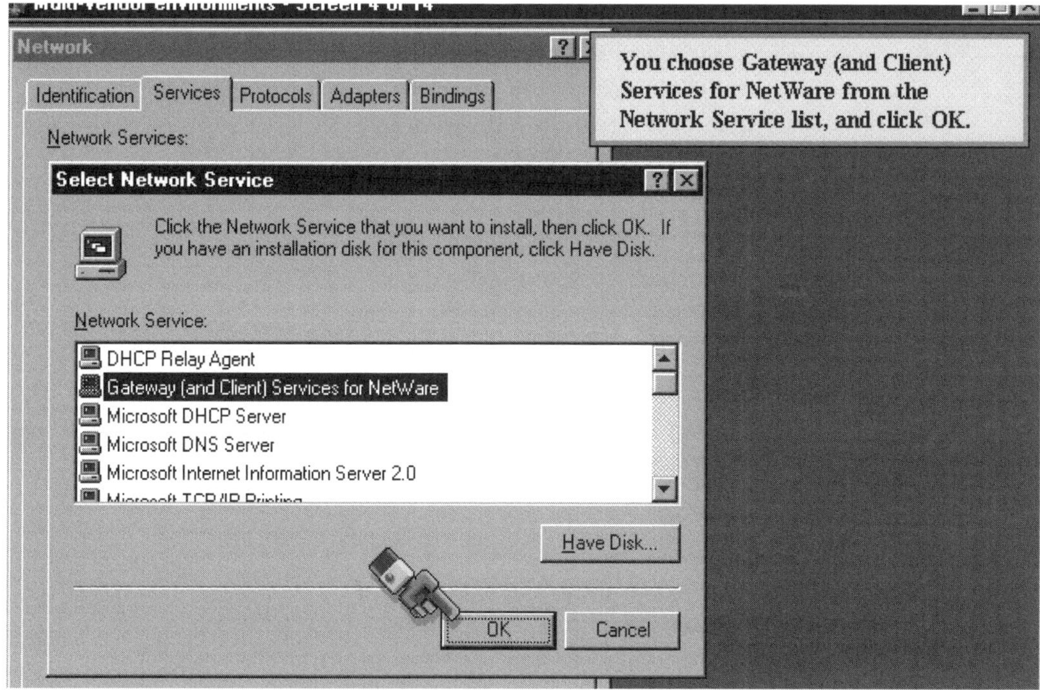

Figure A–78. *Highlight Gateway (and client) Services for NetWare.*

Click the Continue button to return to the Services tab
Click Yes to restart your computer

Information You Need To Know About Network Printers

- NT printing terminology is different from conventional printing terminology.
- A printing device refers to hardware that prints to a physical printer.
- A printer refers to a print queue.
- Applications print to a local printing device, which is a printing device that is connected to a workstation. Print job designated for a network printing device must be redirected from the local printer to the Network Adapter card.
- Printing on the network is a two-step process. First the client's redirector sends the print job to the Network Adapter card addressed to the network print server. The network operating system sends the print job

from the network print server to the printer where the job is queued with the other jobs waiting to print.

- Some networks use a print spooler that stores print jobs in memory in the print server, then the job is passed to the printer when the printer is ready to receive the next job.
- Print jobs sent to a print spooler are also stored in a spool file that stores print jobs on disk in case of a power failure.
- The print spooler can overflow if more print jobs are sent than can be stored. Those jobs that cannot fit on the print spooler are lost.
- Printers are installed and managed by using the Printer folder found on the Printer window.

How to View information About a Printer Queue

Click Start
Click Settings
Click Printer to display the Printer window
Double-click the icon of the printer you want to view
All the information about the printer is displayed (Figure A–79)

How to Audit a Printer

Click Start
Click Settings
Click Printers to display the Printer window
Double-click the icon of the printer you want to audit
Click File from the menu bar
Click Properties from the submenu to display the Properties dialog box.
Select the Security tab
Click the Auditing button to display the Audit dialog box (Figure A–80)
Check the auditing events you want to audit
Use the Event Viewer to see the audit log (See **View The Event Viewer Log File**)

How to Pause a Print Job

Click Start
Click Settings
Click Printers to display the Printer window
Double click the icon of the printer you want to view
Highlight the print job you want to pause
Click Document from the menu bar
Click Pause from the submenu (Figure A–81)

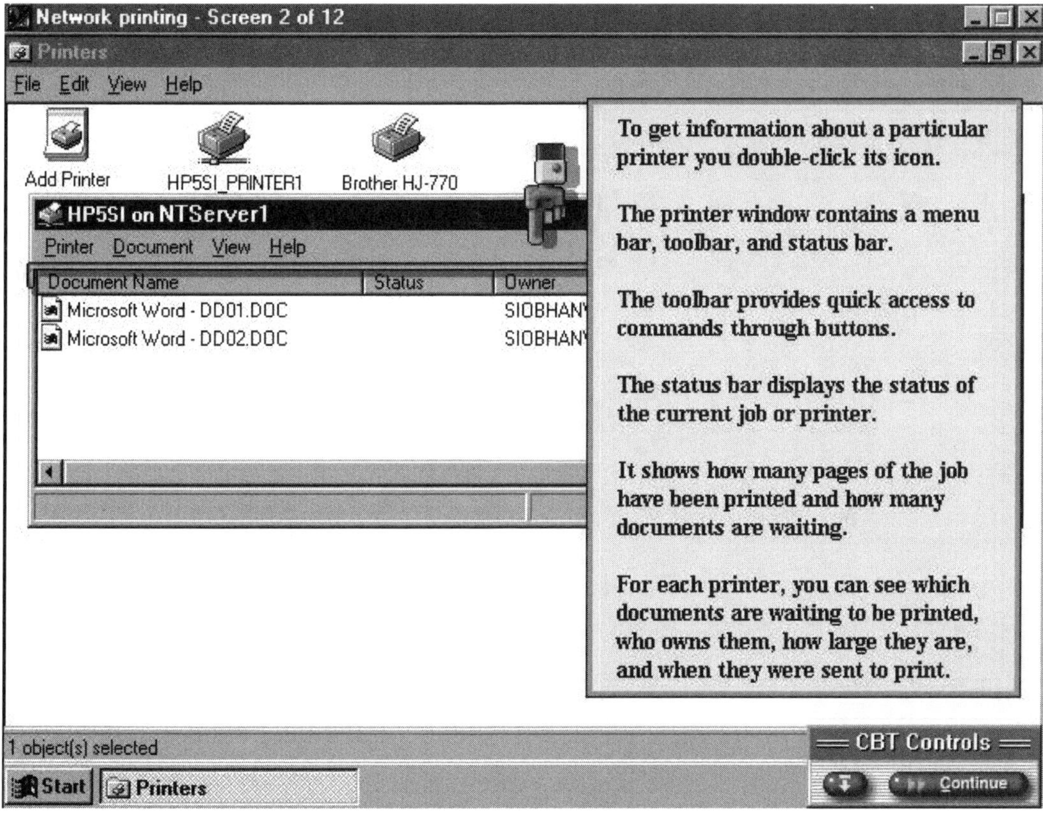

Figure A–79. *Pending print jobs and other information about a printer are displayed in the printer's window.*

How to Restart a Paused Print Job

Click Start
Click Settings
Click Printers to display the Printer window
Double-click the icon of the printer you want to view
Highlight the print job you want to pause
Click Document from the menu bar
Click Restart from the submenu

How to Cancel a Print Job

Click Start
Click Settings

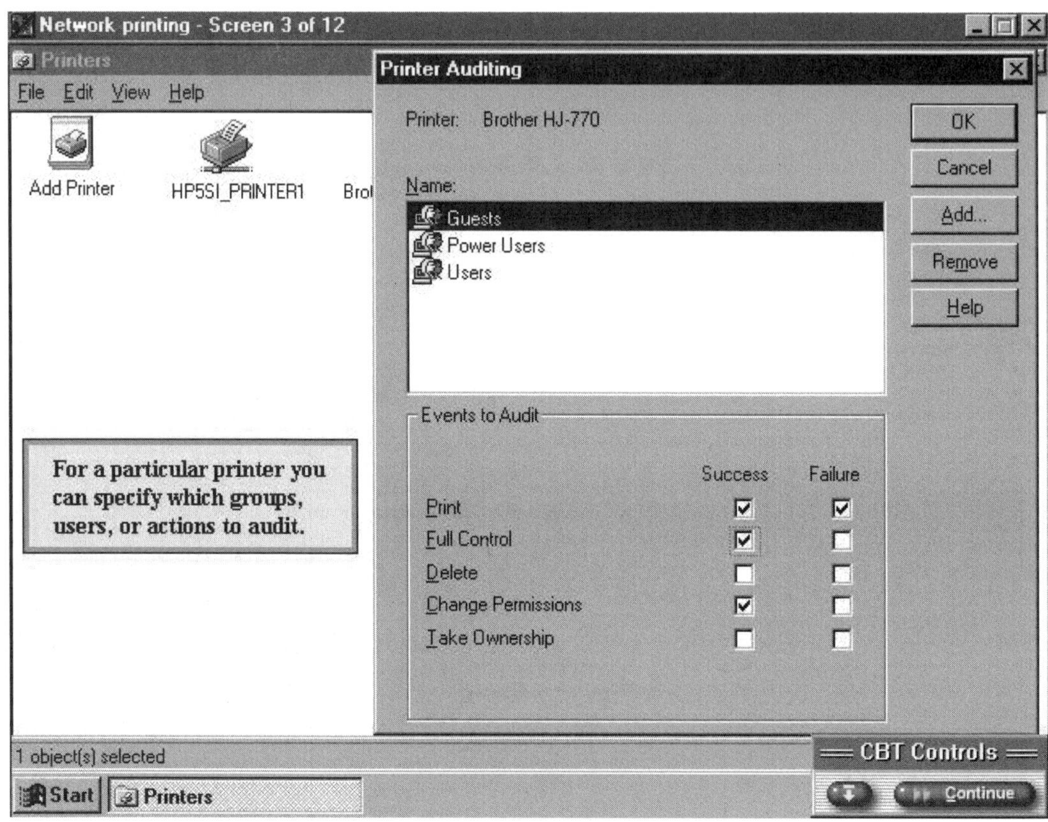

Figure A–80. *Click the auditing events you want to audit.*

Click Printers to display the Printer window
Double-click the icon of the printer you want to view
Highlight the print job you want to pause
Click Document from the menu bar
Click Cancel from the submenu

How to Add a Printer

Click Start
Click Settings
Click Printers to display the Printer window
Double-click the Add Printer icon to start the Add Printer Wizard
Select the server that is linked to the printer.
Double-click the printer you want on that server (Figure A–82)
Highlight the manufacturer of the printer and the name of the printer you want to add

Click OK
If the printer driver isn't installed, then click the Have The Disk button and use disk or CD supplied by the printer manufacturer to install the driver
You may be prompted to insert the NT Workstation CD. This CD contains files necessary to complete the installation of the printer. If you do get prompted, you'll be asked to provide the path that leads to the files.
Click OK
The Printer Properties dialog box is displayed (Figure A–83).
Click OK
Click Yes if you want to use the printer as the default printer
Click the Next button
You can configure the printer now or accept the defaults
Click the Finish button to complete the installation

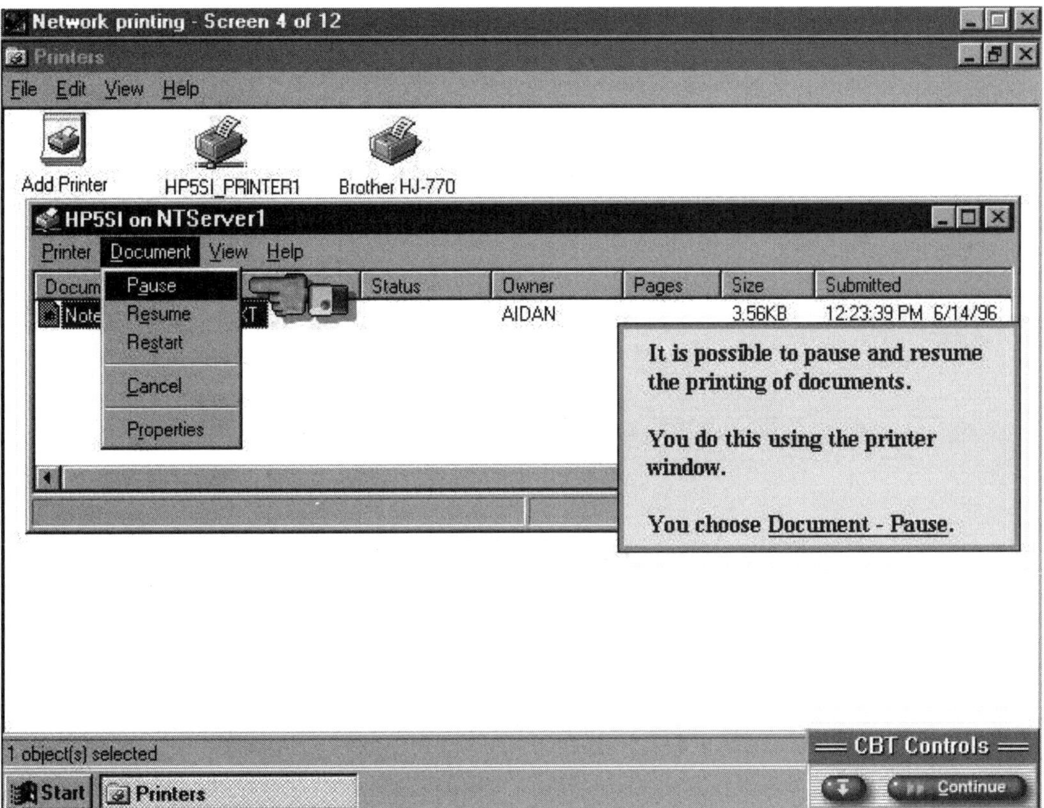

Figure A–81. *Select Pause to suspend the print job.*

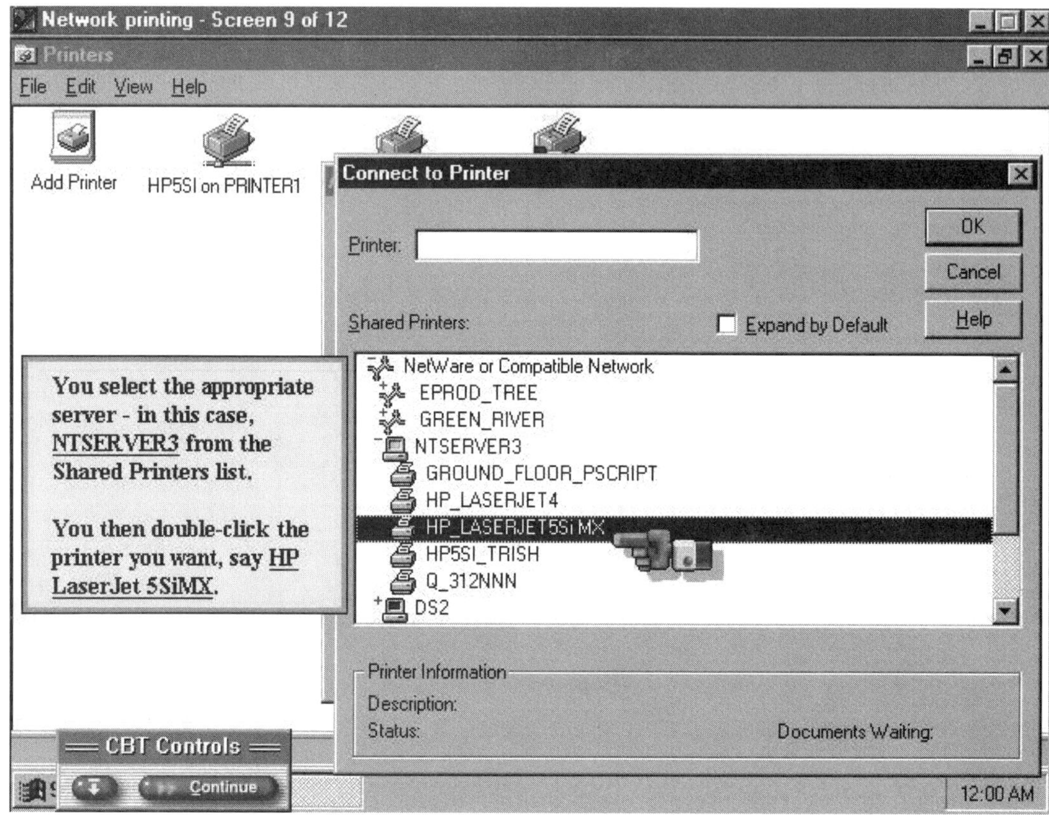

Figure A–82. *Double-click the printer you want to add to the system.*

Information You Need to Know About Shared Printers

- The network administrator must grant users permission to use a shared printer.
- Users with Full Control permission can move their print job ahead of other print jobs on the printer queue and delete print jobs other than their own.
- Most network operating systems provide a tool for managing printers from a remote location.
- Windows NT uses the same utility used to manage a local printer to manage a remote printer.
- You can optimize printing by creating a printer pool that enables a user to a pool of printers rather than a single printer. The printer pool

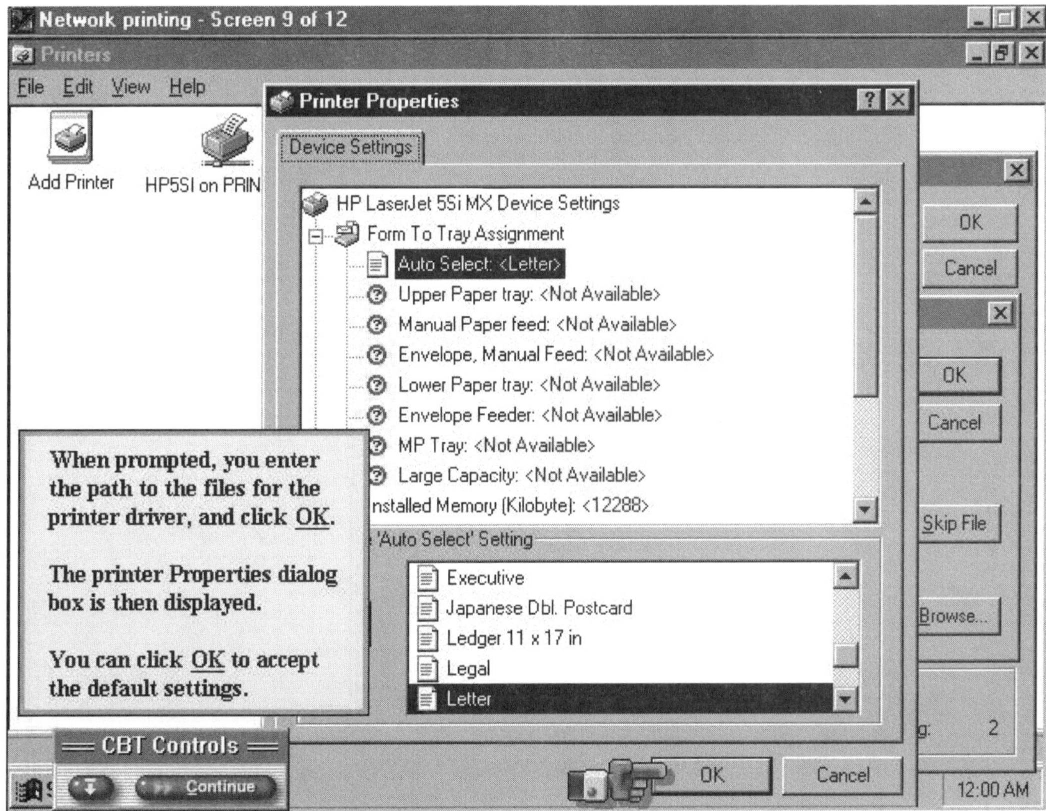

Figure A–83. *The Printer Properties dialog box is used to configure the printer.*

is identified to the user as a single printer. However, the print job is sent to the next available physical printer in the print pool.

- Changing the properties of a printer pool affects all the printing devices in the printing pool.
- Only printers that use the same printer driver can be included in the printing pool.
- The order in which you select the printer ports for the printing pool is the routing order when documents are printed. The first printer port check is the first printer used to print a document. Be sure to check the most efficient printers first since they will receive most of the print jobs.

How to Create a Printer Pool When Creating a Printer

Click Start
Click Settings

Click Printers to display the Printer window
Double-click the Add Printer icon to start the Add Printer Wizard.
Click the My Computer option
Click the Next button
Check the Enable Printer Pooling check box
Check the ports where you have connected the additional printers in the pool (Figure A–84)
Follow the Add Printer Wizard prompts to complete the creation of a new printer
Click the Finish button to complete the installation

How to Create a Printer Pool from an Existing Printer

Click Start
Click Settings
Click Printers to display the Printer window
Double-click the icon of the printer you want to add to the printer pool

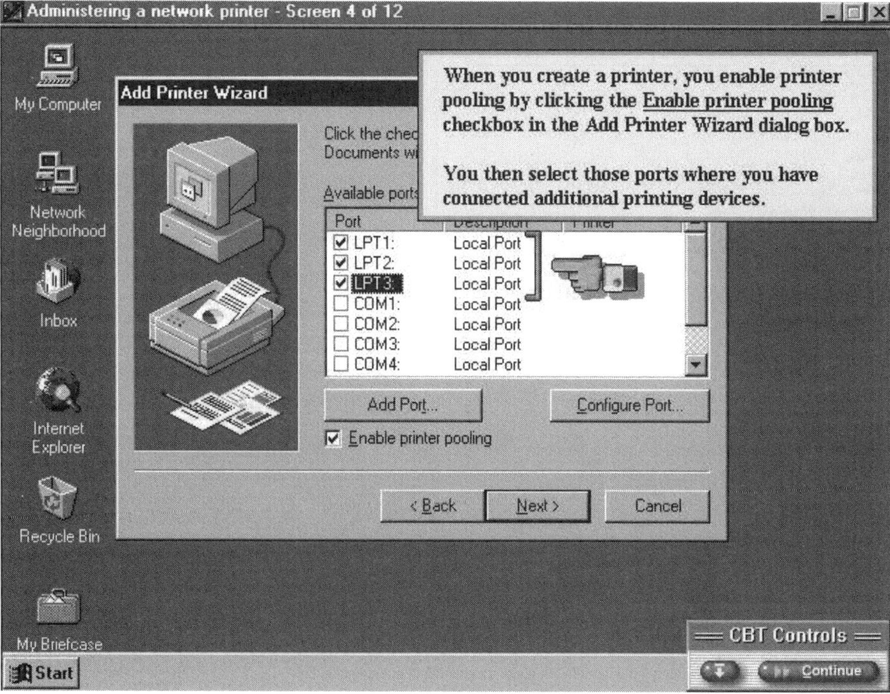

Figure A–84. *Check the Enable Printer Pooling checkbox then select the ports used by the additional printers.*

Click Printer from the menu bar
Click Properties from the submenu to display the Properties dialog box.
Select the Port tab
Check the Enable Printer Pooling checkbox.
Check the ports that the printer device can print (Figure A–85)
If the port you want is not displayed click the Add button.
When the Printer Port dialog box is displayed, select the local port (Figure A–86)
Enter the name of the port you want to add to the port list (Figure A–87)
Click OK
Click the Close button.
The new port appears on the list. Check the port
Click OK

How to Set User Permissions for Use of the Printer

Click Start
Click Settings
Click Printer to display the Printer window

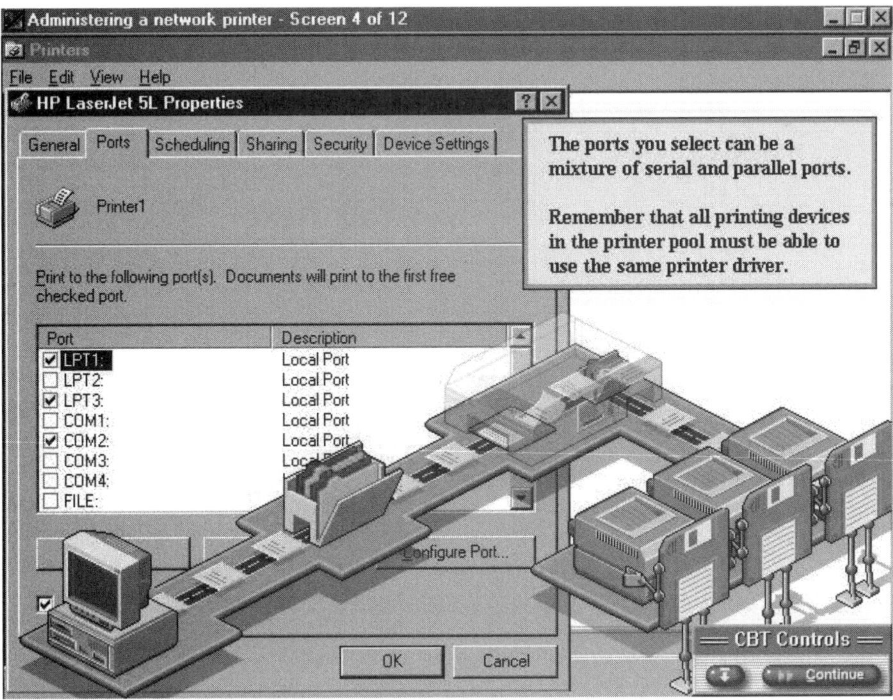

Figure A–85. *Check the ports that the printing device can print.*

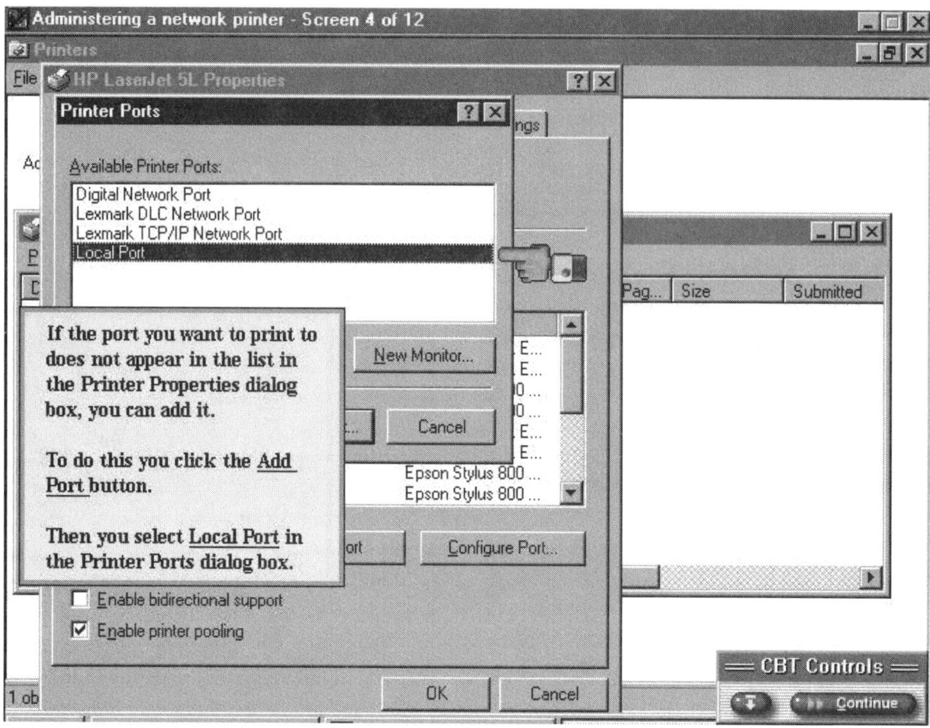

Figure A–86. *Select the local port from the Printer Ports dialog box.*

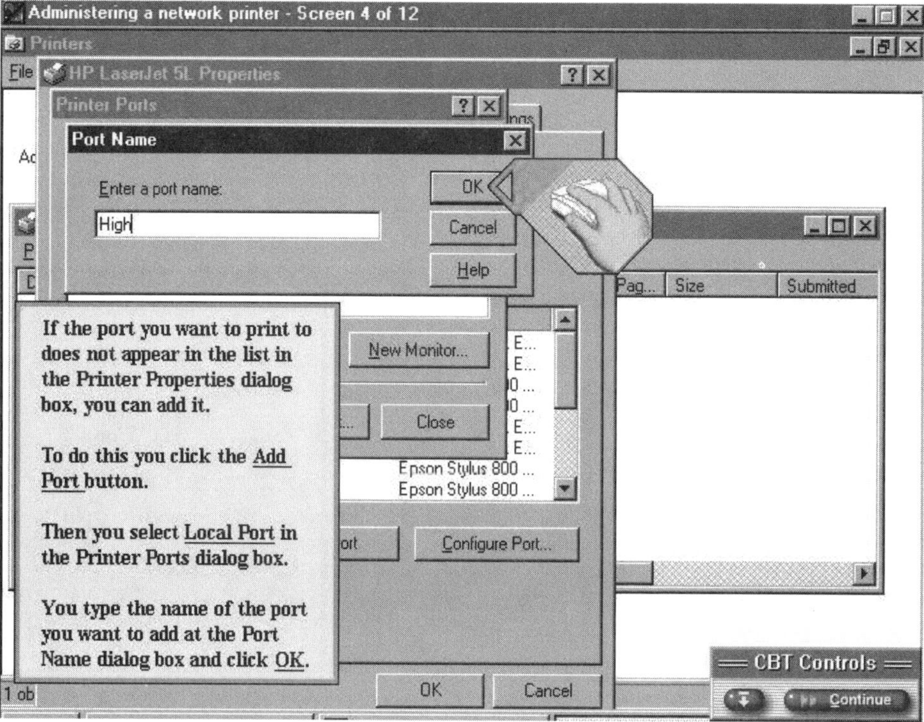

Figure A–87. *Enter the name of the port you want to add to the ports list.*

Double-click the icon of the printer you want to add to the printer pool
Click Printer from the menu bar
Click Properties from the submenu to display the Properties dialog box
Select the Security tab
Click the Permissions button
Highlight the user or group you want to use the printer
Select the access type from the Type Of Access drop-down list (Figure 9–88)
No Access prevents the selected user/group from using the printer
Print enables the user/group to send documents to the printer
Manage Documents gives the user/group reorder printing priorities
Full Control grants full rights to manage the printer
If a user or group does not appear on the user and group list, then click the Add button to display the Add Users and Groups dialog box
Highlight the missing user or group
Click the Add button
Click OK
Repeat step 9 to grant the new user/group permission to use the printer

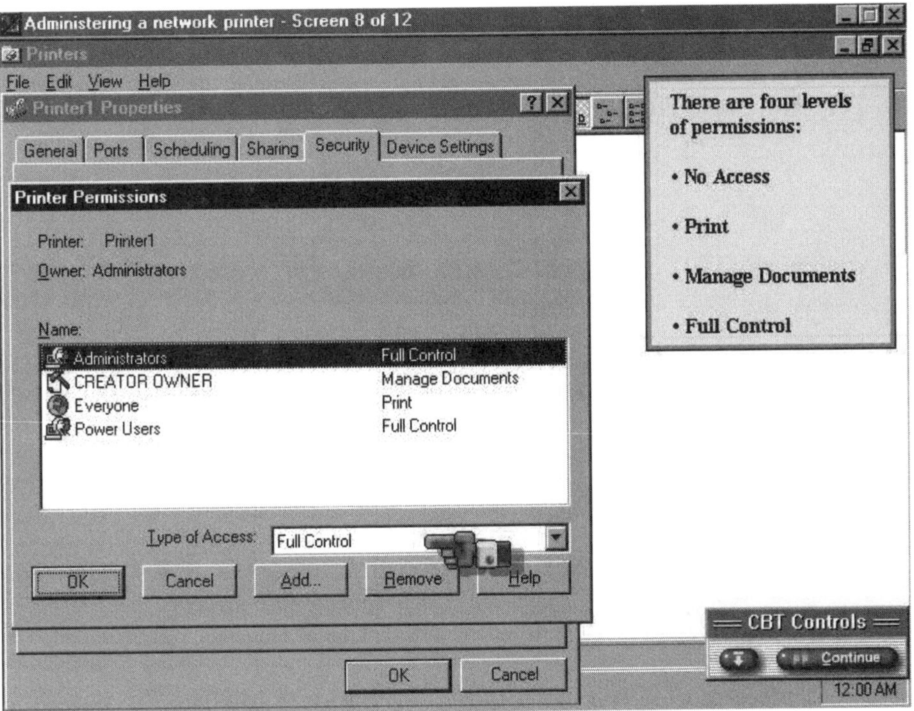

Figure A–88. *Select the access type from the Type Of Access drop-down list.*

APPENDIX B

How to Rekindle Your Test-Taking Skills

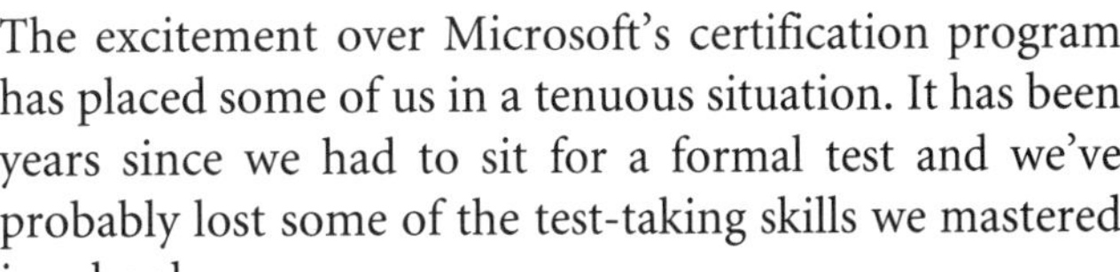

The excitement over Microsoft's certification program has placed some of us in a tenuous situation. It has been years since we had to sit for a formal test and we've probably lost some of the test-taking skills we mastered in school.

Put aside any anxiety you might have about taking the Microsoft certification tests. Throughout this book you have been presented with facts and concepts that will be on the test. On these pages you'll learn how to prepare yourself for taking the test.

We can't guarantee that you'll ace the test by following these procedures, but they'll give you an advantage over those professionals who haven't mastered test-taking skills.

A Little About the Test

You'll find that the Networking Essentials test covers the general topic of networking. Don't expect many hands-on types of questions. Instead you'll be expected to know how to plan and implement a network, then use standard procedures to track down and resolve network problems. And as you would expect you'll be tested on a battery of networking terminology and concepts.

Each test in the MCSE series took a team of professionals about 7 months to develop. Microsoft expects the team to create a test that is relative to the job of a Microsoft support engineer. Therefore, the test development team begins their process by reviewing the tasks they expect an MCSE to perform.

A list of learning objectives is created as a result of the team's tasks review. The next step is to have current MCSE rank each learning objective based upon the relevance the learning object has to performing their job.

Higher-ranking learning objectives are then transformed into a battery of test questions. The first draft called the alpha exam is given to current MCSE who review the test for relevance and accuracy. Their input causes the development team to revise the test.

The next draft of the test called the beta test is given to a larger group of volunteers whose profiles match those who will be taking the test. Questions answered correctly by 30 to 90 percent of the test takers are included in the official copy of the test.

The passing grade varies among the MCSE tests. Microsoft enlists the help of a group of MCSE who determine which questions are important for a MCSE to answer correctly. For example, a network-troubleshooting question might be considered more important to answer correctly than a theoretical question about networks.

Collectively, this group decides the passing grade for each test.

Where to Start

Begin by deciding which test you want to take. I assume you've decided on the Networking Essentials test since you purchased this book.

Give yourself enough time to prepare before you register for the test. Each test costs about $100, so it can become a little expensive if you need to retake the test several times. The remainder of this appendix shows you how to prepare for taking the test.

When you feel you have a good shot at passing the test, then called 800-755-3926 to find the Sylvan Prometic test center closest to you. Sylvan Prometic administers the test for Microsoft. You can also contact them online at www.prometric.com.

You must register for the text at least 24 hours before you want to take the test. You're expected to pay the fee at the time of registration. You can pay by check or credit card. Once registration is completed, you are assigned an ID number that you must be used whenever you communicate with the test center.

A Little About the Questions

The entire test is given on the computer. You'll be presented with mostly multiple choice questions although you might find a question that requires you to simulate the execution of a typical MCSE procedure such as setting up a user account. This shouldn't be new to you since similar simulations are contained in the CBT courseware two of which are included on the CD with this book.

A word of caution. Some questions pose a real life-networking problem that you must solve. These are tricky to answer although the answer is a multiple-choice question. Don't be fooled. Be sure to practice these questions using the sample test included in this book.

Also, more than one answer can be correct. Therefore, you'll be required to choose more than one of the multiple-choice answers. Some such questions specify the number of correct answers to find and others don't give you any hints.

Down to Studying

Knowing what is in store for you before taking a test is important so you can properly prepare for the barrage of questions you'll be expected to answer. The previous sections gave you a glimpse at what is to come, now it is time to give you tips on how to prepare for the test.

Here's what you'll need to do:

- Create a study schedule
- Stay attentive
- Take good notes
- Don't skip over the harder topics
- Tricks the pros use to study

Create a Study Schedule

Give yourself enough time to properly learn the material that will be on the test. Don't procrastinate and put off studying until the night before the test. This technique narrows your chances of passing the exam.

Instead of cramming, create a formal study plan that complements your regular schedule. The study plan will give you time to focus on what you need to learn without being rushed by outside activities.

Here are some tips to follow when creating your study plan.

Determine the test date. Be sure to choose a date far enough in advance so you'll have time to properly study for the test.

Identify all the information you need to learn to pass the test. This information is provided throughout the pages of this book.

- Organize the information you need to learn into lists.
- Review your normal schedule to find time periods where you have downtime. Don't overlook lunchtime, the hour or so between dinner and television, and the time spent on a train or bus commuting to work.
- Assign to each downtime period all or part of a list to learn.
- Keep pace learning these assignments. Make sure nothing else interferes with your studying during those periods of the day.
- Assign yourself a few test questions each day to practice answering.

Stay Attentive

Even the best student can easily become tired of studying especially when the material isn't very exciting. I'll admit there is material you need to study for the Networking Essentials test that fall into this category.

You can't change the material that you must learn; however, you can take steps to reduce the likelihood that you'll get droopy eyed while studying. Here are a few ways to keep attentive. They've worked well for many an A student, so they'll probably work well for you too.

- Don't lose sight of why you are studying. The best motivator is the fact that you'll be a test closer to certification once you pass the test. And to receive a passing grade you must learn the material you're studying.
- Make the subject matter meaningful. I attempted to do so throughout this book. Once you can see how to material is applied in a real-life situation, then it will be easier to keep focus on your studies.
- Create short-term study goals. Break down each topic into digestible pieces of information to learn. Each section of this book is a digestible piece. Concentrate on learning all the terms and concepts within the section, then take a break. Walk around. Do something to get your mind off of your studies. Return and glance over the section to refresh

your memory before moving on to the next section. You'll tend to retain more information in spurts rather than long study sessions.

- Stop and do something else at the first sign that your mind is drifting away from the topic. Your eyes could be reading a passage but your mind is thinking about other things. You're not learning.
- Minimize distractions while studying. Find a place that is conducive to learning. Some like to find a corner of the public library. Others like to don a headset and listen to music while studying. Do whatever works for you, but stop as soon as you become distracted.

Take Good Notes

I associate note taking with being in a classroom, but that's not true. You should also take notes while studying. A trick of many good students is to create a list of terms, concepts, and facts that you think is important to learn. Chances are in your favor that the Microsoft test development team agrees with you.

The quality of your notes depends on your note-taking skills. Some students naturally take good notes, while others need to learn a few basic techniques. Here are a few proven ways to take notes, just in case you fall into the latter category.

- List all key terms followed by a brief definition. Make sure your spelling is correct and the definitions are accurate.
- Outline each chapter. You don't need to rewrite every word, but you do need to write the concepts taught in the chapter into your own words.
- Read over your notes the next day and see if they make sense to you. If you can't make sense out of them, then you need to polish your note-taking skills. Start over. Make sure the notes are organized and your writing is clear.
- Give yourself a quiz based upon material in your notes. Read a term, tell yourself its definition, then read your notes to see if you're correct. It is also wise to compare your definition with that contained in the book. This assures you that your notes are correct.
- Develop your own shorthand. Write clue words as letters in your notes rather than complete sentences and punctuation. A clue word jostles your mind to bring back to the full terminology or concept.

- Create diagrams when possible to illustrate the concept that you are learning. Label the illustration with terms so the terms become a meaningful part of a real-life scenario. You'll be able to associate the flow of the concept with the terms used to describe the flow.
- Be able to teach the material to someone else. This is a very good technique especially if your firm has a certified engineer on staff. You can give her or him your explanation of the concept, then see if she or he agrees. If you're wrong, then she'll put you back on the right track.

Don't Skip Over the Harder Topics

Topics are not hard to understand, you just need to have them explained in a way you can understand. This sounds obvious, but some of us don't go that extra step to seek out other explanations for a topic we don't fully understand.

It is very common for someone to read a section of a book that they don't comprehend then blame their inadequacies for their inability to grasp the material. In reality it is the author's inability to convey the material. Neither person is at fault. It is just that they are not a match for each other.

Here are some tips you can use to better understand topics you find difficult to understand:

- List the terms or concepts you don't understand, then review previous chapters for information about the material. You'll find that advanced topics are built upon knowledge learned in previous chapters. Therefore, the difficulty you are experiencing probably stems from material you didn't learn previously.
- Take a break from studying. Many times your brain is overworked and is not in the proper condition to tackle a challenging topic. Part of your brain has shut down preventing you from thinking clearly. I usually call it a day when this happens, then go back to learning the material after a good night's sleep.
- Draw a picture of the topic as the author explains it in the chapter. I tried this when I first learned about the OSI model. You'll recall the OSI model is a seven-layer protocol stack (a set of rules) for transmitting and receiving data on a network. Each layer does something to the data that is being transmitted or to the data that is received. I drew a picture of the data at each level of the OSI model. The image helped me to see how each layer affected the data.

- Don't give up! If you've tried to learn the topic, but are still having problems, then abandon the method you are using - not the topic. Let's say you don't understand the way I present a topic in this book. I'm the first to admit this can happen. Your next step should be to use the courseware provided in this book. The courseware author presents the same topic using a different approach. And if you're still confused, try asking the networking staff at work for a little advice.

Tricks the Pros Use to Study

I've spoken with a number of students who usually do very well on tests. They shared with me a few tips that I'll pass along to you. Keep in mind these methods don't work for everyone, but they are well worth a try when preparing for your MCSE test.

- Create a master list of facts, terms, and concepts you think will be on the test. Include illustrations you've drawn to help you picture the concept in your mind. Keep this list with you at all times (except when taking the test itself). Memorize the list at every free moment.
- Create rhymes, mnemonics, acronyms, and mental associations with the test material. You probably used these techniques in grammar school. You remember 30 days have September, April, June, and November.
- Try to visualize your master list. Sometimes the term or concept escapes you, but you know you've seen it on your master list. There is a good chance you'll jog your memory by recalling the image on the list.
- Create a study group with others who are taking the MCSE test. You can quiz each other and discuss terms and concepts to reassure that you understand the material.
- Study right before you go to sleep. Some students believe that you are likely to remember something if you read it right before bedtime.
- Take every practice test you can get your hands on. This technique helps to identify topics you don't know and gets you comfortable taking tests.

Test Day

I've given you tips on studying. Now let's assume it is test day. What do you do besides panic and say a few prayers? There are a number of techniques that help to ease your mind about being hit with questions for an hour and a half.

Here are a few techniques used successfully by students:

- Keep the test in perspective. You are not in a life or death situation. Instead, you are taking a test the results of which only you and the computer know. The worst that can happen is you fail the test and you must retake it another time. It will cost you $100 for the experience. The best that can happen is that you pass the test and you are on your way to becoming an MCSE.
- Avoid embarrassment by keeping quiet about taking the test. More than one student has been caught in this dilemma. You brag to friends and relatives that you're taking the MCSE test. Of course, they want to know if you passed or not—and you don't want to say you failed. Wait until you pass the test before you tell the world of your achievements.
- Study no more than a week before the test. You'll lose sight of the goal and have a difficult time remembering the material if you have a longer study period. Test material is typically stored in short-term memory rather than long-term memory.
- Study before going to sleep the night before the test, then get a good night's rest so you'll be fresh for the test the next day.
- Keep reviewing your master list up until test time. This will keep the image of the list fresh in your mind.
- Avoid cramming the night before the test. All-nighters make you exhausted on test day. You'll need at least a good four hour's sleep or more.
- Know the types of questions that will be on the test. I reviewed these in a previous section and provided sample tests. This helps relieve anxiety of the unknown. You may not know the exact questions that will be on the test, but you'll have an idea of the type of questions you'll be asked.
- Eat well before the test. Plenty of carbohydrates will give you an energy boost.
- Give yourself plenty of time to arrive at the test center. You don't want to get lost or be late for the test. I plan to arrive an hour before a test. This gives me time to find the test center, then walk around the neighborhood, relax, and review my master list again.
- Don't talk to other test-takers about the test. Walk away if you find yourself being drawn into conversations about test material. Alarmists who supply you with misinformation can easily sway you from your test strategy.

During the Test

You are on your own once the test begins. You can't ask for help and obviously you are not permitted to review your master list. So what do you do? Panic! No, you should develop a plan before you enter the test room on how to approach every aspect of the test.

Should you skip questions, then come back to them? You can't! Should you skip questions altogether? What if you have a panic attack in the middle of the test? These are just a few of the many questions you'll need to address. Here are a few techniques that will help you address them.

- Try the safe and happy approach to a mid-test panic attack. Stop answering questions for 30 seconds. Close your eyes and think of some place where you felt safe and happy. Breathe deeply and you'll find that your body will be relaxed.
- Read the directions very carefully. Avoid assuming anything about how the test is administered and how Microsoft expects you to answer the questions.
- Read questions carefully. Be sure to know the number of correct answers Microsoft is expecting you to prove. Some questions have a specific number of correct answers such as select the three ways a network can fail. Also look for clue words such as which of the following is NOT a characteristic of a fiber optic cable.
- When you are unsure of the correct answer, eliminate the obvious wrong answers. This will increase the probability of your guessing the correct answer. Let's say there are four possible answers and the questions ask for one correct answer. You have a 25 percent chance of guessing correctly. However, you have a 33 percent chance of giving the correct answer if you can eliminate one choice and 50 percent chance by eliminating two choices.
- Don't ponder the answer once you've decided on the answer. Go with your first instinct. Avoid changing the answer unless you have determined the correct answer.
- Visualize your master list if you're stumped for a term or concept. Close your eyes and picture the list. If this doesn't work, then move on to another question and come back to it later in the test.

APPENDIX C

Terms You Should Know

10Base2 An Ethernet network using Thinnet.

10Base5 An Ethernet network using Thicknet.

10BaseT An Ethernet network using Unshielded Twisted Pairs.

10BaseF An Ethernet using fiber optics.

100BaseT An Ethernet network called Fast Ethernet.

100Vg-AnyLAN Provides speed up to 100 MBPS using demand priority media access method

American Wire Gauge (AWG) A standard that uses wire diameters to define a cable.

Analog A signal that contains many states and is typically found in radio, television, and telephone transmissions.

AppleTalk A network architecture distributed as part of the Macintosh operating system and used to link together Macintosh computers.

Application Layer The layer of the OSI Reference Model concerned with the user interface.

Application Server A network server used to acccss applications.

Asynchronous Communication A transmission method where data transmitted is contained between a start and stop bit.

Asynchronous Transfer Mode (ATM) A transmission method used in WAN that achieves data transmission speeds of up to 622 MBPS by dividing data into 53 byte cells. ATM is considered packet-switched technology.

Attached Resource Computer Network (ARCnet) One of the first networks to use token passing to connect a maximum of 255 computers using twisted pair.

Attachment Unit Interface (AUI) A connector found on the network adapter card in a 10Base5 Ethernet network.

Attenuation The degradation of a transmitted signal on the network.

Backbone The central cable used to connect multiple networks together.

Backup Domain Controller (BDC) The NT server that contains a duplicate copy of the domain security database. It is used whenever the Primary Domain Controller (PDC) fails.

Bandwidth The number of bits that can be transmitted simultaneously.

Barrel Connector A device used to connect together two coaxial cables.

Baseband Transmission A communication channel is used to transmit one signal.

Baud Rate The number of state transitions that occur within a second. A state transition is where a zero to one or one to zero occurs.

Beaconing Each computer notifies other computers that it is no longer receiving the network signal.

Binding The technique of associating a network adapter driver to a protocol driver.

Bottleneck A device that slows the flow of data across the network.

Bridge A network device used to reduce network congestion by combining multiple networks into one network.

Bridging Table A list of network addresses used by a bridge to determine the most efficient way to deliver data packets to network devices.

Broadband Transmission The technique of dividing the network cable into multiple communication channels by using analog technology. Each channel can transmit a bit of data.

Broadcast Packet A data packet that is transmitted to all network computers.

Broadcast Storm The rapid transmission of data packets by a malfunctioning network adapter card.

Brouter A device that has the capabilities of a bridge and a router.

Bus A network topology where all network devices are connected to the same cable.

Bus Mastering A way for the network adapter card to take control over a computer's data bus to bypass the computer's CPU when sending data to the computer's memory.

Carrier-Sense Multiple Access with Collision Avoidance (CSMA/CA) The transmitting computer determines if the network is in use. If it isn't, the computer sends a signal over the network announcing it will transmit data.

Carrier-Sense Multiple Access with Collision Detection (CSMA/CD) A computer transmits data over the network, then listens for a collision with another data packet transmitted by another computer. If a collision is detected, both computers pause a random amount of time then resend their data packet.

Cell A data packet used by ATM.

Channel Service Unit/Data Service Unit (CSU/DSU) A device that connects a digital line to a computer network.

Cladding The glass shroud covering the central fiber of a fiber optic cable.

Client A computer connected to a network.

Client/Server Architecture An arrangement of computers where user requests are initiated at a client computer and processed by a network server.

Coaxial Cable A cable containing a solid copper core wrapped around insulation.

Collision A signal corruption caused by two clients transmitting data across the network at the same time.

Concentrator A central device also known as a hub used to connect multiple network devices.

Contention Two or more devices attempt to use the same network device.

Crosstalk Interference caused by two wires positioned alongside each other during data transmission.

Cyclical Redundancy Check (CRC) The results of a calculation that is positioned at the end of a data packet. The values are recalculated upon receipt of the data packet to determine if an error has occurred during transmission.

Database Server A network server dedicated to store and retrieve data in a database.

Data Link Layer This is the OSI Reference Model layer that packages data into a frame and assures error-free transmission.

Device Driver Software that translates a request for service between devices.

Dial-Up Network Facilitates the remote access to a network.

Digital A signal that consists of two states—zero or one.

Disk Mirroring Data is written to two or more disks at the same time. If one disk fails, data can be retrieved from the other disk(s).

DNS Name Server The network server that houses the domain name service.

Domain A group of network devices that are represented by the same name.

Ethernet A network architecture that uses a bus topology and CSMA/CD access method to transmit data at 10 MBPS.

Fault Tolerance A network configuration that enables network operations to continue when a network failure occurs.

Fiber Optic Cable A cable composed of glass that transmits data in the form of light waves.

File Sharing The technology that enables a file to be shared by two or more computers.

File Transfer Protocol (FTP) A protocol that enables files to be transferred between two unlike computers.

Frame Relay The creation of virtual packet switching circuits between two points on the network used to transmit variable length packets.

Frequency-Hopping A method for jumping frequencies during data transmission. The transmitter and the receiver need to jump to the same frequency.

Gateway A computer that connects two networks and translates unlike protocols during data transmission.

Geosynchronous Satellite A satellite stationed at a fixed location over the ground.

Hop A path between two end points stored in a routing table.

Hub The central connection point in a star network.

Impedance A wire's resistance to a signal that is measured in ohms.

Integrated Services Digital Network (ISDN) A digital network that uses two 64Kbps channels to transmit up to 128Kps of data.

International Organization for Standardization (ISO) An international organization that establishes standards such as the Open System Interconnect (OSI).

Internet Protocol (IP) The network layer protocol used to address TCP packets.

Interrupt The disruption of CPU processing. The event that caused the disruption is addressed by the interrupt handler.

Interrupt Request Lines (IRQ) A line on a circuit board or CPU that is used to transmit an interrupt signal.

I/O Address Known as the port, the I/O address of a device is used to send and receive data from other devices.

IP Address An address of a device on a TCP/IP network.

IPX/SP The Novell Network transport protocol.

Leased Line A telephone line between two locations that is permanently opened.

Local Area Network (LAN) A network of computers that spans no more than a building.

Local Printer A printer that is connected to a client.

LocalTalk The cabling system used for an AppleTalk network.

Logical Link Control (LLC) A sublayer of the Data Link Layer of the OSI Reference Model that maintains the connection between computers.

Logical Ring Clients are connected to a hub that is configured into a ring topology.

Map The assignment of letters to a file server directory.

Media Access Control (MAC) The sublayer in the Data Link Layer (IEEE 802 network model) that controls computer access to the physical network.

Multiplexor (MUX) A device that combines signals from several communications channels and transmits them as one signal. MUX also reverse the process when the signal is received.

Multiport Repeater A device, also known as an active hub, that amplifies the signal when retransmitting the signal along the network.

Multistation Access Unit (MAU) A hub used in a Token Ring that is wired as a logical ring.

Name Registration The reconciliation of a client's name with a client's network address.

NBF Transport Protocol The NetBEUI frame protocol.

NetBIOS Interface A presentation level interface that hides the network from the user.

Network Adapter Card The interface card that connects a client to the network cables.

Network Architecture The structure of a computer network.

Network Basic Input/Output System (NetBIOS) Software used for network communication.

Network Device Driver The software that manages data transmission between the network adapter card and the computer.

Network File System (NFS) The service used to distribute a file system.

Network ID The segment of the IP address that identifies the network.

Network Layer The OSI Model layer that addresses and routes data over a network.

Network Operating System (NOS) The operating system used on network servers.

Network Protocol The protocol used to transmit and receive data across a network.

Noise Interference that distorts the network signal.

Open Systems Interconnect (OSI) The OSI Reference Model of network architecture consisting of seven layers: Application, Presentation, Session, Transport, Network, Data Link, and Physical.

Packet Encapsulated data that is transmitted over a network.

Packet-switch Network A network where data is encapsulated into several small data packets that are transmitted via different routes to the same destination.

Parity An error-checking method where the number of 1's must be even or odd.

Peer-to-Peer Network The network architecture where computers share local resources with other computers.

Performance Monitoring A method of measuring the performance of a network.

Physical Layer The layer of the OSI Model that transmits the signal over the network.

Plenum The space between the false ceiling and the actual ceiling in an office building.

Point-to-Point A dedicated connection between network devices.

Point-to-Point Protocol (PPP) A protocol used to connect to a remote network service and the replacement for the SLIP protocol.

Presentation Protocol The layer of the OSI Model that translates encrypts and formats data.

Protocol Rules that specify how two devices communicate with each other.

Protocol Analyzer A monitoring device used to measure network performance.

Redirector Network software that enables a computer to access the network.

Redundant Arrays of Inexpensive Disks (RAID) The method of using a number of hard disks to provide fault tolerance processing on the network.

Repeater A device that receives a signal, amplifies the signal, and retransmits the signal on the network.

Ring A network topology where all devices are connected to the same cable.

Routable Protocol A protocol used with a router such as TCP/IP.

Router A device used to connect multiple networks.

Routing Table A table used to redirect data packets to the proper network address using a router.

Sector-Sparing The method of checking the hard disk before writing or reading data to the disk.

Server A device that provides resource sharing to clients on a network.

Session Layer The layer of the OSI Model that manages network communications.

Shared Directory A directory that can be accessed by clients on the network.

Shielded Twisted-Pair (STP) Twisted pair cable that is surrounded by mesh shielding to reduce interference.

Simple Mail Transfer Protocol (SMTP) The protocol used for e-mail service.

Simple Network management Protocol (SNMP) A protocol used to manage network components.

Socket A communications channel used to transmit and receive data.

Spooler Software used to schedule printing.

Spread-Spectrum A method of using multiple frequencies simultaneously to transmit data using either direct sequence modulation or frequency hopping.

Star A network topology where network components are connected through the use of a hub.

Station Identifier (SID) An address of a computer on an ARCnet network.

Subnet A section of a larger network separated by a router or bridge.

Subnet Mask The portion of the IP address that identifies the network ID from the host ID.

Switched Virtual Circuit (SVC) A temporary network path in a packet-switched network that connects to devices.

Synchronous Communication A timed coordinated data transmission method.

Synchronous Optical Network (SONET) A fiber optic based WAN used to simultaneously transmit voice, data, and video.

Systems Network Architecture (SNA) A mainframe network architecture created by IBM.

T Connector A connector used to join two coaxial cables.

T1 Line A digital line that provides 24 channels that can be used for data or voice.

Terminator A device that traps a signal at the end of a bus network.

Thicknet A thick coaxial cable that can transmit data up to 500 meters.

Thinnet A thin coaxial cable that can transmit data up to 185 meters.

Throughput Data flow over a fixed point in the network.

Time-Domain Reflectometer (TDR) A device used to transmit a pulse signal over network cables in an attempt to locate a break in the cable.

Token A data packet that is passed to clients on a token-ring network. A client can transmit data across the network only when it receives the data packet.

Topology The arrangement of devices on a network.

Translation Bridge A bridge that connects two networks that use different protocols.

Transmission Control Protocol (TCP) A protocol used to divide data into data packets.

Transport Layer The layer of the OSI Model that delivers data in the proper sequence error-free.

User Account Information that identifies a user to the network operating system.

User Name A unique identifier of a user.

Vampire Tap A device used to connect a transceiver to a thicknet cable.

Wide Area Network (WAN) Multiple networks covering a large distance using a long distance network.

Wireless Bridge A device used to connect to the network without the use of a cable.

APPENDIX D

Chapter Review Answers

▲ Chapter One

▲ Fill in the Blanks

1. *Peer-to-Peer*
2. *BIT*
3. *ASCII and EBCIDIC*
4. *Cable*
5. *Address*

▲ True/False

1. *False*
2. *False*
3. *True*
4. *False*
5. *True*
6. *False*

▲ Multiple Choice

1. *D*
2. *B*
3. *A*

4. *D*
5. *B*

Chapter Two

Fill in the Blanks

1. *Protocol*
2. *Originator (or sender) and the destination (or receiver)*
3. *CRC, calculation, trailer*
4. *Header, information/data, trailer*
5. *Packet*

True/False

1. *False*
2. *False*
3. *True*
4. *False*
5. *True*
6. *True*

Multiple Choice

1. *B*
2. *A*
3. *C*
4. *A*
5. *B*
6. *A*

Chapter Three

Fill in the Blanks

1. *Bus*
2. *Token*
3. *Up Linking*
4. *Attenuation*
5. *Terminator*

True/False

1. *True*
2. *False*
3. *False*
4. *True*
5. *False*
6. *False*
7. *True*
8. *True*
9. *True*

Multiple Choice

1. *C*
2. *B*
3. *A*
4. *D*
5. *A*
6. *C*
7. *B*

Chapter Four

Fill in the Blanks

1. *10BaseT*
2. *Segmented*
3. *Creates the token*
4. *Multistation access unit (MAU)*
5. *Repeater*

True/False

1. *False*
2. *False*
3. *False*
4. *True*
5. *True*
6. *True*
7. *False*
8. *True*

9. *True*
10. *True*
11. *False*
12. *True*
13. *False*

Multiple Choice

1. *C*
2. *A*
3. *B*
4. *B*
5. *E*
6. *D*

Chapter Five

Fill in the Blanks

1. *Multitasking*
2. *Domain controller (PDC)*
3. *Binding*
4. *IP address, subnet mask, default gateway*
5. *SQL*

True/False

1. *False*
2. *True*
3. *True*
4. *False*
5. *True*
6. *True*

Multiple Choice

1. *C*
2. *E*
3. *D*
4. *B*
5. *A*

6. *D*
7. *C*

CHAPTER SIX

Fill in the Blanks

1. *Group*
2. *Fault tolerant*
3. *Bottleneck*
4. *Virus*
5. *Uninterrupted power supply (UPS)*

True/False

1. *False*
2. *True*
3. *True*
4. *False*
5. *True*
6. *False*
7. *False*
8. *False*

Multiple Choice

1. *C*
2. *E*
3. *D*
4. *B*
5. *A*

CHAPTER SEVEN

Fill in the Blanks

1. *Bridge*
2. *Router*
3. *Hop*
4. *Router and Bridge*
5. *Gateway*

▲ True/False

1. *True*
2. *False*
3. *False*
4. *True*
5. *False*
6. *False*
7. *True*
8. *True*

▲ Multiple Choice

1. *C*
2. *A*
3. *A*
4. *B*
5. *B*
6. *A*
7. *B*
8. *B*
9. *C*
10. *D*
11. *B*

▲ Chapter Eight

▲ Fill in the Blanks

1. *Access permissions*
2. *Backup device*
3. *Risk analysis*
4. *Failure rate*
5. *Maintenance schedule*

▲ True/False

1. *True*
2. *False*
3. *False*
4. *True*

5. *False*
6. *True*
7. *True*
8. *True*
9. *True*

▲ Multiple Choice

1. *B*
2. *A*
3. *A*
4. *A*
5. *A*
6. *E*

INDEX

CBT Systems develops, publishes, and markets a comprehensive library of interactive training and educational courseware titles that teach mastery of client/server, intranet, and Internet information technologies. This courseware is education on demand, in the form of convenient, self-paced information technology training. Our courses are designed to keep people current in mission-critical business applications. Because these applications change at an accelerating pace, we are committed to updating and expanding our product line accordingly.

To order additional CBT Systems courseware today call 800.789.8590 or visit www.clbooks.com/training/cbt.htm

Congratulations, Now You Have Courseware From CBT Systems, That Employs the World's Most Proven Training Technique: Reality

The most effective learning begins with the reality of doing. Now you have CBT Systems™ comprehensive reality-based training.

With CBT Systems you get the leader:

- superior quality products
- more IT titles, from end-user level to system administrator and beyond
- real expertise in information systems technology—it's all we do
- the largest and most experienced in-house courseware development staff in the world
- consistency—a student-friendly intuitive interface
- applied skills training, as well as full certification compliance
- course content regularly updated to keep pace with the rapid changes in IT applications
- highly interactive, learner-centered approach
- several deployment options

CBT SOFTWARE LICENSE AGREEMENT

IF YOU DO NOT AGREE WITH THESE TERMS AND CONDITIONS, DO NOT INSTALL THE SOFTWARE.

This is a legal agreement you and CBT System Ltd. ("Licensor"). The licensor ("Licensor") from whom you have licensed the CBT Group PLC courseware (the "Software"). By installing, copying or otherwise using the Software, you agree to be bound by the terms of this Agreement License Agreement (the "License"). If you do not agree to the terms of this License, the Licensor is unwilling to license the Software to you. In such event, you may not use or copy the Software, and you should promptly contact the Licensor for instructions on the return of the unused Software.

1. **Use.** Licensor grants to you a non-exclusive, nontransferable license to use Licensor's software product (the "Software") the Software and accompanying documentation in accordance with the terms and conditions of this license agreement ("License") License and as specified in your agreement with Licensor (the "Governing Agreement"). In the event of any conflict between this License and the Governing Agreement, the Governing Agreement shall control.

You may:

a. (if specified as a "personal use" version) install the Software on a single stand-alone computer or a single network node from which node the Software cannot be accessed by another computer, provided that such Software shall be used by only one individual; <u>or</u>

b. (if specified as a "workstation" version) install the Software on a single stand-alone computer or a single network node from which node the Software cannot be accessed by another computer, provided that such Software shall be used by only one individual; <u>or</u>

c. (if specified as a "LAN" version) install the Software on a local area network server that provides access to multiple computers, up to the maximum number of computers or users specified in your Governing Agreement, provided that such Software shall be used only by employees of your organization; <u>or</u>

d. (if specified as an "enterprise" version) install the Software or copies of the Software on multiple local or wide area network servers, intranet servers, stand-alone computers and network nodes (and to make copies of the Software for such purpose) at one or more sites, which servers provide access to a multiple number of users, up to the maximum number of users specified in your Governing Agreement, provided that such Software shall be used only by employees of your organization.

<u>This License is not a sale. Title and copyrights to the Software, accompanying documentation and any copy made by you remain with Licensor or its suppliers or licensors.</u>

2. **Intellectual Property**. The Software is owned by Licensor or its licensors and is protected by United States and other jurisdictions' copyright laws and international treaty provisions. Therefore, you may not use, copy, or distribute the Software without the express written authorization of CBT Group PLC. This License authorizes you to use the Software for the internal training needs of your employees only, and to make one copy of the Software solely for backup or archival purposes. You may not print copies of any user documentation provided in "online" or electronic form. Licensor retains all rights not expressly granted.

3. **Restrictions**. You may not transfer, rent, lease, loan or time-share the Software or accompanying documentation. You may not reverse engineer, decompile, or disassemble the Software, except to the extent the foregoing restriction is expressly prohibited by applicable law. You may not modify, or create derivative works based upon the Software in whole or in part.

1. **Confidentiality**. The Software contains confidential trade secret information belonging to Licensor, and you may use the software only pursuant to the terms of your Governing Agreement, if any, and the license set forth herein. In addition, you may not disclose the Software to any third party.

2. **Limited Liability**. IN NO EVENT WILL THE Licensor's LIABILITY UNDER, ARISING OUT OF OR RELATING TO THIS AGREEMENT EXCEED THE AMOUNT PAID TO LICENSOR FOR THE SOFTWARE. LICENSOR SHALL NOT BE LIABLE FOR ANY SPECIAL, INCIDENTAL, INDIRECT OR CONSEQUENTIAL DAMAGES, HOWEVER CAUSED AND ON ANY THEORY OF LIABILITY., REGARDLESS OR WHETHER LICENSOR HAS BEEN ADVISED OF THE POSSIBILITY OF SUCH DAMAGES. WITHOUT LIMITING THE FOREGOING, LICENSOR WILL NOT BE LIABLE FOR LOST PROFITS, LOSS OF DATA, OR COSTS OF COVER.

3. **Limited Warranty**. LICENSOR WARRANTS THAT SOFTWARE WILL BE FREE FROM DEFECTS IN MATERIALS AND WORKMANSHIP UNDER NORMAL USE FOR A PERIOD OF THIRTY (30) DAYS FROM THE DATE OF RECEIPT. THIS LIMITED WARRANTY IS VOID IF FAILURE OF THE SOFTWARE HAS RESULTED FROM ABUSE OR MISAPPLICATION. ANY REPLACEMENT SOFTWARE WILL BE WARRANTED FOR A PERIOD OF THIRTY (30) DAYS FROM THE DATE OF RECEIPT OF SUCH REPLACEMENT SOFTWARE. THE SOFTWARE AND DOCUMENTATION ARE PROVIDED "AS IS". LICENSOR HEREBY DISCLAIMS ALL OTHER WARRANTIES, EXPRESS, IMPLIED, OR STATUTORY, INCLUDING WITHOUT LIMITATION, THE IMPLIED WARRANTIES OF MERCHANTABILITY AND FITNESS FOR A PARTICULAR PURPOSE.

4. **Exceptions**. SOME STATES DO NOT ALLOW THE LIMITATION OF INCIDENTAL DAMAGES OR LIMITATIONS ON HOW LONG AN IMPLIED WARRANTY LASTS, SO THE ABOVE LIMITATIONS OR EXCLUSIONS MAY NOT APPLY TO YOU. This agreement gives you specific legal rights, and you may also have other rights which vary from state to state.

5. **U.S. Government-Restricted Rights**. The Software and accompanying documentation are deemed to be "commercial computer Software" and "commercial computer Software documentation," respectively, pursuant to FAR Section 227.7202 and FAR Section 12.212, as applicable. Any use, modification, reproduction release, performance, display or disclosure of the Software and accompanying documentation by the U.S. Government shall be governed solely by the terms of this Agreement and shall be prohibited except to the extent expressly permitted by the terms of this Agreement.

6. **Export Restrictions**. You may not download, export, or re-export the Software (a) into, or to a national or resident of, Cuba, Iraq, Libya, Yugoslavia, North Korea, Iran, Syria or any other country to which the United States has embargoed goods, or (b) to anyone on the United States Treasury Department's list of Specially Designated Nations or the U.S. Commerce Department's Table of Deny Orders. By installing or using the Software, you are representing and warranting that you are not located in, under the control of, or a national resident of any such country or on any such list.

7. **General**. This License is governed by the laws of the United States and the State of California, without reference to conflict of laws principles. The parties agree that the United Nations Convention on Contracts for the International Sale of Goods shall not apply to this License. If any provision of this Agreement is held invalid, the remainder of this License shall continue in full force and effect.

8. **More Information**. Should you have any questions concerning this Agreement, or if you desire to contact Licensor for any reason, please contact: CBT Systems USA Ltd., 1005 Hamilton Court, Menlo Park, California 94025, Attn: Chief Legal Officer.

IF YOU DO NOT AGREE WITH THE ABOVE TERMS AND CONDITIONS, SO NOT INSTALL THE SOFTWARE AND RETURN IT TO THE LICENSOR.

About the CD-ROM

The enclosed CD-ROM contains the following computer-based training (CBT) course module from CBT Systems, specially chosen to accompany this book on MCSE Course number 70-058:

Network Essentials: Network Troubleshooting

The CD can be used on Windows 95/98 or NT systems. To access the CBT course, launch the SETEUP.EXE file. Further information about the installation can be found in the README.TXT file.

If you recieve the following error message during installation: "Setup was unable to communicate with the Program Manager to add the Microsoft Test Items," click OK or hit RETURN Key.

Technical Support

If you have a problem with the CBT software, please contact CBT Technical Support. In the U.S. call 1(800)938-3247. If you are outside the U.S. call 3531-283-0380.

Prentice Hall does not offer technical support for this software. However, if there is a problem with the media, you may obtain a replacement copy by e-mailing us with your problem at:

disc_exchange@prenhall.com